THE
LITTLE BUDDHA
AND THE COSMOS

Eva Prem

Acknowledgements

Thank you to all the beloveds and friends
who have inspired us and supported us.

None of the characters in this book is real.
If you recognize yourself in one of them,
it is because they are universal.

CONTENTS

Prologue	SHAMBALA	5
Chapter One	THE BUDDHA OF LONG HISTORY	19
Chapter Two	OPERATION CHARAVEDI	27
Chapter Three	THE AKASHIC RECORDS	35
Chapter Four	METAMORPHOSIS	41
Chapter Five	SOUL PARENTS: THE INDIGO COUPLE	49
Chapter Six	MEETING WITH A REMARKABLE GIANT	59
Chapter Seven	A SECOND CHANCE	69
Chapter Eight	YOU GAVE ME BACK MY GRANDFATHER	79
Chapter Nine	A SPECIAL MORNING IN THE COSMOS BAR	89
Chapter Ten	MAYA AND HER MASTER	101
Chapter Eleven	A LONG LOST FRIEND: THE ENLIGHTENED MONKEY	111
Chapter Twelve	A FAMOUS HEALER	125
Chapter Thirteen	THE DARK NIGHT OF THE SOUL	139
Chapter Fourteen	IN THE PLANES OF SIBERIA	151
Chapter Fifteen	THE YOUNG SHAMAN	159
Chapter Sixteen	THE PERUVIAN MUSICIAN	169
Chapter Seventeen	THE PERUVIAN MAGICIAN	179
Chapter Eighteen	SHADOWS OF THE PAST	191
Chapter Nineteen	ISTANBUL: A TALE OF LOVE	201
Chapter Twenty	A HEALING PRAYER	213
Chapter Twentyone	ZEN: FROM NIGHTMARE TO NIRVANA	219
Chapter Twentytwo	LAUGHTER AND TEARS	229
Chapter Twentythree	THE FINAL HEALING	239
Chapter Twentyfour	ALL IS WELL	251
Chapter Twentyfive	JOURNEY TO THE MANSAROVARA AND BEYOND	259
Chapter Twentysix	VISIT TO SHAMBALA	267
Chapter Twentyseven	REBIRTH	275
Chapter Twentyeight	ALL ROADS LEAD TO GOA	285
Chapter Twentynine	THE DWIJA CIRCUS	293
Chapter Thirty	SOULMATES	301
Chapter Thirtyone	MARRIAGE	309
Chapter Thirtytwo	THE MYSTERIOUS ADVENTURES OF MISS SWUPI	317

Prologue

SHAMBALA

Test...test...Okay, here we go....
The sweet notes of an Indian raga swirl for a moment in the air...
"Good morning to all of you loyal listeners! Here is Radio Manali, broadcasting from Manali, state of Himachal Pradesh, India...
Today our special Guest in the studio is the Big Buddha, formerly known as the Little Buddha. As some of you might have heard, about a year ago his name made it to the international headlines as one of the co-inspirers of the "Little Planet", a highly advanced ecological project. We hear that the "Little Planet" is a step-by-step transformation of garbage into a highly concentrated fertilizer that could reverse the toxic state of the Earth. So far, no specific details of the experiment have been disclosed. Is it right, Big Buddha?"

"Ehmmm..."

"You might or might not have heard his voice right now, but from here I can see the Big Buddha making a clear "Let's change the subject" sign...So we won't pursue this any more....

Where were we...ah, yes, Greece. After completing his part in the "Little Planet" experiment, he retired to a Greek island, where he promptly became famous for his healing abilities. This time the news of his skills reached the world through Facebook and New Age websites, making him once again world famous.

Some of you might remember how after a while all news of him stopped. Very little is officially known about what happened since he disappeared from the newspaper headlines.

I have here a very interesting photo of your time as a healer, Big Buddha, where you appear...ahem, as a child, at the most one fourth of your present size, with a little monkey on your shoulder...Given the fact that these photos were taken less than a year ago, we are very puzzled by your physical transformation: now you are big and there is no monkey with you...Are we free to talk about this particular subject?

Ladies and gentlemen, you cannot see him, but I can: the Big Buddha, a handsome and tall blond blue eyed young man, with a dazzling smile, has just nodded "yes"! From wherever you are listening, please give a big hand of applause for the Big Buddha!!!"

A recorded applause is immediately followed by the jingle jangle of cymbals and bells in a playful crescendo…Fade…

"So dear Big Buddha, welcome to our live program 'Who and what is new in the State of Himachal Pradesh'. My first question:

What brings you here in the Himalayas? Tourism or business?"

"Hello everyone, and thank you, friend, for inviting me to this program. I heard only good things about it. To answer your question, I am neither a tourist nor a businessman. The Himalayas have been my home for eternity. Their purity and transcendence have inspired my meditations for lifetimes…"

"So you remember your past incarnations?"

"That's the reason I have been called here this time. The University of Mystery and Science in nearby Kulu has invited me to give a few talks to a selected group of students about my personal journey through different incarnations."

"And what about the Monkey, your steady, how can I put it, childhood companion of the photo? Forgive me for my curiosity. We here in India have no trouble with the concept of past lives, but the idea of growing up in the same body from child to full adult in the space of one year seems to be out of our league…"

"I am sorry, there is so much to explain and so much to be silent about…Anyway, the Monkey is still my best friend. He has just married his sweetheart. A few days ago I had the great pleasure of accompanying them to a very sacred place high up in the mountains where his beloved and he went through a special ritual of purification and initiation. By now they should be on their way to the secret "Little Planet" location where he has family."

"This sounds reassuringly normal for all of us…hey all of you out there, you can draw a big breath of relief. The sweet monkey of the photo is still alive and well with his family…but…has he also grown up, like you, into a mature male in such a short span of time?"

"Indeed. But I will not reveal any more details about him because I know how he cherishes his privacy during his honeymoon…"

"With your permission, we would like to move on to the next question. It is rather personal, so you are free to gesticulate if you do not want to comment…I'll stop on my tracks.

You look handsome enough, and are obviously wise and cultured enough to be invited to lecture in a very prestigious University. I am sure that women like you. In fact I see our female sound technician blushing right now through the glass partition… sorry Rani for drawing you in! My question is: is there a significant other in your present adult life? I am sure that specially our female listeners would be interested to know…"

"Well… it's true, it is a very intimate question, and a while ago I would have been embarrassed by it. But in this last period of my life a lot of things have changed, quite obviously…I have become a man!"

"I see that our guest is blushing a bit…I can stop if you like…where were we…"

"It's OK, I am not ashamed. In my long train travel from Delhi, the beauty of Indian women really captured me. However poor they might be, they carry themselves with such dignity…but more intriguing to me is the attraction that I felt towards their soft and playful nature, their secret giggles and their sweet fragrance. I saw them all like princesses from a thousand and one nights. Since my focus has been for centuries on meditation only, I hadn't seen them in this way for very long. I can only say that this is refreshing…"

"Thank you, Big Buddha, for such a poetic and honest answer. You honor our land with your words. And what will be next, after the talks at the University?

"In the long hours of the train ride I have also been toying with the idea to write a novel about my experiences. Anecdotes and illustrations have been playing in my head. To be honest with you, I have no clue of how to write a book, but I have a good story that could entertain many in a good way…"

"Where would you start your story?"

"Way back in time, in a mythical land called Shambala…"

"The Land of the Buddhas?"

"Forgive me the giggle, friend, I am just anticipating your next question, which will be 'does Shambala really exist?' I can only answer to it by saying that writing a novel will allow me to leave this question as unanswered as it should remain, and yet hint at the truth in a poetic way…"

"We look forward to read it! What will the title be?"

"I don't know yet. Maybe the Little Buddha and the Cosmos…I trust that in due time someone will appear and help me put the story on paper…"

"Editors, ghost writers of the Valley of the Gods! Do you hear the Big Buddha's request? If any of you wishes to help him in his literary endeavor, step forth…I am sure many will answer, because we all want to know more about the fascinating character of the Little-Big Buddha!

And one last question for all our listeners. Has the famous Princess Swupi already invited you to attend the Annual Waltz Night at the University next week? What is your relationship to her?"

"We just met yesterday to discuss the possibility of her editing the book I would like to write…but I did not know about the Waltz Night… Did you say Waltz Night? I had a dream about it in the train coming here…"

The notes of a beautiful Raga cover his last words, and immediately after it's time for commercials.

One year later…

THE LITTLE BUDDHA AND THE COSMOS

By The Big Buddha

With special thanks to a most wonderful editor, Princess Swupi

Introduction

My story starts far back in the mists of history…
Somewhere amongst the Himalayan peaks and long past any sign of civilization, a group of ragged travellers is steadily crossing mountain range after mountain range, following a hardly visible narrow path.

It is not easy to detect that beneath the many layered clothes, dirty with the mud and snow they have been walking, sitting or resting on, and stiff with their own frozen sweat, is concealed a group of awakened beings that have gathered for a special purpose.

They are twelve, men and women, all coming from different spiritual traditions.

Well, to be precise, thirteen, including myself.

I am known by the Twelve as 'The Buddha of Long History'.

Although my name speaks for itself, I have to add that it is a true Dharma name[1]: it indicates that I have been on the spiritual path for immeasurable time, seeking and searching for the One and Only Truth that passes through everyone and everything, and that I somehow got there in the end.

But let the past be the past…

And what of my future?

The time to come shall reveal to my utter surprise that the Path is not finished; it never began and it will never end. I will enter another new incarnation, this time under the mysterious name "The Little Buddha".

---

1   Spiritual name

But let's not spoil it for our readers and get too much ahead of our story…

Let's go back to this endless trek through the mountains. As the Buddha of Long History, I am walking, or rather stumbling and sliding, on the narrow path. The world around is dazzling white and empty: I can barely detect a thin division line between the snowy earth and the milky sky.

All around me there is absolute silence, except for the occasional gust of wind that blows tiny sharp icicles into the open slit of our hoods. It hurts, but at the same time it keeps us alert, because even the peak of spiritual awakening cannot stop us from wanting to give in to our bone tired exhaustion, lie down and doze off.

Luckily we are all well disciplined. We had to learn to stay present to get to the ultimate state of consciousness. We keep going, knowing that this too will pass.

I can hear the laborious breathing of my companions as they climb next to me, but I can also feel their silent Buddha nature, so perfectly mirrored by the majestic silence of the Himalayas.

This is the main reason we all came: to drink from this pure and immense source of peacefulness that surrounds us here on the roof of the earth…

But there is also another reason: although there is no mention of it during the long hours on the trek, we are looking for a sacred place. Some of us have called it Garden of Eden, or Jannah, or Nirvana, and many other names according to our different spiritual traditions.

We Buddhas call it Shambala. It normally indicates an inner space achieved through deep meditation that results in the opening of the third eye. But this time we are taking a new step: we are looking for it on the outside, as a physical location. We want to find a place where we can all live together in that inner space as a Sangha: a Commune of enlightened ones.

My twelve fellow travelers had met each other long before their enlightenment, and shared a great variety of experiences in many incarnations, sometimes as men and other times as women, sometimes as family members and other times as friends or lovers.

The only thing that they had not been able to share was the last stretch of their individual journey to awakening. Back then, it was believed that to attain enlightenment one had to be alone: just like with any other attachment, also friendships had to be left behind.

But in spite of all, the friendship amongst them survived the ultimate test. Once they all attained, existence called them back together.

Scattered as they were all over the then known world, the Twelve started to have the same recurring dream. They all saw a tropical valley surrounded by high snow covered peaks: it emanated a bright and vast light that reached to the furthest corners of the Earth.

It did not take long before each one of them, through visions, gossips and tales from faraway lands, discovered about the other eleven. They all set off at the same time to find each other. Given the distances and the language barriers between them, they came together in the miraculously short span of a year.

They gathered in the ancient University town of TakshaShila, on the continent now known as India, a place swarming with Pundits and scholars.

All of them recognized each other instantly, and all cried, laughed, and joked about each other's new outer appearance. Their bond was renewed.

They started sharing about their dream in earnest. Each one of them added some detail, until a full picture emerged: Shambala, they all agreed on the name, was to be a place of immense inner and outer beauty.

They decided to set off immediately. The following day, in the utter darkness before dawn, twelve shadows with two fully loaded yaks slipped out of town, heading for the mystery. They travelled light, carrying in their bundles just a few special objects and some dried fruits.

This is when I joined in.

Although they would have gladly accepted me if I had wanted to be included as a founding member, I was not one of the Twelve. I had no desire for status: that's how I was.

I did have a long history, though. In my many incarnations, enlightened or not, I had gone through uncountable adventures and misadventures.

Just at that time, I had reached the point in my life where I needed a break: my greatest wish was to live with friends, far away from the world, surrounded by nature, in a silent and meditative way.

I was alone travelling through the South of India, meditating on the sacred design of the ancient Hindu temples, when a message reached me from the inside. Suddenly, in the silence of a shrine, I distinctly heard the clipped northern voice of an old friend and teacher of mine from the Eburones tribes, known as the German Buddha[2]: "As the Head of the newly formed Council of Twelve, I am pleased to let you know that we are in TakshaShila. You are already with us in our hearts. We are looking for a place to live together. Care to join us?"

I immediately understood who the Twelve were. The bonds between them and I ran as deep as the connections they had with each other. It was just that I had a reserve about being defined, so I always tried to remain the odd number outside.

But even if I preferred to do things on my own and had never joined any organized religion, I had to give it to them: they would be a fantastic team, and sometimes, to achieve something greater than oneself, it is good to work together…

I really had no choice: my yes came fast and easy.

I made it to arrive just before their departure, and took my place almost invis-

---

2   Buddha is a general term that means the Awakened One

ibly in the last minute chaos. It was dark, and everyone was focused on fighting the nightly chill. But as light came, all their faces bore a warm smile of welcome for me.

After a relatively easy first part of the journey, we reached the ancient city of Kantipur, known in the modern days as Kathmandu, the capital of Nepal. Back then, it was the only civilized place in the Himalayas.

The city was bustling with life, and it did not take us long to arrange for more provisions. After a good rest in a local inn, still warm from the heat of the animals in the stables below our pallets, we set off into the mountains with no precise destination.

And here we are, still walking through the eternal snows…

After a couple of months on the road, our long walks through cloudless sunny days have reinvigorated us; the altitude makes us happy, and we are stunned at the beauty of the landscape. There are of course also misty and cloudy days, where the majority of us feels lost and wonders about our dreams.

But the worst days by far are the ones on which we feel literally attacked by liquid ice or frozen snow. We have to stop our progress and huddle all together under our blankets, shielded by the broad backs of our two friends: the yaks. While the wind howls around us, we cheer each other up and rekindle our dream.

On such "bad" days, I spend a lot of time with my old friend the German Buddha. Enveloped in the warm scent of the yaks, we chat about our recent incarnations as disciples of Gautama the Buddha, and our endless traveling to spread his words far and wide.

"Remember our first Sanghas? When we used to travel in groups, penniless, to teach the Dharma, the Universal Law of the Spirit?" he tells me, "I had a secret name for us, I called us the Dharma Bums…"

"I did not last long on that path. It was a bit too regulated for me…" I have to admit, accepting gratefully a steaming cup of yak milk from his hands and passing it on after sipping from it.

"Thank existence for Mother Yak," says a thin female voice coming from a hood that lets through only some unruly wisps of blond hair, as a delicate hand reaches for the cup, "All the rest of the food is frozen…"

"But we are free…." The German Buddha says, winking at me.

When the snowstorm is over and night comes, we finally set up camp in a more sheltered place under a huge boulder. Everyone settles down with a cup of Tsampa Butter Tea in his or her hand and a nice old yak bladder filled with heated snow under their feet. It's the right moment for me to share my love for Gautama[3] the Buddha's Heart Sutra[4]. Just yesterday I rediscovered in my traveling bundle a rice paper transcription of it, tightly wrapped in oilcloth. Everyone listens intently.

---

3   The historical Buddha, known by everyone
4   The Heart Sutra is often cited as the best-known and most popular Buddhist scripture of all.

"According to the tradition of Gautama the Buddha's traveling monks", the German Buddha says at the end of my reading, "we are not supposed to overstay the length of three days in the same place in order not to get attached to anything. I am asking you all, friends: how does this reconcile with our desire for a permanent place?"

While the fresh cold snowflakes dance around us, we launch into a heated discussion.

"Non attachment doesn't mean poverty!"

"But how to avoid complacency?"

"Listen up friends, true religiousness writes its own credo every moment anew…"

And so on and so forth…meanwhile, I can feel that in the heart of our hearts we are all one, and that we are following a choiceless path that will lead us into some totally unknown direction. Shambala.

"I have a suggestion…" I jump in, "why don't we call ourselves the Shambala Buddhas? In that way, we honor Gautama as the first human being that realized the divine in himself, but we also honor our new dream…"

Everyone cheers and agrees. Honor has been done, and the future is open.

In the late hours of the evening, just as everyone is about to lie down huddled around the warm embers of the campfire, one of the Twelve, known by all as an endless source of technical information, suddenly sits up and gives a little shout. We quickly gather around him, concerned.

"No, friends, it's nothing bad. I think I found something. There is an ancient tale about some mysterious tropical valleys hidden amongst snowy peaks…" he is holding in his hand some dirt that he just dug from under the snow, and sounds increasingly excited, " Look, this earth is steaming…. there must be ruptures in the soil around here that let through thermal water from subterranean hot springs …the exact conditions for a tropical microclimate somewhere nearby, sheltered between the mountains!"

An excited conversation breaks loose. We are all so tired of this eternally white surrounding that we long for some luscious green. But it seems such an impossible dream…

"There we go, some hope," sighs the German Buddha, relieved to have some hint at last.

"They are not easily accessible," the technical Buddha adds, "because they are well hidden amongst the eternal snow. I'm not a hundred percent sure that we can find them…"

But a few days later it happens.

On a particularly cold afternoon, after climbing up through a very narrow and steep ravine, we reach a high plateau with an open view to the endless mountain ranges that stretch in all directions. Suddenly, a young woman, known by all as the

Waif Buddha, shouts out loud and points towards an area between two mountains, lit up by the last rays of golden sunlight.

We can all see it: the deep green of a valley against the stark white backdrop of the mountains. It is a large valley filled with huge trees, whose majestic crowns leave no gap in between each other.

We are all very excited, but we have to wait because it's getting dark. While sitting through the night around our blazing campfire on the plateau, we all agree: we caught a glimpse of the green natural beauty of the mysterious valley. This must be it.

Early the next day, light headed from the night of talking and planning, we gather our few belongings and set off for 'our valley', as we already call it...

We reach its entrance in the early afternoon. Like a pair of huge sentinels, two tall cedars stand on each side, their crowns interwoven in an arch. Behind them, in the distance, the snow-covered peaks are still visible. Once we cross the cedars, though, the scenery changes dramatically: we have entered a lush green valley.

Ancient pines, slim white birches, and tall cedars are circling green meadows with flowering rhododendron bushes in red, fuchsia and purple, pearly lilies of the valley, and wild orange roses. The temperature is perfect: mildly warm, like eternal spring.

We don't hesitate one minute.

We all take off our by now really smelly robes and shawls and pile them up at the entrance of the valley. Wrapped in our last clean cloths, we spread around to explore, each one on his or her own.

I follow a path that leads me to the far end of the valley, and stop at a warm water spring that bubbles out of a rock formation.

I bow, dip my hands in the water and rinse my face. After my long hike, it's pleasantly cool. I continue washing my whole body in the ritual Buddhist way.

While gently patting myself dry, I look around and see a tall cedar standing on a nearby small mound, covered with bright green soft moss. I sit there and soak in the delicious sunlight that envelops me like a blessing.

Time passes, or rather becomes irrelevant in such a place as this one. At some point, I see the snow peaks in the distance gloriously lit up by the late afternoon sun.

The trickling sound of the warm water spring is so soothing.

I close my eyes, and turn inwards.

Then I hear something. It's coming from inside me. It's a long forgotten music, a sacred tune that fills my soul and erases all the hardship I went through in the last months.

I start singing, a bit tremulous and insecure at first. Then, like a prayer, my chant starts soaring towards the sky. I am pure joy.

When I stop, a royal response comes from the other side of the valley. This is no human voice: it is a nightingale, its melodious notes touching the strings of my heart. It's telling me that this is my place.

I show up back at the entrance of the valley when the moon is already high in the sky.

Meanwhile, the Twelve have all come back. They returned at different stages of the afternoon, each one nodding a solemn yes to the ones who were already there. Everyone has found his or her own place.

The last of them to come back is the German Buddha. He is well known for being very thorough. We occasionally giggle about his Germanic perfectionism, but in fact everyone trusts him as Head of the Council exactly because of this trait. When he saw the other eleven waiting for him, he thrust his thumb up, provoking a loud laughter and a great sense of happiness in everyone.

When I get there, my friends are all buzzing with childlike excitement.

Everyone turns towards me. My vote is not decisive, but my opinion is important to them. When they see the huge smile on my face, it's final: this valley is to become the land of the Buddhas, the Sacred Shambala.

We gather in a circle under the open sky, full of bright stars, and the German Buddha speaks out:

"Beloveds, we made it. Existence celebrates this new stage of Buddhahood, the Sangha. It is a total new experiment in sharing consciousness. We will call this valley Shambala: this word indicates a state of consciousness: Sham means tranquility, Bala means virgin -- virgin tranquility. That is the space of enlightenment, which always remains virgin. There is no way to corrupt it.

Let's celebrate tonight. Now there is no need to return to our countries anymore. This is our new home; tomorrow we will start settling in. In time, our friends and fellow travelers will find Shambala and join us. In the future, this will become the largest gathering of Buddhas."

"I can see many buildings here…" jumps in a rather imposing older woman Buddha with visionary eyes, "Bungalows, meditation huts, a large Buddha Hall, a library, a market and an inn…. But there is no rush," she adds with a smile, "It will all happen in synchronicity with existence…Shambala will build itself…"

"Over the next period of time," the German Buddha continues after smiling at her, "we will send into existence an invitation for our awakened friends from all over the planet to join us. This new communal quality of enlightenment will become stronger. It will spread in mysterious ways to the furthest corners of the Earth.

"Times will keep on changing on this Planet… there will be periods of darkness as well as glorious eras of enlightenment. We need to learn to remain equally unaffected by both. But we need to protect our Sangha from the darkness. For this reason, our well informed friend who guided us here, who will one day be known as the Buddha of Technical Support and Maintenance, will device soon a system to make Shambala invisible to the outside world. It will be simply impossible to come here uninvited.

"Friends, I bow down to the Buddha in each one of us, I bow down to the Sangha in us, and I bow down to the Ultimate Truth.

Let the celebration begin!"

Much Much Later...

Since those early days, Shambala has truly developed into a Buddhaland. All its inhabitants are enlightened.

Throughout all the centuries that followed its foundation, I became an honorary resident, in and out of Shambala as I pleased to follow my adventures in the outer world, which I kept on finding exciting. In Shambala I remained the Buddha of Long History so long, that in fact I sometimes felt as if was made only of light.

But let me tell you a bit more about the Buddhaland...

No one outside Shambala has ever found a map to get here. Up to these days, for the outside world its name remains a legend, and its location shrouded in mystery.

In the centuries that followed its foundation, many seekers journeyed through the Himalayan Mountains trying to find it. But Shambala has eluded the majority of them. Even if everyone on this search found important truths and experienced significant insights, most of them came back to the world without finding Shambala. Throughout many centuries, only few seekers managed to reach and take residence here.

There is a small exception, though: family members. I personally have none, but some of the resident Buddhas here have large families that visit from time to time. I like it: it always creates some kind of welcome diversion to the serene routine of the place...

Shambala is a country built by Buddhas for Buddhas. No war has ever occurred here. Whenever any negative energy tries to invade, Shambala disappears into the Himalayan mists.

It is also the first community without internal conflicts. Everyone chooses to take any disturbance amongst the residents as a device to step out of one's individual perspective and wake up to the larger picture.

The newcomers that trickle in, fresh from the struggles of the outer world, are always amazed at the serenity of the Shambala population. It is as if the whole sacred valley is filled with a radiance of peace.

As travel and communication became increasingly easy with the passing of time, the population of Shambala has steadily increased. To house everyone without spoiling the purity of the place, The Buddha of Technical Support and Maintenance was appointed to draw a town plan under the supervision of the German Buddha.

The resulting design is still in use now, after quite a few years, but constantly improved by the latest findings in environmental science.

All private dwellings are small dome-like homes, built with natural materials gathered in the valley. The single rooms inside are circular, with no corners, to let energies circulate and renew. Their interiors, floors and furniture, are made out of local pale birch wood. Each one has also a porch where the Buddhas that are used to a more nomadic lifestyle can sleep under the stars.

The buildings are all painted in a soft pearly white: they gleam with liquid light against the eternal white of the snow-covered peaks of the Himalayas at the horizon. They look simple and comfortable, elegant and spare.

Now...

By the beginning of the 21st century, Shambala has become a place of great creative expression through painting, music, dance and martial arts, and deep meditation, through the many techniques brought here by seekers of different spiritual paths.

There are several large communal spaces that cater to the needs of the whole Sangha: Magdalena's Vegetarian Restaurant, Chiyono's Hair Saloon, Jesus Winery, and a Caravanserrai Guest House for family visitors at the foot of the hill, next to a large stream. Close to it, stands the Gopala Kindergarten for the youngest Buddhas and the rare small guests.

But the Buddha Hall, the communal meditation place, is the heart of it all. At certain times of each day and night, the Shambala Buddhas gather there and sit silently, broadcasting positive intentions to the whole Earth.

Everyone in Shambala is beautiful. Unlike in the outside world, no one tries to improve on his or her appearance with artificial means: their beauty is a grace that comes from within. The Absolute shines through every single one of their faces.

As you can feel and imagine, Shambala has become the perfect refuge for those who have reached the highest level of consciousness and do not wish to seek further.

Although I never decided to reside in Shambala on a permanent base, I always kept my own house here.

For a very long time, I went on traveling around the world. Human beings and their customs kept on fascinating me long past my enlightenment. But I was always happy to come back to Shambala, drop my earthly disguises and resume being the Buddha of Long History.

Everyone rejoiced at my return, knowing that I had wondrous stories to tell and a load of contagious enthusiasm to spread.

After that, I normally spent some time contributing to the Community in a kind of disorganized but supportive way: I spent a day cooking in Maggie's restaurant, and then maybe the next day I threw myself full heartedly into weeding or planting or watering in the veggie fields.

But the day came, exactly one year before the Little Buddha came to this world, where I felt a great need for emptiness and rest after a particularly exhausting and dangerous travel. No more adventures, I told myself. I decided to take time off, and stay around Shambala without any schedule or agenda.

At first, this period of freedom turned out to be very satisfying. I developed the habit of waking up before sunrise in order to be already well on my way when the first rays of sunlight touched the peaks of the tall cedars, trekking through the surrounding snow covered mountains. After my wanderings, I spent the rest of the day at home, improving on my cottage and tending my pretty tropical garden with free flying exotic birds, descendants of the original fauna of the valley before our arrival. My visits to friends became increasingly infrequent, but everyone around left me in peace: they respected my choice to retreat as one of the most commonly spread spiritual practices in Shambala.

I spent time for what felt like an eternity in this way. I completely fell in love again with meditation, and forgot about the world outside Shambala. At least for a while…

This is where my story begins…

Chapter One

THE BUDDHA OF LONG HISTORY

One day, on his way out for his customary predawn walk, the Buddha of Long History stopped on his tracks. He suddenly felt like breaking what was becoming too much of a routine.
He turned around and decided to stay home instead. Gazing from his large window into the last shadows of the night, he felt in a vacuum, as empty as the darkness surrounding him. He sat a bit forlorn, waiting for sunrise.

But when the first light came, his mood drastically changed. He couldn't understand why: he suddenly felt excited, aflame, as full of colors as the majestic sunrise in front of him.

Then he understood: existence was showing him something. "A new dawn…" he whispered quietly, and bowed down in a gesture of surrender.

Later that morning, a message was slipped through his door. The envelope bore the seal of the Council of Twelve.

He was surprised to receive news from them. As the months of his retreat rolled by into almost a full year, he had taken more and more distance from them. Although he still considered them his best friends, he did not want them to see him in his present state.

Truth was that lately he had been feeling increasingly bored, and very ashamed to admit it to himself, let alone to others.

Boredom had crept on him slowly: he first noticed it as a kind of dullness in his system, and thought it must be a side effect of too much choiceless awareness, some kind of occupational hazard on the path of meditation.

But he knew better than that: he had experienced choiceless awareness uncountable times, and this was not it. He soon realized that what he felt now did not have that quality of lightness and freedom that came with meditation. This was a heavy and lethargic state of mind that made him want not to move any more. After struggling for quite a while with the definition, he finally had to admit it: he was stuck.

Not a suitable mood for an inhabitant of Shambala, he told himself, but that did not help either. His boredom continued growing stronger by the day, and his struggle to hide it was consuming all his energy.

Away from public view, he had kept on watching fear and shame closing in on him, breathing bravely through them until the next attack would set once more his nerves on fire.

Now he realized that the Twelve must have noticed from afar what was happening to him and decided not to interfere up to this moment. They trusted him, he sighed shaking his head, and they were convinced that watching one's thoughts would be the winning method to defeat the restless mind. But, to be honest, he was starting to doubt it.

He sat down with the unopened envelope in his hands. He could not deny that the Council had been a fantastic leading team for Shambala on all levels, both practical and spiritual, and he admired their capacity to keep up with the latest technologies. It was just…that sometimes they appeared to him as a bit too comfortable, too settled. "They might be stuck too, for all I know," he said with a last shrug before breaking the seal.

With his heart beating a bit faster, he opened the message. As he read and reread the one and only word in it, he kept on scratching his head in disbelief.

It said:

CHARAVEDI.

He knew what the word meant:

"Keep on moving".

It was one of the essential teachings of Gautama the Buddha.

But why? Why him? He went blank. He had lost his cool and could not think straight.

Then, his thoughts came back flooding in all at once: "Is this how the Twelve see me? Unable to move on my own accord? Stuck? Why couldn't they say it straight to my face?"

He felt an unbearable heat rising to his face. It was more than blushing: it was burning with shame.

He took time to cool off. After a while, still holding the paper with a trembling hand, he started to take in the implications of the message. The worst had happened: his boredom had been exposed. In the eyes of his beloved friends he must look no more than a comfortable recluse, safely hiding away to conceal his boredom. This shocked and repelled him.

He tried to close his eyes and meditate, but the tranquility that had always come natural to him in Shambala was no longer there.

He tried to keep himself busy with household chores, but he could not think of anything else than the message.

He decided to give up and just sit at his window, waiting for guidance, but nothing came.

Exhausted, he fell asleep early, but woke up soaking wet from sweat only a couple of hours later. While struggling to free himself from the knotted sheets and sit up, he remembered his dream: he was back in his childhood, desperately crying because his favorite dog had disappeared or died. He could feel that same sadness and loneliness right now.

He sat up in the dark for the rest of the night, mulling over his situation in futile circles of thoughts. He found himself swinging from one extreme to the other, first getting really angry at the Twelve and at their patronizing attitude, then suddenly turning that anger towards himself, feeling like a hypocrite and a coward, and then raving once more against them and so on so forth…

But in the early hours of the morning something new started happening. His heart started smiling. It was a funny phenomenon: a sweet but also sad sensation in his chest that made him want to laugh and cry at the same time. But the rage did not subside. It kept on running parallel to that feeling, like a smoldering underground volcano.

When the first sunrays came through his window, he did not move. He still felt completely split between his anger and the sweet sensation in his chest: he could not bring himself to face anyone just yet.

His inner fight reached its final peak in the late morning: it was like being caught in the violent clash of opposite air currents. He had lost all direction.

"I have to move now", he thought, straining to get out of his trance like state. Just then, a knock came at his door.

Through no more than a tiny open sliver, he checked who was standing outside. It was his neighbor.

She was a normally composed and silent lady, who had attained Nirvana, salvation, through the path of Yoga. This path was very regulated, and so was she. She always got up at four in the morning and did her exercises.

But today she looked completely different: her face was beaming with excitement, and her voice sounded much louder than usual.

"Hello," she almost shouted, handing him a paper identical to his, but addressed to her. "Can we talk?"

"Dear neighbor," she continued, stumbling over her fast words, "Usually I am not… Ehmmm… over emotional... But this time I need to speak up, and you need to listen to me. This note", she said, showing him a piece of paper that looked alarmingly identical to his, "is exactly the same as the one I see crumpled on your floor.

I also received it yesterday, as I assume you did too... when i first saw it lying next to my entrance door, I didn't even look at it: I thought it was some kind of publicity.

But last night I had a dream, for the first time since very long. I would not have dared intruding your privacy, but you were strongly present in it. I saw you finding a dog and showing it to a very happy little boy that was standing next to you. I was very glad for that little boy and I ran to hug you out of gratefulness..." a touch of blush appears on her cheeks, but her serious expression quickly erases it, "But you immediately stepped away from me and pretended as if nothing had happened..."

There was a gap, long enough for the Buddha of Long History to realize how many things had remained unmentioned between them. They had been neighbors for so many years, and yet he could count on the fingers of one hand the times they had spoken to each other beyond saying 'good morning'. He had no idea how to respond...

But he need not worry, because the Yoga Lady resumed talking: "You always look so serious and a bit bored with the activities that ordinary enlightened people like me are contented with..."

Boredom, this word was really haunting him, the Buddha of Long History thought.

"In contrast to all of us, you appear so wise and so perfectly detached... your venerable age and experience are visible to all", she continues, while he lowers his eyes, "but I want to tell you something that you might not even remember. A couple of months ago I felt inspired for the first time to break my Yoga routine and go to Samba lessons at the Meera Dance Studio.

I asked you to come with me. You answer was like a cold shower. You mumbled something like 'I have other appointments' and ran off, looking very busy. Guess whom you reminded me of?" And there she paused until he felt compelled to look back into her unsettling eyes.

"Right, of my father. He also never responded to any of my dreams. He was too busy making lots of money..."

The Buddha of Long History, no longer used to direct confrontation, went completely blank while she carried on: "After you pushed me away in the dream, I noticed that there was a little girl next to me: she looked like me as a child. As I was about to talk to her, the notes of my favorite Samba tune filled the air. The little girl shrieked with happiness, and grabbed my hand to dance with me. I noticed that you and your little boy were still standing a few steps away, watching us. I waved at you, inviting you to join us, but you didn't respond much. You just smiled politely. I was already retreating in my hurt when your little boy jumped up and asked me: "Why?" Before I could say anything, my little girl answered him with a giggle: "Why not?" and they both started laughing...I woke up to the inner sound of children voices..."

As she kept on talking, the Buddha of Long History started to see her in a new way: her lithe and sensuous Samba body and her flushed cheeks made her really beautiful. A sensation that had not stirred up in him for thousands of years suddenly woke up, shocking him. He took a long breath and replied: "So, let's go dance sometimes..."

She looked at him, blushed, and smiled:

"Aren't' you lucky that I won't keep you to your words! I have made other plans: I am going to keep on moving, Charavedi. I have had enough of waiting here for eternity: I am already enlightened anyway! I found a Soul Family in Brazil and I am going there."

The Buddha of Long History tried to imagine himself in Brazil and smiled. It was not his story, but he really admired her for her bold choice. She smiled back, and continued: "Yesterday evening, a rumor was going around the whole community…"

For the Buddha of Long History this was like waking up from a self centered trance: while he was locked in his room, the world around him had continued moving…Well, he had always been a bit of a loner, anyway…

But now he was curious, just like anyone else: "What kind of rumor?"

"One that proved to be true, if you ask around. The gossip was that last night all Shambala Buddhas would dream of themselves as children, and that each one would find in his or her dream a key for how to move on to their future…"

She stopped and made a cute puzzled grimace, continuing: "You can imagine everyone's reactions at the word future…we are supposed to live in the here and now!!! And moving…I myself do every day my yoga and get up always at the same time, and I move enough as it is…"

The Buddha of Long History smiled. He knew exactly what she meant.

"But my dream of the Samba girl turned everything around. When I woke up, I picked up the note on the floor and read it: Charavedi…and it felt like a blessing for my deepest longing."

The sweet feeling in the Buddha of Long History had meanwhile won over the rage. Now he knew: that soft ache in his chest was called longing…

"Before last night's dream I had almost entirely given up on my longing," she continued, answering to his silent comment, "Your refusal to my invitation was the last drop. Maybe once in a while I still would Google the word Samba and enjoy watching Samba videos and pictures, but that's all.

Already as a child I had to give up dancing, which I loved so much, for competitive sports. On my way to training, I passed each day by a Samba school. The music would draw me in. I slowed down and look through the glass window at the dance hall, full of Latino boys and girls my age, dancing in abandon. But I never went in…"

A cloud of sadness shadowed her lovely features. She let it cross her face until it dissolves. She is back again, wonderfully radiant, a sensuous Buddha with red cheeks and bright eyes: "In my second childhood I want to have the opportunities I never had in my first childhood. If I can find a way to fulfill the longing of that little girl, I am ready. In my new Brazilian childhood I want to include both: the love for Yoga, which has brought me to enlightenment, and my passion for the Samba in all its divine beauty, with as many different boys as possible. Maybe in the end something like YogaSamba will be born out of this experiment…"

"But…" the Buddha of Long History heard himself interrupting her. It was as if the last embers of his anger were suddenly glowing again, "One essential question remains unanswered: what is the place of the Council of Twelve in all this?"

She took time to look intently into his eyes, and when she answered it was the wise and experienced yogic woman speaking, not the lighthearted Samba girl: "Enlightened beings have come and gone from Shambala as long as it has existed without anyone ever deciding for them. As long as you are enlightened, you are free to come here and go away as you please."

She kept on holding her gaze while talking: "And no Council, nobody else than yourself can know if you are enlightened or not. In that regard the Twelve have no spiritual authority and I guess they wouldn't want it either."

How could I have judged her as naïve, the Buddha of Long History thought, amazed at the clarity of her answer.

"It's up to each one of us how to honor the gift of enlightenment. We can stay out there in the world, or even dissolve into existence once for all, if we like. We can even come back from that. And the Twelve are amazing at keeping track of all of us. Even the ones that go away for millennia will always have a place to come back to in Shambala…"

"Charavedi, Charavedi…" the Buddha of Long History whispered with a bow,

"Yes, there is no beginning and no end to this Great Journey, and always something new to learn…" the Yoga Lady concluded, closing her eyes for a moment. When she opened them again, they were full of tears: "I am touched and grateful to you," she said, "for listening and understanding."

Then she shifted back into her more girlish Samba attitude and lowered her voice to a whisper: "It is also rumored that we will be offered a new possibility to come into the world as already grown children, skipping all the hardship of all the preliminaries like birth and the womb… in this quantum physics era, new incarnation techniques are available. But you can only find out more about this by visiting the Council of Twelve…I am so excited about it! Being such a recent newcomer, I always tried to model myself on the older ones and started to act like a prudish old lady that cannot tolerate chaos. But this is not me…"

Chaos…the word stirred some visceral fear in the Buddha of Long History, enough to make him realize that what was happening was truly a wake up call. But before he could reply, she stopped him and whispered to him in a soft and loving voice: "Keep on moving, dear Buddha of Long History, keep on moving…"

With those final words, she gave him a slightly awkward peck on the cheek and ran off to her home.

Standing there at the door opening, the Buddha Of Long History felt suddenly empty. He almost felt that by letting her go he had missed some very important opportunity.

He sat on the floor in the middle of his round room, not knowing what to do.

It took him quite some time to realize that the deep sobs that he was hearing were his.

At dusk, when the crying subsided, he got up and looked at himself in a small mirror close to his washbasin. He was surprised: instead of the long sad face that he expected, he saw himself relaxed and rosy. His lips were gently parted in a shy smile. He looked like a child.

Superimposed to his adult male features, he started recognizing the expression of his much younger self. He nodded a welcome to the child that had been invisible for so long.

That night he did not sleep well again. He was usually a sound sleeper, but the looming sense of chaos inside and around him was making him feel restless.

He got up and sat. The soothing darkness of the night helped. Although his confusion remained, his heart started to beat in a more relaxed rhythm, as if it had begun to accept the big change ahead.

As soon as the first rays of morning sunlight came, he looked out of his window. He took a moment to remember the area as it had been when the Twelve and himself arrived here for the first time. It was so long ago…

The tall cedar he had sat under was still there. It was even taller now, but the spring of warm water had dried up and disappeared long ago.

He looked appraisingly at his tropical garden with the colorful birds…

For a moment he felt paralyzed by his attachment to Shambala and his home. But then he suddenly remembered his adventurous spirit, and how every single one of his journeys had made him richer in his soul.

He looked around, reviewing all the changes that had happened around him throughout the years. He felt open to the new, interested again in life.

"Charavedi, Charavedi" he heard his own voice saying out loud, and smiled.

That smile remained imprinted on his face while he was dressing up and afterwards preparing his light breakfast.

Finally, dressed in a bright hand-woven orange cloth, and a pair of beautiful matching velvety slippers, well groomed and warm inside his belly, he was ready to face the world.

Chapter Two

OPERATION CHARAVEDI

The main street of downtown Shambala was buzzing. Something was clearly going on: far in the distance, the Buddha of Long History could see an unusually long line of Buddhas in front of the Council Hall at the end of the avenue. Some of the bypassers coming his way after their visit to the Council looked uncharacteristically smug, as if they were treasuring a private joke.

The Buddha of Long History sighed: he did not like queuing up, but there seemed to be no other choice. He had to get an explanation from the Twelve; he was after all their odd founding member...

But this official title did not match the goofy smile that he did not seem to be able to control. He suddenly felt too exposed, and decided to try and sober up. On the long walk through the main avenue he kept on massaging his face and even tried to think of all the sad events in his many lives.

Nothing seemed to work. By then, he had reached the large Enlightenment General Store, the first and most ancient commercial enterprise in Shambala. Its back garden, normally crowded with Buddhas sipping the hot cocoa he himself had introduced after a journey to the Americas, and taking a break from their meditation practices, was empty. He sat down on a bench and closed his eyes.

Suddenly freed from the struggle, his whole being started smiling. This time he did not try to stop it, he allowed it instead to spread all over. It tasted familiar: like berries and cherries, like his childhood. Like moments of great happiness, of going on unknown adventures. Yes, to keep on moving was exactly what he had been longing for, without realizing it, since quite a while! It was time to show that smile ...

Inwardly, he whispered a goodbye to all the dear friends with whom he had spent such lovely times in this backyard over the years: Jesus, who often came by after working the land in his olive field, looking good and no longer like some emaciated superstar. Kabir, who hang out there at the peak of the heat of the day, drinking a cocoa fredo while reciting his poetry to people, dogs and cats. And sweet Lao Tzu, who shared his truth with anyone willing to listen, while drinking a spicy hot chocolate in the tranquility of a late afternoon. How much they all loved lounging on the Zen wall, the low stone bench under the large mulberry tree, and enjoy each other's company.

After these public gatherings, they would make a later appointment by the local hot springs, to simply commune in silence. That was his favorite time with them. Unluckily those springs had dried up in an earth shift during a minor earthquake a while ago.

But soon enough, he was taken out of his pleasant reverie. None of them was there now. The place looked empty and out of stock. The Buddha of Long History couldn't stop smiling about such a solid routine being interrupted.

He stood up and walked on, listening to the soft swishing sound of his velvety slippers on the cobblestones, until he arrived at destination. He stopped in front of a handsome tall building, slightly taller than the others, with a big polished copper sign on its front door saying: SHAMBALA TOWNHALL, Council of Twelve. He couldn't believe his luck: the queue was gone.

He took the lift to the upper floor. The thick ebony doors opened straight into a large airy room. On an elegant buffet in the corner, the remains of a large breakfast were in view, still warm and enticing.

The Twelve were sitting around a highly polished table, having just finished eating.

As he came in, all heads turned towards him. Before they all stood up to greet him, he had the time to notice that in front of each one of the Twelve was an Ipad - open on a page displaying in capital letters:

OPERATION CHARAVEDI. They didn't look surprised. In fact it looked as if they had been waiting for him.

As soon as he sat down on the empty chair around the table, a fresh selection of delicious food was presented in front of him. He felt more and more intrigued, curious and ready to hear all about it…

The Head of the Council spoke up.

His German accent sounded a tiny bit harsher than the Buddha of Long History remembered, but it still had that unmistakable warmth that went straight to his heart. He was after all one of his best friends ever.

"Beloved," he said, "We thank you for coming exactly on time, and we thank you for accepting our offer."

The Buddha of Long History was completely mystified: on time? Accepting their offer? He had not talked to any of them for what seemed like ages…was he dreaming?

The German Buddha continued on cue: "We know that you might think this is a dream, but the truth is that we all just woke up. Right now everything might seem in a chaos, but Shambala is no average place.

We have been aware for quite a while now of how things are undergoing a tremendous acceleration on the whole Earth. The stress is such that everyone is increasingly afraid for his or her survival. More and more people start acting blindly out of that fear. This attitude is very dangerous: it can erase consciousness and cause self-destruction. We Buddhas need to help: those amongst us who are willing will have to step out of their comfort zone and mix again with humanity to bring back the flavor of Buddhahood in the world. Operation Charavedi is for those who are ready to take this quantum leap..."

His words were making the Buddha of Long History happier and happier. He felt a click inside, an excitement, just like a child...

The German Buddha continued: "You saw with your own eyes the transformation in your Yogic neighbor. Inside her there is an incredible amount of sensuousness and celebration that has lain dormant for a very long time: Operation Charavedi has activated it. She will share it now through the Samba in Brazil, and the people around her will feel much more positive and stronger, without even knowing why. She will be radiating joy, a very much-needed quality for the survival of the planet."

The Buddha of Long History looked at his twelve ancient friends sitting there. He felt them all inside him, deeper than in his heart, as if they belonged to the texture of his soul. He also felt there his Yogic neighbor, and then slowly all the Shambala Buddhas, whether they would be staying or moving on. They were all connected, including him, by a golden web of consciousness, each one fulfilling their individual purpose. He bowed down at the masterfulness of existence, and to the Twelve that had kept this connection alive.

"We Shambala Buddhas are all a living invitation for humanity to evolve," continued the German Buddha, "But at this moment only some of us feel ready to go into the world and embody this invitation. This will be the fastest way to the human heart: anyone who will be able to experience directly the energy of a Buddha, will look from then on at the world with new eyes. Their new state of consciousness will continue rippling outwards, affecting those who surround them, like a soft cloud of kindness and positivity and many other enlightened qualities."

"But there is a catch..." intervened the Buddha of Technical Support and Maintenance, " It will all need to happen in the time span of a summer season..." There was a hush and a turning of chairs as he continued explaining, "Due to the obvious lack of time on Earth, I have been experimenting, under the supervision of the Head of the Council, with new possibilities of faster reincarnation. So far, the best technology we have come up with is to project the "Charavedi Buddhas" as holograms to the home of the humans chosen as their "Soul Parents". Each couple of Soul Parents will possess the special skills needed for switching the hologram into a human being, avoiding in this way the lengthy procedure of traditional incarnation..."

There was a very impressed "Ooooh" coming from the majority of the Twelve, not all as technically bent as him...

"But we have a problem. We don't know for sure if the molecules of this new type of body will hold for more than one summer season. After three months, anything could happen. Now you understand why the short time span..."

"The Soul Parents won't know the real identity of their guest," the German Buddha added, visibly amused by the idea of a surprise, "We selected them from a list of applicants to an exchange program that we posted a while ago on Internet. They will just be informed that someone will come to them in an unusual way. Things will happen mysteriously from then on..."

He left a long gap for the Buddha of Long History to absorb all this information.

"It is a lot," he said in the end, "but I am open to it".

"One last thing... our current technology doesn't allow us yet to create holograms of adult human size..." added the Buddha of Technical Support and Maintenance with a somehow apologetic tone, "Everyone will incarnate into a five-six year old child..."

"It will be easier for you as a Buddha to be a child anyway!" added the Waif Buddha, leaning over to him with strands of honeyed hair covering her face, "a child lives in the moment, like a Buddha..."

Everybody present giggled approvingly at her innocent remark.

Maybe because of all the excitement, or maybe just out of happiness, the Buddha of Long History felt suddenly very thirsty and hungry. He found this funny and incongruent, but before he could do anything about it, a Chinese porcelain cup of fragrant green tea was presented to him. From another side, appeared a tray with two deliciously fresh croissants.

"Sustenance for the long journey ahead..." whispered a husky woman, known as the Dark Buddha, with a jolly smile. He relaxed, and ate with gusto, while everyone seemed more than pleased to have a little pause from what looked like a very intense morning of meetings. Only towards the last morsel of pastry he realized that everyone had been intently watching him.

"And how did your holographic breakfast taste...?" the German Buddha asked him with a sly smile...

"Remarkably tasty, and probably much lighter to digest...", replied the Buddha of Long History, surprised, wondering how becoming a hologram would feel...

As that thought crossed his mind, the Twelve seemed to respond in unison. They all closed their eyes in meditation, leaving him to begin his quest.

He also closed his eyes. He felt as if the light of his inner smile was guiding him towards a whirlwind of translucent colors that were moving and pulsing in search of a configuration. As his vision settled, the dancing particles slowly descended like gentle rain, forming a shape.

He saw a child Buddha. He had sky blue eyes. Blond unruly curls bound in a topknot framed his sweet face. He was wearing his same hand-woven orange cloth, and his feet were clad in a smaller version of his own soft velvety slippers. He emanated grace and innocence.

When the Buddha of Long History opened his eyes again, he noticed a notepad right in front of him, open on an empty page. He quickly sketched the image of the Little Buddha, wondering all along how impossible it was to capture innocence in a drawing...

Just as he finished, the Twelve opened their eyes and relaxed back into their comfortable seats. The Buddha of Technical Support and Maintenance stood up and took the sketch from his hands. He came back with it to his seat, produced a scanner and a laptop out of some invisible drawer under the perfectly empty table, and proceeded to scan the drawing.

The Buddha of Long History had so far mostly shunned from technology: only rarely had he allowed himself to use emails to communicate with fellow Buddhas on their journeys into the world. But this new concept of incarnation felt irresistible to him.

Picking up on his curiosity and jumping on the opportunity to divulge his inventions, the Buddha of Technical Support and Maintenance told him with a slightly distracted smile: "Now that we have saved this image, we can open our large database: "New Incarnations". It's a compilation of the thousands of contact addresses of those who responded to our Internet ad promoted by one Shambala Foundation. Each contact has a profile, with spiritual history and special skills. All of them have declared themselves ready to host a "special" child for a summer season..."

By now almost everyone had gotten up, and was crowding around the computer screen. The only one remaining sitting was the German Buddha, who seemed to know as much as his technical friend. Comfortable in his chair, he explained with his phlegmatic tone: "Now he has entered the image of the Little Buddha into the database and is searching for possible matches...."

Everyone stopped chattering when the screen halted to a name:

"The top result of the query is a couple living in Greece, next to a spiritual Center," declared the Buddha of Technical Support.

"They are known as the 'Indigo Couple', and live on an Island" continued the rather large bejeweled Empress of Poetry Buddha, famous already since founding times for her channeling skills, "I can see them: the true color of their aura is Indigo Blue. Their special skill is manifesting things through drawing. Indigo," she softly added, "represents a wakeful state of consciousness that comes with a strong penchant for a unique lifestyle...more and more children being born these days on Earth are exhibiting this quality. They seem to often get in trouble because they are determined to have it their own way. They are not easily prey to the fear that makes humanity so easy to manipulate..."

"This makes me like them instantly!" commented the Buddha of Long History, now scrolling through the information, but barely registering any of it through the loud thumping of his heart...

He stopped at their last additional paragraph, and read it out loud: "Being fully aware that the biological role of parents entails karmic responsibilities which we are no longer ready to take, we would like to be blessed by becoming substitute Soul Parents of a young child. We would like to provide this child with the right care, with a sense of being protected and a feeling of inborn freedom. We would like to restore its birthright to be loved unconditionally. We feel that in this way we will learn the precious soul lesson of caring and nurturing our own and the child's potential."

The Buddha of Long History caught a glimpse of the expression of longing on the face of the German Buddha, and wondered if also the Council would end up sooner or later joining the ' Operation Charavedi'. It seemed to him that this whole event had much deeper implications even for the Council …

But when he held his gaze a fraction longer, the German Buddha looked as unflappable as ever, and declared with his usual dry humored voice: "You have just been liberated from the crushing weight of the biological process of reincarnation, and you are now given our blessing to do whatever your soul needs and wants.

In this incarnation you will be known as the "Little Buddha". If you wish so, you may refer to the couple that is going to host you as your Soul Parents." He stood up, saluted the Buddha of Long History with a Namaste, and then hugged him warmly.

The rest of the Council followed his example. Hugging everyone took quite some time, but as far as the Buddha of Long History was concerned, it was just fine.

Finally, the German Buddha drew the meeting to a close with a solemn gesture and said:

"Now we want you to start opening up to your new form. As you tune into it more and more, you will reach a moment in which you will be neither your old self anymore, nor the Little Buddha yet. This is a very important time in the life of every seeker. It's the doorway through death into a new life."

The Empress of Poetry Buddha took hold of his hand and added: "We suggest you go now to our Library, and start gathering as much information as possible about your future life, the place of your spiritual rebirth, your Soul Parents. Maybe in this way you will also be able to get a hint of the lesson that you will learn…"

On his way out, the Buddha of Long History turned one last time towards them and declared: "This is going to be something completely different than anything I experienced before, and I feel ready for it."

He walked down the avenue with purpose and happiness.

Chapter Three

THE AKASHIC RECORDS

The Library was a short walk away from the Town Hall. Its beautiful domed building also stood high above all the other roofs, spreading pink light from its rose quartz roof tiles. The door was ajar.

Entering the Shambala Library was like entering a Temple. The Buddha of Long History could hear his own footsteps on the hall marble floor magnified by the silence, and he inwardly bowed down to the immense treasure of knowledge and wisdom that this place contained. Anything that had to do with spirituality was here, neatly catalogued, from ancient treatises written on palm leaves to the newest eBooks, all safely kept away from warmongers and power trippers.

A soft swooshing sound interrupted his thoughts, and he saw a whirling shadow briefly appear in his field of vision.

The chant "La Illaha Ill'Allah Hu!" reached him, repeated in a never-ending sing-song of peaks and valleys...

It was the Dervish, the Librarian on duty, whirling around the hall, fully absorbed in his own prayer. He didn't seem to be affected by the turmoil of Charavedi Operation, the Buddha of Long History observed. But this was no surprise to him: the Dervish had his own path to follow...

Coming to a halt right in front of the Buddha of Long History, the Dervish bowed down, and then slowly lifted his gaze towards him. He looked intense. He appeared at first sight as severe as the tradition he originated from, Islam. His eyes were blazing like the hot sun.

But the Buddha of Long History knew where to look in those eyes. At their core lay an oasis, a spark of happiness that the Dervish could never fully hide.

His true being, thought the Buddha of Long History as he met the Dervish's eyes, reminded him of a desert after an unexpected heavy rainfall, a barren landscape suddenly turning into a real Garden of Eden. The aura around his lean body, toughened by hardship and endurance, was surprisingly golden and sensuous, and emanated wellbeing all around him.

Knowing that this might embarrass him, the Buddha of Long History restrained his impulse to embrace the Dervish. His outer form remained gruff, prickly, like desert figs. He was not one for social meetings. Although everyone around knew that he was the most widely read Buddha in Shambala, he was famous for dismissing erudite questions with a shrug. If somebody got upset at his rejection, he would say: "God is everywhere. God is in your anger, God is in your curiosity, and God is in your love…"

"I came here for two reasons, my Dervish friend," the Buddha of Long History softly spoke out, "The first is to inform you that I will take leave from you until our paths cross again. The second is to consult a tome of the Akashic Records and gather some information about my pending rebirth on Earth, specifically on a Greek island…"

"Will you continue practicing what I taught you?" Asked the Dervish, his only focus being his practice.

"Inch 'Allah, my dear friend, I am sure there will be a chance to continue, and, who knows, maybe our paths will cross even there, in the most surprising way…" the Buddha of Long History answered, sounding for a moment completely Middle Eastern, like his friend.

The Dervish's eyes responded by lighting up, and giving out a rare shower of bliss that only a few intimate fellow travelers were allowed to see.

The Buddha of Long History realized just there and then, standing in the Library Hall, that it was not the first time that he had felt stuck in Shambala. His friendship with the Dervish, mostly made of very short sentences and a lot of shared silence, had begun a few years before exactly for that reason …

"I am afraid to confess, my dear Dervish, that for the last few months I have been finding myself in the same situation as I was when I first came to you a while ago. I have been feeling stuck again…"

The Dervish nods, remembering very well how then the Buddha of Long History had come seeking for help because all his usual sitting meditation techniques had stopped working.

"You taught me to whirl in the ceremonial way…"

"Yes," the deep and melodious voice of the Dervish filled the high vaulted hall, "The simple system through which my Master before me, Jallaluddin Mevlana Rumi, and myself, have reached enlightenment."

"I loved to whirl until dawn together with your group of students…and I liked so much the green costumes that you designed for us, with those full skirts that seemed to float mid air when we turned…" the Buddha of Long History stopped. He had never exchanged so many words wit the Dervish, and wondered if he was talking too much.

But it was the Dervish that picked up the conversation with a trace of mischievousness in his smile: "Remember the hats?"

"This is how I fell in love with you!" shouts the Buddha of Long History, his voice echoing through unseen corridors, "that time when you ran to the Enlightenment Store and grabbed a pile of green shopping bags to replace the Sufi hats that had gone misplaced upon delivery!"

"God is everywhere, also in the Supermarkets…" commented the Dervish with a distant gaze, his attention slowly drifting back to the divine…

Before losing him completely to ecstasy, the Buddha of Long History quickly repeated his second request: "Can I now browse into the Akashic Records? I am looking for a particular book that will give me useful hints for my next journey"

The Dervish looked at him for an intense moment: "The Akashic Oracle…" he said with certainty.

The Buddha of Long History smiled: his friend knew every single volume of this Library, probably including the ones that were not yet written…

Beckoning him to follow, the Dervish went down through a spiral staircase dug out of Himalayan rock, and stopped at a huge entrance door of solid teakwood. The Buddha of Long History could barely hear him murmur some enchantment. Immediately responding to his command, the door slowly opened.

They entered a large hallway that opened into an ancient maze of corridors, halls and high ceilinged vaults. The place was suffused by a soft light, and felt dry and safe. Its walls were entirely covered with books. The Dervish in the lead, they went further, through another smaller door and down another spiral staircase. Their footsteps were now inaudible, as if they were gliding through the stone floor. Ahead of them was what looked like a very ancient place, with its whitewashed walls retaining the imprint of prehistoric graffiti and symbols. By contrast, the space was beautifully furnished with modern tables and comfortable chairs, and equipped with the most sophisticated photovoltaic diffused lighting. The most precious and ancient texts were kept here, underground. The dry cold weather of the Himalayas acted as a perfect natural preserver, and only a few trustworthy people had access to this area.

In one of the most secluded rooms was the full collection of the Akashic Records, which dated far back to the beginning of human history.

"The Akashic Records" said the Dervish, "are as you know a comprehensive record of all spiritual events, from the smallest individual's path towards enlightenment to the largest collective shifts of consciousness that redirected evolution. They reveal many esoteric secrets that could only be known after long and complex teachings. But few know of the existence of the Akashic Oracle, an esoteric treaty within the Records that contains the algorithms of all what could happen in anyone's future."

He drew one of the ladders towards the section "Future Lives" and pointed to the upper shelf to the Buddha of Long History, "it's up there," he said, and softly sighed, "Good bye my friend…Charavedi…"

In a rustle of green fabric, he whirled out of The Buddha of Long History's sight. Climbing to the top shelf, The Buddha of Long History stopped at a beautifully bound book with the title embossed in gold: "Akashic Oracle".

"This is what I was looking for," he said softly, with reverence. It was a heavy tome, and he had to balance it carefully while climbing down. He placed it on a well-lit table, and started leafing through it. The book spoke in riddles, numbers, complex calculations and symbols, all leading to a few facts and many cryptic sentences about one's future path. Whoever could read beyond both facts and words would store that information in their deepest unconscious. This information would then resurface to his conscious mind as an inner guidance when needed.

After completing all sums and solving all riddles, the Buddha of Long History read aloud: "Your future life will be one of extremes. You will experience great friendships and great loneliness, great curses and great healings". As he continued reading, his voice echoed through the corridors eerily amplified:

"The Final Transformation will happen to you when you shall take your share of blame for the past, and find the place where love and meditation are one.

"In the end, you shall discover that being small is truly great, but being fully human is even greater ..."

The Buddha of Long History carefully closed the book, placed it back on its shelf, and sat for a while on a stool, eyes closed in deep meditation, absorbing the words without questioning them.

On his way home, he thought about the mind-blowing technology described by the Buddha of Technical Support and Maintenance. It seemed that now science and spirituality had finally found a meeting point, right at the edge between energy and matter... His sketch of the Little Buddha would soon turn through a play of lasers into a hologram, to which his light consciousness could easily attach itself. Later on Earth he would materialize through the loving intention of his Soul Parents... He felt a strong sense of anticipation and curiosity: he could only compare this journey with his previous slower incarnations, but this time it would be a conscious and fast jump...he frowned, realizing that he would be wavering between matter and spirit for an indefinite while, and how disorientating that could be...

Only then he started realizing all the implications. He spoke out loud: "How will it be to come as a ready-made child? Will I retain my wisdom? Will I forget why I came? Will I be me?" He remembered the smile of the Waif Buddha, her words, and everyone else giggling. His essence would be intact, that much he knew, but for sure he would have to let go of his middle-aged mannerisms and aura of wisdom ... maybe his child brain would not even remember many things...

Arriving at the gate of his tropical garden, he was startled by the brightness of a cluster of Hyacinths: Indigo, like his future soul parents. He caressed the flowers, bent to inhale their fragrance, and felt a great peace descending over him.

Back inside his home, the Buddha of Long History took a last look at his surroundings. He removed some specks of dust on the windowsills, watered his orchids, lit an incense stick and sat on a meditation cushion right under the skylight at the center of his domed roof. As the sun descended and evening came, a whirlwind of spinning lights started surrounding him. With a grace that defied gravity, the light particles gathered themselves into the shape of a child. The Buddha of Long History bowed down to it, and with a deep last inbreath allowed his consciousness to detach from his body.

Instantly, each one of his subtle bodies started taking on his future shape. He felt like a child, defenseless and small, but also brimming with vitality and freshness. He looked at his feet; they were translucent, immaterial, clad in a smaller version of his slippers. At last, he experienced how increasingly hard it was to identify with the old man sitting in meditation right in front of him, and then, also that image was gone.

Now he had to find a way to get to his new home and the new life waiting for him. He went out into the garden and looked for something that could carry him to destination: something light, with an easy shape. Something air borne.

Suddenly, a cool mountain breeze blew through the valley, casting loose leaves and dry branches on his path. The Little Buddha cheered, and saluted the wind.

He noticed a large banana leaf, almost as large as him, that had just fallen nearby, and with a graceful hop sat on it.

A gust of wind came down the mountains, swiftly lifting the leaf with the etheric Little Buddha on it. He just held himself to the sides, and his new vehicle started undulating upwards. It had all happened so fast...

He looked down, at the panorama below. A thing of rare beauty was happening...

The Council of Twelve and the whole remaining population of Shambala had come out in the open.

They were standing all together, each holding a candle or a torch, in absolute silence. It looked like a shimmering sea of light, flickering in synchronicity.

The Little Buddha felt tears in his eyes. His friends were sending him off. It was like a tribute that marked the ending of an era. No one knew what would come next; whether Shambala would still continue existing, and if the Little Buddha would ever return.

In the flickering light of the candles and the smoky glow of the torches, he looked at each one of them, honoring their courage to surrender to the unknown.

Then he set off on his journey.

Chapter Four

METAMORPHOSIS

Full Moon in Scorpio-Transformation

It's springtime, and a Greek Island, set somewhere in the North Aegean Sea, is just waking up after a long trying winter.

Tourist season has not yet started. The terrace restaurants at the sea village, battered and partially demolished by the violent sea storms, are being slowly repaired for the summer. The villagers themselves are still living up on the hill away from the tides.

Only few people have remained through the winter in their cottages scattered amongst the fields at sea level. They are the ones who work in summer, the waiters and waitresses who charm tourists with their easy smiles, the artists who sell their paintings, clay objects, and handmade jewelry. Some of them are musicians, Yoga teachers, Reiki Masters, healers of the heart and soul, silently creating a positive field of coolness around.

They have spent their winter safely warm in their small cottages doing their winter crafts or simply resting while the ferocious wind outside attacked the cold stonewalls and rattled their roofs.

But when spring comes, and the gates to the winter underworld bang shut for another year, they all open the creaking doors of their winter cottages to a new land, entirely covered by tiny purple natural orchids. The sky above them is polished clean and bright.

On such a glorious spring afternoon, high up in the hills that border the settlement of the locals, a tall couple, a man and a woman, are walking hand in hand down a dirt road bordered by flowering oregano bushes hand in hand.

They seem to be engaged into a passionate discussion. The man started it: he seems now to emphasize a point with his free hand. The woman, standing for her opinion, stops on her tracks and replies. They simultaneously let go of each other's hands and begin gesturing emphatically. But they don't seem to take it too serious: they are also laughing and taking dramatic pauses to catch their breath.

As they resume walking, he says: "Isn't it surprising how the name Shambala keeps on recurring in our lives lately? First that beautiful article that someone shared about the mythical place called Shambala where the Buddhas, the awakened ones, were said to come together after their enlightenment. Like a Buddhist Paradise…And then, just right after, that reportage you found on Internet that argues that this is all a legend, because nothing of the sort appears on the areal maps of the Himalayas… But don't you think," he slows down, long enough to catch her eyes, "That enlightened Buddhas can make themselves undetectable by computerized equipment, if they want to?"

She smiles back at him, and says: "I don't think that Shambala exists on the material plane. It is a metaphor; it simply indicates the field of enlightenment, the inner space we all would like to be in. I imagine it just like that special atmosphere that blossoms around an Enlightened Master. Except that in Shambala everyone is supposed to be enlightened, Master and disciples alike. That would be the ultimate, don't you think?" she pauses and sighs: " But I'm afraid it doesn't really exists…"

The man's deep blue eyes twinkle: "Who knows? I am not so sure. I think that there are more mysterious places in the world than we know…"

They keep walking down the road in silence for a while, until the man has again something to say: "But you must admit that it's really funny that Shambala is also the name of that Himalaya based organization that contacted us a couple of weeks ago! Such a beautiful name for an exchange program!"

"And this one it is for real, for sure…" smiles the woman, "They search for couples with special skills to host gifted children…I wonder if our experience in psychology and meditation qualifies us … it was worth applying for the program anyway. İt's just one of those perfect coincidences that we took the summer off from work and that we have the time for something like this…It would be so exciting to host one of these kids for three months! We would become his or her 'Soul Parents' for a season, that's what it said… there would be so much to give and to receive!"

"And…" she continues, sounding hopeful, "there is one more coincidence…many of these new gifted children are known as…Indigo children! They are kids who have somehow stumbled onto the next evolutionary step. Schools don't know how to deal with them, and parents are often overwhelmed because they don't seem able to discipline them! It's easy to imagine that some of them have already gone through quite some trouble."

"I like trouble!" concludes the man, with a happy smile….

Long after Shambala has disappeared from his view, the Little Buddha still feels for quite some time the presence of the Buddhas down below sending him blessings. He is so touched by their tribute that he barely notices how the wind is carrying him further and further away. At some point, he feels a shiver: an invisible boundary has been crossed, and he is all alone, in the vast sky.

This time, he decides, he is not going to teletransport like he did for centuries: too risky in his present etheric state. He feels like slowing down and drifting a bit, letting his banana leaf be lulled by the winds. It is a beautiful night, and the stars are shining so brightly that it feels like bathing in the light of a midnight sun. Together with the sound of the wind, as the winds carry him higher and higher, he begins to hear a celestial music: the "Choir" of the Planet Earth, a sound akin to joyful dolphin songs and free bird calls. He is delighted to be on the move again, and feels one with everything.

He would like to steam ahead, explore the vast cosmos around him, but when he tries to stand up he almost faints. He is not yet used to move his holographic body. He perceives it like a delicate whirlwind of circular patterns of light and color crisscrossing each other. It has no solid boundaries; every sensory input enters straight to his core. He definitely needs more time to adjust.

He spends many hours in this state in between worlds, getting used to his new reality.

When he finally thinks of looking down, beyond his banana leaf, he feels dizzy. But then, he steadies himself and gazes at the faraway Earth beneath him, the blue Planet, shimmering like a jewel of immense proportions. He sees sapphire, cobalt, aquamarine, turquoise, and many more shades of blue, in a whirling and dancing kaleidoscope of light.

The view is so stunning that he almost falls over the edge. Trying to steady himself, he grabs the borders of the leaf. His sudden movement causes a shift of balance, and a downward moving current catches the leaf. The Little Buddha holds on: his descent has started…

He recognizes a Mediterranean landscape, suffused by the surrounding glimmer of the sea reflecting the sun already low at the horizon. As they roll towards the sea, the red mountains in the background become hills upon hills of olive trees, figs and almonds.

He slowly approaches the green hills standing on his banana leaf like on a surfboard, flying so low that he can smell the fragrance of thyme, oregano and mint in the open fields.

Then he lets the last soft breeze take him gently to the ground.

He gets out of the leaf, bows down to the wind and stretches his limbs.

A couple is walking ahead of him. They are having a stroll in the hills. They are talking animatedly. From the fragments of conversation that he catches, he understands that they are headed home to change clothes before their Evening Meditation, which will take place somewhere else nearby.

He is almost sure that these are his Soul Parents, but he decides anyway to continue following them unseen a bit longer. There is no hurry, he tells himself, slowly walking behind them…

The woman looks quite grounded. She walks at a steady pace. She emanates both softness and natural authority. She is youthful. The clothes she wears are loose and sensuous. Her hair has a deep chestnut hue with streaks of bronze.

He loves her instantly.

The man has silvery hair, and the way he moves makes the Little Buddha smile. He does not walk in a straight line like most people: he sways from one side of the path to the other instead, as if drunk. But for some mysterious reason his movements still appear graceful and elegant to the Little Buddha.

They both talk a lot. From time to time, she distracts him from his words by pointing out at something along the path, like a flower or a bush of oregano.

They don't look like anyone the Little Buddha has ever known. As he silently comes closer, he can see it: a shimmering Indigo light dances around them. They are his Soul Parents! He had imagined them just this way, and yet to feel them in reality is new and different...

He keeps hiding few steps behind them. He might overwhelm them by suddenly appearing as a hologram claiming to be their soul child...

It seems that their debate is over. They are moving slower now. Their focus has gone inwards, the Little Buddha can tell: they are on the spiritual path. But they don't appear austere or ascetic. On the contrary, there is a feeling of enjoyment around them.

This time he almost calls them out. Without even noticing it, he gains speed and comes very close.

Just then they stop. He stumbles to a halt in between the bushes right behind them. They have arrived home.

Their cottage lies on a large piece of land high up in the hills, with an open view to the sea. As soon as he slides through the wooden gate behind them, the Little Buddha notices a big change in the atmosphere.

Everything here feels sacred.

A few steps up on the gravel path, there is a long pink wall. On each side of it stand two huge almond trees: their entwined branches frame an archway entrance. Peeping from behind the archway, the Little Buddha can see an inner courtyard with more almond trees, its floor painted in multicolored big flowers. All around it, there are terraces covered with roses, jasmine, geraniums, hibiscus and oleanders, and sheltered corners for sitting and enjoying the view according to the time of the day. He catches only a glimpse of what seems to be the corner of a stone cottage beyond the trees.

The Little Buddha hesitates. His first impulse would be to follow them into their house, but he realizes how tired he is from the journey: he needs some space to relax and let his new subtle body settle. There will be time enough when they come back from their evening meditation.

As he watches his Soul Parents leave again, the Little Buddha, hiding behind a tree, silently blesses them and wishes them a lovely evening. Alone again, he looks around for a safe place to rest and turn inwards. He will visit the house later...

He enters the garden, full of blossoming roses: he deeply inhales the early evening air, pregnant with their scent, and lets out a contented sigh.

He ventures a bit further in the field, where the ancient fig trees create all kinds of comfortable nooks and corners for someone as light as him to nestle in. A beautiful long branch that bends inwards with a graceful curve seems to be the perfect choice…

He takes his shawl, spreads it over the foliage, and climbs in. He is reminded of his summers in Shambala, when he used to sleep outside, under the stars. Like there, here also the evening is alive with the divine calls of the nightingales, singing to each other songs of love the whole night through. Before he knows it, he is asleep.

Later on, the Indigo Couple returns home. They look happy and rested after their meditation.

While the Indigo Man brews a pot of delicious Lotus Tea, the Indigo Woman checks their emails on her Ipad. "Wow!" she exclaims, "Shambala again! The Foundation has sent us a very cryptic message… 'You application has been accepted. Be ready for surprises…. Charavedi….' I wonder what that means…"

"Great! We'll soon find out, but let's relax for now," says the Indigo Man, placing a steaming cup in her hands. They are lounging in their colorful kitchen, on a large wooden Balinese couch full of cushions in front of a big table, with their cup of tea and a bowl of healthy biscuits.

"Shall we paint?" the Indigo Man asks her after a while.

The Indigo Woman nods a happy "yes", and slips out of the couch, returning with paints, brushes and pencils. She places one large piece of paper for both on the table.

"Together?" she asks, already intently looking at the blank paper.

There is a peaceful glow around them as they each start drawing on opposite corners in absorbed silence. When they reach the middle of the paper, they merge into one design.

"Remember when we discovered that we could call friends to us by simply drawing them? How they would come unexpectedly, even from abroad? " She speaks without lifting her gaze.

"Yes, and I remember very well how overwhelmed I felt when we realized we could do the same with objects…"

The woman giggles, remembering: "We had to learn the hard way that it's best to be playful and unselfish with what you manifest..."

"It's done…" They both say at the same time. It is complete. They first look at each other with a smile and then at the drawing: it's the picture of a Buddha child, with blond hair and blue eyes.

"So utterly sweet…" she says, "Do you think that this is how he will look?"

"It could very well be", he replies thoughtful.

Still mystified by their drawing, they decide to let it be for tonight and sleep over it.

They leave the paper on the kitchen table and switch off the light. Soon they are quietly sleeping on their loft.

Outside, deep in the heart of the night, the Little Buddha wakes up. He looks at the sky above, where the silvery rays of a pure full moon are playing hide and seek behind a blanket of spring clouds. He likes this time, when everything is silent, and the whole world is enveloped by the soft luminosity of the moon.

In the garden ahead, the roses look almost fluorescent.

He descends from the branch and starts walking up towards the cottage.

Suddenly, he becomes aware of a very subtle smell surrounding him.

Glimmering in the moonlight, he sees on the ground countless little purple fragrant orchids, forming what seems like a purple milky way pointing towards the house beyond the courtyard.

This makes him smile. It's as if existence is creating for him the most beautiful path to enter his Indigo parents' home.

He crosses the arched entrance and sees across the courtyard a simple but masterly built stone house. Its entrance stands theatrically a few stone steps higher that the courtyard, giving visitors the feeling of stepping upon a stage.

To his great luck the door is left slightly ajar…

As he slips inside, he hears a gentle rumble above him. He freezes and listens carefully: it's the regular deep breathing of the couple, sleeping on the loft right above him. It changes for a moment, but then reverts to its steady rhythm.

The Little Buddha wonders what to do next. He is at the right place, but his body is not yet fully there. It's a similar sensation to the intense experience of disintegrating when teletransporting at the speed of light, but this time he has no control over it…

He has had enough by now: he really would like to fully enter his new body. He feels the call of the beautiful Greek earth, but doesn't know yet how to respond…

Then he catches again the delicate scent of the tiny purple orchids in the field outside. Their fragrance reminds him of his life in Shambala, when he was still the Buddha of Long History. He suddenly remembers a boy in an odd Tyroler outfit with leather suspenders and a feather in his green cap, who used to visit his tropical garden for a few summers. He would enter shyly, sit somewhere and sketch for hours the flowers and the birds on his pad. On one of their rare conversations, the boy had confided to him that the fragrance of wild orchids was what guided him in his art…

He wonders for a moment why he remembered that child just now, and shrugs. It's time to move on, Charavedi…

He starts looking around, careful not to make any noise.

A few steps down, right underneath the loft, there is a lounge area with an open fireplace, a comfortable couch, and a window with sea view.

He instantly falls in love with this house. It's cozy. And even if it's not so big, it feels spacious.

He turns to look the other way towards the open kitchen, and notices a large piece of paper on the dining table. His pulse starts beating faster.

Just at this moment, the moon appears in full glory from behind the clouds, and its light streams like a laser beam through the window above the table, casting a dense silver light on the drawing. Climbing on a chair, the etheric Little Buddha looks at the paper and instantly recognizes his own image: "It's just like the one I sketched for the Buddha of Technical Support and Maintenance…" are his last stunned words.

It all goes very fast: after feeling a nanosecond of intense nostalgia and heartache, the Little Buddha lets go of the last residues of attachment to his previous life. He experiences a huge shock, and for an instant doubts his own choice: A blond and blue eyed little boy?

A timeless voice, right from the core of his soul, replies from within, urging him on: "Charavedi, Charavedi"

He looks again at the drawing. This is the moment: there is no way back.

He moves forward and bows, surrendering to the moonlight streaming over his etheric body, until his forehead touches the paper.

Light bounces from one whirlwind of particles to another. He feels as if he is going to faint. All energy runs out of him. It's similar to dying…but different…

When he feels as if the last drop of life has drained out of him, everything stops, abruptly. All is silent for a while.

Then he can almost hear wheels turning, and the first sensations of a new energy start filling him. This time it's a physical experience. He can sense: life has a taste and a tridimensional existence.

It begins slowly, and then becomes like a roaring waterfall, overwhelmingly delicious and blissfully warm, orgasmic. It is such a delight, that the Little Buddha almost passes out again.

His whole body is vibrating and buzzing in utter contentment. When the waterfall of energy reaches the extremities of his body, the sensation becomes excruciating, on the border between pain and pleasure. Then the energy bursts out, surrounding him like a rainbow aura.

"Life is so sweet", is his last thought before disappearing into some unknown dimension.

He doesn't know how long this lasts, but when he comes to the first thing he notices are his hands: they are the hands of a real child. The aura around them is dense, vibrant: he knows from past experience that this is a sign of healing powers.

Suddenly he embraces his tinier self. He feels so happy: he did it!!

"One last step to go", he tells himself: "bowing down in gratefulness to my old self, so that my new heart will carry no trace…

"Farewell, Buddha Of Long History" he whispers "Thank you for the long and precious life I had as you. Now you can dissolve into oneness. I take all the many gifts you gave me into my present life as the Little Buddha. Thank you!

For the very last time, the image of the Buddha of Long History disappears with a smile. Gone for good.

The Little Buddha is suddenly aware of a change in the sounds around him. The first morning birds are starting to call each other in the dark. The moon has set long ago. It is shortly before sunrise. He decides to wait on the large Bali couch for the sleeping couple. Soon he enters a dreamless sleep.

Chapter Five

SOUL PARENTS: THE INDIGO COUPLE

At dawn, the Indigo Woman opens her eyes with a great sense of anticipation. She looks surprised at the curve of her sleeping husband's back: he is usually the one who wakes up earlier to watch the sunrise over the mountains. But today it's different: she feels wide-awake, like a child on the morning of her birthday.

Descending the creaky wooden stairs as silently as she can, she goes to the kitchen counter. It's still dark inside, but she won't put the light on: outside the large window the almond trees already dance in the morning breeze, and the light is gently taking over. She starts preparing a delicious smoothie, a deep green brew of spirulina, fresh figs and rice milk. She sighs contented. Everything is perfect as it is.

Just as the first light enters the kitchen, she remembers last night's drawing on the table behind her, and turns around to look at it one more time. She cannot see it clearly yet.

She draws a bit closer, wondering how their picture will look in the morning light. As she leans over, she notices a bundle on the Bali couch. It must be my husband's clothes from last night, she thinks. But when she leans to gather the bundle in her arms, she notices that it seems to breathe. Whatever it is, it's alive. She steps back, not knowing what to do.

Just at that moment, the sun rises above the mountains and shines in through the window above the couch. She can see him now. It is a sweet-faced child with golden curly hair, wrapped in an orange shawl, deep asleep. He is here.

She turns away on tiptoes not to wake up 'the Little Buddha', as she already calls him.

Once out of his earshot, she runs up the stairs to her sleeping husband. All excited, she starts to shake him: "wake up, beloved!" she urges him, barely keeping her voice down, "there is a surprise downstairs!"

He opens only one eye. When he sees the expression on her face, he briefly opens both. Then he closes them again. She looks around in a hurry. Lifting a nearby pitcher full of water, she pours the content all over his face.

He instantly sits up: "What's happ…" he starts saying, but she clasps her hand over his mouth.

"Sssssshhhhh," she whispers. Only when his eyes show that he is finally listening, she lets go of him.

"Beloved, we have a guest..."

He looks at her open mouthed: "From the drawing...?"

She nods emphatically and kisses him on his nose. Still all wet, he takes her in his arms and hugs her passionately.

"I love you," he whispers in her ear.

"Me too", she whispers back.

"Let's go down and welcome our divine guest."

Just then, the Little Buddha starts surfacing from his deep sleep. He is feeling disorientated and drowsy. When he finally opens his eyes, he does not understand where he is. As he pulls himself up and rubs his eyes, the events of the night start slowly returning into focus. He stretches his newly acquired limbs with delight.

Just as he is wondering what to do next, he sees two people coming down the wooden stairs in front of him. He wonders who they are: "I am supposed to know them", is the nagging thought at the edge of his waking consciousness, but it feels as if it was long ago, and he was someone else. While his child's brain is working overtime to reactivate the lost connections, one of the two, the woman, walks towards him.

Their eyes make contact.

She stops and looks very intensely at him. He cannot suppress a yawn, but keeps looking. As they both keep on staring, a gap occurs: their minds go blank. In this emptiness, a sweet feeling of intimacy comes over both of them.

Then, as if they woke up from an unknown reality, their eyes blink at the same time. A big smile lights up the Little Buddha's face, sparking off the same response on her face.

She looks in awe at the drawing on the table, and realizes that this time it might have been something more than the usual manifesting of friends or objects. She feels as if they invited the divine in their home… "Now it's not the time to try and understand", she realizes, not wanting to break the magic.

This is definitely not an average child, she knows right away. He looks graceful, both outside and inside: his turquoise eyes reveal a harmonious inner world. But there is something else: he looks like a true Little Buddha…suddenly, the word Shambala has a new ring of truth for her: maybe it's more than a myth after all…

She silently takes back her mixer, completes her smoothie and pours it into three large glasses.

Meanwhile, the Indigo man, now dry, has reached and put his arms around the Little Buddha.

"Hello little guy", he says, "welcome to our small abode."

The Little Buddha looks up at the tall man. He likes him. There is a sparkle of laughter in his eyes. And around him, a dark blue shimmering aura. He smiles back and remembers: these are my Soul Parents!

The Indigo Woman returns to the table with three mugs and a big bowl of fresh fruits. She puts everything down and reaches out with both hands to the other side of the table, connecting with both her husband and the Little Buddha. The boy and the man join hands too, and they all sit silently for a moment, merging into one circle of energy.

When they let go of each other's hands, the Little Buddha lifts his arms skywards, in a gesture of blessing and surrender.

The Indigo Woman is visibly touched. Her motherly feelings are being awakened, but she is also experiencing something else, subtler, less personal: devotion.

The Little Buddha gently touches her heart center, in the middle of her chest. She experiences a sense of sweet benediction and a healing current expanding through her whole body. She can almost hear the sounds of inner organs relaxing while her blood happily rushes through her veins.

Then the Little Buddha turns towards the Indigo Man. He gently brings his little hands to his face and rests them on his forehead in an ancient gesture of blessing. The Indigo Man responds after a while by enveloping him in a long big hug.

When they move apart, the Indigo Woman is standing there, offering them a smoothie. They all laugh when they realize that the mug is far too big for the Little Buddha: it looks like a bucket in his hands... She goes to the cupboard and returns with a handful of colorful straws.

Nobody talks much in the hours that follow. As his new Indigo Parents try to make him feel at ease with cuddles and nice snacks, the Little Buddha's initial clumsiness gives way to the movements of a normal child. By the early afternoon they look like an unusual but still plausible family.

By late afternoon, the Indigo Couple decides to venture outside with the Little Buddha for a stroll, to show him the surroundings. All is green, sparkling under the sudden outpours of rain, and life is gentle. As he follows them with his little footsteps through the fields, he notices overgrown shepherd houses in ruin, barbed wire left to rust and many weeds. This makes him sad.

He turns to the Indigo Couple with tears in his eyes: "Why...?" They respond with a sweet smile. They talk to his soul, without the mannerisms that adults too often use for children: "You know, Little Buddha, also our land looked like this when we first saw it. But just as it is now, the earth was festooned then with daisies and orchids, and the air was as pure. We felt a great potential in this land: it looks neglected, but it is also safe from worse forms of chemical pollution... "

The Indigo Man looks with pride at his wife and adds, "We installed right behind the cottage several solar panels that supply all the electricity, and big tanks for the water that we gather with a pump from a reservoir down below…"

The Indigo Woman adds with obvious passion, "There are no high tension cables or water ducts close to our home…we still live on the edge of the wilderness that was reclaiming our property."

The Little Buddha is impressed: so that's how it's going to be for him too…right from scratch…

As they make their way back home, the Indigo Man continues: "I am convinced that it's possible to have a comfortable life in this simple way. I have started appreciating the art of recycling, using what would be normally cast off in new creative ways."

"And we are not the only ones doing that. Just a few weeks ago we were in Denmark for our work." The Indigo Woman says while they reach the arched entrance of their cottage, "While strolling in the streets of Copenhagen, we saw a poster that drew our attention," she says, opening the door, "Here it is…" and hands him a flyer that is resting on a pile of magazines near the entrance.

"Congress on the Creative Use Of Garbage", the Little Buddha reads the title on a colorful piece of recycled paper, followed by a long list of what seems an impressive collection of world experts. His Soul Parents are again stunned. He speaks and reads with unusual accuracy. But that's to be expected, they both think, he is a specially gifted child…

"We went, and met a man who is popularly known as the "the Garbage Collector'. His solutions are incredible, "continues the Indigo Man, "His projects are very daring: he wants to create a new little planet, entirely made out of recycled trash from the Earth. This sounds like true twenty-first century alchemy …"

The Indigo Woman makes an almost invisible gesture to her husband, and interrupts the conversation: "Ahem…Little Buddha, you look like you need to refresh a bit, would you like us to wash you?"
"No, no thanks..." he answers blushing, "I am ok to do it on my own…"

While he rinses his child body in their aquamarine bathroom, the Little Buddha ponders over the destiny of this overexploited Planet.

As he scrubs the mud out of his feet and legs, he notices small rashes and cuts, and a bloating in his gurgling belly…in clean and pure Shambala he has never gotten sick like this…

He feels that he wants to take time before going out again. He still needs the protection of the Indigo Land to get adjusted to so many sensations. He falls into a dreamless sleep on the Bali Couch, feeling safe in this peaceful home.

The following morning early, the Indigo couple is drawn out of the main house by a loud shout of surprise. Rushing into the field, they see the Little Buddha running towards them, obviously excited, gesturing them to follow. He has just discovered the Zen Hut, the elegant wooden meditation cabin at the edge of the property. The Zen Hut has a very silent presence. Built underneath a large oak, it is shaded by its leaning branches, which create a cupola of leaves that always remains cool. It is resting on a wooden platform with well-concealed high poles that give the impression that it's floating amongst the greenery. The air around is filled with harmony and sacredness. It's made to just relax in it. Once he sees them coming, he quickly runs back: by the time they arrive, he is already sitting inside, his eyes closed, on the tatami floor.

They look at him, at each other, and then simply sit with him, in communion.

After a long time they all open their eyes. The Hut is luminous. They can almost hear their hearts beating in synchronicity. After a while, the Indigo Woman stands up and whispers: "I have things to do…", and leaves. The Indigo Man lingers a bit, but then eventually signals that he also has to move on. The Little Buddha gestures in return that he is going to remain a little longer. He feels happy here. It is as if a piece of Shambala has landed in this oak grove…

The Hut instantly becomes his place. In the next days, he spends most of his time there, looking into the books he borrowed from the Indigo Couple that expound new amazing theories, or simply resting with his eyes closed.

The Indigo Couple soon realizes that this place has been created for him long before he came. They can see that their guest is no ordinary child: even though he looks like one, there is a much more ancient feel to him, an aura of insight and wisdom. His presence provokes transformation...

"Little Buddha…" the Indigo Woman asks him after a few days, while bringing him breakfast, "Are you…coming from Shambala?"

The Little Buddha grins and nods a happy "Yes…It was about time you asked. Please go and call my Soul Father too, I have a story to tell…"

They all sit in a circle on the Hut floor, and for the rest of the morning they listen rapt to the Little Buddha's tales about Shambala and Operation Charavedi. The only thing he omits is who he was before. He doesn't want to linger on that.

The Indigo Woman is speechless for a while. "I am so touched and happy that the Land of the Buddhas really exists" she says, almost out of breath, "and I am deeply honored to be part of it in this way…" The Indigo Man smiles and remains silent, as if he always knew.

"Please tell me about you, now" the Little Buddha asks them, "What is your spiritual affiliation?"

They both have to smile at the unique mixture of his tinker bell voice with a language that sounds a bit formal, "Where do you go for your Evening Meditation?"

"Would you like to join us?"

And so it is that they take him to the Center of the Controversial Master, nestled close by in a peaceful valley facing the sea.

"It's a large place," the Little Buddha notices, entering the compound, "and people seem friendly and peaceful enough…" he says, waving back at a girl sweeping the faded dance floor of an open lounge with rickety chairs.

"Everyone is busy preparing the place for summer," says the Indigo Man, pointing at a young man cutting the tall grass.

"What a garden…" whispers the Little Buddha

"Yes, pure natural art at work…" the Indigo Woman replies, sweeping her hand over an incredible variety of overgrown bushes, rose plants, palm trees, pines, planted over the years with no apparent design: now they all embrace each other, almost calling one another, creating peculiar compositions.

Finally all activity around stops, and they hear music coming from an area beyond the lounge.

The Little Buddha is for a moment speechless at the beauty of the marble open space they find, surrounded by bamboos and shaded by a huge oak tree. Slowly, everyone around comes, showered and mostly dressed in white. The music goes into a crescendo, until even the hoarse evening calls of the shepherds are drowned by the drumbeats. Then, a softer melody follows, and everyone sits down. "It's lovely. I like this unusual mix of celebration and meditation…" whispers the Little Buddha to his Soul Parents while everyone adjusts on their seats for the next stage of the meditation.

"Now comes a video discourse of the Controversial Master…" the Indigo Man whispers back with a wink.

The Little Buddha listens intently to the talk that follows: he cannot help wondering whether he has personally met this Controversial Master on one of his spiritual journeys. He is intrigued by him, so modern and so ancient both, and amused by his irreverence and penchant for doubtful jokes.

"I love this new way of spirituality", he says on his way home, squeezing gently the hands of his Soul Parents on each side of him.

Days roll by in leisure for our three friends. The Little Buddha soon comes to know that beach time is the favorite early morning ritual for the Indigo Couple, and starts joining them.

The three of them climb on their scooter. The Little Buddha sits in front, on the lap of the Indigo Man, nestling on to the warm chest of his Soul Father and shrieking with delight at the wind in his hair.

The water is cold and transparent. They always all jump in without hesitation as soon as they arrive, and the Little Buddha loves it. It's like bathing in liquid crystals.

One day, while parking at the seashore, the Indigo couple notices that the Little Buddha is lingering around the scooter, looking at it from all sides…

"What is it? Do you like it?" the Indigo Woman asks him.

The Buddha smiles a bit shyly. Teletransportation, with zero carbon imprints, has been his favorite way of traveling for millennia. The thought of these new vehicles leaving streaks of smoke in the air doesn't appeal to him very much. But now he is part of this new world, and has to adjust to the normal ways of moving. He will do it wisely, without overdoing, he decides.

"Yes, you observed rightly." He says, "to drive vehicles that do not use animal power is a dream we all Buddhas have cherished for a long time. Now you made it come true".

It's the Indigo Woman's turn to smile: she just loves his mix between innocence and wisdom.

When they get home after the sea, in the pleasant coolness of the kitchen, the Little Buddha picks up the subject again: "But why do all vehicles come in such strange and ungainly shapes? I don't understand. They could be designed differently, with more imagination. They could look like apples, or clouds, or…" He stops. His smile spreads from his lips to his whole face. "Or like…a Lotus, a pink Lotus!" He looks as pink as his imaginary vehicle…

"No problem, Little Buddha," the Indigo Woman says, touched by his effort to update and be part of the modern world, "we will design for you the most beautiful and harmonious pink Lotus".

The Little Buddha replies quietly: "Thank you!" and then looks down. No need to mention teletransportation for now, he thinks. Better to focus on how to create a really good modern vehicle.

"Please Indigo Mother, do not take this as greed from my side," he adds, "But I would like a vehicle that can fly: this is the way I dream to travel: either on a lotus or just airborne, riding the winds. In fact, I am surprised that your Vespa cannot fly: am I too curious if I ask why?"

The Indigo Woman, visibly adoring him for his sincerity, takes him by the hand and replies: "My beloved Soul Child, this is a fantastic idea: it simply never occurred to me. I am still bound by conventions and habits, so I just travel by land like everyone else, or take airplanes…I would be happy to create a flying Lotus for you!"

"I am honored…" he replies.

The Indigo Man is on the terrace overlooking the sea. He is in the middle of carving a mask when he hears them calling. By the excitement in their voices he can feel that some new creation is brewing.

When he joins them, they are already sitting around a large piece of paper on the kitchen table, the child silently watching the woman drawing. A thousand-petal lotus is beginning to take shape. The Little Buddha looks at it in full admiration. Then, the Indigo Woman sits back, and nods. The Indigo Man opens a large pencil box and starts coloring: rosé, shocking pink, a little orange, some red, a little shade of blue … the lotus takes on body and fills up with essence. Finally, in the middle of it appears the seat for the Little Buddha, in the softest pink.

When the drawing is complete, they all step back to appreciate it. Then, the Little Buddha touches the drawing and speaks out his blessings.

Right in front of them the image of the lotus starts glimmering, decomposing into a whirlwind of light particles that settle after a while into a three dimensional Hologram Lotus, the size of a toy car. As The Little Buddha steps gracefully inside it and tries its seat, it slowly solidifies: it is made of a mysterious substance that seems durable and very light. The Buddha feels comfortable: the petals around him support him perfectly.

"But how can we make it fly?" whispers the Little Buddha,

"I have an idea. Shall I draw a touch-screen for driving it?" the Indigo Woman asks. Without waiting for his reply, she dives onto another piece of paper and starts drawing, while her husband colors it right behind her in all hues of metal gray, anthracite and silver.

"Thank you," the Little Buddha says, "this is enlightened intelligence in action: no limits to what is possible…"

In the same sequence as before, the Little Buddha touches it and blesses it. As soon as it becomes tri-dimensional, the touch screen settles precisely in the center of the pink lotus.

The Lotus Mobile becomes the official mean of transportation of the Little Buddha. It takes some time before he can master it: in the beginning, he is very awkward. Both our Indigo friends run behind him trying to catch it just before colliding with an olive tree or nearly falling into the well … But each time, the brave and alert Little Buddha steers out of danger with a last minute turn.

Soon he becomes an expert driver. He masters the art of making his vehicle move gracefully and slowly, sliding silently along the air currents, like the shadow of a passing cloud. He grows very fond of his Lotus Mobile. First thing every morning, as soon as he wakes up, he goes where it's parked underneath the Zen Hut. He usually finds the Indigo Man, who loves the early morning too, already there.

One morning, a week or so into his stay, the Little Buddha finds the Indigo Man waiting for him right outside the Hut. He takes him by the hand, and leads him to the Mobile. He has polished it. It shines so brightly that it competes with the first fiery rays of the morning sun over the mountains. The little Buddha runs to him and gives him a big hug, whispering in his ear: "Thank you Soul Father…"

"I guess you'll soon need it for a longer journey…" the Indigo Man answers, with a cryptic smile.

Chapter Six

MEETING WITH A REMARKABLE GIANT

New Moon in Gemini – Time for Travel

It's dawn. The Little Buddha is already awake. Two weeks have passed since his arrival, and he feels at home.

He loves the coolness of the beginning of the day, when everything is fresh and young.

Soon the sun will rise above his favorite mountain, the Ancient One, as he calls her, and then another hot day will start.

From the garden terrace where he sits he can still catch a glimpse of the sea at the horizon. Most of the view is taken by large bushes full of roses in a riot of colors: red, yellow, orange, pink and all the varieties in between. They surround him in an alcove of fragrance.

The Indigo Man is already outside for a slow and unfocussed walkabout, as he calls it. He moves around the orchard, letting the traces of the night lingering around his sweaty body evaporate in the morning coolness.

Inside, the house is still quiet. The Indigo Woman is up in the loft; she likes to hang out a bit longer in bed, letting the day arrive slowly and enjoying the breeze from the open windows.

But as soon as the first rays of sun enter the house, she comes out in her long morning robe to water the plants, her favorite early morning meditation.

The Little Buddha looks at both of them, the man and the woman, each performing their rituals, silently connected. He can see that they are not born to this island. He is like the North Sea, sometimes calm and quiet and other times passionate. She is one of those who carry in their blood many different nations and cultures, which makes her look and behave in an ever-surprising variety of ways, sometimes northern, then suddenly southern.

"They anyway belong to my world," the Little Buddha thinks, "a world where everyone is on the path, travelling from lifetime to lifetime, moving towards more and more grace and consciousness".

He is starting to wonder, though, if it will ever stop. There seem to be always new mornings to awaken to, and what appears as a fairytale in one life becomes a manifest reality a few lifetimes after.

"There is no end to the journey, nothing is ever final or perfect," he giggles, "even enlightenment…"

He is already learning something new, now, here on the island. Since his first walk through the surrounding to his latest visits to the sea village, he has been noticing how everyone carries gadgets and consumes a lot of everything. What confuses him the most is that there is no way for him to decide if it is for the better or the worse. It's unknown territory for him, and he does not want to judge hastily…

He loves his morning contemplation, watching his train of thoughts. Letting himself be surprised by the insights that come and go…

Meanwhile the sun has reached the corner of his terrace. Soon the white Hellenic light will ban all shades. He feels a subtle tension, an edginess.

He is just bracing himself against the impending heat, ready to retreat indoors, when it dawns on him: he needs absolute coolness, he misses the dark space of the cosmos, he longs for emptiness. He suddenly becomes aware of how tired he is.

Returning to his Zen Hut he sips some cold Green Tea and lies on his futon, resuming his contemplation.

He realizes how he has had to come to terms with the fact that so many things he expected to find back on Earth are gone; whole civilizations, whole cultures have disappeared. Everybody seems to be more streamlined, more the same. Before, changes were rare events, going over many lifetimes. Now constant changes, upgrades, updates and improvements are happening at a dizzying speed.

"Is it a deep fear of boredom that drives this new humanity?" he asks himself, well aware that boredom is what he had been feeling in Shambala before the Charavedi Operation. For the first time, he empathizes with the new humanity: boredom is something hard to watch and contain, and modern people seem to have zero tolerance to it. They would rather be entertained all the time, do, consume. They have forgotten what they really need. They discard love and prefer compensation…

"I am on dangerous ground, …" the Little Buddha warns himself, "feeling better than them won't help. What is in it for me to learn?" he closes his eyes. "Maybe simply that it's worth experimenting and sharing rather than holding on to what you already know…"

From what he sees and reads, from the videos he watches on the Indigo Woman's Ipad, he has to admit that he likes quite a few of the new people: even if they might lack some depth, they are more colorful and playful than the ancient ones. Life is a party in this time and age, he thinks with a smile.

He stretches out his body and yawns, falling into a peaceful nap.

When he wakes up, the sun is setting behind the ocean. From the cool deck of the Zen hut, he gazes at the lower flagstone terraces, bathed in the green shade of the oak tree above them, and leans over the platform to greet his Lotus Mobile parked underneath.

He has grown so fond of it. He goes down and looks at it with affection. It is truly part of his new human incarnation.

In his long enlightened existence, he has always been using teletransportation to move around. But not this time: his journey from Shambala on a Banana leaf has inspired him to enjoy traveling at a more human pace. Now the Lotus Mobile is the next step. He enjoys the whole ritual of sitting in it, letting the touch screen flash, and taking off.

He looks in the direction of the main house. The lights have gone on, and the silhouettes of his Soul Parents are moving inside, visible from the open windows, preparing for dinner.

His afternoon rest has soothed him, but he notices that his desire for a field trip in the vast cosmos is still there. "I need peace and emptiness", he whispers. His Lotus Mobile continues beckoning him from under the platform, glowing in the evening light. "It won't be a long excursion," he tells himself, "just enough to breathe out and erase so many impressions in such a short time…too many for my child brain…"

He decides to break the news to the Indigo Couple gently. Quick learner as he is, he comes to the kitchen and prepares for them their favorite dessert, Mousse au Chocolat, from a recipe found on the Internet. After their delicious dinner, while they are all savoring the Mousse, he informs them about his plans.

"It is understandable that you need space…"says the Woman.

"And adventure…" adds the Man. The Little Buddha is touched by their trusting response.

The Indigo Woman goes to her storage and takes out a thick saffron colored pullover: "Just in case it is cold out there in the vast emptiness…"

"When are you planning to go?" asks the Indigo Man.

"Now…" he smiles at both of them, and bows down to receive their blessings…

They both love his way: no time to lose, here is the only place, now is the only moment…

In the darkness of a moonless night, they wave at the Little Buddha while he takes off in his Lotus Mobile.

He flies higher and higher, until the outer edge of the atmosphere. Charging full speed ahead, he dives into the mystery.

The dark luminous dome of stars ahead is as beautiful as he remembers it. He feels blessed: entering the vast Cosmos is as sacred as entering the Cathedral of Chartre, or the Taj Mahal on a full moon night. He wonders if what humanity recognizes as universally beautiful is simply what is in tune with the universe and reflects its magnificence.

He suddenly remembers how in his past journeys here he had heard a melody that seemed to originate from the very center of the universe. A deep and melodious humming, that left a subtle healing vibration in its wake.

Just as he tries to catch it back again, he realizes that it is no longer audible. It has been replaced by the electronic sound of millions of bytes of information bouncing around the Earth to cover the distance from satellite to satellite.

"No way to hold on to the past…Charavedi, Charavedi…" he repeats to himself, letting go of another piece of nostalgia...

He decides to honor the new by trying not to follow any familiar path. He steers towards an unknown direction, gazing at the display of endless stars, each one with its unique colored light. It's blissful to be here, bathed in starlight…

Suddenly, the Lotus Mobile starts faltering. The engine stutters.

There is a huge cumulus of clouds ahead. The Little Buddha moves towards them, holding tight against the change of pressure. It stinks here. His whole body reacts to a very unpleasant smell. To avoid breathing what seems to be a deadly mix of toxic mold, he veers the Lotus in the opposite direction.

Just when he is in the clear again, he hears an alarming high-pitched sound. Something is really wrong. His touch screen is blinking, displaying in big letters: STOP!!!!

A rock as big as a house is hurling towards the Lotus Mobile at top speed. At the last moment, he manages to pull the break.

Just as he comes to a shuddering halt, so does the rock. The Little Buddha jumps out of the Lotus Mobile onto what seems a carpet of soft cumulus clouds and edges towards the rock. He studies its surface. It looks like an asteroid. But in that case it couldn't have stopped abruptly …

He circles around it, trying to understand. Then he notices that it's again moving, this time slowly, but steadily, towards him. He is paralyzed by surprise, and stares without getting out of the way.

Just as the rock is about to squash him, he catches a very fast movement at the periphery of his vision. As the rock hurtles an inch away from him, he is unceremoniously pushed aside. His ears are whistling. He closes his eyes.

An angry booming voice brings him back:

"Why didn't you step out of the way…?"

He is stunned. On the cumulus where the rock was, a very large man is standing. And behind him there are many more rocks, looking like mountains of all sizes.

He is a giant. Everything about him looks very large. Even for such an oversized body, his hands are enormous. He looks fearsome: his mouth is twisted in anger, his fiery eyes are penetrating, and he speaks very loud.

The Little Buddha is reminded in a flash of the masks that his Indigo Father sculpts, similar to the ones that he has seen in a previous life long ago carved on a temple door somewhere in the Far East.

"I did not expect a moving mountain here in the cosmos," he says, omitting for now that he expected even less to meet an angry giant here.

The giant looks at him, checking him out and apparently weighing his answer.

In the end, he seems satisfied. His face relaxes, and he looks more curious than angry.

The Little Buddha is relieved.

But then he starts again, with a challenging tone: "But what you called a mountain, is not a mountain"

The Little Buddha does not know how to react. It did look like a mountain to him. But it's also true that normally mountains do not move.

He can feel that the giant wants to tell him more, and he doesn't want this strange meeting to degenerate into a fight. So he complies, and asks the question that the giant seems to be waiting for.

"If this is not a mountain, what should I call it then?"

"Go and look for yourself"

His brusque unfriendliness triggers the Little Buddha, but he again decides to let it pass, and not to react.

He takes a step closer to the rock, and reaches out to touch it. It smells. It emanates the same toxic odor that drove him away from the clouds. It's not made out of stone as he first thought: it is pliable and sticky. It's garbage.

He would like to turn away in disgust, but realizes that it wouldn't be such a graceful response after all. Especially because the giant might have just saved his life...

He opts for a polite answer: "It is interesting to discover that the mountains around here are made of a material that in some way reminds me of the texture of garbage..."

The giant looks for a long moment into the eyes of the Little Buddha. His face turns more and more red, until he cannot hold back any longer. He is giggling.

First his shoulders start to shake, and then he begins to emit muffled sounds of what could be just as well tears or laughter.

"Interesting..." he says, with a shrill falsetto voice, "the mountains around here are made of a material that reminds me of garbage..."

Realizing that the giant is imitating him, the Little Buddha gets enraged. What does this big bastard want from him? He is suddenly blinded by an outrage so big that it takes all his energy to stop himself from screaming: "Do you want me to find a better word for garbage, a word that suits you better? Well what about sh..., since you anyway seem to be full of it?" These words resonate loud inside him, unspoken.

There is a long silence.

The Little Buddha realizes that he is in a shock. If the giant hadn't stepped in, he would have for sure been crushed to death. And now he is silently insulting the man who has actually saved his life. Just as he is about to apologize for his unfriendliness, it is the giant who speaks out.

"I am sorry, I did not mean to offend you. It must be because I spend too much time on my own…I am actually very happy to see you here!

By the way, I haven't yet introduced myself: I am the Trash Giant, also known as the Giant Of Trash And Garbage. I live here alone. And who are you?"

Compared to the deafening voice of the Trash Giant, the voice of the Little Buddha sounds tiny and fragile: "I am the Little Buddha"

The Trash Giant lets out a sigh as powerful as a storm. The Little Buddha pulls up the collar of his pullover against the sudden cold.

"Mine is not a very clean name, but my job is not very clean either. I must look disgusting to you, and I certainly smell bad. For sure, you must have already decided that I am insensitive."

The Little Buddha has indeed thought all that, but he doesn't want to mention any of it now.

"I do have feelings", the Trash Giant continues, "but since I have been living here alone for quite some time, I have not had many chances to share them with others". Something changes in his voice. He does not sound aggressive any more, just a bit wary.

"Don't you have a family to share with?"

The Trash Giant shakes his head, "I did have a family once, but I have left them behind."

"Why did you do that?"

"Because I changed. They knew me as a good person, a dedicated member of the family. I also believed I was. The trouble was that at that time I was unaware of my hidden dark side, and when it surfaced right after childhood I broke up with almost all of my family..."

"Who was it amongst them that you did not break up with? " the Little Buddha, who has now relaxed, asks him.

"My grandfather", the Trash Giant looks happy mentioning him.

"Did you love him?"

"Immensely!" Suddenly a deep veil of sadness descends over his eyes. But it's gone as quickly as it came, replaced by a jolly smile.

The Little Buddha wonders. He is not yet sure about the Trash Giant. He seems to be full of contradictions, someone who at any point might change his mind and attitude,

But there is also something very human about him. He is like a rough diamond, unpolished. After his timeless time in Shambala, where each inhabitant was so sensitive and refined, it actually feels refreshing for the Little Buddha to meet someone as uncivilized as the Trash Giant.

Before his enlightenment, the Little Buddha recalls, he has had so many friends, both women and men. His body suddenly remembers hugging, kissing and touching all of them. He is shocked by his physical response. He feels turned on, excited, alive…

But suddenly his thoughts shift: he feels betrayed by his own body. First it has almost killed him by not moving when the rock of garbage was going to crush him, and now it makes him helplessly turned on...

He quickly checks whether the Trash Giant is aware of his state of arousal. His secret little action shocks him even more. He wonders, "Who am I then, if it is all completely out of my hands?"

The Trash Giant interrupts his reflections, this time gently: "Would you like a cup of tea, before you travel onwards?"

He looks really happy when the Little Buddha shyly nods.

"Okay then, I will go and wash", he says, disappearing behind one of the many mountains of garbage.

The Little Buddha is left on his own. He feels dwarfed by all the surrounding heaps of trash. But then it dawns on him: this is exactly the adventure he was longing for.

He parks his Lotus in a safe place away from the mountains and ventures, hopping from lack of gravity, amongst them. Just as he is getting used to the smell, he picks up an entirely different scent: the fragrance of spices, teas and biscuits…He finds himself at the entrance of a wide area that seems to be the kitchen.

The Trash Giant is standing in front of a large broken mirror, drying his hair and vigorously rubbing his scalp with an old towel. That rag must be coming from some garbage heap, the Little Buddha thinks, but it looks clean.

"Don't be worried my little friend," the Trash Giant tells him, inviting him to sit down on a worn out couch and offering him a steaming cup of tea from a lovely chipped china cup, "if you don't have enough time today to listen to my story and tell me yours, you can still come and visit me again any day you feel like...."

The Little Buddha is touched. This is turning out to be a real meeting. "Thank you", he says sweetly, sipping from his fragrant tea, "I will be back soon". Then he stands up, ready to go.

Before he knows it, The Trash Giant draws him to his large body into a big hug.

Squeezed into physical intimacy with him, the Little Buddha's suspicions are confirmed: the Trash Giant does smell quite a bit. But then, he knows that he cannot apply his Shambala standards to everything and everyone.

Awed by the mystery of his new life, the Little Buddha surrenders, and returns the hug with equal passion.

Flying homeward bound through the clouds in his Lotus Mobile, the Little Buddha has time to regroup. He has had a very uncommon day, with quite some unusual challenges. He realizes that there is no reason to criticize anyone, including himself, for being different. He sits back in his vehicle, which is moving at a comfortable cruise speed. His heart relaxes: all is good.

Suddenly, he hears the deep humming sound of he Cosmos. It's still there. This brings him instantly back to his center. It's all he needs. As he starts descending into the Earth's atmosphere, he feels once again blessed by all the multicolored celestial bodies shining above him.

When finally the Greek Island is in sight, he is delighted. Home. He descends gently, surfing the currents with his Lotus, just as he did on his first landing atop his Banana Leaf.

The Indigo Couple must still be sleeping, he guesses, while stepping out into the dark. He wonders: so little time has gone by, maybe just a couple of hours. He sits outside the Zen hut gazing at the clear night sky. Somewhere in this vast expanse of revolving planets and glittering stars is the Trash Giant. The Little Buddha can picture him in the Cosmos, surrounded by heaps of garbage. He feels for his new friend, all alone up there. He will for sure visit again.

The following morning, while lounging with a smoothie in the shade of the pergola, the Indigo Couple asks him about his night trip into the Cosmos. They laugh at the antics of the Trash Giant, cry for the loss of his innocence, and are awed at his inventiveness.

"You have made a precious friend, I feel it", says the Indigo Man

"And how did the Lotus Mobile hold up so far from the Earth?" the Indigo Woman asks, concerned.

The Little Buddha realizes that the only way to reassure her is to tell her the truth: "Beloved Soul Mother, I thank you with all my heart. The Lotus is gorgeous and I love using it. Just one extra thing needs to be said. I know how to teletransport to any destination; it is just something that I acquired by becoming a Buddha. Even if I adore its design, I want you to know that I do not necessarily need the Lotus Mobile to be able to fly…"

"I suspected this" the Indigo Woman blushes, "I have read about the extraordinary abilities of a Buddha…"

"But I anyway want to make you a surprising gift", she adds, while only the slightest question mark at the end of the sentence reveals her insecurity…

"Thank you " the Buddha says, feeling relieved to be honest about his capacities.

But the Indigo Woman has not finished: "Let's go inside…" she says with a quizzical smile.

Back inside around the large kitchen table, she takes out the paper with the image of the Little Buddha, and draws right behind his shoulder blades a pair of beautiful and delicate butterfly wings. When it comes to coloring them in, the Indigo man tells the little Buddha: "If you want, we can make them multicolored: bright, dark, light... In this new world we are no longer attached to castes and credos: you can be of any color you like".

The Little Buddha bows down, in awe at this unimaginable new world, where garbage is cherished and transformed, and all colors and sizes are welcome…

Chapter Seven

A SECOND CHANCE

"Here they are...the floating garbage mountains," the Little Buddha speaks out excitedly while he shifts the course of his Lotus Mobile towards them. He has been preparing to take off since yesterday, when the image of the Trash Giant appeared in his meditation.

Some of the Garbage Mountains have grown in size during the Little Buddha's weeklong absence. He edges closer: they are almost hollow, the cosmic light peering through their gaps. They all bear human features. Every single one of them is a female representation, looking strong and beautiful. Here's an African Warrior Queen, and there is a Caucasian Peasant Woman, looking proud and graceful. They all seem to reflect the sculptor's love for women.

As he parks his vehicle next to the last Garbage Sculpture, a stately priestess in all hues of blue, he hears the splashing sound of water, and the softer muffled grunts of someone singing: it must be the Trash Giant, washing himself after a day's dirty work.

The bathroom area is right ahead: it's bordered by an array of faded shower curtains of many sizes, and the space is full to the brim with bottles, little pots and dispensers obviously rescued from garbage heaps. It's enough to fill the cosmetics area of a small supermarket.

The Trash Giant, looking like a king in his own domain, is pouring water from a bucket all over his naked body. When he sees the Little Buddha, he waves enthusiastically at him.

The Little Buddha feels a bit shy. The Trash Giant's body is big and pale: it reflects the late afternoon light like a full moon.

Upon departure, the Little Buddha has informed the Indigo Couple that this time he will stay overnight at the Trash Giant's place. He has told them that he wants to watch the sun rise over a million planets in the cosmos.

But now that he is here, he is overwhelmed just like the first time. After all, he does not really know who the Trash Giant is, and everything about him is so oversized, loud and dramatic, that he feels too small, almost non-existent next to him. For a moment he wants to turn around and leave.

Picking up his hesitance, the Trash Giant moves fast. He quickly wraps a towel around his body and runs to hug him.

The Trash Giant's smell of soap and perfume has an instant relaxing effect on the Little Buddha. He starts yawning and stretching his little body, giving in to his tiredness from the cosmic journey.

Ever so attentive, the Trash Giant immediately guides the Little Buddha to what he calls his lounge, a cozy corner with a motley collection of couches and easy chairs. Some of their springs are showing, and some of their feathers are gently floating in the air, but the whole place looks comfortable enough.

"Fresh from the garbage", the Trash Giant says jokingly.

While the Trash Giant busies himself into the adjoining kitchen area, the Little Buddha settles into an old orange couch, whose lumpy and sunken seats reveal the imprints of the backsides of countless generations.

Just as he is about to cross from relaxation into deep sleep, the Trash Giant comes back with some fresh green tea and sits next to him. The Little Buddha cannot but marvel at the unique beauty of the teapot and cups, broken and repaired several times. They look like art pieces.

"Beloved Trash Giant," he asks, "why do you have such attraction to garbage?"

It takes long for the answer to come.

"Garbage is what humanity produces the most. We all try to deny its existence. We respect all kind of things as long as they remain neatly packaged, but as soon as their presentation is gone, we lose interest. Everything ends up on the garbage heap, even the people whom we have no longer use for.

Like most, I spent a big part of my life trying to be what was expected from me by the surrounding. If the world needed architects rather than artists, I would become an architect, and renounce my true call. But the day came when I could no longer bear doing this to myself. I realized that my only way out was to rebel against all obligations. Once all ties were cut and I was alone, I started looking inside myself, and I found out that I was the one creating the heaviest obligations for myself, more than anyone else on the outside.

That's when I dropped out. In my aimless wonderings through the streets, I noticed how all garbage was released from its package, and how it could just stand there, being itself. This felt like the perfect metaphor for the freedom I was searching for. I relaxed deeply, and started enjoying being a nobody, just another heap of trash.

But soon, Little Buddha, I realized that garbage was not useless.

I realized that, because of its lack of definition, garbage contained an immense potential for new life. I started to love trash. It became easy for me to recognize how what others discarded could be put to use in new surprising ways. Trash became my fascination.

I can really tell you now, sweet little brother, that most people become who they really are only when they are given a second chance."

"But before we continue, little brother, I want to show you something: look," the Trash Giant points at what looks like a group of small fluffy clouds not too far from them "these are cushions with a special cloud design that I found somewhere in Mexico. I use them as a camouflage when I do not want to be spotted. Aren't they amazing? Touch them: they are as soft as fluffy clouds. Come," he says sweeping up the Little Buddha from the rickety couch, "Have a taste of real comfort…"

Together they dive into the feathery pile, and lie on their back, looking at the stars.

In the peaceful aftermath, the Little Buddha becomes suddenly aware of a constant slow rocking movement under him, like on a large boat. He reminds himself that this cozy home is in fact free-floating in the vast cosmos. He lets go into this sensation: being suspended in the universe can be very relaxing, a bit dreamlike…

After a while, the Trash Giant resumes his story:

"I originate from a long and distinguished line of cosmic architects and creators. Our dedication to life has always been to make it more beautiful.

We come from Earth, but we live all over the universe, in different stars and planets. Long ago, just before our Planet was almost destroyed by a huge manmade flood, many of my ancestors decided to leave. They used their advanced knowledge of holographic science to project themselves on planets that bore similar conditions for life as on Earth. Most of them made it, and found out that with a lot of care and love they could start a new life there.

My family remained on Earth. Our design firm for luxurious homes is very successful. You can still find us on the Internet under the name Star-Architecture."

The Trash Giant continues, looking down and sighing. The Little Buddha can hear a faint tremor in his voice:

"Those of us who left the Earth during the great flood have also continued to design, but they are not focused on creating rich people's homes. They design on a planetary level.

All of us are born with the ability to create new patterns for the cosmos. What we search for is symmetry, parallels, and connections. We have found many explanations for cosmic recurrences, and we can create brilliant astral rains, or eternal sunrises. My lineage is deeply respected. Our names are written down for eternity in the Akashic Records".

At this point the tremor in the Trash Giant's voice becomes like a gasp, as if he is trying to rein his emotions. He stops abruptly.

The Little Buddha realizes that this story is still fresh for the Trash Giant. His chest is starting to heave, and he is getting restless. He is visibly struggling not to get caught up in his own past.

Things are different in Shambala, the Little Buddha cannot help comparing. There, everyone is dedicated to meditation, which means practicing non attachment to feelings.

He is fascinated. What is happening here now is no less significant to him than what takes place in Shambala, but it is so different…

He edges closer to the Trash Giant, wondering how to approach him. Then suddenly he feels the sensuous warmth emanating from his big body. Sensing that touch must be the simplest way to connect with him, he reaches out and places his left hand in the middle of his chest, where the Heart Chakra, the center of love, is located.

At first there is no response. For a moment, the Little Buddha fears that Trash Giant might find his gesture patronizing…

But then he suddenly surrenders to the Little Buddha's touch, letting out a sigh of relief and pleasure.

He starts talking again, this time very softly: "I already told you that I no longer have a family that cares for me. As a child I was very proud of my parents, but then they disappointed me again and again. After they realized who I was going to become, they tried in every way to stop me. I felt betrayed by them."

The word betrayal touches the Little Buddha deeply. But he does not feel betrayed by his own parents. The Trash Giant's words remind him of his own self-betrayal. He has been denying for quite a while his real longings and desires, especially those that have to do with intimacy, sensuousness and love.

Before he can stop himself, he admits: "I myself miss love and touch in my life…"

His soft voice resonates through the silence that suddenly fills the space.

Placing his huge hand on the Little Buddha's tiny vibrant one, the Trash Giant looks at him with tenderness, "Sweet Little Buddha, love and touch are always available for you here"

Then, he asks: "And you, Little Buddha…where are you coming from?" He is still not able to fully control his voice. He seems aware of how vulnerable it sounds, but unable to change it.

The Little Buddha replies in a whisper: "I originally come from a place situated in the Himalayas. It's called Shambala…"

The whole body of the Trash Giant starts trembling like a volcano just before it erupts.

Barely controlling himself, he asks: "Shambala the Buddha Land?" The mixture of longing and agitation in the Giant's voice leaves the Little Buddha breathless. He feels extremely moved without really knowing why. Maybe it is the name Shambala that does it. He feels a little grip in his heart recalling what has been his home for such an eternity.

"Yes, I do" he says, surprised, "from where did you hear about the Buddha Land?

The Trash Giant's face lights up, a smile of nostalgia mixed with pain on his lips, "Oh, I have more than heard of it. Once it was the most important place for me. It symbolized the pure essence of creativity. It is there that my creative education took really shape. Many enlightened artists, musicians and designers took up residence in Shambala for a while, and few of them decided to stay on a permanent basis. It was pure ecstasy for me to be close to such people, who could express their consciousness through their creations...As a child, I visited them many times. I know Shambala well..."

His voice sounds younger now, " We used to visit because my enlightened grandfather had settled there. My parents took me there to spend time with him."

The Little Buddha sits up, curious: "Do you remember the name of your grandfather? His Dharma name...?"

In the short pause that follows, the Little Buddha can almost hear all the conflicting emotions inside the Trash Giant, who finally says: "Yes, his name is Raidas."

The Little Buddha is surprised: "I haven't seen him for quite a while!"

"Yes, he left Shambala long ago, just when I was entering my teenage. It was a bit of a scandal in my family, my mother told me that he had betrayed enlightenment with sex.

The rumor was that he had escaped to some foreign land with some woman. I was ordered by my mother never to mention his name again."

The Little Buddha looks at the Trash Giant's face. He looks all excited, with bright red cheeks.

Now it dawns on him: "From the first moment we met, I picked up something familiar. I recognize Raidas in you. He was also very tall. Sometimes we called him The Giant. Like you, he loved working with what everyone else considered dirty trash. He was the garbage man of Shambala, the only Buddha that had a strong smell..."

The Trash Giant is visibly proud to hear all this. His face lights up again with a huge happy smile. This is a relief for the Little Buddha: he does not want to shame him in any way. "Please Little Buddha," the Giant continues, "tell me more about my grandfather! During my childhood, my mother always told me that he was a saint, and I believed her. Whenever I committed any transgression, I felt guilty not to be a saint like him..."

Then, suddenly, he looks up at the Little Buddha. The intensity in his eyes is overwhelming.

"May I ask you something very important?"

"Go ahead"

"This needs some explanation first. You can relax while I talk, it's a long story. I haven't met Raidas for years now; I have never received a word from him. But a while ago, an old friend spoke to me about her new Guru somewhere in India. It took a while before I understood she meant Raidas. Although my heart was instantly very happy, I could hear my mother's voice warning me. After praising Raidas and religiously sitting at his feet for all my childhood, her tone had changed completely just before my teenage. She had started to bitterly condemn him, and this was the voice I was hearing.

Something must have gone majorly wrong at some point. I remember the day, at the end of my childhood, when I became aware of the silent stress between my parents. That day we had just come home from shopping, and I suddenly realized that they had hardly talked to each other. The few words that they had exchanged had been unfriendly.

My father was at work away from home a lot. My mother disliked Tyrol, where we lived, and its people, immensely. She was growing day by day increasingly unhappy and frustrated. She often blamed me for everything. I had been a quiet and introverted child, pliable and obedient, but with puberty approaching a new energy had started running through my veins. I wanted to go out. I didn't want anymore to stay at home with my mother, listening to her ever-increasing complaints about me.

'Your father has no authority' she would say, "wait until we meet his father, your grandfather, this summer in Shambala, he will set you right!!"

I had never considered Raidas as a punishing patriarch. But her constant hammering on me took its toll. I tried to be good, I even tried to be better than good, but the more I tried the more she turned against me.

When summer came, for first time ever I did not want to go to Shambala. I begged my father to support me, but my mother reacted so violently that he just left the house. It became clear: it was only between my mother and me now.

"As we arrived in Shambala that summer, my mother's mood changed completely. Not only that, she dressed up for our visit to Raidas in her most expensive clothes, with layers of make up, and arms full of gifts. She went in to see him alone first.

Outside, my father and I did not exchange one word.

After a short while, we heard the door slam. She exited fuming. This was not a good sign. It surely meant that also Raidas was very angry with me.

By the time she stood in front of me, shaking from top till toe, my shoulders were pulled up to my ears.

What happened next really blew my mind.

"That snake", she hissed, "that adder"

Then she turned to my father and commanded him: "Pack our luggage, we are leaving this perverted snake pit immediately!"

If the moment had not been so serious, I would have laughed out loud when I saw my father act like a frightened mouse, scuttling down the stairs to the pantry where we had just stored our luggage.

'And you,' she suddenly turned towards me like a fury, 'you good for nothing, you will never visit this place again! You will never see that Raidas again...!'

Then she sat down, her now calmer tone as sharp as a razor: 'But before you pack your stuff, let me tell you what I think about him. He betrayed us. I was just humbly asking for his opinion. But the fool did not even give me a chance to finish my sentence. Claiming to be helping you, he suggested I would allow you to become some kind of free artist, like himself. I know much better than that: he once used to be a respectable architect, but when he started to be foolishly convinced that he was enlightened, he gave up his job and with it his respectability. And now he would want you, my one and only lovely son, to follow into his footsteps, and fall into the same pit!'.

She sighed, her face becoming the perfect representation of motherly love: 'But he is an old man, too tired to fight. As soon as he noticed my unconditional love for you, he backed up immediately. I know him well' she continued with a conspiratorial smile, 'After all, I have married his son. I am familiar with the greed that runs in his family. So I took my purse, opened it, and emptied it on the floor. While he kneeled down to gather the coins, I told him: My family and I will never meet you again. Not as long as I can prevent it.'

At this point she started to violently sob, 'I did it for you, my baby, my beautiful child....'

I felt nothing. My heart was frozen. I anyway did my duty, and held her until my father came with our luggage. We left immediately.

In the long car ride back home to Tyrol she did everything she could do to please and seduce my father. Soon he gave in, and they started playing their favorite game, the happy couple with their happy happy son...

I felt nauseous, but I convinced myself that it was the car. This was my first little lie to myself, of many more to come. Slowly, I started to deny whatever felt unpleasant and uncomfortable, and lived my life according to my mother's voice in me.

But when after so many years my friend told me about her new Guru Raidas I could not believe her at first. I asked her to tell me about him and his methods for awakening.

Since I had never shown before any interest in spirituality, at first my friend was surprised by my urgency, but then she told me all she knew. This is how her story goes:

'It has happened more than once that the new visitors who come to Raidas on the wake of his fame become a target for his practical jokes. He loves to welcome them disguised as an uneducated low class servant. And they all fall for it, because they cannot associate such a coarse and unrefined appearance with enlightenment. Raidas responds to their expectations by mistreating them, sometimes insulting them, or other times simply ignoring their requests. Then he abruptly leaves the room, as if to announce them to his Master. From behind the door, he improvises a two-voice dialogue, one sounding authoritative and angry, the Master, and another repeating again and again: 'I am sorry, I am sorry...' To top it off, he simulates a fight with banging and smashing objects that he has gathered for this purpose. Then he stops suddenly.

After quickly donning his ceremonial clothes, Raidas enters the room where the guests are waiting, appearing totally unaware of the commotion that has just ended.

By then, his self-important guests are in terror. Their former arrogance has turned into fear. Seeing that Raidas looks like the horrible servant of before, brings them into such a state of confusion that they often run out of the room, never to be seen again, before he reaches them.

At this point Raidas sits down and laughs so loudly that he often ends up falling out of his chair, a phenomenal sight in itself.

When anyone asks him what is the purpose of such a spiritual practice, he simply starts laughing all over again, and says: 'Good riddance...good riddance...'"

With these last words the smile dies on the Trash Giant's lips. When he speaks again, his voice is full of pain and sorrow.

"Do you know what I told my friend? I said to her: 'This Raidas is a cheat of the worst kind. He would deserve to be jailed....'

But after telling you my story, I start having great doubts... That is why I want to ask you my very important question:

Did my mother lie to me about what Raidas told her on our last visit, when I was fourteen? Did she make up her own story? Is the real Raidas this outrageous Guru that my friend told me about?"

The Little Buddha looks at the Trash Giant with overwhelming compassion. He knows that the truth must be told.

"She lied," he says, "your mother lied to you. Raidas is one of the greatest Masters of this time. Nothing can corrupt him. People have tried to buy him with money; they have offered him all the power one can get. All women, old or young, are crazy for him, and he could have all the sex one can dream of. But he remains himself, incorruptible..."

The Little Buddha stops talking. The Trash Giant acts very fast. He starts running to one of the Garbage Sculptures Mountains and starts ripping it apart in total fury.

The Little Buddha understands his rage very well, and feels that nothing can be done to stop it or change it. His presence makes no difference now. He cannot be of any help while the Trash Giant is engaged in such a confrontation with himself.

He notices an empty postcard on the rickety kitchen table. It's a picture of a Buddha statue sitting in deep meditation. Suddenly, he misses the Indigo Couple and their evening meditation. 'It's time to go home...' He smiles, thinking how their home has become also his home, and in such a short time...

He turns the postcard face down and writes on it a little message: 'I will be back soon', and signs it.

Then, he places it in the middle of the table for the Trash Giant to see, and leaves.

This time he decides to leave the Lotus Mobile behind, parked up here. He is not in the mood for technology, and anyway he'll come back soon enough to retrieve his vehicle. He first thinks of teletransportation, but then drops the idea: why not honor the gift of the Indigo Couple and fly back?

Standing on the edge of the lounge, he opens his wings, chooses sky blue as their color, and spreads them open, jumping into the limitless cosmos. The sensation of freedom reaches him all the way to his core; he lets himself slide along stars and planets, through milky ways, all the way to the Blue Planet, descending towards the Northern Hemisphere, pointing to the Mediterranean and then gently descending towards his home with the Indigo Couple. He neatly lands in their courtyard and finds both of them still up, silently listening to the nightingales.

Chapter Eight

YOU GAVE ME BACK MY GRANDFATHER

"You have given me back my grandfather, Raidas...." It is the Trash Giant speaking. He is strolling together with the Little Buddha down a cloud path, illuminated by the multicolored reflection of the sky above. "Is is sunset or moonset?" The Little Buddha wonders for a moment, still dazzled by the different perception of time up here in the Cosmos, and then adds: "I am very happy for you…"

The clouds are soft under their feet, and fluffy like whipped cream. From time to time, one of the two slips and falls face first, bursting into shakes of laughter and throwing the other off balance.

The Little Buddha has arrived on what on Earth was midday, for his third visit to his new friend. Only a couple of days have gone by since last time, but his concern for the Trash Giant has brought him back sooner than he planned.

Anyway, he tells himself, all conception of time is irrelevant here, when you are surrounded by the rising and setting of so many celestial bodies.

The only tribute to Earth Time in the Trash Giant's world is a miniature Big Ben, which welcomes them back to the Kitchen area after their cloud walk by marking the hour with a disco version of its famous chimes.

"I cannot keep up with these chimes," the Giant tells the Little Buddha, "After being up here for a while I started to sleep and wake up whenever I felt like. But the Big Ben doesn't care about this, it happily continues its song…it's a friendly arrangement between me and time…"

After a delicious cup of tea, the Little Buddha goes on his own to check on his Lotus Mobile, which he finds, as a matter of fact polished, exactly where he left it. He feels at ease in the Trash Giant's world, and knows his way around by now. He strolls around the garbage sculptures noticing the improvements that have happened in such a short time. As he crosses the last sculpture and enters into the Trash Giant's work area, he knows well how unwise it would be to walk around unannounced while the Trash Giant is rearranging heaps of garbage. It's a risk not to be taken twice, he thinks, remembering how he almost was crushed to death on his first visit, and decides to wait for his friend in the lounge area.

There must have been huge sales of couches these last days on Earth, he guesses while looking around. A new precarious tower of discarded easy chairs and sofas is dangerously leaning in a corner. It reaches so high that the Little Buddha is reminded of the tale of little Jack and the Beanstalk. High up on the last couch on top of the pile, the Trash Giant has fixed a colorful flag. It is made out of ragged t-shirts, and it looks a bit like a pirate skull flag.

As the Trash Giant enters with a booming salute, the Little Buddha, no longer startled by the antics of his friend, notices that he is also dressed like a pirate. He has changed into a romantic hero outfit made out of throwaway rags, with a laced up shirt, a velvet vest, and a pair of patchwork leather high boots. "It suits you!", giggles the Little Buddha, hugging his friend.

"You rest, and I'll fix up a meal for us…" the Trash Giant tells him, pointing to an almost new rich man's couch upholstered with the latest memory foam…

After a long and very silent rest, the Little Buddha is woken up by the smell of his favorite food: home made palak paneer[1] with chapattis[2] fresh from the oven. He cannot prevent himself from getting up and following the delicious scent.

The Trash Giant is in his cooking area, cutting and whipping and chopping and grating with hundreds of different tools. He must own the best-equipped kitchen in the whole cosmos…

Rows and rows of shelves contain slightly chipped or rusted jars and tins of spices. He must also be a great spice and herbs cook.

The Little Buddha notices with great personal delight that Chili Pepper is occupying center stage on the main shelf. He adores Chili Pepper…

Next to the great array of ground, dried, tinned and sliced peppers, there are also quite a few cooking books from all over the world, each one singing the praise of Chili Pepper in their own tongue, from Peperoncino to Garam Masala, from sambal to cayenne to harissa, and many more. All the books are faded, earmarked and full of spots, proof that they have been read and reread.

"My dear friend," the Trash Giant turns to him making a sweeping gesture with a ladle towards his collection, "This is my philosophy. Any recipe that is so widespread and praised cannot be anything else than the best. Look at my chili collection: I have been religiously gathering every ounce, every bit of chili that has been trashed out by people who hate to be on fire as part of culinary delight. I am now the owner of the largest variety of chili peppers. In fact I should be mentioned for it in the Guinness Book of Records and even in its spiritual equivalent, the Akashic records…"

The Little Buddha smiles at the passionate praise that even only the sight of chili pepper draws out of his friend…

---

1 Spinach and processed cheese, typical Indian dish
2 Hand made Indian flat bread

The food is as impossibly spicy as expected, and both friends love how it makes them sweat, setting their mouths on fire and turning their lips hot and red. They are a good match for each other; each one eats everything on his plate with smug defiance.

At the end of the meal, a lot has changed between them. Their common love for the rebel of all spices, the chili pepper, has created a new bond between them.

They both bolt from their seats shouting like children, and start running from cloud to cloud, jumping and laughing, leaving a trail of red hot energy behind them, until they reach the furthest cloud, a large one, where they stop to catch their breath in what they call their "horizontal reality", on their backs, panting and sighing until peace is restored.

Later, back at the lounge, it's time for the Trash Giant to resume his story where he has left it last time. The Little Buddha makes himself comfortable, eager to listen.

"Little Buddha, my friend," says the Trash Giant," before I resume my story I have to thank you from all my heart. You did the right thing when you left earlier then arranged. I finally had my long overdue emotional release, in which I screamed, hit, kicked, cursed, freaked out and cried endlessly and deeply. When I came back, lighter and purified, I felt such gratitude towards you.

In short, you gave me back my grandfather, Raidas. And in this way I also received an essential part of myself back."

The Trash Giant has made himself a very comfortable seat, with uncountable cushions of all colors and sizes. He has propped himself up, which suits the Little Buddha well, because he can see and hear him from his own lying down perspective.

He starts talking about the kindergarten in Shambala. The Little Buddha knows the building very well, close as it is to the Enlightenment Store, with a large mural that depicts all the child divinities in human history, and a large sign saying Gopala kindergarten.

"I was so happy there, sitting at my little desk simply painting, or folding geometrical shapes out of paper. Later I started studying people's features and proportions and made many portraits and sketches. It was so inspiring to be at the source of enlightened creativity.

In the Southern part of Germany, where we cam from, there was no stimulating cultural approach, no art revolution, and no spiritual breakthroughs, only breakdowns. Already as a child I was an outsider. We were considered strangers especially because of Raidas. My mother tried to erase her daily humiliation by being very proper. As time went by, it became her fulltime occupation. She used to remind everyone all the time of our ancient lineage. She would dress me up in the local traditional Tyroler outfit and then show me off to everyone, making it clear that we were like everyone else, only slightly better.

Everybody would always stare at me. The other kids wore normal clothes, and quite a few of them were often smirking at me.

I started to believe that I really was this odd boy in his Tyroler outfit. It was easier for me to be that than trying to be like everyone else.

The only time in my childhood that I was free of this Tyroler outfit stigma was when we went to Shambala. There nobody made fun of me, I never felt judged…On the contrary, I felt free to express my creativity in whatever way it came.

I was together in a class with some exceptional children born with unusual talents in some field or other. I remember a three-year-old musical composer, some young mathematical geniuses and also a few child artists, who had already produced great masterpieces.

I loved painting. I would leave our guesthouse in the early morning and explore all the different gardens, some with thousands of years old trees. I loved capturing them on my sketchpad in the morning light.

There was specifically one garden that had a magnificent collection of tropical flowers and birds, some of them no longer to be found anywhere else on the Planet.

I would often go there. The owner of that garden was well known; he was one of the original inhabitants of Shambala. A handsome man in his middle age, he would be in his garden at sunrise. I loved that man. Something in him inspired me. For a time I dreamt of becoming like him when I grew up…"

"You were that boy?!" the Little Buddha interrupts him, "Now I remember you! You may not remember me, because I was a different person at that time, but I recall this little shy Tyroler boy. You were sweet, and so talented in your drawings, they were so full of life…" He wonders for a moment if he is going to reveal to the Trash Giant what is his more than intimate connection with the owner of the tropical garden. He clearly remembers the little Tyroler boy who passed by every summer, every day at sunrise, years ago. Tears come to his eyes as he remembers the last time they met. The boy must have been around fourteen years old. One day, at the beginning of summer, he came to tell him that he was going to be sent to boarding school to study architecture. They sat silently in the garden for a short moment. The boy had suddenly grown a lot in the last year, and had started to outgrow the Buddha of Long History himself. One could still feel his original innocence, but anger and pain had already gathered at its edges.

The Buddha of Long History knew his parents. He also knew that especially his mother felt that Shambala was no longer a safe place for her son, because there he was given too much freedom, and many strange ideas were put into his head. The Buddha of Long History had even tried to talk some sense into her before, but as soon as she had felt that he might be on her son's side, she had withdrawn from him and told her son to watch out for him.

As that morning came to a close, the boy and the Buddha of Long History had exchanged helpless looks. Both somehow realized that this was the last time they would meet. They hugged goodbye amongst tropical bird sounds and exotic flower fragrances.

To meet him here again after all this time as the Trash Giant leaves the Little Buddha speechless. On a closer look, he starts to recognize his young friend. But what a change has happened to him: from the sensitive young boy he was, he has become now a rough- tough young man...

The Little Buddha notices that the Trash Giant has stopped talking. His soul has recognized him, but not his conscious mind. A shy smile appears on the face of the Trash Giant, just like the one he used to have as a child...Then the moment passes, and when the Trash Giant asks him if he wants to hear more, the Little Buddha simply nods.

"I remember our teacher, he was fascinating! A very serious looking Dervish..."

"No, not the Dervish!" the Little Buddha says: "Was he teaching?"

"Yes, he was, and he was always saying 'God is everywhere' while whirling ... I did not understand him at all..."

At this point, both the Little Buddha and the Trash Giant start to laugh. It is obvious that they share a real fondness for the Dervish.

"Now I remember," the Little Buddha says, "he caught everyone by surprise when he offered to volunteer as a teacher for the kindergarten, and even more when it became clear that in spite of his stern appearance all the children absolutely loved him. His divine madness had something innocent that no child could resist."

"My time there was the happiest of all my childhood," sighs the Trash Giant, "Whenever we returned from Shambala to Tyrol it took me a long time to adjust back to the ' normal world '. It was then that I discovered that drawing and painting brought me back to myself. Whenever there was an opportunity to contact that creative source in me, I was totally happy again.

But even before I was out of my mother's womb my parents were already convinced that I would continue the family trade. They started showing me buildings and monuments before I could even count to ten.

The problem was that architecture did not interest me at all. I did not like geometry and calculations... I loved painting: having an empty paper or a canvas in front of me, and selecting pens, pencils or brushes to paint with, was ecstasy for me. But my parents were adamant: I would become an architect.

Whenever they would catch me painting free hand, they stopped me and marked on the paper the correct proportions and perspective.

Especially my father did this. It was amazing to see the difference between him and Raidas, his own father. Unlike him, there was nothing of the artist in my father; he was a born bureaucrat, unimaginative and controlled.

He took me with him into his studio, where he showed me papers upon papers full of lines and notes that together constituted the plan for a whole building. I could feel how proud he was of his skills, and how much he wanted me to follow.

One time we went on a fieldtrip. When I failed to respond for the tenth time to one of his remarks, my father got very irritated. I was just daydreaming about the expressive painting on a large canvas that I was making in the privacy of my own bedroom. He lost his temper and slapped me. The physical pain and the shock that I felt were nothing compared to the feeling of humiliation that took me over.

He felt instantly guilty and started to apologize: 'I am sorry, my son, I lost my temper… but please trust me, I did it for you. I don't want you to become a free hand painter, because your life would be a very hard one.

His effort to undo the wrong done touched me. I wanted him so much to love me. I understood that he could never live up to his father Raidas, and realized that what he wanted now from me, his son, was the approval that his father had never given him.

I felt so sorry for him, that there and then I decided to renounce my artistic side, and to follow his footsteps as an architect instead.

I never completed the painting that I had left at home.

From then on, I left my paints, pens and brushes in boxes in a corner of my room, where they gathered dust for many years. Finally, when I graduated from boarding school, my mother emptied all the boxes into the garbage with a big sigh of relief.

Now I had proved myself to my parents. They were delighted. It was time for me to receive the legacy of my lineage, 'the Gift', as they called it, and become an architect. So it was that this 'Gift', given to me by others, started replacing my natural gift as an artist. My grandfather Raidas, the other artist, went unmentioned for a long time.

But one day my parents surprised me. They called me in our best room, sat me down on the armchair like a grown up, and talked about Raidas for the last time ever.

My father started off: 'Your…ehm…grandfather had the Gift too. After declaring his…ehm…enlightenment, he designed a highly idealistic model for an ecological and spiritual new planet. He gave us all the information needed to create it, from water system to recycling, from temples to forests…'

'We received the legacy of his project with due respect, but we could already see that he was becoming odd…' my mother quickly added, and lowering her tone, she continued: 'you know, he was losing it. Instead of using his power to support us, his real family, he kept company with all sorts of weird people. At some point he even volunteered to collect the garbage in Shambala. We lost all respect for him when he started raving that we were completely in our head.'

'Please, beloved son,' my father stepped in, 'do not think that we are not capable to continue the work my father started before he lost all sense…the Gift is more than just designing homes,' he looked with faint defiance at my mother before lowering his eyes, 'it does not grant us the power to actually create planets, but it allows us to contribute to their creation by imagining them in detail. Existence will respond to us, at the right place and at the right moment, and manifest our design or a similar one.'

Rising a few inches higher for a glorious moment, my father added: 'This is what my father told me when I was your age, and this is what I pass on to you, remember it: 'We believe in the power of manifestation. Mankind is constantly manifesting. Whether it is heaps of trash and pollution, or beauty and love, whether it is poor hovels or magnificent palaces, it all depends on the consciousness of the creator…'

This was truly exciting. I swept away my personal doubts about Raidas, my favorite grandfather, being crazy, and listened more attentively to my father.

'To master this art, beloved son, you will need to attend a special training held at the Esoteric University in Copenhagen, the pretty capital city of Denmark. If you feel ready for this next step as we feel you are, we would be glad to continue supporting you financially.'

My mother, all animosity forgotten, looked at me proudly when I nodded yes.

It was decided: during the school year I would leave Tyrol and go to the University. During summer we would reunite and spend some family time at home, where my father would teach me more about architecture.

'Even though I understood their enthusiasm and went along with it, deep inside I remained cold and frozen, in a shock. Up to that moment I had kept alive a little hope that one day they would see me and support my dreams. But now I realized that this would never happen...

I felt angry at them, but specially at myself, for not having the courage to go my own way. I promised myself that I would confront them during my next holiday at home. But deep down I already knew that I had given up for good. I had no strength left to stand up against their expectations.

I did go to Copenhagen, and I have to admit that the training there was fantastic. I met lots of new and interesting people in and around the Campus. I started to move my own way. I did not think about being a painter anymore. Once in a while I still had dreams of it, and woke up in tears. On those occasions, I judged my behavior as childish, as if I was clinging to an old fairy tale. It was much better to be a grown up, I told myself.

I did become an architect, and a very self-confident one. I could not wait to start, I felt ready to design anything, up to the finest details. The first job offers started to come; they were many, enough to allow me freedom of choice. For a while, I was content with being a designer for luxurious homes.

But then it all took a different turn...

Each half century, the Esoteric University extended to all its students, past and present, an invitation to join a friendly competition. It was about creating and designing the most ecologically advanced and beautiful new planet in the cosmos.

The contest required a wide range of skills and a great sense of imagination. This was what I had been waiting for, I thought: a chance to freely create... I joined the contest immediately.

We were granted half a year to prepare our pitch. We needed to describe in detail our vision of the new planet and its layout. We also were asked to produce an estimate for labor and material costs.

Out of this first round, three contenders would be chosen for the final. The selected ones would be asked, with a crew of skilled workers at their disposal, to show their design as a holographic tridimensional projection.

After their presentation, the three would engage into a debate, using every inch of their genius to win votes from the board of professors. There would be only one final winner. The last decisive factor for victory was the capacity of the contestant to remain meditative and conscious in highly competitive situations. Every one knew that the contest was really a stimulating excuse for everyone to give their best. In such an atmosphere of wisdom and learning, even losers would be winning. What mattered was full abidance to the Law of Grace, where only a surrendered mind could manifest in synchronicity with the Divine. Humility was what was truly respected.

As far as I was concerned, these high principles went over my head. I was instead eager to show off my skills and use them. I managed to reach in this way the semifinal, with little doubt that I would win.

When I was selected for the semi finals some of my former teachers did not agree. They argued that I was much too young and inexperienced for meeting the challenge of manifesting a whole planet. I would for sure become competitive, and soon lose my meditativeness.

I thought it was just their envy speaking and ignored their opinion. My mother also heard about their misgivings, but kept on fully supporting me. 'She deserves to be proud of me,' I thought, 'after all she has given me…'

The other two competitors were scholars, with a great respect for hierarchy.

They both presented very solid plans, thoroughly discussed with their former teachers, following their instructions to the letter.

I, on the contrary, had not asked for any guidance. I had just kept my focus on the little quote that had come to me the night before the contest.

It had spoken in a familiar voice. At that time I did not recognize it as Raidas's. It said: ʃUnderstand where humanity has gone wrong and turned against its surrounding, and find ways to restore its creative impulse to manifest a better world on all levels'.

I felt ready for everything.

Truth was that by then I was living in complete denial. I could not see myself, or even less others. I started a new model of the Earth, the Blue Planet, and named it The Jewel Of The Cosmos. I applied to it all I had learned. I enjoyed being totally involved, from the broadest outline to the finest detail. I loved creating continents with more pleasing and harmonious shapes. At one point I became totally engrossed in the creation of rice fields on the shores of large watercourses that would supply constant irrigation. I went to some lengths to find out how to create a new different type of skin that would repair by itself and never age.

Finally, when I felt totally satisfied with what I had done so far, I started thinking of what kind of humanity I would want in my planet. I felt that my creation was too special to be given to people that might not be able to appreciate it.

Had I been still visiting Shambala, I sometimes secretly thought, I could have put my design at the feet of the Sangha, but now I was left on my own.

I was convinced that common people would not understand what I wanted to express. I did not want any feedback. The idea to have to listen again to others giving their useless opinion about my creativity was unacceptable to me.

That's when the old pain surfaced again. But this time it came with a new partner: anger. This time I would not let anybody influence me. Nobody could harm my baby planet. This time I would be the one to decide what was right and what was wrong!"

The Little Buddha can literally see wheels of fiery red energy spreading outwards from the Trash Giant's navel. He must have been very angry at that time…

Suddenly, he remembers. He is back in Shambala on the 'Charavedi Day'…He can see his old self going on fire because of that one word message. From his present angle, it seems ridiculous that something so small could trigger such rage in him. But he can also remember how devastating it felt while it was happening…

He reaches out with a compassionate hand to the Trash Giant.

For a long moment he doesn't respond. His eyes are glazed, fixed ahead. He looks as if he is back in the past, facing a great dilemma: 'is it worth giving a whole new world to the same humanity that has just finished destroying the old one? Or is it better to start completely afresh?'

But then he wakes up out of his trance, meeting the Little Buddha's eyes.

"I am so happy that that time is over", he says.

The Little Buddha nods.

"Let's take a break", he suggests.

"Pancakes, anyone?" the Trash Giant asks, with a wink and a smile.

Chapter Nine

A SPECIAL MORNING IN THE COSMOS BAR

Later on, over a large pile of fresh pancakes with maple syrup, the Trash Giant continues: "I used to come together with my crew at night, in the local pubs, and discuss with them how the work was progressing. We soon went into increasingly heated arguments about who would be worthy of this new planet. In the beginning, it all felt like a joke to me, but I soon realized that it wasn't for them. They were dead serious. Many of them were born in less developed countries, and had no use for utopias. Where they came from it was all about survival.

They started claiming their share of my creation. They wanted to know if in the end they would also profit from it, or was it all only mine? They accused me of drawing a separation between humanity and myself: as if I wouldn't be human too, just like them.

I had not expected this. In my life I had never had real opponents except my parents. I had given up my painting for them, and since then I had simply done everything to be praised. Now my crew was questioning my authority and my status. I felt insecure and scared, but I didn't show it, of course.

I started to make promises that I knew I would never fulfill. Different promises to different people, about bigger shares, higher salaries and less working hours. I had to juggle from one secret arrangement to another, making sure no one would find out.

Instead of enjoying being creative, I used most of my time to survive through my lies. I soon lost touch with my true self.

"The model of the new planet started reflecting this. The conflicts with the crew were creating a tense overcharged electro magnetic field around the delicate web of holographic patterns that constituted my Jewel Of The Cosmos.

My holographic planet was all the time threatening to fall apart.

When I finally designed a new humanity, I imagined it colorful, warmhearted, and intelligent. The kind of people I secretly dreamt of belonging to...

My design was coming to an end. I was exhausted from all the conflicts and the compromises I had made. It had come to the point where I couldn't have an honest talk with anyone. I felt increasingly lonely. Yet, I remained proud of my first planet.

Just then, I received a message summoning me for a talk with my former teachers.

I was afraid of their questions and opinions, but I could not ignore the invitation. I went.

When I entered the conference room, they were all sitting around a table. Many of them had also been my private tutors. Disappointment and disapproval were clearly visible on their faces. I tried to explain what had been happening to me, but I was only met by their antagonism.

The Principal talked for all of them: 'we were the ones who recommended you for your excellence. Thanks to us, you have been able to join the competition…"

I realized that I had never acknowledged this, let alone thanked them for it. Because of their support, I had become the youngest ever to participate.

'We realize that you think that our choice was based on your undeniable brilliancy, but this is just one part of it. We thought that in this way we could continue teaching you. You rejected our wisdom and experience by wanting to do it all on your own. During these last six months you never came to us for guidance. The other two competitors have never stopped consulting us…"

I realized that I had never even acknowledged the existence of this board.

When I told them that I had been discussing the plans with my workers instead, several of them stood up and left in fuming disagreement.

I had failed. I felt deeply ashamed. Suddenly, the anger that had been fueling me vanished; I was left behind, utterly collapsed.

I did realize the truth of what they said, and I felt exposed in my lack of love and respect. But for me they were all outdated, ancient. I was younger, and more daring than them: as far as I was concerned they had nothing to teach me.

At the end of our meeting, the members of the board who had not left asked me if I still wanted to carry on with my project. 'Or should we maybe pass it on to the other two contestants, who will follow our guidelines to complete it?' concluded the Principal with a sigh.

In a flash of awareness I knew they were right. I would never create a model for a living planet. I lacked experience, true, but if I had been really motivated and inspired, I would have learnt. It was something else in me preventing it: I knew deep down that I would never be happy as an architect, even a cosmic one.

Maybe this was the true insight that I had been missing. I should have stepped back earlier, and admitted that I did not want to become what others wanted from me. I had lacked the grace of knowing my limits.

As I understood this, a part of my heart broke off, and I faced my forgotten pain.

I thought, 'Now I will become a nobody', and for the first time in my life I felt free. I was ready to resign. I returned to the University all the tools I had borrowed. I still did not like how my teachers had maneuvered me out of my work and replaced me with less threatening students. But I could also see now how dedicated the two other contestants were to architecture and design, and how deeply uninspired I was by the very same things...

"For a while, doing nothing was healing for me. I let days pass by without any significant action.

Inwardly, I had to face the anxiety caused by dropping out. Some days I woke up and automatically packed my backpack to go to work. Then the shock came, delayed. I had no focus, no goal.

Although I had made a lot of work acquaintances, I had no real friends. This became painfully clear to me when, after several weeks out of work, I still had met nobody, and nobody had yet contacted me.

The financial support that my parents had been providing had enabled me to live in relative luxury. When they heard about the circumstances of my resignation, they put an immediate stop to it. My funds quickly shrank to almost nothing. My parents did not contact me and I did not look for them. It felt as if they did not care for me any more.

The day came when I could no longer afford my current living standard. I received a note from the estate agent putting me in front of an ultimatum: either I would pay now or evacuate the premises immediately. If I wouldn't, the police would be notified.

I had to smile when I recalled how sure of myself I had been just a little more than six months before, when I had won the semifinals. I had felt so much younger then... I would have definitely had enough energy to fight back and win. But now I had none. It was as if with losing my identity as an architect I had lost all sense of myself."

The Trash Giant's voice sounds far away, almost from the other side of the universe. The Little Buddha feels for him. Becoming who you are truly meant to be is not easy.

Just as he is about to share this with him, the Trash Giant turns towards him and says: "Growing up is not easy. I had to move on, and let go of my financial dependency from my parents. I saw that if from their side this was a way to keep me bonded, I also used this situation not to take full responsibility for myself.

I took a little low-rent pied-a-terre in a back alley of Copenhagen. I furnished it with what I could find on the streets. Every month on a special day the local population was allowed to leave on the corner of certain streets whatever objects and pieces of furniture they wanted to discard. On that day, the poorer students were all there, browsing through the piles of second hand wares that had been rejected by more affluent people.

I started joining in. I found out how much I loved trash: old stuff, faded textures, overused couches, boxes full of old CD's or cassettes, family photo albums, clothes of all kinds.... for me they were mementoes of many stories.

I found out that I really liked sorting out garbage, collecting things by color or size. Being a non-ambitious activity, it helped me to remain centered while my life fell apart around me.

On one of these browsing trips, I had the good luck to find a large paper box full of books by the Controversial Master. As I had nothing else to do, I decided to spend some time leafing trough them. Soon I was reading whole chapters, going quickly through all the books. It was as if I had hit upon the one fruit that could save me from starvation. I found answers to so many questions, even to those I didn't even know I had.

This Master's saying: ' it does not matter what you do, but how you do it', really stopped me on my tracks. It was precisely expressing into words what I was starting to understand. This much I was learning, from all the mistakes I had made.

It was a bittersweet time for me. Sometimes while reading I found myself fighting again, while other times I felt transported into a straight communion with existence. All in all, it was like being bathed in essence.

At the end of my reading, I felt deeply cleansed. I was back on my feet. The waiting was over. I had to move again. I realized how stiff my body had become with all that soul searching, and decided that it was time for physical activity and pleasure."

Here the Trash Giant stops. He mightily yawns, stretches his whole big body, and stands up. It is late. The Little Buddha is still awake, but barely able to listen any more.

Noticing his sleepy and uncoordinated efforts to sit up, the Giant scoops him up in one sweeping gesture and holds him close to his heart.

The contact with his warm body and the sound of his heart quietly thumping relax the Little Buddha completely. He is already asleep before his head touches the pillow.

Much later, the Little Buddha wakes up to the disco chime of the Big Ben and looks at the clock: 12 o' clock, noon. It's a shocking: he never gets up that late… but then, he has to laugh. Waking up before dawn is after all just a habit that he has kept alive for what seems forever. Old habits don't die easily, he realizes, and giggles again. Still, it's time to go back home, he thinks.

Just when the last notes of the disco chime are playing, the Trash Giant enters the lounge. "Wake up, you lazy bum ", he says, with a big smile, "A surprise visitor will be arriving here in a couple of hours, and I have to tell you his story before you leave…" and disappears into the kitchen.

The Little Buddha has already noticed before that sometimes the Trash Giant appears to him like an oversized child with boundless enthusiasm. He is always on the go, and allows no time for any dust to gather. So much like his grandfather Raidas…

"Who is this surprise visitor…someone I know?"

The Little Buddha is now trying to get the Trash Giant's attention, while he keeps on jumping from one side to the other of the kitchen area. Dressed up this time in full cook gear, with hat and all, he is carrying armloads of kitchen tools, obviously preparing what promises to be a colossal Brunch for the coming visitor.

"No, beloved Little Buddha, not someone you know..."

The Little Buddha can hear the subtle tremble of disappointment in his own voice when he answers back: " Fine then..." He was not aware of how much he misses his Shambala friends …

The Trash Giant smiles at him, and suddenly, in that smile, the roles reverse. For the first time, the Little Buddha feels like a child, and his friend looks like an adult.

In the Trash Giant's smile, joy and optimism are very visible, but together with them always comes a trace of sadness for having lost his childhood dream. One can read it all in the lines of his large face: trust and pride, regret and sorrow. He has grown into a mature man.

"You do not know this person, and I would have loved to introduce you to him. Maybe I will next time you come. He is my best friend. He came into my life when I had finally made friends with myself. During my spontaneous retreat in my little apartment, I had the time to realize that others were not just a reflection of me: they actually existed. I would like to tell you about him…"

Sensitive as he has become, the Trash Giant notices an ever so slight reaction in the Little Buddha's face, and adds: "I have started to love you too, Little Buddha, with my body heart and soul. This means that now I have two best male friends…is it ok if I call you my best friend too?"

The Little Buddha nods solemnly.

"Let's celebrate this great occasion with a little late breakfast treat, fruit salad, with fresh fruit, not gathered from the garbage heap... While we eat our treat, I will tell you the story of how love for garbage can change a man's life. Okay, Little Buddha?"

"Okay, Trash Giant!" the Little Buddha leans back, ready to surrender once more to the Giant's story telling.

"Picturesque roads and alleys, canals, rivers, vegetable patches, the city of Copenhagen had it all. It managed itself very well in a calm and peaceful way with little excitement. Life was normal, quite uneventful.

I started walking around town. I noticed that by just moving my body, my mind started to clear out. I could see that walking brought me also into a much lighter mood. I had been sitting around too much and for too long.

One morning, as I was strolling down the main shopping street, I heard a loud noise behind me. I turned around on my heels to see the bumper of an enormous garbage truck right behind me. The dirtiest man I had ever seen descended from the vehicle and came quite close front of me. He looked straight into my eyes with a big mischievous smile. Every single part of his body was covered in filth; his overall was already grimy at this early hour.

When I saw how he could walk with no shame in his smelly and unwashed gear through the main street, happily smiling, something very important happened to me. I suddenly felt like a child again. I had regained my energy by reading and walking and eating healthy, but I hadn't yet managed to let go of my subtle mistrust towards others.

This made me look serious.

But right there and then, in the middle of the decent town of Copenhagen, the child in me suddenly reappeared on the stage of life. It was this child who really saw the Garbage Collector. And it was love at first sight.

It was as if I was seeing myself, the way I had been as a child, completely absorbed in my painting, not even noticing when I was full of paint in my hair, on my face, all over my body.

Now I saw the same focus in the Garbage Collector's eyes, the same passionate love for what he was doing. In that light, the dirt that covered him was perfectly fitting to him. He moved around his truck like in a primitive dance, looking like a strange apparition in the neat and controlled streets of Copenhagen.

His eyes bore deep into mine. In them, there was none of the fear or restraint that I saw in the eyes of the other bypassers. There was wildness instead, like in the eyes of a free animal, both daring and soft. And tender.

I realized that this was the kind of freedom that I would have wished for the inhabitants of my new planet… But now that I was meeting someone who was truly living it, I realized that it was not possible to give this freedom to others. It was up to each individual to grab it and live it.

I found myself smiling back. For a while we just stood there, grinning like fools at each other.

Then, without saying one word, the Garbage Collector handed me the keys of his truck, turned around and left. Caught by surprise, I lost track of him as he walked briskly away through the shopping crowd…

As more and more people passed by, I started to shrink. Many of them looked first at me and then at the garbage truck, and then at me again. All they saw was failure. They quickened their step and walked away, afraid of contamination.

This made me angry.

Suddenly I realized how I still depended so much on others' approval. I needed to do something about it. I walked to the back of the truck and rubbed my hands, arms and chest into the trash, wiping myself off on my faded jeans. Right at that moment, I realized I also wanted to become a trash collector.

I looked in the rearview mirror of the truck, and I saw someone different than my usual self.

The eyes looking back at me were as clean and sparkling as a child's. In them, I could recognize my long forgotten sensitivity and wildness. This time I did not hide when I walked back to the front of the truck. I felt proud and free.

It took what seemed a long time before the Garbage Collector came back. When he did, he looked very smug. I did not want to embarrass him and myself by asking where he had been. He simply scratched his head extensively, rolled a cigarette, opened the door, jumped behind the stirring wheel of the truck, and drove off.

I was left standing like a hobo in the middle of the street. I did not care: I felt completely happy.

The next day, I was 'by accident' walking down the same shopping street at the same time as the day before. I heard a loud honk behind me. Sure enough it was the Garbage Collector, gesturing to me from his truck. He came out with some urgency, dropped the keys once more in my hand, and disappeared.

This time I went inside the truck. I pulled myself up on the empty driver seat and sat there.

When he came back after some time, he bowed to me as I came out of the truck and shook my hand. I was surprised: I myself was very big, and I had always felt guilty about the fact that my father was much shorter than me: when I shook his hand, my own hand would feel enormous, too big... But here the opposite was the case. My hand felt really small, like a child's, in his much larger hand. When our eyes met again, something in me had relaxed very deeply.

This unusual ritual between us went on for quite a few days. We never spoke: it seemed to be enough as it was. Day after day, in a subtle way, a big breakthrough was happening for me: I was letting him in, allowing him to see my soul. I started calling him secretly "My Best Friend".

In my childhood, the slightest bit of dirt would send my mother into frenzy. Sometimes she would get too hysteric, and my father had to take over from her. He would take me to the bathroom and try to clean me nervously. I hated his touch in those moments.

But even though I had suffered much for the lack of intimacy, I had also taken over my parents' fear for it. Only now, in my solitary retreat, I had started feeling how lonely I had always been.

My new best friend had his own fragrances and smells; he was dirty, and obviously he did not care. But his touch was warm, sensuous and friendly.

After a few weeks, the Garbage Collector did something new. He showed up at our usual rendezvous, but this time instead of leaving me, he reached out and pulled me up in the passenger seat. The cabin was clean. The Garbage Collector was wearing his usual overall, but this time it was laundered.

Before I knew it, my first best friend ever gave me a big bear hug.

My body could not reject this physical declaration of friendship. For the first time in my life, I allowed myself to fully respond to another's embrace. Something unlocked in me, and I started feeling trusting and open. Time stopped, and we remained in a silent embrace for very long.

When we finally let go of each other, we both laughed loudly. Such big guys as us looking so ridiculously pink and innocent...

Then the Garbage Collector suddenly gave me a big shove, and jumped on me, toppling me over. I went blank. My mind could not make sense of what was happening.

It stopped. Right here, and now.

In this gap that could have lasted as well an eternity as few seconds, I felt a big upsurge of energy flooding my whole body. I felt both incredibly ecstatic and totally still.

Then, in an uncontrolled response, I pushed him back. His door opened, and we both tumbled out of the truck, down the slope into the gutter.

I was again caught by surprise by the craziness of it all. Sprawled out in the gutter, we both didn't move, and in that stillness all separation between us fell away. We became one. It was the lightest experience I had ever felt.

Then that experience too disappeared, and only a sense of dissolving remained. At that point, I knew: this was my path.

When the Garbage Collector pulled himself up, he looked exactly like his usual Self: really dirty. When it was my turn to sit up, I looked as dirty as him.

Both of us were vibrant with energy. We crawled over to help each other to stand up.

We brushed off each other's clothes, and started walking.

As we walked to into a narrow alley, he spoke out for the first time. His tone, not very loud, surprised me as melodious and cultivated. It was a highly cultured man speaking, with a voice rich in modulation, as if it could tell many stories at once.

"Beloved" he said.

I could only reply with the same word: " Beloved…"

We stood in front of a non descript building at the end of the alley. The only thing that interrupted the monotony of its façade was a faded sign over a grimy window. It read: "The Cosmos Bar".

Once we stepped through the door, we entered a different world.

Outside it was a late morning on a bright and sunny summer day. Inside it was dark and shady. I could hardly see anything. I held on to the hand of the Garbage Collector, who seemed at ease in this environment.

When my eyes got adjusted to the dimness, I could see on the back wall a glass display with alcoholic beverages, some soft drinks and a few snacks.

Some old-fashioned slot machines stood close to the entrance, and in the middle of the room there was a small dance floor. All in all, it looked like an average Pub: invisible.

Although it was early and wonderfully sunny outside, the pub was packed full with very animated people. Some were involved in passionate discussions, others were chatting up girls and flirting. It was difficult to define the clientele: they were of all ages, from all over the world, with no specific common traits. It was impossible for me to feel left out or different.

What surprised me most was that everyone seemed to know the Garbage Collector. Both men and women looked very happy to see him.

A small crowd gathered wherever he stopped, and wherever he was the discussion seemed to intensify. He took the time to connect with each one of the people. Together with his natural charisma and sensuality, a perfume of love lingered around him. Each time someone stood in front of him, his or her features became aglow with a golden aura, and a big smile appeared on their lips.

I could not stop myself from staring at this phenomenon. Was this my Garbage Collector friend, who usually smelled like sweat, tobacco and trash? What was happening around him?

Then I heard the deep vibration of a big Japanese Gong coming from the furthest end of the room. Everyone's attention was drawn to the back wall. A liquid crystal screen had replaced the glass display. Against its backdrop, a small stage with two chairs had been quickly assembled. The play of lights on the screen gave it the appearance of floating in mid air. The Garbage Collector took a seat on the stage.

He looked very different. Gone was the dirty image that I had grown so attached to.

He was wearing an exquisitely tailored suit, a silk shirt with diamond cufflinks, and Italian shoes in the softest leather. He looked stunning.

Next to the Garbage Collector sat a beautiful woman. She and the Garbage Collector made a great couple. Her dress was matching his: a long gown, sky blue and sleek, definitely a designer piece, and diamonds sparkling around her neck, wrists, and ankles.

I found a barstool and sat somewhere in a corner of the pub.

I heard the Garbage Collector's voice for the second time in one day, this time through a microphone. I could hear authority in it. He obviously knew what he was talking about.

'Beloveds', he started off, 'thanks for coming here today. I would like to introduce myself, and my dear wife, a divine teacher and master in her own right. The reason I have chosen this old bar in the heart of Copenhagen for this important meeting is that lately I have taken up work in this neighborhood as a garbage truck driver. It has been a real breakthrough for me. This job is providing me with an endless source of delight.

I am not someone who is normally used to do these kinds of jobs..."'

The Little Buddha jumps up from the Trash Giant's couch with sudden realization: "Wait a moment! I have heard this name before! Yes, the Garbage Collector! My Soul Parents mentioned him, I think they even went to one of his conferences in Copenhagen!" For a moment, the meeting of his two present worlds feels to him more than anything like a loud and unexpected clash. He is dizzy.

The Trash Giant smiles: "Nothing surprises me any more about you, dear friend… we are obviously connected in many more ways than we know…"

It's the Little Buddha's turn to smile, thinking of the little Tyroler boy and himself as a middle aged man…he asks for more fruits and relaxes again into listening.

"He went on speaking about his background," the Trash Giant continues, "by then I was not surprised to hear that the was highly educated, with several PhD's to his name, and a title. Recently, he had developed a reputation in the environmentalist circles as an expert on the growing problem of waste. But the way he had introduced the beautiful woman next to him as his wife and divine teacher did surprise me. I wondered who she really was…

Almost as a response to my thoughts, the woman on stage smiled in my direction, her whole face lighting up. Had she heard me? I was not prepared for the great joy that flooded me when I saw her smile…"

"Little Buddha", the Trash Giant says, "you must be familiar with the sensation of lotus petals descending on you, but for me this was a new experience"

Tears are flowing over his cheeks.

"In that very moment, I surrendered to the divine feminine grace, the lady, the mother, the master, and I knew that my life would be dedicated to Her, whose grace and wisdom surpasses all."

"After this experience I lost focus for a while: I was just delighted and full. I came back to the sound of the Garbage Collector's voice closing the conference with the words: 'I love garbage, I hope you do too!'

The public was enthusiastically clapping. I wondered what next. I was so full of impressions that maybe it was a good time to leave.

I was intercepted on my way out by someone waving a piece of paper right in front of me. A message. It read: 'Wait for us please. Your friends, the Garbage Collector and Maya'. Just the sound of her name was melting my soul…

"What to do, Little Buddha, I would have waited for her till the end of time"

The Little Buddha is puzzled. Even though women mystics have been his friends and companions for many different lifetimes, he has always remained more connected to the male path of meditation. With its focus on improving the outer world, the female path has always appeared to him a bit superficial and frivolous.

But looking at the Trash Giant now, it's striking for him to see that his love for the divine female is not effeminizing him. On the contrary it makes him more male, in a colorful and juicy way. For a moment the Little Buddha experiences a sense of envy, but it soon disappears. He loves the Trash Giant.

"After that, everything started moving very fast. I waited for them to change clothes in a room at the back of the emptying bar. They came back dressed casually, both in jeans and a black pullover. They invited me for an early dinner.

Chapter Ten

MAYA AND HER MASTER

"We went to a beautiful Indian Restaurant right in the middle of town," the Trash Giant continues, "amongst the flashing lights of cars, cinemas and casinos. Once inside, the atmosphere was hushed, with a swarm of jolly Indian waiters moving around the heavy set gilded tables and chairs, and a delicious smell of spices permeating every corner. My nostalgia for the Himalayas was rekindled.

It was during that dinner that I heard who Maya was. A direct descendant of the mother of Gautama the Buddha, she had met the Garbage Collector at Berkley University, U.S., were she was studying Free Arts. Born in the Himalayas, near Lake Mansarovara, already at a very young age she had been declared a Divine Being. When she met the Garbage Collector, they had instantly recognized each other as soul mates and married soon after.

I understood well that if my love for her had been of the earthly kind, I would have ended up in a competition with the Garbage Collector. But it wasn't so: I didn't feel possessive: my love felt more like devotion. It magnified my friendship with the Garbage Collector too.

A deep longing awakened in me when she spoke of her Himalayan teacher, who was living in a little Zen hut at her birth lake. She was still communicating with him telepathically over any distance.

It was her Master who had initiated this garbage project. Needing to heal his heart in peace from a bad break with his family, he had decided to move to the furthest regions of the Himalayas, and had ended up settling on the shores of the Mansarovara Lake. It must have been around fifteen years before, when Maya was still a child. In the beginning, he had just slept out in the open. In his daily walks around the Lake he had slowly started to collect pieces of bleached and gnarled wood along the water line, and had used them to build a very simple shelter.

From there, he started noticing more and more the debris that was washed to the shore, and realized how most of it could be ingeniously put to use. In the end, he had a very comfortable and elegantly designed hut made out of driftwood, old car tires, bleached bones of yak, and rubber shoes of different sizes...

He had created furniture, knitted a rough jacket out of old entangled ropes, and carved for himself a beautiful bowl of dark teakwood. Some of the trash he collected seemed to have mysteriously landed from very distant shores: it was difficult to imagine how it could have been transported from halfway across the globe.

Maya met him for the first time at his hut.

I can still hear her telling me the story:

'I used to be very curious as a child,' she told me, "Even though I was already considered a Divine Being, this did not stop me from being a mischievous little girl too.

My family was living in a matriarchal way, and as a little girl this allowed me lots of freedom. One of my favorite games was to search along the shore of the lake for things that I could use to for creating dolls: little branches, moss, and different colored pebbles. I created a whole tribe of them: one looked like my mother, one like my uncle, I had even made our yaks and dogs. I used to choreograph with them whole rituals, like the ones that I saw my mother and grandmother perform, passed on through endless generations of our women. Life was still peaceful in my tribe, and I felt totally protected. No fear infiltrated my upbringing. Already as a child, I knew that demons and negative entities were projections of an inner disbalance, and that unknown travellers, especially those who could tell a good story, had to be always welcomed by our tribe. That's how news of the world arrived: in the shape of well-told stories. It is the women's way.

My Master's hut was not far from our settlement. His arrival at the lake was soon followed by all kinds of tales about him. Some told that he was the 'incredible snowman'; others described him as a huge giant with round blue pebbles as eyes and flossy hair the color of a silvery winter afternoon…"

As Maya's story unfolds, the Little Buddha realizes that he is no longer hearing the voice of the Trash Giant telling it…he is back there, in the cool serenity of the Himalayas, feeling at home, and also for some reason very excited about the meeting ahead.

"Are you still there, Little Buddha?" he hears the Trash Giant ask him, a bit puzzled. He comes out of his reverie, but cannot shake off the excitement, "Go on, " he says. You are such a good narrator, I was deep into the story…"

"Maya continued: 'on the base of the stories I was told, I made a big doll in his image. But when it came to giving it the moon white skin that I heard he had, I was at a loss. I asked around, until I found out that the special white clay I was looking for could be found only in one place along the shore. Exactly where he had settled.

I immediately felt that this was the best excuse to visit him…

I asked my beautiful mother to dress me up in my favorite ceremonial outfit, the one with lots of turquoise in it. She did so without asking any questions.

Then I went to my favorite uncle. He was the beekeeper of the tribe, and his incredibly tasty honey contained a potpourri of wild herbs that only grew in our area. I asked him for a small jar of his honey to take with me as a gift. He also didn't ask why when he gave it to me.

"You see," Maya told us, "we children were never treated differently than the adults. The only difference between us and the grownups was the amount of life experience, but not always. Some children were born wise, or highly talented, and they were deeply respected for it, though never favored above others.

Dressed in my turquoise clothes with my little jar of honey in a pouch, I set off along the shore of the sacred lake Mansarovara. It was quite a distance for a little girl like me to walk alone.

But my beloved lake had always been my best companion. I used to talk to her, to her being. I felt her like the Divine Mother, deep and peaceful. It was impossible for me to imagine stepping into the lake. Only on special ceremonies my mother, the Head of the Tribe in her ritual outfit, immersed herself into the lake for only one moment, honoring the great womb of the Divine Mother.

I often heard the lake speaking to me, giving me guidance. On this walk, it told me the story of the man I was going to visit.

When I arrived at his hut, he was there. He looked magnificent. He was wearing a long saffron robe, with a sash around his belly. He was truly a giant. Everything about him was large.

It was the first time I saw somebody with light hair and skin. He was with his back towards me, standing at the shore, his hands joined into a Namaste.

He only heard me when I was just a few footsteps away. When he turned around I became for a moment insecure. He looked like a living mountain. I felt tiny in comparison, but I was determined not to let fear overtake me.

He said something to me in a language that sounded like my favorite yak when he wanted my attention.

Without any words, I thrust my doll at him. He took it tenderly in his hands, just like my mother held my baby brother.

He looked at it, and a big smile appeared on his bearded face. He looked at me, pointed at the doll, and then pointed at himself. I vigorously nodded.

As a response, straight from his belly came the loudest laughter I had ever heard. It sounded like the big gong of the nearby Buddhist monastery. For a moment, I froze. Then my own belly started to shake and rattle with laughter. I sounded like the silvery sound of cymbals…"

Again, the Little Buddha jumps up to interrupt the narration: "Have you met her Master, yet?" he seems unable to stop himself from barging in.

"No, although I know much about him, I haven't. I am told that it is going to happen in the next days…"

"But does he have a name?"

"No, Maya refers to him as her Master, why?"

"He might be someone from Shambala that I used to know…" the Little Buddha wonders how it has not yet occurred to his friend that this Master sounds very much like Raidas. But he decides not to pursue the sensitive subject.

"It has occurred to me that he sounds a lot like my grandfather," the Trash Giant says, intercepting his thoughts, "But wait until the end of Maya's story. The Raidas I knew of until recently would have never taken so much trouble to save the world …"

The Little Buddha smiles at him quizzically, and resumes his listening position, sitting back on a pile of cushions. Now he knows why he is so excited…

"Maya's story continued: 'Together we went to the place of the white clay. He gave me a very thin paintbrush and showed me how to dip it to paint the face of my doll white. After that, he dipped another thin brush into a darker pond of mud and painted his own features on the doll's face.

We soon became inseparable. I walked everyday the distance along the lake to his place, where he would be waiting for me, to teach me how to create objects out of nature's gifts.

After a while, my mother became curious. One day she asked to come along. The moment their eyes met, I witnessed something yet unknown to me: they instantly fell in love. Although my mother had already several other husbands, this was no problem for either of them. My Master remained in his Zen hut, and my mother kept her position as Head of the Tribe in the settlement. They only met when it happened spontaneously.

In due time, my mother gave birth to his son, my brother. We painted the skin of his doll with a mix of two different hues of clay, white and deep brown…"

"That would make you related in some way…" the Little Buddha is again poking at his friend.

"Just wait, let me complete. Maya and her Master remained best friends, bonded by their common interest for debris. But as Maya grew up, her sacred lake started giving the first signs of sickness. When she finally left on her study grant to the US, the trash that washed ashore smelled bad and wouldn't decompose. Tourism, foreign nuclear debris buried deep in the land, plastic everywhere, had started to defile this once pristine land.

She came back to the Lake a few years after, on honeymoon with the Garbage Collector, who was already quite involved in environmental causes. It was a great shock for her: she couldn't talk any longer with the divine being of the lake. She responded to her remarks only with silence. Her shores were lined with cheap shacks with blaring music on.

Only her Master's hut stood like an oasis amongst all the other soulless plots. When they visited him, he was by no means dispirited. Nothing could drag him down. He showed them some scientific experiments he was conducting with trash. By adding certain chemical components, he had managed to break down the garbage that was officially non-degradable, and was now experimenting with the resulting substance, a kind of plasma which he called 'Elixir', that had proved to be the main component for an endless variety of life sustaining products.

The Elixir had a similar chemistry to lava and was as fertile, but without being hot. A seedling palm growing in it could reach its full height already after a maximum of two weeks. The Garbage Collector had immediately caught on to its potential, realizing that this could be done on a larger scale. The two men talked animatedly about the possibility of creating a whole new little Planet with the Elixir.

'As long as you can collect enough garbage to fill up a medium sized planet in a minimum of time…' was the sentence that, from initially being just a joke between them, became their motto for the next period of time.

That's when the Garbage Collector took his big jump. He made some calls to some of his committed environmental science friends, and found out more and more about the plague of the millennium. Garbage would soon be covering the entire globe.

The Garbage Collector's friends, a group of highly educated and extremely intelligent people, were involved in all sorts of research projects to find some solution to this terrible predicament. It was clear to all of them that this was no longer the time to sit back and pay others to do the dirty jobs. They understood that they themselves had to set the example.

It was the Garbage Collector that took the first step in that direction. He started visiting big trash dumps all over the world. Most of them were so highly toxic that it was dangerous to come too close to them. The third world countries were the ones most at risk, because they were completely unprepared for the sudden impact of so much plastic and chemical waste.

It was Maya's Master that urged the Garbage Collector to believe in the impossible. Every difficulty on the way had to be accepted as a stepping-stone, he said. Whatever small change could be made, they needed to trust that each single pebble moved could cause an avalanche in the end. He never tired of repeating to the Garbage Collector: 'Remember, my friend, this too will pass…'"

With those last words, the Trash Giant stops, and the two friends fall into a contented silence. When the Trash Giant interrupts it with a loud belch of satisfaction, they laugh.

"It's time for you to ask your Garbage Collector friend for the name of Maya's Master. Some loose threads in your life are about to be picked up again…" says the Little Buddha when they hug for the last time.

A quick shadow of ancient grief passes the Trash Giant's face. But he is smiling when he replies: "I'll tell you next time…."

The journey back to the Greek island is very pleasant. The Little Buddha lets his Lotus Mobile cruise lazily amongst the few clouds. He enjoys the view of the sunset on the sea as he approaches home. His vehicle is glittering in the pink light, and down below he sees the streetlamps of the sea village coming on. He notices that the imperfection of the landscape has become in some way part of his soul, and that he is no longer discriminating between beautiful and ugly…

The Indigo couple welcomes him back with a delicious dinner and many questions.

"We did see him," the indigo Woman tells the Little Buddha when he mentions the Garbage Collector, "quite a giant of a man, very driven and very funny…"

"His wife was stunning," adds the Indigo Man, " noble in a natural way, and so pretty!"

"There is little doubt left about the identity of her Master", she adds.

"If it truly is Raidas, he was wise to wait….", concludes the Indigo Man.

That night, the Little Buddha dreams of his old friend Raidas and his mighty laughter. He wakes up refreshed in the morning, with a new hope dancing in his heart.

The next two days no one mentions much the Trash Giant. It is as if both the Indigo Couple and the Little Buddha are silently holding the space for a very important meeting to happen somewhere in the cosmos. They go on about their daily business and meditations, but there is a subtle anticipation in the air.

When the Little Buddha finally decides to take off again at the end of the second day, everyone is relieved. It's time to know what happened…

As he descends with his Lotus Mobile on the Trash Giant's cosmic patch, the scenario has drastically changed. He is amazed: the trash mountains, the garbage statues, the piles of second hand furniture and all the other apparels are all gone. The Trash Giant is peacefully sitting on a cumulus, as if he had just been waiting for him.

"Beloved little Buddha", he says, inviting him to sit close, "Of course you were right…to hear the name Raidas from the Garbage Collector's mouth stopped my mind. For all these years I had missed him so much, secretly even to myself. But I wouldn't have been ready to meet him until I met you, Little Buddha. I was still too entangled with my mother's opinions, and unaware of my own grief. You healed my heart.

And now, as you like it so much, I will try to tell you word by word what the Garbage Collector has told me on his visit here…"

"Go on," says the Little Buddha, eager to listen and to put the last essential pieces of the story together.

That's what he told me: 'Beloved friend, Maya informs me that now your heart is whole again, and that you are ready to know the facts. Your grandfather Raidas sends you greetings from his hut in Lake Mansarovara….'

"Isn't it amazing, my friend, that my grandfather has conceived with the mother of Maya a new child, a baby boy, who is simultaneously my uncle and the half brother of Maya?" The gigantic man is as happy as a little child when he talks about Maya's and his joint lineage…

Then, suddenly, he looks older, more mature, more focused, run through by life, with a new air of wisdom around him: "And then the Garbage Collector went on to explain to me what led to our meeting in the shopping street of Copenhagen. He told me:

'A few months ago, Maya and I were sitting together with Raidas on his wooden deck overlooking the lake. The conversation came to the topic of family. Raidas spoke about his son and his grandson. He told us how much he loved the little boy and how sad he had felt when the boy's mother had prevented him from seeing his grandson ever again. He was very human about it; he did not hide the sadness that lingered after his outrage and grief had long been consumed.

This reminded me of a beautiful Zen anecdote I heard in my travels.

When a Zen Master died, one of his disciples started crying so loudly that the others felt disturbed in their meditation. They told him: 'Don't you know that only the body of the Master dies, not his being?' But the disciple cried even louder, and said: 'I know, but my body does not know. It cries because it will never see the Master again in its human form'...

I decided there and then to find out what had happened to Raidas's grandson. Through different sources, I retraced his steps until his conflict with his teachers at the Esoteric University in Copenhagen. I decided to go to Denmark. I instantly fell in love with the quaint atmosphere of the city, especially the old center. Everything was so civilized, clean and pretty.

When I met up with some American environmentalist expatriates who loved this town just like I did, I decided to stay a bit longer. It was a good chance for me to study Denmark's management of garbage through a very modern recycling system.

Of Raidas's grandson there was no trace. He had given up his expensive apartment and there was no other record of his whereabouts.

As time passed, I developed the crazy impulse to do some very daring field research: how would it be to enter for a while the life of a trash collector, and explore the issue from the insider perspective? The idea made me really excited...I followed the necessary steps to obtain work permission as a garbage truck driver. In some respect, it was more challenging for me than taking a third PhD.

It was the first time I was in such close proximity to real large quantities of trash. To my own surprise, it was an instant love affair. I could hardly wait each morning to put on my work overall, which to my great delight was becoming filthier and filthier by the day. Coming as I did from upper class, this was one of the greatest breakthroughs in my life. I loved the smell of fermenting garbage more than any of the very civilized scents of my childhood home.

At the end of my round, when the garbage had been delivered to destination to be divided, I loved to stay a bit longer in my working clothes and stroll through the backstreets, like a real nobody. Sometimes I would also visit the park and lie down in the grass, to breathe in the smell of the earth for a while, before disappearing again in the large field of anonymous humanity.

After a while I was ready to invite my beloved wife Maya, who had stayed with her family back at Mansarovara Lake, to come and visit. I found a Pakistani run Internet Café in a side street, and sent her an email.

Her reply was instant. I had just pressed, "send" when my inbox started blinking. It was her, explaining that her visit must wait for one more month. She wrote that Raidas was close to completing successfully the formula of his Elixir for the new planet. She just needed to stay and help until the end. So much was at stake...I knew my Maya, fully absorbed into some project, giving all of her soul to manifest it.

On a lighter note, she also wrote how Raidas and herself had turned into ancient alchemists, forgetting about everything else. If her mother had not supplied them with spicy samosas and momos, they would have certainly starved. I just smiled at the picture of them, and relaxed into waiting and enjoying myself.

It was exactly around that time that you, my friend, started roaming the streets of Copenhagen...'"

The Trash Giant stops for a moment: he looks still partially in disbelief, afraid that it all might have been a dream: "Little Buddha," he says, "the perfection of it all left me speechless. I had been moving towards Raidas all along...Little did I know that before being able to meet him again I had to let go of everything that was false in me ..."

"But you never really lost your trust..." the Little Buddha adds.

"True, even when I was walking a bit numb in the city streets...but let's get back to our story. The Garbage Collector continued telling me:

'When I saw you for the first time, the main thing I noticed was how different you were from the average bypassers. You looked a bit haggard, as if you had gone through some very tough times that had torn apart your soft emotional tissue. But your resemblance to Raidas was unmistakable... I did recognize you instantly.

Why I instantly fell in love with you, I don't really know. But it was certainly mutual. In the beginning I had to hold myself back from pulling you in my arms. You had something of a stray dog, a little unreliable. But eventually, we did hug... I took you to the Cosmos Café on the day that I picked up Maya from the airport..."

The Trash Giant stops again, and in the gap that follows, the Little Buddha takes his hand and holds it tight. His friend has found back his true family. He becomes aware of a longing inside...something that has to do with family, with brothers and sisters. He remembers his feelings towards the Twelve. This brings up such conflicting emotions in him that he decides to let it be for now.

Lost as he is in his introspection, he suddenly becomes aware that the Trash Giant is telling him something important: "Raidas had now completed his Elixir. The final component has proven to be some extract of immense power that they found exactly in the white clay at Lake Mansarovara. The result is beyond anything they could have hoped for. Now the garbage is going to be mixed with the Elixir that will transmute it into life giving plasma.

All that is needed afterwards is someone with an artistic inclination to sculpt out of that plasma a certain number of huge goddesses that will function as the matrix of a little new planet. Charged with feminine energy, the soil will yield the most beautiful and healing flowers, plants, bushes and trees. The mountains and valleys of the little planet will maintain the beauty and abundance of the female goddesses that they originate from. They will host different animals and birds, especially those risking extinction on Earth. It will be a tribute to the path of transformation, where garbage can turn into life-giving matter.

That's where I come in.

I have been asked by Raidas to be the artist that will fashion the sculptures for this new planet. Unknowingly, I have been practicing for this moment. But from now on, the sculptures that I will create will be imbibed with Elixir; they will be teeming with life that wants to manifest itself…

It's time for me to leave my retreat. I have a task now: the Garbage Collector has found a system to send all the trash from here to the location for the new planet. I will also leave. Together with Raidas, I will paint my sculptures in vivid colors. We will practice creating together as one, in reverence to life. With Maya, I will learn the ancient art of telekinesis, how to move heavy masses and shift mountains with the blink of an eye… "

As the Trash Giant completes his last sentence, the Little Buddha is fully aware that their special time together is coming to an end. The Trash Giant is joining his Sangha, and he himself needs to follow the unraveling of his own surprising path…

It is with a mixture of true joy and regret that he gracefully gets up, bouncing on the cumulus towards his friend.

Just as he is leaning to hug him for one last time, the Trash Giant adds: "If you ever go back to Shambala, and meet the Buddha of Long History, please send my love and gratitude to him. He was in a way my first best friend. Sometimes I was so overwhelmed by his unconditional love, that even the most refined drawing paper became too thick, too dense to draw the lightness of being that I felt in the early mornings in his enchanted garden…"

The Little Buddha's smile spreads out all over his face and continues expanding until his whole being smiles into the vast and peaceful cosmos.

"I will do that, and I am sure that he will be very touched. Good bye, Trash Giant…"

"Good bye Little Buddha…"

Chapter Eleven

A LONG LOST FRIEND: THE ENLIGHTENED MONKEY

Full Moon in Sagittarius- Journey into New Dimensions

Daily life resumes on the Greek island. Summer has arrived, and the sea village is teeming with tourists. In their peaceful hill retreat, the Little Buddha and the Indigo couple spend time indoors, protected by the coolness of the stonewalls against the blaring heat. The silk saffron curtains are drawn closed against the light, creating an intimate space for them to write, read, paint and above all share.

"Don't you miss your friend the Trash Giant?" the Indigo Woman asks the Little Buddha, visibly restless in this confined space.

"I wouldn't even know where to find him…" he replies, clearly having thought this through several times already.

"I wouldn't be so sure," replies the Indigo Man

"When two hearts meet like yours did, there is an inner thread that binds you. Why don't you just follow that thread and visit him in his new place? There might be more surprises waiting for you there than you can imagine right now…" adds the Indigo Woman.

"Do you really think so? I have lost many friends for centuries before finding them back…but will never know if what you say is true unless I try…" says the Little Buddha, always impressed by their capacity to reflect his wishes and support him to follow them.

That evening, when a fresh breeze announces that the sun has gone to sleep, the Little Buddha is ready for a new journey. As the Lotus Mobile takes off, the first rays of a full yellow moon set it aglitter. He is excited.

For a while, he lets his vehicle drift with the currents, but then decides to start from where Trash Giant and he parted last time.

Later, after arriving at the former den of the Trash Giant, he sits alone on the cumulus, pondering his next move. The universe is big. Just then, he notices the screen of his Lotus Mobile parked nearby blinking furiously.

"The wonders of this day and age are endless," he whispers while staring at the display of the navigator. An intermitted luminous arrow is pointing to a path though a map of stars. "My ancient heart has to still get used to this kind of fast communion…" he sighs, jumping back on the seat.

The travel to destination turns out to be shorter than he thought. Before he knows it, the new Little Planet, nestled in the diffused light of the cosmos, is in sight. It appears indigo blue with large areas of emerald green.

He slowly descrends into what from above seems a huge tropical garden. It does remind him of his garden in Shambala. As he comes closer, he notices that there is a big difference here: this garden is not solid. It is tridimensional but see-through, as if painted in the air with light.

Just before landing, a giant transparent beanstalk that seems to be growing upwards by the second brushes him on his cheek. He looks down incredulous, and sees the Trash Giant standing right underneath, busying himself with something. Gone is his scruffy street urchin look. He is wearing a pair of immaculate cotton pajamas, his hair is glossy and curly, and he looks tanned. He is so engrossed in his activity that he seems not to hear the sound of the Lotus Mobile approaching.

His whole attention is focused on an intricate composition of creepers growing in big pots. With his huge hands he is delicately rearranging it, highlighting the different colored blossoms that sprout at dizzying speed from different branches.

Around him there is an array of brushes and open pots with an endless variety of colors. But there is no trace of paper or canvas.

As he silently steps out of his Lotus Mobile, the Little Buddha finally understands: nature itself has become the Trash Giant's canvas and creation. The shimmering paintings are his, colorful lights slowly turning into matter.

He is standing just few meters away, awed, when the Trash Giant finally notices him. Without turning his head away from his creation, he barely whispers: "Shhh…" and signals to come closer.

The purest full moon the Little Buddha has ever seen in any of his lives is just rising above the Little Planet. Her light is an unpolluted reflection of thousands of suns, as unblemished as a Buddha's heart.

Then the moment passes, and the Trash Giant turns to his friend, pointing with an open mouthed grin at the images dancing in the sky above.

"Look," he says, while the tropical garden slowly materializes around them, covering the rich soil with all sorts of plants.

"You did this…?" the Little Buddha asks him.

"Yes I did…" the Trash Giant replies with a touching hint of modesty, "and guess what, Raidas and Maya bestowed upon me the new title of Cosmic Creator. Now that all the Garbage I gathered is in the service of life on this new little planet, my old name has become redundant. Now I interact with colors and shapes. They inspire me and I make them alive...would you like to see how I work?"

The Little Buddha is barely able to keep up. The former Giant, now Cosmic Creator, has achieved so much in just a couple of days. Earthly time seems very slow in comparison. He feels dizzy.

"Come, just trust me and relax," his friend whispers to him, taking his hand. Moving through the now thick foliage, they finally come to a green meadow. The Cosmic Creator lets go of the Little Buddha's hand and looks up, scanning the sky in all directions.

"I like this piece", he says, pointing to a particular area above them, with a small silver lined cloud, and runs to get his paintbrushes.

The Little Buddha sits on the silky grass, admiring his friend. The Cosmic Creator starts painting images that move as soon as they are complete. It looks as if the little silver lined cloud is playing with them, altering their form and changing their colors...

"However much we change, certain rituals remain part of our essence," the Cosmic Creator says, between one mouthful and another, "I still love good food...". They are now sitting in his new kitchen area, as well equipped as the previous one. Several pancakes with large dollops of heavenly syrup are towering on their plates.

"And I am as curious as always," joins in the Little Buddha, "after food, I would like to explore this whole little Planet..."

"It will be my pleasure to be your guide..."

After washing down the food with a delicious Green Tea, they set off for an excursion. The little planet is filling with more beauty and life as they walk. Jungles have sprouted overnight, with a completely renewed flora. Never before the Little Buddha has witnessed such large orchids, such green... One can almost hear the hum of nature growing.

Then something else catches his attention: animal calls. They sound slightly different: there is a note of joy and celebration that the Little Buddha has always associated only with human voices. They follow the sounds until they reach a clearing in the middle of a valley, where the Little Buddha cannot help but gape in amazement at what he sees. There are birds performing complex dance steps with each other, a giraffe swinging lazily on a trapeze, a zebra floating mid air and singing, and a bear hanging upside down.

"This new animal population seems to be free from the bondage of repetition", says the Cosmic Creator, "It has developed the capacity to try out new behaviors..."

Then he takes a deep breath and takes the Little Buddha's hand, "and this is where our ways part, until we meet again, my beloved friend..."

The Little Buddha is confused, and doesn't quite understand the timing of his friend, "But weren't you supposed to be my guide?"

"I was indeed, my dear Little Buddha, and this is exactly where I needed to guide you. The Little Planet has an invaluable gift for you, right here in this valley. And remember: an invisible thread that will never break binds our hearts. Trust me, we'll meet again…"

After joining his hands in a Namaste and bowing down with surprising grace to his much smaller friend, the Cosmic Creator turns around and disappears into the jungle. The animals, almost in unison, retreat too, each one to their nest or den.

Alone in the valley under the full moon, the Little Buddha is feeling strangely free and exhilarated. Now he can really let the Cosmic Creator go his own way. He spreads his iridescent wings and lets himself free float for a while above a landscape of already huge trees enveloped by vines and surrounded by wild bush.

Then, suddenly, the sound of children playing makes him look down below. Amongst the foliage, there are signs of a village. He wonders if anyone lives there, and decides to land on the branch of an ancient looking tree. On a little distance below, he can see almost human-looking animals moving around the place. Then, as his eyes adjust to the perennial twilight of the jungle, he suddenly realizes that he is looking straight at someone, sitting right in front of him on the same branch.

It is a small being. A monkey. He doesn't appear restless and noisy like an ordinary monkey. His silence makes him almost invisible. The Little Buddha is intrigued. He moves a bit closer, but no response comes. After scraping his throat twice with no success, he takes courage, and reaches out with one hand towards him.

Calmly, the monkey opens his eyes. They are of a rare sky blue, clear and peaceful like a mountain stream. The Little Buddha is captivated. He gazes straight back at him and a strange phenomenon happens. The monkey's eyes seem to grow larger and larger, soon covering the rest of his face. Then they shrink back to size again, revealing an ancient, familiar face. It's the face of an enlightened Tibetan Lama that had been one of his revered teachers lifetimes ago.

"This acceleration is getting at me," whispers the Little Buddha, "I am starting to hallucinate. A Tibetan Lama turning into an animal, this is never heard of…"

"Fear not, ehm…honorable ex student…", the monkey speaks out with a rasping voice. His vocal chords are obviously not used to human language, but he makes quite an effort to be understood, "It is me, now called the Monkey, and it's a long story. But before anything else, forgive me but my newly acquired monkey nature compels to embrace you, can I?"

The Little Buddha opens his arms with a confused but happy enough smile, and the Monkey nestles into them. He smells like jungle, fur, bananas and something else…a very vague familiar undertone of incense…

"I always regretted not to be there when you died, my revered Lama…"

The Monkey looks at him with a mischievous smile, simply signaling towards himself with his tiny hairy hands as if to say: "I am still here…"

They sit for a while, taking each other in, the Monkey and the Buddha child, letting old memories slowly wash away and making space for this new meeting. Then they close their eyes. The quality of his presence has not changed one bit; the Little Buddha has to admit.

Other members of the tribe slowly gather around them. There is none of the chattering that monkeys are normally associated with. They seem to just be happy being around the two friends, silently.

Still a bit awkward, the Little Buddha tries to start a conversation: "What meditation techniques does this tribe of monkeys use?"

There is a silence. And a giggle. And many more giggles...the whole tribe is laughing wholeheartedly and uttering nonsensical sounds...

Suddenly, his friend the Monkey bursts out into a kind of improvised language, made of guttural, hissing, clacking sounds. He is so expressive with body and soul that the Little Buddha starts catching on. After a moment of hesitation, he starts improvising too. Soon they are both joyously shouting at each other, while the rest of the tribe continues shrieking and laughing.

Then, as suddenly as it had started, the mayhem stops, and everyone closes their eyes.

"This, my friend," says the Monkey in his guttural broken voice, "is Gibberish, the meditation technique which has led me here, to be reborn as a free, natural and happy monkey. Come back with me to my parents' hut, we will offer you some refreshments and I'll tell you about my adventure."

The others, still seated, part to let them descend from their branch and then line up behind them to escort them.

The hut is close by, a simple but clean shelter made of palm leaves woven into a beautiful design. "How did..." the little Buddha asks, pointing at the pile of utensils and spoons neatly laid on a polished rock.

"We are a tribe of fellow seekers who have decided to follow an unusual path, but we all have retained our human good manners" grins the Monkey, getting more fluent by the minute in human language, "and this is my father," he adds, slightly bowing to a round bellied monkey with silver streaks in his fur, "and my mother", a female with round dark brown eyes and a perfect denture. The Little Buddha gladly accepts from her a large tray of coconut slices and bananas, while the father beckons him to sit on the place of honor in the house, a comfortable hammock made of thick vines.

Eventually, while his parents gently shoo away everyone else, the Monkey comes and nestles into the Little Buddha's lap. "For many lives since we last met I kept on being reborn again and again as a monk of the highest rank, honored from the moment I came to my new life. Signs of my rebirth always led the Lamas back to me in my new incarnation, and I was invariably taken back to a Monastery to perform my service. But, believe me, my friend, I got tired of it." The Monkey lifts up his liquid eyes and sighs.

The Little Buddha can only whisper: "Charavedi..."

"I haven't felt an ounce of boredom since I came here..." the Monkey adds, playfully scratching his dumfounded friend, "But let's not get ahead of ourselves. My last human parents treated me with all the due respect, but they kept physical distance from me because they knew that I was anyway destined to the Monastery. But the dam they had built around themselves broke just on the day when the retinue of Lamas came to pick me up. I was a small and confused child trying to be brave, and they took me in their arms, moved and sorry. For the first time, I felt such a warmth coming from their bodies that the memory of it kept soothing my heart for a very long time after. It became my secret treasure: whenever the cold walls of the Monastery would get too oppressive for me, I would remember that warm hug, and feel happy. But I was afraid to be seen as impure and attached by the ones around me, so I kept it very quiet"

The Little Buddha nods, and holds the Monkey tightly around his own little body: "We are proving it right now: being enlightened does not exclude love and touch…" He suddenly realizes how much has moved in him through his friend, the Trash Giant. He would have never said such a thing in Shambala…

The Monkey seems to hear his thoughts, and start mimicking himself in that previous life. He seems at least four feet taller, and starts strutting around as if he had swallowed a broomstick…his monkey parents laugh full heartedly, and the Little Buddha joins in, strangely relieved by all this joking.

"I am also tired of being serious," says the Little Buddha, provoking another fresh peel of laughter. He suddenly realizes what they see when they look at him: a blond child with iridescent wings: little to be serious about...

"In the Monastery," continues the Monkey, "I kept to myself and studied a lot the texts I had always loved before, while in the privacy of my cell I kept on dreaming of the vast green expanses where my nomadic tribe was moving through each summer. When I became old enough, just before my last initiation, I explained my predicament to the Elders. They decided to grant me permission to visit my family for one whole summer. 'Great service is expected from you, Rinpoche,' they told me, 'maybe this is part of a greater plan…' The Elders' proved to be right. During that summer, I found my calling.

Meeting my parents and siblings was a very sweet experience, warm and touching. My brothers and sisters had grown up into smiling men and women, and my parents had gone white, their skin was like parchment. But after a while into my stay the daily routine settled back into the tribe, and I started again feeling alone, different. I offered to tend the animals of the tribe, because I felt peaceful around them.

That's how I made friends with…" suddenly, the eyes of the Monkey overflow with tears, "Emotions in a monkey's body can be overwhelming…" he sobs, while his parents from afar start clucking their tongues in a consoling sound. The Little Buddha joins into the clucking until the Monkey steadies himself and giggles again: "I made friends with a monkey. I never quite understood how he had gotten there amongst our Yaks," he adds with a shiver, "As a matter of fact I don't want to think about it right now…" he quickly looks at his father, who shakes his head in a silent 'no, don't'. The Little Buddha has intercepted this exchange, and wonders. Before he can ask, the Monkey moves on with his story: "I liked him very much, and he responded well to me. I soon found out that he was very lonely, just like me. We started to spend more and more time together, until we realized we could communicate with each other easily in Gibberish, nonsense language. Just like you and me did before on the tree branch," the Little Buddha is enjoying this tremendously. It's the child in him taking over his old soul…

"It became our ritual. We met every day at sunrise," continues the Monkey, "and for half an hour we would talk in Gibberish. Sometimes it got very loud and cathartic. Hearing our strange and loud sounds, some of my relatives started to get intrigued, and eventually joined us, gibbering away in full content. I soon added a silent half an hour sitting at the end of the loud part. By the end of the summer, half of our tribe was with us in the morning.

I was stunned by the results my method had on them. People that rarely smiled could not stop laughing for the whole day, and severe pains in their bodies disappeared. Shy and introverted persons like me started to talk and joke.

In fact, I could not stop talking any more, especially to people of my own age and younger kids…

When summer ended, I said goodbye to my family and went back to the Monastery. Now I had a purpose. Soon enough, I introduced my new meditation technique to the Committee of the Elder Lamas. The outcome was surprising: they granted me a very special privilege: I was invited to experiment with my Monkey Gibberish Meditation and study its results on my fellow monks. It was the first time that a new technique was allowed entrance in this strictly Buddhist order.

Very excited, I ran back all the way to the nomadic camp of my tribe and took the monkey with me back to the Monastery.

We demonstrated our first Monkey Gibberish session in a large windy storage hall, and the whole Monastery came to see.

Quite a few came to see the experiment fail. Knowing this, I had hand picked a number of monks that would stand in the front row and create a field of protection against any malevolence.

At the scheduled time, I brought in the monkey. The audience went silent. After whispering some nonsense to each other and towards the audience, we let our energy go. By the end, we were screaming in Monkey Gibberish at the top of our lungs.

After some hesitation, a few monks joined in. And then some more. By the end of the meditation, everyone was screaming chaotically. The silence that followed the bells that marked the end of the active part of the meditation was very peaceful and deep."

"I did experience this too just before," the Little Buddha says, "when a whole tribe of chattering monkeys stops, the silence is truly very deep…" and looks at the Monkey. His friend's tone has changed, now. He sounds like a young enthusiastic man, the way he must have sounded back then…

"The whole thing was so different from anything anyone had ever seen that it could have easily turned into a scandal. Luckily, positive responses started flooding in that same day. The majority of those who had participated was elated. It was such a relief for everyone to release all their withheld emotions and craziness through the Gibberish. In the following days, many reported how healthy and alive they felt again.

From then on, every full moon night the whole Monastery would come together to do one hour of cathartic Gibberish followed by one hour of sitting silently. The monkey and I conducted the meditation together. Our way of communicating became more and more fluent, until one day we started to understand what the other meant …."

There was a long gap of silence. This was exactly what was happening between them, thought the Little Buddha. But the roles were reversed, now...

Then, the Monkey continued: "Soon I became well known all over the Himalayas, and a whole new school of meditation created itself around me. But as I grew older and more tired, I found myself dreaming again of an ordinary life, without the stress and the heavy responsibilities I carried towards so many souls. I longed for a simple life, a woman, a family and nature. Sometimes this longing was so strong, that I had to painfully hold it in my muscles and nerves. My body became so badly affected by this that I got sick. Nobody knew why I was wasting away so quickly." As he speaks, the Monkey gently pushes away his mother, who seems to be worried by the stressful tone that colors her son's voice, "Do not worry, mother, I learnt my lesson…" he tells her with a giggle.

The voice that resumes the story is now ageless, no longer monkey or man:

"When I felt there was only a very short time left, I made my plan. I did not want to be reborn once more as a monk. As a matter of fact, I did not want to come back at all as a human being. In my time with the monkey, I had heard many stories about his life in the monkey tribe. How he had felt so free until he had been caught. They took him to a strange and scary place where they sold him. I cried with him. I knew the pain of losing one's family and having to live a life that was not your choice.

It was then that I made the decision to be reborn as a monkey.

I knew very well that within the monastic system I would have no chance to die and go my own way. They could still reach me and guide me through the Bardo, the transition period after death. They would certainly prevent me from becoming a monkey and going astray …

As hard as I tried, I could find no solution. As my last resort, I turned to my monkey friend. He was staying with me in the Monastery, but most monks ignored him. They had remained prejudiced against animals. Some of them had even started to order him around, demanding from him to do their little errands. The monkey tried to ignore them, but the whole situation started entering under his skin. He started complaining about aches in his bones and loss of his hair. His body missed the warm sun and the moist air of the jungle.

One day, he came to me announcing that he was going to leave. He wanted to find back his family and start one of his own. For me, this was the last drop.

That night I could not sleep. In the early morning, I called him again. I told him that I also wanted a new life, just like him. He hugged me and offered whatever help he could give to get me out of my spiritual imprisonment..."

The monkey parents are broadly smiling. They are holding each other tenderly.

The monkey looks at them with benevolence, and continues: "As part of my esoteric education, I had been taught how to determine the best moment for me to die by just stopping my breath. I gave the monkey my chosen time and date, explaining to him that my physical death would immediately be followed by the Bardo, the seven-week transition cycle before the next rebirth. I told him that the end of the cycle would coincide with the rising of the full moon during the collective Monkey Gibberish meditation. Exactly at that moment, he would need to take the great risk to replace the usual text of closure and blessings read by the Head Lama with the new one that I had written.

In the new version, I guided myself away from the human form, into the body of an enlightened Monkey. Since the words monk and monkey could easily be mistaken for one another, the change in the text was minimal, but immensely powerful. I handed the new scroll to the monkey, who took it and quickly disappeared with a conspiratorial smile.

And so it happened that the Lamas who had so far been guiding me through the Bardo could not access me any more. I had erased any sign of the direction that my soul would take...

It was a big risk: I was ready to face the possibility that the universal laws would not let me get away with my alteration of the text, but it wasn't so. Everything went well for me.

When the end of my Bardo was declared and my soul could no longer be found, the whole Monastery went into a big upheaval. In all that chaos, the monkey quietly slipped out of the compound. It was a beautiful spring morning. He took a deep inbreath of pure Himalayan air, made a soundless yodel of joy, and disappeared...

After many days of searching in vain and performing all kinds of rituals to retrieve my soul, the monks settled for a half-truth: it was declared that I had attained the state of Arhatta: an enlightened one whose journey was complete, who would simply dissolve into the cosmos after dying."

The Monkey lets his last sentence hang in the silence for a while, and then continues: "When I had previously announced the time of my death, my own disciples came to me in tears, and pleaded me to let them gather around me again, wherever or however I would return.

I told them something. I could not simply lie to them, but I didn't say the full truth. I did mention as a half joke my dream to become a monkey, marry and get children, but most of them laughed. Some decided to leave, and some remained for a while longer. Only few stayed with me till the end. To those, I taught my new method for deviating from tradition…"

Just then, the deep silence is interrupted by a swooshing sound in the foliage outside. All the tribe members have gathered around the hut, in respectful silence.

The Monkey acknowledges them by putting a hairy hand on his heart, and continues: "After my death, I entered a truly blissful period of transition. I met many different deities, some positive ones and some negative ones. I recognized them for what they were: projections of our own collective unconscious… there were so many sex goddesses! I remained detached from all of them, and in the end only a great sense of bliss remained, carrying me gently onwards. I felt ready to be reborn in a monkey tribe.

The gentle, some would call it angelic force that was guiding me, brought me right here, to this little planet. Here I have experienced a new kind of happiness. I instantly recognized my new father. It was my most beloved friend and partner of the Gibberish experiment, the monkey…." His father bows down to him in a sweet teasing gesture of reverence, and the Monkey laughs back at him, "My mother, his long dreamt of companion, is as you see a very sweet natured female. And another breath taking surprise was waiting for me: the tribe of monkeys that welcomed me was constituted for a great part by my former misfit disciples! For the first nine months of my new life I was in such ecstasy, that all I could do was smile…" A wave of giggles crosses the crowd outside as a response.

The Little Buddha is caught up for a moment in a futile attempt to make sense of the density of time on this Planet. From an earthly perspective, only two days have passed since the Trash Giant, no, the Cosmic Creator… how can the Monkey have spent a whole childhood here already…But then he surrenders.

After what seems to be a long, long time the Little Buddha slowly brings the palms of his hands together in a Namaste. His body slowly bows down until his forehead touches the ground. There he remains for another long time.

When he finally comes up again, His face is wet with tears.

"I am humbled by the mysteries of life. Thank you, my friend…"

The news of the arrival of the Little Buddha quickly spread throughout the whole Little Planet. All the other new animals gather from every side. In the beginning there is mayhem, lots of reunions and new meetings. There is a festive atmosphere: all animals love a good party… A long necked giraffe is instantly infatuated with a sturdy bear from the Amazon, and a monkey is explaining love postures to an adoring bunch of young female hippopotamuses.

But after a while the noise fades, and slowly everyone becomes silent. They all close their eyes and enter into meditation. The Little Buddha is deeply touched. Not only has he witnessed the natural birth of a new planet, he is also experiencing right now how this living organism, born out of transformed trash, is attracting a new type of consciousness.

But compared to the renewed friendship between the enlightened Monkey and the Little Buddha, everything else pales. By the end of the evening it's clear that separating is out of question for them.

"It's time for me to take my leave from my parents and move to my next adventure with you, my dear Little Buddha," the Monkey tells his friend, "since you came a deep call has awakened in my heart, and I know that I will have an important place in your new life, as much as you will have an important place in mine. I am so grateful to my parents and to my tribe for giving me the opportunity to experience true belonging, but now I will have to take leave from my father and mother." His liquid eyes fill with tears, "I honor them as my parents, even if in our previous lives our roles were different. My soul doesn't belong to them, but I will always have a special place for them in my heart…"

The Little Buddha notices some hesitation in him, and asks: "Beloved friend, would you feel better if I was the one to ask your father if I can take you with me?"

After such a long and prolonged effort for his mind and vocal cords, the Monkey seems to have returned to just being himself. He wrinkles up his whole face, thinking deeply about his answer. The Little Buddha has to smile: he really looks funny. His friend is really a monkey now, not the eloquent lama that he used to know. He feels protective of him.

Finally, the Monkey answers: "Yes, Little Buddha, yes, please do that!"

After the Little Buddha is granted permission by his father to take him along, the Monkey goes to his parents and thanks them, with tears in his eyes, for the great love and care that they have showered on him.

Saying goodbye to the rest of the tribe takes quite some time. After much hugging and kissing and more of it all over again, the Little Buddha and the Monkey depart at dawn.

On their journey back to Earth on the Lotus Mobile the Monkey is very quiet. He is contemplating over what he already knows from other lives: on Earth, monkeys are considered lower forms of consciousness. They are regarded as empty-headed chatterboxes. Even the great Buddha Gautama used to compare man's mind to a monkey that chattered all the time in an endless flow of unconscious gibberish.

The enlightened being that now lives in a monkey body knows by direct experience that it is not like this, but he also knows that if he wants to communicate with people other than the Little Buddha, he needs to train his voice to utter human sounds. This will be a real challenge for his monkey brain.

In the end, he decides to happily surrender for the time being to speaking Gibberish, trusting that he will be able to communicate when needed.

After a pleasant and timeless flight, they finally reach the Mediterranean home of the Little Buddha's soul parents, the Indigo People.

The little Monkey is shy: for the first days in these new surroundings, he keeps to himself in the Zen Hut, hiding from everyone except the Little Buddha, who takes good care of him, bringing him suitable delicacies like rice, honey and milk.

One morning, with a full little belly and a sweet feeling in the heart, the Monkey finally relaxes. Seeing him so trusting and happy, the Little Buddha feels that this is the right moment to tell his Indigo soul parents about him. They respond very lovingly: "When you both feel ready, bring him here. We are very happy to include your friend in our lives".

On a cloudless afternoon, the Monkey is introduced to the Indigo Couple. They start making friends right away. With them, he begins to practice the art of human language. With incredible patience, they train his little voice until it can utter all sorts of words. Together, they sing devotional songs, and the singing helps the Monkey to relax his heart and throat and speak more and more fluently.

Chapter Twelve

A FAMOUS HEALER

"Life is sweet on this island," the Monkey keeps on telling the Little Buddha in the next days. He feels totally at ease in the Zen Hut that they share.

Since they got here, the two friends have immediately started functioning like a small Sangha. They have both spent so many past lives in religious institutions and esoteric Mystery Schools, that making schedules of who is in charge of the meditations for that day, and arranging specific times dedicated to inquiries into the nature of the Divine, comes natural to them. They love discussing enlightened scriptures and their application in this new surprising world.

That's not quite how it appears from the outside. Every morning, the Indigo Man loves watching them both walking along the perimeter of the property: what he sees are a child and a little monkey, sometimes shrieking and gibbering to each other, sometimes walking with their hands behind their backs, looking like old Greek philosophers. But there is no mistake about the golden light they emanate...

One early morning before dawn, the Little Buddha gets up. He moves very carefully not to wake up the Monkey, who is gently snoring on his own futon.

He steps unsteadily outside the hut, in the velvety twilight, and for a moment trembles uncontrollably. He has noticed for this whole week after his return from the Little Planet that sometimes one side of his body feels suddenly on fire, while the other becomes numb. He wonders if it's the effect of the acceleration he has experienced on the Little Planet, or if his fast reincarnation without the soothing rest of the Bardo in between lives has some unforeseen side effects. It almost feels as if he is lacking some essential substance in his system, as if he is burnt and numb.

He looks with great affection at the bundle lying in the hut under a blanket. He loves how the peaceful sleeping presence of the enlightened Monkey supports him to find out more about his own unusual incarnation. He slowly stretches his limbs, and feels better.

Outside the hut, there is a small but well equipped kitchen area, shaded by an umbrella of palm leaves. The counter is full of neatly stacked steel bowls and plates, a memento of the Indigo couple's journeys to India. In the flickering light of an oil lamp, the little Buddha makes himself a delicious cup of yogi tea. He finds himself wondering what will be next.

He carries his steaming mug to the nearby terrace overlooking the whole curve of the bay, and slowly sips from it. Sitting in his easy chair, he notices that the daylight is coming; there is just the first hint of it at the horizon. He finally puts his cup on the ground, breathes in deeply the first scent released by the roses, and closes his eyes.

Suddenly, reality shifts around him. He sees a very vivid and alive picture unfolding in front of his inner eye. Then, it is no longer an image: he is there, with all his senses. He can smell the familiar pure air of the Himalayan peaks and feel its cool prickle on his skin. He sees the pure blue sky reflected by the calm waters of Lake Mansarovara.

He looks at the shore: there is a hut just a few steps away. With no doubt in his soul, the Little Buddha recognizes it as Raidas's place. It looks just as Maya described it to the Trash Giant. But it is not fully of this world. It is shimmering, luminous. As he comes closer, the door opens by itself. Once inside, he realizes that he can still see the spectacular view of the Lake and of the Himalayan mountains through the walls: the hut has become transparent. The Little Buddha is sure now that he has stepped into another dimension, closer to the original source.

A large gathering is slowly forming at a short distance from the hut. The Little Buddha squints for a moment, blinded by the concentration of light that this group of people seems to emanate.

Then he sees them. The whole population of Shambala is there. He is pleased to see amongst them the sensuous Samba Yoga Lady, and the German Buddha together with all the other members of the Council of Twelve. Even the Dervish is present.

From the distance, he notices another group of shorter beings walking slowly towards the gathering of Buddhas. The light around these beings is dark and soothing. As they come closer, he can see them clearly: it's the whole monkey tribe, wise old ones and children in the front.

The Little Buddha feels relaxed and trusting. He somehow knows he shouldn't attempt to move unless a signal is given, so he waits inside the transparent hut.

The Himalayan silence is gently penetrated by a familiar hum interwoven to the sound of prayer bowls. With a rustle of saffron and maroon cloth, a whole procession of Tibetan Monks joins the large group on the shore.

Then the Little Buddha sees his soul parents, the Indigo Couple, their faces wet with sweet tears of longing. Behind them is their very colorful and crazy tribe of lovers and devotees of the Controversial Master.

Then something surprising happens. From all directions, strings of scientists in pullovers and shamans in full ritual gear, together with musicians and dancers of every race and color, move towards the main gathering. When they arrive, their different streams of music dance, modern science and ancient magic finally join into a new symphony that contains them all.

"It's like being in front of a living rainbow," the Little Buddha whispers, enjoying so much the undiluted wonder that he can experience inside a child's body. "There is no trace of boredom in my body", he realizes.

Then, as all sounds fade, someone steps away from the gathering towards the Little Buddha. He recognizes Raidas, as always a giant with a mischievous twinkle in his blue eyes and a surprising grace. He beckons an older woman to also come forward. She is wearing a ritual outfit with strings of coral around her still swan like neck, and emanates the gentle and firm authority of a matriarch. Maya's mother, the Little Buddha thinks, also mother of Raidas's new son. But the greatest joy comes over him when he sees right behind her his Giant friend, the now Cosmic Creator, with a broad and proud smile on his face. With him are Maya and the Garbage Collector.

"No more Garbage Collector, Cosmic Alchemist, now..." the Cosmic Creator whispers loud enough for the Little Buddha to hear, winking conspiratorially. Even the modern clothes that this couple wears cannot mask their timeless quality.

The little Buddha is unable to respond in any way. The only thing he can do is to open his arms and let wave after wave of utter blissfulness and gratefulness wash over him.

Then Raidas gives the signal. He beckons the Little Buddha to come closer. As he does so, the walls of the hut become visible again, and he finds himself seated at the feet of Raidas, leaning with his back on his legs. Everyone else has disappeared, except for the Cosmic Creator and the new Cosmic Alchemist with his wife Maya and her mother. They all listen for a while to the lulling sound of the waves lapping on the shore of the Lake.

Then the Little Buddha hears Raidas's voice. He turns to look at him. He is smiling, and his sky blue eyes are transmitting pure love.

"Beloved Little Buddha. We have summoned you here to meet all of us who love you for what you are now and for what you will become later in this life." He makes a sweeping gesture —so much like his grandson- towards his soul family.

"Being a Buddha, however little," Raidas's humor is received with an uncharacteristic giggle by the rest of the company, "makes you a herald of the hopes and dreams of humanity. This planet evolves thanks to beings like you. What you learn on your path seeps into the ordinary state of consciousness of human beings through their dreams and visions, and veers the course of their lives towards the true, the good and the beautiful."

Then Raidas's eyes change, and so does his tone of voice: "As we all know, growing can be very painful, sometimes. By really listening to his story, you have made it possible for the Cosmic Creator to realize that he had to let go of his defenses and open up again..." he smiles affectionately at his grandson sitting nearby on the earthen floor, and continues, "A clean mirror is all it takes for seeing oneself. We all thank you for what you did from the depth of our hearts."

He looks around the room and his eyes fall on Maya, whom he beckons forwards, and resumes talking:

"It's our turn now to give something back to you, Little Buddha. We know that great challenges are waiting for you on the Earthly plane. But before it's too late, we would like to offer you some possible alternatives.

You have heard of Maya, my beloved spiritual daughter. She is raised in the matriarchal way of total acceptance and unconditional love. Like her, Little Buddha, you will need to become a servant of love, and embrace through understanding what you before judged…"

His last words enter the Little Buddha's heart like a piercing arrow. He doesn't understand why he is suddenly feeling a wave of great sorrow. Then it's gone. The intimate atmosphere settles again, and Raidas continues:

"Maya has been trained by the female elders of her mother's tribe in divination. Women know how to contact people's souls without being invasive. It's like tending to children, and instinctively knowing what is happening to them. We men are more aggressive. We have more outgoing power in our solar plexus, we have ideas…" he adds, bellowing with his famous laughter while rubbing his stomach, "but women… women have a lunar plexus, that can reflect the light in others, their potential, just like the moon reflects the sun rays.

Men like to conquer. When in the service of life," Raidas looks with tender respect towards his younger male friends, the Creator and the Alchemist, "male energy can move mountains and realize impossible dreams. But women…" and he gazes with adoring eyes towards his smiling wife, "women have a clear intuitive power. They can read all the big and small signs of life, from the yearly migratory flight of birds to the signs left by the black bear when he gathers honey, from the position of the planets in the sky to the cryptic oracles of the Akashic records. They have the power to follow any deep trace of woundedness that needs healing. That's why divination was born out of women…"

Maya steps forward, and addresses the Little Buddha in her American drawl: "Beloved, when I asked existence to send me signs about your immediate future, the message I received spoke to me clearly.

I was told that the solidifying of your holographic shape into a denser physical body has released a new great skill in you, the power of healing…"

The Little Buddha, unable to utter words in this trance like state, remembers silently the first time he saw his hands while incarnating, "the luminous aura…healing powers".

"Yes, you did recognize it right from the start," she replies to his thought with a smile, "Your healing power is still growing, but it will become very big and difficult to manage. We all want to remind you that you do have a choice. The signs told me that your delicate system has the tendency to easily burn.

Look at this buttercup I found…" she says reaching out with the palm of her hand to show a small yellow flower, radiating pure light, "It's beautiful and delicate and has very strong healing powers, just like you. Expose this flower to too much heat and passion, and it will whither. Nourish it with love and coolness, and it will share its healing properties with joy."

Then she steps back, and her expression changes. Her eyes are humid with compassion when she tells him: "Beloved, we would do anything for preventing you from experiencing the pain that you will soon feel. But we cannot. It is part of a Karmic teaching that we have no right to alter…"

Although the Little Buddha feels no trace of fear in his soul, his body sets off into an uncontrollable trembling. Speechless, he wonders what is happening.

Maya gently touches his check and replies: "Our advice, Little Buddha, is to take it slowly and to listen to the signs of nature, like all of us should do. Remember that trees and animals have as much need of your presence as human beings in distress…" and with these last words she moves away, joining her hands in a Namaste and slowly vanishing.

All the others seem to have disappeared too. The Little Buddha stands for a moment in the empty hut before it also dematerializes. For what seems an eternity, he closes his eyes and sits alone at the shore of the Great Mother Lake Mansarovara.

Then he remembers the last words of Maya, and his heart fills with care and respect for his new friend the Monkey…He suddenly becomes aware of a gentle breeze softly caressing his face, and opens his eyes…

He is looking straight into the smiling face of the Monkey, who is fanning him with a large fig leaf. While they watch together the glorious sunrise above the ancient mountains, The Little Buddha can see that his gentle friend knows, but won't invade the preciousness of this moment with questions.

The day after, while washing his favorite saffron Kurta[1], the Little Buddha feels a lump in a corner of its pocket. It is a small dropper bottle.

The label reads "Cosmic Elixir, from Raidas with love. Use it well"

The little bottle glows with life. He takes it gingerly in his small hands, and calls everyone for a meeting. Soon after, he is sitting on the Bali couch of the cool main house with the Indigo couple and the Monkey.

"This Elixir is enormously fertile …" the Little Buddha starts, showing everyone the glowing bottle, and tells them about his vision the previous day.

"What touched me the most in your vision, beloved friend," says the Indigo Man, "is that it reflects the new spirit of this time, in which Buddhas and monkeys, Lamas and musicians, scientists and shamans, are able to create together a new healing symphony for this Planet…"

"It is this new spirit that brings me to you, my beloved soul family…" the Little Buddha, says, including the Monkey with a sweet smile, "I feel that together we can create something greater than what we could individually …"

---

1 Long Oriental shirt

Everyone nods. The Monkey sits up and asks eagerly in almost perfect human language: "Where shall we start?"

"With drawing a colorful map of the Earth," the Little Buddha says, looking at the Indigo Couple, "with all the different countries, mountain ranges, oceans and rivers on it."

The Indigo Couple are more than happy to be included in this magical adventure, and in no time they draw a beautiful round map of the globe in all colors. Everyone stands around it, the Little Buddha and the Monkey on the Bali couch, the man and the woman on the flagstone floor.

"I have been told by Maya that plants and animals need me as much as people in distress. I would like to dedicate my new healing power to nature…" declares the Little Buddha.

"Let's make a list of the places on the Earth that need most healing", the Indigo Woman promptly opens her Ipad and starts a search.

When the list is done, the Monkey produces a box of colored pins. To everyone's surprise, he puts them exactly on the corresponding places on the drawing of the globe: "My intuition remains the same, animal or not…", he giggles back with a flashing full teeth monkey smile.

While all four look proudly at what they all feel is a potential masterpiece of global healing, the Indigo Man utters a blessing:

"Beloved Mother Earth,

Here are your four children speaking.

We want to offer to you a very powerful healing Elixir

Made by Raidas, your divine servant

Please accept our healing intention

To remove all the scars we can from your Planet

And to make it green again

Thank you, Blessed Mother"

"Time for your healing force to act…" he says after a gap, slightly bowing to the Little Buddha.

"There is not enough of it to cover the whole planet, but these are the places that have really suffered the most…" the Little Buddha says, carefully placing a few drops of the Elixir at the base of the red pins on the map. The result is immediately visible: wherever a drop has landed, a green glow starts appearing, first intermittently then steadily.

"Now we can only wait and see," says the Indigo Woman, moving towards her kitchen to prepare a smoothie for everyone.

The news travels fast. Within a couple of hours, everywhere on the web are posted new pictures and videos of rainforests growing again where they had been exploited and destroyed, and of vast landscapes turned into deserts being miraculously irrigated again by the appearance of sudden streams, and becoming meadows of blossoming flowers.

"We are trying to determine if this change is due to some unforeseen effect of the change of the axis of the Planet, or…" the reporters comment, while showing images of once barren mountains now freshly covered by greenery, "The latest reports coming in are also talking about a sudden purification of the ocean waters in the areas where oil had spilled. They are teeming with life again…"

Later during the day, the four see shots of people in different parts of the world celebrating, splashing each other with water in former barren lands, hugging each other in tears where trees are suddenly growing at an incredible rate.

"Songs are already being composed to celebrate this event, but the truth is that we do not know its source, and the scientists maintain a skeptical attitude towards this unknown phenomenon…" says a cheerful US anchor woman on the net, inviting an older distracted looking gentleman to speak, "Until we have ascertained the stability of this change and its source, we cannot comment…" he says, and adds with an unexpected wink, "but in the world of quantum physics anything seems possible…"

It's a matter of hours. By the end of the evening, the big change in the ecosystem seems to have stabilized. The green glow on the map fades into a green spot wherever nature has regained territory on the Planet.

Speculations run high everywhere, from the scientific to the esoteric circles to the political scene. "Look at this one!" laughs the Indigo Woman, showing a diagram on a website that proves the connection between the latest events and the political platform of an Italian presidential candidate…

"I am certainly happy to be out of public focus…" the Indigo Man adds, happy with their little secret.

But in these modern times information is quickly gobbled and digested. Apart from the tribal populations who have benefited by the great change in their surrounding, people soon forget about the great events to make space for the next sensations…

Within a couple of days, the four friends are again enjoying the slow pace of their life on the island. The Little Buddha, lounging on his easy chair, sends out his gratefulness to Raidas and his soul family. "Our advice, Little Buddha, is to take it slowly and to listen to the signs of nature…" he remembers Maya's words; he can almost hear them again in the peaceful birdcalls before sunset.

That evening, an unexpected visitor shows up. Just as the four are settling for their supper, a knock comes at the door. A lanky and unkempt man is standing at the entrance.

"Remember me?" he says, drawing the Indigo Woman in a sudden hug.

She is good with names and faces, and gently but firmly stepping back, she exclaims, gaining some time to remember his name: "Aren't you…? Weren't you together with…"

"Well, I am her ex husband," he says, while lowering his eyes for a split second, "but I am here just to say hello. I am new on the island, and would like to start fraternizing right away…"

The Indigo Man stands up to greet him, but his reserve is visible in the way neither he nor his wife invite him in. Now the stories about him are coming back to their memory.

"And what on earth is a Monkey doing here," the uninvited guest says, barging in and barely acknowledging the Little Buddha, "Don't you know that monkeys are dirty? They spread lice and flees, and on top of it they are little thieves, I do remember when they stole my backpack in the jungle…"

The Monkey cannot stop himself from releasing a whimper coming deep down from his animal soul. The Little Buddha hears it, and turns to the Indigo couple: they are meanwhile looking at each other, making slight grimaces of disgust. They are almost managing to maneuver the Ex Husband out of the door with the excuse of showing him the orchard, when his eyes fall on the map, now neatly hanging on the wall close to the kitchen table, pins, green spots and all.

"And what would this be?" the Ex Husband asks, with a sneer on his face "geography lessons for the monkey?"

The Little Buddha notices the blue eyes of the Indigo Man getting a few shades darker, as if a storm is brewing in them, "How would you know," he tells the Ex Husband in an outburst of anger, "You have never created anything new in your whole life! This," he points out at the map, "is the source of planetary healing that every one was talking about a few days ago…", and then stops, regretting immediately what he just said.

After cowering for a second under his attack, the Ex Husband straightens up, grabs his mobile, points at the map and takes a few snapshots that include a wide open eyed Little Buddha standing next to it with open arms, trying to conceal it, and the Monkey at his side.

Then in one step he is out of the door, quickly saying, "See you guys, good luck with your fantasies!" and is gone.

The four stand there in a shock, not knowing what to think about what happened.

"I am sorry, friends…" the Indigo Man whispers.

"He anyway stank…" murmurs the Monkey, relieved and worried at the same time.

The following morning they crowd once more around the kitchen table, ready to watch the latest news on the Ipad while breakfasting on fresh fruits.

"Breaking news", a big lurid red strip announces on top of the latest edition of an online international newspaper, "A world famous chemical concern specialized in fertilizer is offering a fabulous sum of money for whoever can locate the originators of the incredible plant growth that occurred a couple of days ago in some areas of the Planet."

"It wasn't forgotten after all…"says the Little Buddha,

The Indigo Woman stops reading: " I get goose bumps…"

"I have lost my appetite," adds the Monkey, shivering.

Just then, the Ipad screen is flooded with Facebook notifications. They gather around the small screen. The homepage of the Indigo Couple is full of snapshots of their home and of the map of the globe with the open armed Little Buddha and the Monkey next to him. There is also a close-up of the Ex Husband, obviously proud to be the one who has unveiled the mystery, with a link to his recent interview. The Indigo Woman spends the next hour erasing all photos and comments, but they all know it's too late. The word is out.

"There is my watch!" is the only thing the Indigo Man can say when he watches on line the Ex Husband being interviewed by a horde of journalists. He is wearing it at his wrist.

By mid afternoon, though, it becomes clear that the Chemical Concern has dismissed the information offered by the Ex Husband. "After extensive research, our Board dismisses the information received and declines payment of the reward", reads a fresh press statement that no longer covers front page.

"Humiliation is what hardens the soul most," sighs the Little Buddha, feeling compassion for the lanky con man.

"Our source was referring to a small settlement in the North Aegean," the press statement continues, "where no trace of advanced technology except for the usual gadgets is recorded. We prefer to fund our research elsewhere."

The Indigo Man smiles: "What can two ageing hippies and a little child and a monkey do that could be of interest to them?"

But journalists are less picky than a multinational. Before our four friends can draw their breath of relief, they start hearing sounds at the edge of the property.

As they step out, they are welcomed by the buzzing of voices and the incessant clicking and beeping of digital cameras. They quickly close the door again, and look at each other stunned.

"Better go and face the journalists now, when they are still fresh, than letting them grow frustrated and aggressive…"says the Indigo Man. They all nod, and then quickly discuss what their line of answer will be.

"Let's talk about my healing capacity," the Little Buddha volunteers, planning to cover everyone else by this partial truth, "this will keep things in an imaginable proportion, and people's heart will be happy with the news, and I feel ready to share it…"

A long look passes through the other three, and those few seconds seem very long. "It's a big burden you are taking on right now, Little Buddha," the Indigo Woman says.

"I'll stay by your side no matter what," adds the Monkey passionately.

As the four exit the arched passage of the courtyard wall, the Indigo Couple in front and the Little Buddha with the Monkey behind them, mayhem breaks loose; questions are fired simultaneously in several languages, flashes from all directions blind them, and nobody seems to care about anyone else.

The Indigo Man steps forward and raises his arms in a firm gesture. It seems to work: he has everyone's attention.

"Dear friends of the press, we would like to introduce to you a great healer, a beautiful friend from the beyond…" he starts.

There is a murmur in the crowd:

"Is he from outer space?" an incredulous female voice shrieks. It's the signal for another cross fire of questions about UFOs and such.

The Indigo Man lifts one arm again, and continues as they all fall silent:

"His name is Little Buddha. This child…", he says, stepping aside and allowing the Little Buddha to walk forward, "belongs to a new type of humanity, dedicated to healing and love."

Right on cue, the Little Buddha, accompanied by the Monkey, walks towards the gate, meeting flashes and video cameras.

"What's the relationship between these two?" asks an effeminate male voice with a sneer, "Can you cure my hangover?" bellows a hoarse Scandinavian man in the back.

The Little Buddha ignores all remarks and simply stands there, breathing peacefully, flanked by a dignified Monkey.

Everyone is mystified, and quite a few leave angrily after a while. Some remain, and slowly a peaceful atmosphere settles over everyone. The Indigo Woman, ever so resourceful, comes out with jug after jug of cold lemonade for everyone, and small talk is happening here and there. Tired cameramen take a few more shots of the Little Buddha serenely standing with the Monkey, and then put their equipment aside. The gate is opened, and slowly everyone sits on the lawn, enjoying the glorious sunset that turns the mountains pink.

By the evening, everyone quietly goes. The Little Buddha stretches his arms, smiles a bit tiredly at the concerned Indigo Couple, while the Monkey asks: "What's for dinner?"

The following day photos of the Little Buddha appear everywhere on the Internet. "There are very few angry commentaries," remarks the Indigo Man, "most are in praise of you, Little Buddha. Look at this caption: 'The new Sat Guru', or this one: 'An Angel?'"

The Little Buddha is not used to so much focus on his persona, and doesn't feel at ease with it, "It's a bit like being tugged at inside your own soul…" he whispers, feeling too visible…

The next day, he has to renounce his afternoon stroll with the Monkey and the Indigo Couple at the seashore. Friends have told the Indigo Couple that new loads of paparazzi are lurking in the "tavernas" downtown waiting for his appearance, and that miniature statues representing him have appeared overnight in the local thrift tourist shops. His three friends will do their best to discourage the press and calm everyone down.

The Little Buddha remains alone, in the Zen Hut, contemplating becoming a recluse or even returning earlier to Shambala. But his musing is interrupted by some soft sounds outside. "Not the press again!" he is just sighing, when an unknown force drags him out of his comfortable lounging chair into the open, to face a small group of people loitering at the gate.

None of the aggression or the invasiveness he has so far experienced is there, when a middle-aged woman steps out of the group and greets him:

"Respected healer..." she addresses the Little Buddha, and then turns towards a sad looking young man, "my son here is wasting away with some unknown disease, can you help us?"

From that very moment, a new world of sharing opens up for the Little Buddha. It all happens in a heartbeat. Opening his arms towards the woman and her son, he dives into the experience of being a healer.

"He will get better soon," he hears himself saying to the woman with new authority, after placing his hands on the young man's heart and throat and softly murmuring a blessing, "his endocrine system is rebalanced, now..." the young man feebly smiles, and bows to embrace the Little Buddha, who welcomes him in spite of his pungent sweaty odor, feeling only love.

A few more people follow the woman's example, and move forward either bringing a sick relative or friend, or coming to receive healing themselves.

By the end of the afternoon, when everyone is gone, the Little Buddha is filled with a new joy, something that he had been aware of missing since hearing the beautiful stories of cooperation and love told by the Trash Giant.

"I feel that for the first time since very long I can actually do something about the suffering and the pain of the Planet. I can heal its children..." he tells his friends when they come home from their mission in the village. They are overjoyed to find him glowing with energy, pink in his cheeks and brimming with enthusiasm. The paparazzi have been meanwhile misdirected to the other side of the island, and a great feeling of purpose fills the air when the four discuss their new plans around the evening meal.

"There is quite some shade around the Zen Hut for most of the day. People who will come and seek healing can sit around and meditate while you treat your patients. The Monkey can act as a host and receive them, while we will be taking care of the supply of cool water and lemonade for the visitors", says the Indigo Woman, foreseeing large numbers.

"Shall we put a limit to the visitors?" asks the Monkey a couple of days later, standing at the entrance of the Zen Hut with a large Jug of cold tea. The Little Buddha is inside, stretching his tired limbs after twelve hours in a row of treatments.

"I cannot possibly reject any of them," he replies, "I used to be so sensitive to smell and touch, but now only love seems to matter..."

The Monkey sighs, recognizing his friend's burning passion, "Certain things can't be stopped, beloved Little Buddha, can they?"

So the work continues. The opening hours are stretched to the limit, and more and more people come for treatment. The Little Buddha turns out to be a very creative healer. Sometimes he touches people, other times he prays with them or for them. With many he talks and shares. The Monkey always sits close to him, enjoying the many stories he tells, the metaphors he uses to point at the inexpressible, and the absurd koans he produces to stop people from thinking too much.

Each person walks away feeling seen, understood, and healed.

Soon there is not enough space left for people to wait in the shade of the Hut. Awnings are improvised around the orchard to protect people from the ferocious heat, and small tents are planted here and there. The dirt road outside is clogged with cars and motorbikes.

"I honestly don't know what to think…", says the Indigo woman to her husband while they walk hand in hand across their property, dodging running children and dogs, and stumbling over forgotten cushions, "what he is doing is truly special, and he looks so happy. But he is becoming so fragile…"

"I am afraid that he is ignoring his limits," replies the Indigo Man while disengaging his foot, trapped in the rope of a small tent hidden under a large fig tree, "he is starting to absorb too many of the toxins released by his patients…"

That evening they go to the Zen Hut and try again to make their point with the Little Buddha, but to no avail. "Avalokitesvara, the Buddha of compassion, is working through me at this moment," he tells them with large tired eyes, " I cannot stop the flow of my compassion."

The Monkey, unwavering in his support, smiles at the Indigo Couple: "I am staying close to him, and I will make sure that nothing bad happens…We have devised a security system," he adds, with a sly smile, "If I see or feel anyone approaching that could be of potential harm, I will let out very loud monkey shrieks that will alert the Little Buddha and discourage the potential aggressor…"

The Indigo Man and Woman look at each other, not knowing whether to laugh or cry: "But that's not what we were talking about…"

"Don't be misguided by appearances, my beloved Soul Parents," the Little Buddha adds, "the Monkey is talking about negative vibrations and evil intentions. He can pick them up from afar and warn me with great accuracy…"

"I will also warn him with joyful shrieks when the person approaching has a very good aura and a great potential for meditation…"

"Thank you, sweet friend, we hope this will be enough of a protection for our generous Little Buddha…" the Indigo Man concludes, casting a quick doubtful glance at his wife. They leave the Hut to the sound of the two friends quietly discussing the events of the day.

Chapter Thirteen

THE DARK NIGHT OF THE SOUL

New Moon in Cancer – Total Eclipse of the Sun

"It's only a week since it all started, but it feels like ages," says the Little Buddha to the Monkey, getting up with difficulty from his futon.

The Monkey is starting to worry. His friend whimpers in his sleep, and doesn't look any less tired than last night: "Are you sure you don't need a break? Shall we call everyone off for the morning?"

But before the Little Buddha can reply to him, they hear the soft voices of the long line of people waiting outside the gate.

The Little Buddha sits on his easy chair, ready to receive them. His gaze becomes intense and a bit distant. "I want to continue," he tells his friend. As soon as the first patient sits in front of him, he is glowing again with happiness and purpose.

For the next few hours, he touches, talks and listens to everyone.

The Monkey is standing outside the Hut, tapping his feet restlessly. He feels uneasy. Too many people are crowding the place, and he feels cut off from the Little Buddha. "If anything would go wrong now," he thinks, "I would not be able to protect him. He is too busy to hear my signals…" He shakes the thought off, but the worry remains. Then he looks at the people waiting silently, some of them with eyes closed. For many of them this is the first taste of meditation, he realizes. He finds solace in this new thought, and sits down.

Suddenly there is a lot of noise coming from the end of the line. People are screaming at each other. The Monkey dashes towards the angry voices.

There seem to be two parties arguing about their position in the waiting line. At the center of the mayhem there are two women shouting at each other, each one backed by some supporters. One is a dark haired peasant woman that he recognizes: she has already come several times with different family members. She looks outraged, gesticulating with her hands and clicking her tongue: "You came after me," she is saying in broken English, "with all these other fancy people, and you all stepped in front of me without asking. Ellare[1], c'mon, who do you think you are…?"

The other woman keeps her chin up in disdain, as if slightly irritated by the smell of her opponent. She looks at ease in the conflict, as if she is used to boss her way to whatever she wants. Her snobbish attitude and perfect inflexion clearly indicate her class.

She is wearing a slightly outdated Chanel two-piece suit. The Monkey jolts back when his sensitive nose catches a whiff of mothballs coming from her jacket. Although her hair color is a professional melee of honey blond and ash grey, undoubtedly the work of a very expensive hair stylist, her complexion reveals that she must have been much darker. She could be Middle Eastern, observes the Monkey, remembering some traders that used to visit the Monastery when he was still a monk. But she is no trader, thinks the Monkey, this tall woman is powerful, she is a Madame…He somehow even likes her, and briefly wonders what sort of life has made her so hard.

Just then, the Madame changes her tone of voice. There is no arrogance when she addresses the dark haired peasant woman again: "Dear woman, I am deeply sorry for the inconvenience my group has created, but let's not argue too much about this point. While we are arguing out here in the heat, it's a man, as usual, that keeps us women waiting outside, fighting with each other. He is the real problem, not us…"

The dark haired woman looks completely confused. She has not quite understood her words, but the Madame's appeasing tone is clear enough. She turns away almost apologetically.

Completely ignoring her now, the Madame turns to what seems her retinue of followers. "Darling", she says to an overly well-dressed man next to her, "can you call the organizer, whoever that is, and remind him that not all of us have that much time to waste?!"

The man instantly answers, "Yes Madame, I am your devoted secretary…" and turns towards the hut, where the Monkey has meanwhile resumed his guarding position at the entrance. The Secretary squeezes his eyes almost shut to verify if what he is seeing is real, "Madame," he says apologetically, "there is an animal standing there, I think it's a monkey…"

The Madame gets upset with him instantly: "Of course, you fool, don't you read the newspapers!?!?" she also narrows her eyes, but in contempt, "It's typical for a "religious" type like this one! He is of the worst kind. He has declared himself all over the world press and the Internet as a World Healer coming from a supposedly sacred valley in the Himalayas to save the world.." she says with a sneer.

"Yes, Madame, I apologize for my stupidity. Now I recall: I also read that he said that this animal over there is his best friend from lifetimes ago…"

"But don't you wonder why such characters almost always have no powerful woman next to them," the Madame adds, "but favor instead the company of young male

---

1   C'mon in colloquial Greek

acolytes who obviously adore them and believe everything their so-called Master says?"

"Don't you think, Madame, that it is just a case of hidden homosexual feelings?" the Secretary asks, with renewed interest in his eyes.

"Let's go and confront this acolyte, then," the Madame ends the conversation by cutting through the line towards the Monkey. By now, everyone has given up trying to stop her.

The Monkey, alert, stands up ready to receive her.

"Young man," the Madame tells him in a slightly shrill voice, "can you go inside and tell your so-called Master that I have arrived, and that I want to see him now? And can you remember what I told you, or should I send my secretary with you?" The Secretary, who meanwhile has been staring with hungry eyes at the Monkey's hips, swallows deeply: "Well Madame, if this is really needed, I could..."

That's too much for the Monkey.

He runs inside the Zen Hut, where the Little Buddha is just completing a healing on the scar on an old man's back. But before he can explain to the Little Buddha why such a rush, the Madame has sneaked ahead of him.

The Monkey is furious, but when he notices that she has made eye contact with the Little Buddha, he stops behind her. He sees her shoulders relax, and her self assured posture change. She looks smaller, almost like a child. "It's the Buddha Rain," he says in a whisper, having seen it happen now uncountable times around the Little Buddha. People who have experienced it directly describe it as a shower of blessings flooding over them.

But the contact is soon over. The Madame straightens up her shoulders and stretches to full height. She is obviously again in control of herself, thinks the Monkey, worried. Then she politely reaches out to shake the Little Buddha's hand. But he doesn't respond as expected. The Monkey can see the Little Buddha's eyes looking deeply into hers. He notices a subtle shiver along her straight spine, as if she is shocked by the intensity and compassion in his gaze.

Then the Little Buddha responds joining his hands in a Namaste. The Monkey would pay anything to see the expression on her face, but doesn't dare to interrupt. From behind, it looks as if something is compelling her against her own will to do the same gesture. Her hands, slightly trembling, join in the salute.

But this doesn't last long. The Madame opens her arms and makes a signal with her right hand. Instantly, the Zen Hut fills up with her whole retinue, cutting off the Monkey from view. He quickly pushes himself forward, in the small space between the Little Buddha and the Madame, but soon the Secretary draws in close, putting his hand on the Monkey's thigh. The Monkey recoils, and loses his place. From a back row he sees the Madame sitting down on the patient easy chair in front of the Little Buddha. Everyone else sits on the floor, his or her closeness to the Madame's chair reflecting their degree of importance for their Mistress.

Sitting with the Little Buddha eye-to-eye makes her more confident, notices the

Monkey, straining to see. She is sitting straight up, like a bird of prey.

The Little Buddha looks relaxed, waiting for her to start speaking. He is meanwhile enjoying the little dish with fresh fruit that the Indigo Couple has brought earlier.

Her voice is bitter when she speaks: "Once I would have believed in this whole set-up," she says, pointing at the Zen Hut and then at the Little Buddha, "As a little girl, I used to draw angelic beings that looked like you, Little Buddha. But this was long ago. I soon learnt my lesson: beings like you are not real. You can deceive everyone else around you, but I will not buy into it.

It is specially for men like you, who pretend to be innocent, that all women including my former self fall"

The Little Buddha's expression doesn't change, but his gesture reveals that he has had enough. He puts his dish aside and replies softly but firmly: "Dear woman, I do not know you, and you do not know me. Let us remain unprejudiced towards each other." He opens his arms towards her, and continues, "If you need healing, I will do what I can for you. But please be respectful towards the sacred space that is being created here."

This makes the Madame really angry. "Nobody dares telling me what to do or what not to do," she hisses.

The Monkey sees real danger. The Madame's aura changes in front of his eyes: it becomes too vivid; too charged…he recognizes the power of magic at work…

He starts shrieking his monkey signals, but the Little Buddha doesn't seem to register his voice at all: his eyes are glazed. Then he hears a rumble…and the Madame's warning rising above it: "This is MY gift for you, Little Buddha, an ancient spell that will stop you from being arrogant and knowing better…."

With these words, she draws herself up in a powerful stance, points her index finger towards the Little Buddha, and utters mysterious sounds in an ancient tongue:

QUED POR STAZ

REFUS AD MORPED!!!

The last word hangs in the air. Then everything happens all at once.

The Little Buddha slowly falls out of his chair. It looks as if some tremendous force is pushing him down to the ground. The Monkey scratches, bites and pushes everyone ahead to get to him. He is on the floor, his body painfully twisted, completely paralyzed.

The Madame stands there, shocked: "This was meant as a mild curse, no more than kitchen magic…" she quickly turns to the Monkey who is holding his unmoving friend, "It was meant to make him feel a bit numb for a day, well, you know, like being stung by a scorpion? What is happening is too extreme…" She looks in a panic at her Secretary, who appears as helpless as her.

The Madame's last words unlock the Monkey's rage. He jumps towards her with bare teeth, snarling at her: "Do you want to play around with psychic powers?!

Experiment on me, then!" and pushing her out of the Zen Hut with all his might. She literally flies out of the door, over the porch, down in the fields amidst the brambles. She quickly gets up and, ignoring her torn Chanel suit and all the scratches on her body, she runs for her life and disappears.

Then the Monkey is ready for the Secretary: He dives on his legs, blocking him from escape, pouncing ferociously on him. After a vain attempt to fight back, also the Secretary flees. Simultaneously, the whole retinue of the Madame escapes amidst the confused crowd outside.

The Monkey stands outside the Hut. Everyone lets him through, looking in amazement at this usually peaceful small animal who has just turned into a wild beast. When no trace of the Madame's clan is visible, he goes back inside and looks at the devastation: there are strands of his fur everywhere, upturned chairs and broken vases. In the middle of it all, the Little Buddha is still lying, limp and lifeless.

Meanwhile, the Indigo Couple is driving back home from a visit to a friend. They are right in the middle of discussing how the current solar eclipse can influence the psyche of human beings, when they see a disheveled tall woman running towards them down the road, her face in a grimace of fear. Behind her is a small group of people, led by a man wearing what must have once been a fancy suit, now completely in tatters. He has quite some bruises on his face.

The Indigo Man stops the scooter on the side of the road, but by the time he calls out for them they have already passed by in a cloud of dust. They seem in too much of a terror to stop anyway. They are actually running faster, and soon they are out of sight.

The Indigo Man looks at the Indigo Woman. Looking alarmed, they mount the scooter again and rush home. There is such a crowd at the gate that they cannot enter with their vehicle. They drop it there and push their way through to the Zen Hut.

They run inside to find the Monkey in the middle of upturned chairs and broken vases trying to revive his friend, now lifted back on his easy chair. But in spite of all his efforts the Little Buddha appears out of reach. He looks empty and ravaged. One look at the wounded Monkey is enough for them to imagine the cause of that woman's fear. He is wild with rage and grief, wounded and bruised, begging on his knees the Little Buddha to come back.

They each sit on a side of the Monkey, hugging him close while he trembles and sobs: "It's all my fault, I was not alert enough…"

The Indigo Woman whispers to him: "just tell us what happened, beloved loyal friend, there might be no time to lose…"

The Monkey understands the urgency, and with admirable flexibility returns to a calmer version of himself. While he tells them what happened, the shock on their faces is visible. But even in the middle of all the drama, the Monkey manages to draw out of them an amused smile when he describes his adventures with the Secretary. He is back to himself.

Just then their attention is drawn to the Little Buddha, who has not yet moved at all yet. They hear a desperate whimper coming from him, as if he would want to say something, but he cannot utter a single word. His face twitches uncontrollably, and he has a desperate look in his eyes.

They sit around him, the Indigo couple and the Monkey, touching his feet and head very gently, just waiting, until the warmth of their presence starts having an effect on him.

"I don't know what is happening to me…" when he finally speaks out, his voice sounds different: it's flat, very low, with no trace of his typical ring, usually so similar to the silvery sound of meditation bells. He sounds tired, defeated.

Signaling everyone else to stay where they are, the Indigo Man stands up and goes out, meeting the confused gaze of the people waiting outside.

"Beloved friends, due to unforeseen circumstances, the visits of today are postponed. Please be assured that they will resume as soon as the Little Buddha recovers from what seems a very sudden ailment. We will do our best and keep you informed"

That evening, in the village downtown new myths are created, about the epic battles of the ferocious Monkey and the evil spells of the blond witch. The morning after, the older local women, with a vast knowledge in the field of the evil eye, gather to pray for the Little Buddha and do their brand of kitchen magic.

But no local counter spell seems to erase the devastation. In the days that follow, the Little Buddha tries every technique he knows: he meditates, hums, darkens the windows of the Hut to be surrounded by soothing blackness, but in spite of his efforts he continues to feel numb and totally over lighted at the same time.

"It's still me," he speaks barely audibly to the Monkey, "My being is untouched, I am still conscious, I can still watch what is happening to me, but I cannot function…"

The Monkey sighs, trying to lure him into eating some delicious Indian dish specially prepared for him, "You see, I don't even know if I want to eat," the Little Buddha continues, trying to nibble out of the plate with no appetite, "it's hard for me to feel any purpose…"

"Last night he woke me up asking me what his name was…" the Monkey confides that day to the Indigo Couple, "I simply told him, and he thanked me. Only after, in the silence that followed, I felt how scary this was…"

The small Soul Family finds relief in the daily care of the Little Buddha. Every day they rekindle their hope: maybe this herb, or maybe this supplement, or maybe a massage, or maybe a new delicious cake will bring him out of the deep hole he seems to be in. New phenomena start happening: he is shivering in spite of the heat, and complains about severe aches in his whole body.

The line outside the gate is dwindling to nothing. Every day the Indigo Man and Woman talk with the people outside, one by one, apologizing for the delay in their visit, and receiving their good wishes. Some of them take time to be appeased: they have traveled far, and they are angry at what feels to them like a rejection of their hopes. But in the end everyone leaves with an open heart and a fresh lemonade.

The Little Buddha, barely able to stand on his feet, has never stopped protesting. He wants to continue helping, he says, collapsing back in his chair immediately after.

In the end, hoping that this might bring him back, the Indigo Couple relents, and allows him to see the last remaining patient, a young man that has kept on coming every day for the last week. But when they see the young man emerging from the Zen Hut after a while, zigzagging in a strange foggy space, they realize beyond doubt that the Little Buddha is in no condition to help anyone at the moment. They decide to try to get some sense into his tortured psyche. They speak frankly with him: "You need to take space, something really bad, which we do not understand, is happening to you. Together with the Monkey we have looked up on Google under Curses. If he remembers the words of the curse correctly, we have found the one that the Madame used against the Little Buddha. It is used against religious arrogance."

For the first time, the Little Buddha is paying attention: "But I am not arrogant..." he says, with a feeble voice.

The Indigo Woman continues: "But what is most stunning is that this curse is reported as a minor household one, specifically used for restoring humbleness."

"The effect it had on you is far beyond its potential," adds the Indigo Man holding his hand, "we know out of our own experience how negative energies can infiltrate inside you while you are open and unprotected, but we have never witnessed anything close to the devastating effect that this curse had on you..."

The Monkey, now looking far more like a Lama than like an animal, looks at him and adds: "Please look inside yourself, and try to find out what makes you so extremely vulnerable to negativity..."

Accepting the unavoidable, the Little Buddha nods. "I have to stop, I understand..."

But it is not a restful stop. Day after day, the Little Buddha just sits, listless, on his easy chair. His life spark is gone, and with it, all meaning.

"It's the Dark Night of the Soul..." he murmurs to his concerned friends, "I cannot prevent it from happening. No peak of consciousness can erase the limitations of my body and brain..." he concludes with an abysmal sadness in his voice. The Indigo Couple can feel the truth, however hard, of what the Little Buddha is saying, but they still shed many tears out of his sight.

From his side, the Monkey has tried everything he could imagine to cheer him up, like joking and making faces, or driving him around with the Lotus Mobile, even if he can barely control it. But the Little Buddha has remained passive and taciturn, and the Monkey still keeps on blaming himself for it.

"We have been playing and replaying the events of that day long enough", whispers the Indigo Man, sitting at the end of the first week on the raised platform outside the Zen Hut, together with his wife and the Monkey. It's sunset, and there is a general atmosphere of dejection amongst them. The Little Buddha is lying inside, in a bundle, not wanting to eat.

"We have tried everything we could, and it's really hard to admit that it's out of our hands," adds the Indigo Woman, still browsing on her Ipad for the thousandth time through the sites listed under 'spells'.

"We have one last chance," the Monkey says, suddenly jumping out of his brooding mood. The Indigo Couple, never ready to give up hope, turns to him intently.

"My enlightened monkey tribe on the Little Planet!" he says, with a toothy smile, "We have exhausted all possible human sources of information. Maybe now it's time to find out if the transformed animal consciousness can help us where humans cannot…"

There is nothing to lose, they all agree on that. Even the Little Buddha, from inside the Hut, whispers a soft: "Yes…" that brings a gentle excitement in everyone's heart.

After a short and tearful goodbye, the Monkey takes off with the Lotus Mobile, holding on to its sides with apprehension. As he crosses the spectacular starry dome of the sky, he is happy. For a moment, the vastness of the Cosmos seems to absorb and dissolve the intense despair he has been feeling for the last week. But when the Little Planet comes in sight, he is well aware that his mission here is not just for leisure.

When he gently descends towards the jungle clearing, he can see all his tribe standing there, baskets laden with fruits and delicacies, children cheering, everyone ready to welcome him.

As soon as he lands, he happily surrenders to the many hugs, belly scratching and wet kisses. But soon enough, everyone is aware of his state: by the look in his eyes and the subtle trembling in his body they can all feel that he came for support. They gently step back, and accompany him to his family hut, where his monkey mother and father welcome him.

When the whole tribe is settled around him, the Monkey first thanks everyone for the great welcome, and then narrates in a very colorful pantomime the events that have led him back here. He cries, and snarls, and becomes the Madame, and finally becomes the Little Buddha lying listless on the floor.

They all listen to him very attentively. When he finally sits back at the end of his tale, a wizened elder with long beard and sunken eyes, speaks out in guttural ape language from the back row: "I have heard of a great Shaman who lives in a big cave very far away from here," he says, pointing at the horizon with his bony hands, "somewhere on the Planet Earth, in a country called Russia, in a region called Siberia. You should visit him. He might be able to do something that neither us enlightened animals here on the Little Planet, nor you and your spiritual family on Earth can do. Enlightenment cannot help where the body is concerned. What the Little Buddha needs is a human healer, somebody who can heal on a human spirit level".

"What about the Little Buddha's friends, Raidas's family at Lake Mansarovara? Couldn't they help?" the Monkey asks him, while he sits down at his feet, wincing from the pain from his still fresh bruises.

The Wizened Elder smiles at him, and gazes at some invisible point in the distance: "Those friends belong to the archetypal beings called the Gods. My little friend, let me tell you about their place in the large and colorful diversity of beings inhabiting a planet in this cosmic system…"

The tribe murmurs, getting ready for a wondrous tale, "The Gods have grown out of the heroes of mankind. Since the beginning of human history, a Hero could reach the status of God for his fellow human beings. By being honored in this way by so many, Heroes would achieve a position that was far above ordinariness, until their Godlike nature would survive their mortal life. It was well known that when they left this world they simply moved to their final abode, either amidst the highest mountains or even higher, in the sky above them. Gods have changed with time, and their image has adjusted to the ideals of their contemporary humanity. At every generation different Heroes become Gods, and every time through them new wonders of evolution happen on the Planet. The Lake Mansarovara family is one of the new groups invested with God like nature: they can predict the future of others but as far as they are concerned, they remain unpredictable. But they cannot help with healing, that's not their function: they can help with guidance…"

There is an audible shift in the audience. Some are leaning forward, unashamed of being curious monkeys…

"Gods often answer your questions through good dreams or nightmares. One of their common traits through their whole history is that they all are masters in creating illusions, from thunder and lightning to beautiful spring weather…"

Then right in front of his eyes, he sees the face of the Wizened Elder filling up, while he enormously grows in height. A different, human voice speaks to the Monkey: "Tell the Buddha that he needs to stay alert: at the right moment, we will send him a dream that will reveal the source of his karmic entanglement…" It is Raidas, standing just where the Wizened Elder was: "Please greet him for all of us," he continues, "and tell him not to take all this too seriously. He is a Buddha, after all, and he knows that ultimately all of human life is a dream, an illusion."

"And you, little Monkey," Raidas addresses him very gently, "all of us here in Lake Mansarovara bow down in respect for you. Know that we will protect you on your journey…"

Then Raidas fades away, and the Wizened Elder is back in front of him, giggling with amusement.

The Monkey bows down amazed, but once more his curious nature gets possession of him. Dutifully raising his index finger, like in school, he asks: "Old wise one, are there also animal gods?"

The Wizened Elder laughs: "Yes my dear little Hero," he answers, " even amongst the humans some animals that have done acts of great courage or compassion are revered as Gods." He winks at the Monkey, his eye disappearing into the parchment of his lids, "But let me tell you a secret, also animals have their Animal Hero Gods. Occasionally, even a Human Hero or a Buddha are included in their pantheon…"

"Thank you, wise one," the Monkey says; "I hope to become as wise as you when I grow older..."

The following morning, after a good rest in his rope hammock, the Monkey is ready to depart. As he takes off in the Lotus Mobile, he realizes that his journey in search of the Shaman will be very challenging, but also an incredible adventure into the mysteries of the Planet Earth. He suddenly feels tremendously excited, and in spite of his sore battle wounds, he jumps up and down on the vehicle, letting out a very loud shriek of happiness. The whole tribe, becoming smaller and smaller as he rises upwards, responds with equally loud shrieks and jumps from the clearing.

"Do you really feel ready to cross half of the world to go to a mysterious shaman living somewhere in the vast planes of Siberia?" After being instantly relieved by the fresh hope that the Monkey has brought back with him just a couple of hours before, the Indigo Couple now asks, concerned.

"It looks like this is my quest," the Monkey replies. There is a new pride in his stance, he is now standing very straight, chest forward, and seems unafraid to show his animal power, "your task as the Soul Parents is to stay here with the Little Buddha, and keep him in his body while I am gone..."

"But how can we help making your journey easier?" the Indigo Woman asks, wondering meanwhile if she can produce another small pullover against the Siberian cold.

"I have not traveled much in this Monkey body: in fact, I only know this place here and the jungle on the Little Planet...how do I get to Siberia?"

"Take the Buddha's Lotus Mobile for as long as it is needed," suggests the Indigo Man, but the Monkey refuses agitatedly: "I cannot sit in a pink Lotus! It has forever been the symbol of a Buddha! And anyway it drives too fast for me!"

"Don't worry!" says the Indigo Man, enjoying the liveliness of the Monkey like a ray of sunshine after a hard winter, "we can do something about that! What would your dream vehicle be?"

Before he can stop himself, the Monkey hears himself say: "A slice of watermelon!"

The Indigo Couple laughs: "A watermelon slice! It fits so well with you!"

It's quickly done. The Indigo Woman draws a juicy watermelon slice, and the Indigo Man colors it in all the deepest reds and greens.

"It's so inviting...it looks so tasty..." she tells him, noticing his hungry eyes. "But dinner will be later!"

They instruct the Monkey to touch the drawing. Once again, the miracle happens: the drawing becomes first tridimensional and then turns into a solid sturdy vehicle, just the size of the Monkey.

He steps tentatively on it and they encourage him to try it out immediately. He swallows with apprehension. His monkey synapses are working overtime to figure out how to start it. He touches the screen repeatedly, but nothing seems to happen.

Then he literally jumps on it with both hands and feet, monkey style, and finally the watermelon slice starts bouncing up and down, zooming left and right, hiccupping its way up…

It is so good to laugh for all of them. The Indigo Couple has almost forgotten how to, such has been the gloom hanging in the air. Even the Monkey, hanging disheveled onto the control panel of the watermelon, is laughing hysterically…

After many antics and emergency landings, out of sheer determination to save his friend the Monkey starts getting used to the vehicle. After that, it doesn't take long for him to fall in love with it and become an excellent watermelon driver in few hours.

By the afternoon everyone feels safe enough with the Monkey's newly acquired driving abilities.

"There is no time to lose," he tells his friends, "I have to go…"

The Indigo Couple loads him with bags of cookies, bananas and cartoons of banana milkshake for the long journey.

"Open it later," the Indigo Man says, handing him a small backpack, "it contains some extras that you might need in your travel…" he adds, with a quizzical smile.

Then the Monkey goes alone to the Zen Hut to say goodbye to the Little Buddha. Sitting quietly on the side of his Futon, he delivers Raidas's message to him. The Little Buddha silently weeps.

The Monkey's heart is about to break. He holds his friends until his quiet sobs subside. Then they look at each other, silently, for a long time, until the Little Buddha lifts a shaky hand and places it on the Monkey's head: "Journey well, my dear friend and fellow traveler," he says with effort, "Enjoy seeing new things, and explore them with your passion for life. I give you my blessings. Take good care and come back when you feel your mission is accomplished."

Then, taking his hand away and joining it with the other one, he salutes the Monkey: "I will enter into a Zen retreat now. I will remain alone for as long as my being needs it. I am in the right place for this. The Indigo Couple will feed me with rice, dhal and miso soup so that I can stay light and detoxify. I will not allow any visitor. The friends of the Indigo Couple will help them to create around this property a field of protection. One of them, a Martial Art expert, will be around the Hut on a daily basis. I can let go now."

The Little Buddha closes his eyes. He looks so tired and vulnerable, like a very small and sick child, thinks the Monkey standing up.

"Remember, watch your dreams," he whispers on his way out.

The Little Buddha feebly nods, and the Monkey steps out, with an excruciating ache in his heart.

"Thank you," he hears the tiny voice whispering from inside the Hut, "thank you!"

Within moments, the Monkey is up in the sky in his Watermelon Mobile. He flies once in a circle over the main house and sees down below the Indigo Couple waving to him.

"Goodbye sweet Monkey", are the last words that the winds carry to him.

Chapter Fourteen

IN THE PLANES OF SIBERIA

After a whole day of flight, even in his comfortable Watermelon Mobile, the Monkey feels tired. He has been keeping a general northeast direction, flying against the sun, and is pretty sure that he is not that far from destination. As evening approaches, he decides to stop for the night. "Better be rested for my important meeting," he tells himself, waving away for now his concerns about how he is going to find the Shaman. He starts his descent on an open strip of land. There are not many inhabitants in this part of the world, he notices looking at the few large tents, garishly colored, that dot the vast landscape. He recognizes from above the peacefulness of tribal life: women carrying children on their hips, proud looking men riding horses, and old people sitting peacefully at the entrance of the tents.

The Monkey doesn't immediately realize the effect that his descent in such a peculiar vehicle has on the local population. What they see from below is an ancient God descending on a wondrous flying object backlit by a gigantic moon. And he cannot imagine either that his arrival is considered by all the tribesmen as a very lucky occurrence, reported to happen only every thousand years…

He is simply pleasantly surprised when upon landing everyone in this tribe outdoes himself to welcome him. They surround him, all talking at the same time, patting him on the shoulder and inviting him to follow. The Monkey quickly realizes that, if he wants to gain their hospitality, he needs to rise to the occasion. He bows and accepts, flashing a smile that provokes an "oooh" in all the pretty girls standing in the back.

An old toothless grandpa, who turns out to be the head of the tribe, beckons him in some ancient language to sit next to him around a blazing fire, and everyone else joins in a large circle around the flames. While a constant flow of unfamiliar delicacies is brought to to him, he strives to find a way to communicate with the locals. After a while, a peculiar mix of English, ancient Tibetan and sign language seems to do the job. By bedtime, he has learnt a lot about the customs of these simple people, and heard and told many stories.

That night, lying in his cot of woolen blankets in a strange tent, the Monkey has a restless sleep, full of nightmares. He dreams of the Madame, her face a mask of wrath, resembling the Goddess Kali, Mother of Death and Destruction… He wakes up with a start, sweating profusely. He still doesn't understand why all this happened…

In the morning, while munching on his fruit and nuts, the Monkey opens his backpack, browsing through all the items that the Indigo Man thought useful for the Monkey's journey. There's a water filter, a small thermos for tea, a Swiss pocketknife, an almost weightless thermal sleeping bag and a few other smart gadgets for survival. He smiles thinking of the Indigo Couple and their world, such a blend of high tech and eternal…

Then he feels at the bottom of the backpack a well-padded square object. He draws it out with care and notices the note glued to its front.

"This is a gift, a surprise for you from us, dearest Monkey. When you open it, find a way to let us know how you are… And please watch out for curses!!!! With love, the Indigo Couple"

The Monkey turns the parcel on all sides, remembering now how it had arrived with the mail the day before. When he had entered the main house right after the mail delivery, both the Indigo Man and the Indigo Woman looked for a moment like two kids caught doing something secret. It had been like a sweet note in their otherwise sad attitude…the Indigo Man had quickly put the parcel out of sight, taking great care into placing it carefully inside his personal drawer…

The monkey unwraps the parcel with humid eyes, and finds inside a sleek black Ipad, just like the one the Indigo Man is always keeping nearby.

The Monkey jumps up and down in delight. He loves information. It used to be called gossip before, and monkeys knew about it long before mankind.

"It's our inborn curiosity that has kept us alive: we heed signals, not like the Little Buddha that did not pay attention to me…" the Monkey for a moment feels angry at the Little Buddha, thinking how just one missed signal of danger has provoked his downfall…This would have never happened to a monkey.

Then he shrugs, and sends blessings and love to his friend, grateful for all the gifts received in his company, and excited about the adventure ahead.

After a short exchange with his host, a taciturn bearded middle-aged man, the Monkey finally understands that this remote tribe is in possession of a Wi-Fi device. His host smiles broadly for the first time when he shows him his perfectly functioning IPhone. Speechless, the Monkey simply opens his Ipad, and lets his nimble fingers go randomly on the touch screen. By now, he has learnt to trust the way they move, faster than his animal brain, and how they seem to touch exactly the right places. He hits the icon of Facebook and checks into the account created for him by the Indigo Woman. There are many comments to his post about finding the Siberian Shaman, but not much to go by; everyone is just sending him good wishes. Just as he is about to close the Ipad, he hears the beep of another incoming message. It's a map of the southernmost part of Siberia, with no words attached. A blue intermittent dot seems to point to a specific place in the western part of Khabarovsk Krai, inland but not far from the ocean. Scratching his head, the Monkey wonders who is the sender. He inhales deeply and relaxes: he doesn't smell danger anywhere, and this is enough for him. He will follow the directions given on the map.

After some shoulder patting, hot butter tea and more shoulder patting, the Monkey is released by his Host, and accompanied by the whole tribe to his Watermelon Mobile.

In a couple of hours of rather chilly flight through the northern skies, the Monkey finally arrives in sight of his destination: Siberia.

Just looking at the endless expanse below, he realizes that to find a Shaman in this wilderness will require a lot of trust and a good dose of miracles even with a map. As he browses the panorama below shimmering with frost, he feels lost: he suddenly remembers all the stories he heard about people coming back empty handed from their quest. He shivers: he would not be able to live with that shame. "Time to gather myself together," he mumbles, while looking for a landing spot.

But suddenly the vast expanse below is filling up.

Groups of people, some on horses, some driving vintage Russian Jeeps, many jammed in small pickups, are suddenly converging towards the area below the Watermelon Mobile.

The Monkey is getting a real sweet tooth for warm welcomes. There is no doubt that the people waving at him from the ground expect him. He wonders how much of this is due to social networks and how much of it is a simple miracle.

"We want to help your quest," a broad boned tall man with blond hair tells him when he dismounts. We come from different areas of this region, and when we heard that the mysterious ones have directed you here…"

"The mysterious ones?"

"They are told to be four…" one beautiful older woman interjects, with a smile.

"Don't pay too much attention, my friend", butts in a youngster, "your arrival was announced in Facebook…"

Before he can ask for more explanations, the Monkey is escorted to an improvised banquet of Siberian delicacies around the fire. "These are Momos…" the Monkey almost swoons savoring a dumpling, "They remind me of Tibet…"

"Not exactly, they are Pelmeni with vegetables, specially for you…" giggles the girl who is offering the tray.

When the food has all been eaten and the vodka is being passed around, a short mercurial man comes to sit next to the Monkey; one look is enough for both to recognize each other as kindred spirits. "I am the story teller of this clan, the end of a long line. We are famous all over Siberia, in fact you can Google us," he adds with a giggle, "Our clan is very proud of us, and needs us very much, specially in the long winter nights when there is not much else to do than listening to us…"

"I am here to take you with me to a magical place in the forest where you will receive the information you need to continue your journey…" he adds, leaning closer to be heard over the laughter and singing that is happening all around.

The Monkey is ready. Leaving behind the warmth of the fire and the chatter of the tribe, they walk together into the forest that surrounds the camp. It is silent, full of shadows and mystery.

They finally arrive at a circle of stones. They pause in front of it, and the Storyteller, lifting one of the stones, invites the Monkey to step after him inside the circle, putting the stone back behind him.

As soon as the circle is closed, the Monkey feels suddenly showered with energy, and bathed in light: he is so contented that he only wants to give in and relax.

The Storyteller's voice changes. It takes on a hypnotic tone, and his words seem to merge and melt into each other. But somewhere in his trance, the Monkey still understands him clearly: "Now I want to tell you about the lineage of the Shaman that you are seeking for," he starts. "The best way to absorb the story is through deep relaxation. Relax deeply, and don't try to remember anything I tell you. When you need to remember this information, it will be made instantly available tto your conscious mind…"

The Monkey nods gratefully and lies down. In no time he is softly snoring

The storyteller continues happily. He is used to it, and always uses the opportunity to embellish and change his stories without having to discuss any details with his listeners.

The Storyteller continues: "I am touched and honored, little Monkey, to be able to tell such a quintessentially Russian story to such an exotic creature like you…"

The gentle snoring of the Monkey becomes steady, and the Storyteller continues:

"Dear Monkey friend, I will talk to you about Shamans…do you know that you look like one yourself? You say that you are an animal…. But you look so civilized…"

The Monkey, stirring in his deep sleep, sighs and murmurs…."Bananas are expensive in Siberia…"

"Very good" continues the Storyteller, "Shaman is a word that means 'he who knows'. Throughout the many regions that later constituted Soviet Russia, Shamans were once very respected: their healing arts and their reverence for nature were considered highly. They were the spokespersons of existence and of the mother Goddess, and therefore had much power, which they were reported to never abuse.

The story I will tell you is an example of how the Shamanic spirit has survived all persecution and stigmas, and has adjusted to these modern times to continue speaking out the voice of nature, healing, and peace.

The Shaman that you are seeking is a young man, in his thirties, but his knowledge is ageless, deeply rooted in the traditions of the land…

His Grandfather, a big bony man with deep liquid eyes from Caucasus, was born shortly after the Revolution. He spent the first years of his life away from all the turmoil, in his ancestral village where things were still pretty much the same as usual…

the wise ones noticed him early: his otherworldliness, mixed together with the physical power of a bull and a poetic talent, indicated already at a young age that this boy would be a great Shaman, someone capable of carrying on the tradition of his people even under severe danger. Under cover, always at night and in a place in the wilderness away from the village, the boy received several initiations. Some of them required a lot of mental focus, others submitted him to extreme physical duress, and some others challenged his artistic capacities. He reached his twenties as an already wise and powerful Shaman..."

"This period of simple and peaceful tribal life did not last long for him.

When he was twenty-three, the police caught him and many others at an illegal gathering to celebrate the spring equinox. He was sent right away to Siberia, in one of the work camps where most prisoners disappeared or died."

A subtle change of tone in the Storyteller's voice causes the Monkey to open one glazy eye and whisper: "Camps...do they have showers there...?"

"Very well...continues the Storyteller, "Life in the camp was miserable, but the spirit of our Shaman did not break. Knowing somehow that his task was not complete, he kept himself alive.

When a young female inmate, a dissident economy professor from Moscow, showed up in his life, something that had gone cold stirred again in his heart. He saw her from afar, beautiful and proud, with another work team that was taking care of the toolsheds. It was not so difficult for him to find an excuse to talk to her. From there, the attraction between them contained enough despair and passion to drive them all the way from furtive kisses into dangerous sex...

They were never caught...The young woman, brought up as a pragmatic materialist, started realizing that her beloved, whom she had considered a peasant, was in fact a real Shaman. He slowly taught her all the tricks and enchantments to survive and move freely in a camp teeming with guards.

When the big Soviet machine started exposing the abuses of Stalin, the Shaman and the Economy Professor had reached their mid thirties. All around them was the deep unrest and confusion brought on by this unexpected sudden change, and everyone was distracted by the events. They decided to take their chance. One morning, they just walked out of the camp, invisible to the eye thanks to a Shamanic spell.

They escaped to a faraway village in Siberia, not far from the coast. She became the local teacher, and he slowly made his way into the relatively easy job of tending to the machinery used for the mines. This left him enough time to tend his vegetable garden and secretly practice his Shamanic Arts.

Once they felt accepted as part of the village, the couple fulfilled their last desire: at forty, they gave birth to their only child.

Their son grew up to be a strong boy, like his father, but with no inclination towards spirituality. He loved working on the land, eating good food and enjoying the company of pretty girls. He married early, at twenty, with a beautiful sixteen-year-old blond. She immediately gave him a boy child, doted by its grandparents and everyone in the village. It was a big boy with a gentle soul.

When the boy finished primary school, the whole world around him turned upside down...not only did he start falling in love with girls, he also witnessed the fall of the Soviet regime, and saw the big uncertainty that followed. Even in remote rural areas like his home village, food became scarce. No villager was prepared for facing the competitive modern world knocking and pushing at his door.

Everyone in the family worried that their boy's future would become too uncertain there. His Professor grandmother came up with an idea. Throughout all the events of the past half century, she had kept contact with a few surviving siblings in Moscow. Being more reserved and less passionate than their sister, her siblings had managed to maintain their positions in the University. They were all retired now, but they still had good connections within the academic world. Thanks to them, the boy was admitted to the best schools, and granted a fresh start in this new age.

He fell in love with philosophy, and already at 18 he became known for his pamphlets. But soon enough he started wanting experiences, not just theories. With a new wave of young seekers that started traveling to India, the land of mysticism, he set off on his existential quest. It is rumored that he lived for a while in the Ashram of the Controversial Master, experimenting with all sorts of meditation techniques, like whirling, sitting silently, crying, even talking Gibberish..."

The Monkey stirs from his slumber and giggles: "Gibberish...the Monks...the full moon...the monkeys..." and snores again.

"Very well" the Storyteller continues, "He came back to Russia deeply changed. It was as if his eyes were filled with a smile and a depth that had not been there before.

He did not return to Moscow: he followed the call of the winds and silences of Siberia, and his strong impulse to reconnect with his Grandfather, the Shaman.

The Shaman immediately took his young hippie-looking grandson as his apprentice. He was overjoyed to be able to finally pass on all his wisdom and precious information to the new generation. He had understood well his own son's wish for an ordinary family life as a balance to his peculiar childhood, but he had always hoped that his gift would remain in the family.

Grandfather and grandson spent the next few years together, practicing and polishing the Shamanic arts. You could often see the two of them going into the forest in the morning, the old man still perfectly straight in his large bony frame, and the young one, with long blond-reddish dreadlocks and exotic clothes, but with the same large frame and proud stance. On special full moon nights, the rare bypassers could see them in the backyard of their home, sharing a ritual pipe with special herbs that were said to open the gates to the world of visions.

The Monkey stirs at the word 'vision': "television? Do they have television here...?"

"Yes, yes, very well..." continues the Storyteller, amused, "For the young man, this was the fulfillment of all his dreams. His soul responded to all the teachings he received with a deep sense of homecoming: this was where he truly belonged.

Shortly before dying, his grandfather took him to a place in the woods, not so far from where he lived; it was so well hidden amidst foliage and large stones that even after all his years of training he could have never seen it by himself. It was a large underground cave, accessible only through a narrow and well-hidden opening. They let themselves into the opening, and silently slid downwards through a narrow tunnel, and landed onto a vast space. The opening from above shed a dim light onto ancient paintings of long extinct animals. It was a sacred spot, the Young Shaman could see, as old as humanity. Grandpa's mere whisper sounded amplified, like in a cathedral. He simply said: "This is my true legacy". The Young Shaman instantly knew that this would be his dwelling, the place from which he would start his work in earnest. It was dry, well insulated, and not too far from the village. He would even be able to capture through the opening in the ceiling the electromagnetic waves that would connect him through the web to all corners of the Planet…

After his death, the Young Shaman took all his grandfather's notes, herbs and essences, healing potions and talismans, and moved into the cave. He became quickly known for being both deeply rooted in the ancient world and up to date and playful in the modern one.

He is now 30, and is part of a global network of highly respected Shamans working for the healing of this planet.

He has heard about the Little Buddha from Facebook. Even though he could have made it simpler for you, little Monkey, to find him, he wants to stick to the saying of his ancestors: 'if you seek a Shaman, you will always need to meet some hardship before finding him'…."

With these last words, the voice of the Storyteller fades, and the only sound left in the darkness is the soft contented snoring of the Monkey…

Chapter Fifteen

THE YOUNG SHAMAN

The Golden Essence

When the first rays of the morning sun enter the stone circle, the Monkey wakes up alone. He starts rubbing his eyes and stretching his little body, but then he suddenly stops. He remembers the evening before. He looks around: no trace of the Storyteller. Puzzled, he walks through the clearing.

He starts wondering if it was all a dream. Maybe the deep relaxation he thought he was feeling was just pure exhaustion. Maybe it was all a fruit of his overactive imagination, until his eyes fall on a folded note carefully placed over his backpack.

It contains a detailed map of the way from the stone circle to the Young Shaman's underground cave. At the bottom of the page, the Storyteller's elegant handwriting reads: "Hope you enjoyed the story…Good luck, my dear friend!"

He gets up at once, ready to go. Following the Storyteller's directions, he finds the path easily, and follows it up and down through a hilly-forested landscape.

He finally descends into a protected valley with a beautiful meadow along the shores of a large lotus pond: he has arrived. It takes him a moment to locate the entrance of the cave, but after disentangling some branches and moving a few heavy stones, he finds the dark and narrow tunnel leading underground.

With no moment of hesitance, the Monkey jumps. He slides down the passage into the darkness below until he lands on the ground with a loud thump, while his belongings scatter out of his backpack all around him.

He stands up, rubs his sore backside, and looks around. This is a large cave: in the beginning he sees only darkness, but as his eyes get adjusted he can detect the walls around him reflecting the dim light coming from the opening above. It looks like a corridor. In the distance, he notices another light flickering, coming from a fireplace beyond the arched entrance leading into the main cave.

Now that he is getting closer to his goal, he feels suddenly full of doubt. He is not so sure if this Young Shaman that lives underground can really help him. "Too late to think about it anyway," he tells himself, rubbing his bottom for one last time. He starts tiptoeing through a wide corridor towards the main cave.

He is not fully prepared for the wonder ahead: the circular main cave is huge. There are a number of skylights in its vaulted ceiling: the last sunrays entering through them, in all their violets, pinks and oranges, create a stunning light show on the floor.

Even more spectacular is the symphony of different fragrances and smells that suddenly surrounds him: so many scents, mostly unknown to him, are mixing and merging in the dry air of the cave. There is no other way for him than to allow each individual smell to enter and spread all over his body. But it's hard to process so many smells at the same time: some are yummy, others are disgusting, some are sweet, some pungent, and some sour. He catches the whiff of sulfur and arsenic. He swoons, and then gets energized, then feels romantic, then dreamy…some of the smells are visibly hanging in the air, like clouds. Some come from above, some from underneath…He cannot really decide whether this is too much, or it is beautiful in the way a symphony can be when it includes the most contrasting sounds.

Throughout this whole sensory overload, the Monkey remains alert: he remembers that Shamans are still close to nature, and that their sense of smell is as acute as his. "If modern people would pay more attention to what they smell," he giggles in between a whiff and an aroma, "they would probably make happier choices…"

Meanwhile, the sun has set. It takes him a moment to adjust to the flickering light of the fireplace surrounded by the pitch dark of the cave. Then, he sees him, sitting in front of the fire with his back to him. A tall man, sitting on a stool, backlit by the crackling flames in front of him. As the Monkey stands there without making a sound, the man slightly turns: his profile is handsome and intense in a very Russian kind of way. His flaming red blond hair is hanging in dreadlocks. Suddenly, he makes a full turn and looks straight into the Monkey's eyes.

The Monkey feels defenseless against the intensity of his gaze. It's as if the eyes of the Young Shaman are scanning him and assessing his health situation, his body temperature, all his different pulses, even the smell of his body…

For a moment, the Monkey feels it like an invasion, but then he remembers again: it's the same amongst animals, it's wise to assess each other, and to smell each other out…

Without moving his eyes from him, the Young Shaman bows his head slightly and says to the Monkey: "I have been waiting for you".

The Monkey jolts and looks behind his shoulders. "Are you talking to me?" he asks, surprised about his own boldness, "How would you know about me?"

"I have been waiting for you", the Young Shaman repeats, "I have been knowing since a while that you, the Monkey, would come seeking here for help for one of our most precious beings on this Planet. But it took you longer than I expected. I started to worry that you had lost either your way or your courage… I am relieved to see you here in my cave! Welcome, man…" He stands up, walks to the Monkey and gives him a big hug.

The Monkey almost faints from all the smells that the Young Shaman's body emanates. He must have rubbed on his skin thousands of different herbs, flowers and god knows what else. At the same time, his warm embrace makes him feels accepted and at home. He is touched, and all the tears that are pent up in him are now threatening to pour out. He feels instantly embarrassed and out of place. This is his healing quest for the Little Buddha, he reminds himself, gently pulling away from the embrace. The Young Shaman seems to understand what is happening, "Don't worry, man, just make yourself at home and I'll help…" he says to the Monkey with a wink.

"You must be someone who is capable of loving deeply and generously many different people," the Young Shaman continues, sitting back and inviting the Monkey to take another stool in front of the fireplace, "you have an amazing love field around you. I also know that it was your free decision to reincarnate as a Monkey, and I respect you for it…"

The Monkey's body relaxes while he starts absorbing the pleasant warmth emanated by the flames. He feels seen. It will be easier for him to be himself, from now on…

After a short silence punctuated by the cozy sounds of the fireplace, the Young Shaman's attitude changes. He looks more his age, now, and has a funky twist to his jargon: "Come on, dude, let's have a nice evening meal". He gets out of the folds of his sarong a remote control. He presses it and suddenly the lights go on. With a swift gesture, the Young Shaman is up and moving through another archway on the side.

The Monkey follows him into another room, smaller and very well lit. It is a kitchen, surprisingly practical and modern.

"Help yourself, it's cool," the Young Shaman tells him, "I have a whole stash of supplies for you. I'll make my own stuff and you make yours. I thought you might like to prepare your own porridge…" he says, indicating a neat display of jars with nuts and raisins and a bag of oat flakes and a cask of bananas nearby. This revives the Monkey, exhausted as he is after all the surprises, long enough to cut some bananas and crush some nuts for his warm porridge. Meanwhile, the Young Shaman prepares a nice meal of vegetables seasoned with many different herbs and wild rice for himself.

By the end of the meal, the Monkey is sleeping with eyes open, nodding off in between spoonfuls.

"Time for a nap," says the Young Shaman, "your journey was exhausting, I can see that, take a break for now. We'll deal with the other stuff later in the evening…"

He gently lifts the limp Monkey on his shoulders and takes him to his cozy alcove of furs, cushions and blankets on the furthest side of the main cave. Gently placing him on one side, he fluffs up one of the biggest cushions, and slides it under the Monkey's head. He grabs a handful of covers for himself and relaxes next to the Monkey.

Waking in the middle of his nap, the Monkey feels for a moment confused: how did he get here? But then he sees the resting shape of what he starts considering his new friend quietly lying on his side, and relaxes again.

After dozing in this way for a couple of hours, they wake up. It's still evening. The Young Shaman tells him: "I am going to prepare a smoke. Care to join?" he produces a long-stemmed Dutch meerschaum pipe with an aromatic mixture of herbs. The Monkey refuses, on the ground that not smoking is the best way to deal with his health, and that he has never smoked in his life. But the Young Shaman is not convinced, and almost shouts: "Yes, Da! You have to!"

A bit intimidated, the little Monkey takes a few puffs from the pipe and, to his surprise, he likes the effect: it mellows him, he is not so hyper vigilant and worried. He wonders what herbs are in the pipe: they could actually be very useful for the Little Buddha's condition…

Then the Young Shaman gets up and goes to a sandalwood trunk in the opposite corner of the cave. He opens it, and draws out a long un-dyed robe of the softest hand-woven hemp. It is decorated with many ribbons and pieces of metal. As soon as he puts it on, the atmosphere in the cave changes. Everything vibrates with a new strong presence. The voice that comes out of the Young Shaman is no longer his: it sounds ancient and powerful.

He says: "I am the Voice of Nature, of everything that is wild. I transmit the Spirit of Nature. I embrace everything on this Earth. I reject nothing; everything is part of the greater unity, of the greater truth. I am the Voice of Healing for this Planet"

Then he slowly moves to a corner altar, decorated with a few statues and some photographs, and murmurs: "Dear Grandfather, I am honored to stand in your lineage. Please help me today to bring healing to the Little Buddha's condition. Support me to act wisely. Please give me guidance in my dreams tonight".

The Monkey is very touched. For a moment he thinks of his own monkey tribe, of everyone's concern for him, how they all tried to help him.

"Animals are often much more loyal and friendly than people…they never cheat or betray…" he says to the Young Shaman, while he replaces the robe at the end of the ritual. The Young Shaman nods and adds, "Time for dreams now, little friend, let's sleep a bit longer and see what visions I have invited…"

The Monkey, still under the soothing effect of the pipe, cannot think of a better idea.

In the morning, when he wakes up, his favorite bananas and nuts porridge is waiting for him next to his bed.

He gets up, and stands below the opening that leads outside. Only now, in daylight, he can see the prehistoric graffiti on the walls. He also realizes that right in front of him there are stairs, carved in the rock, to make the upward climb to ground level easier. He takes two steps at a time, and comes out in the clearing.

It's early morning, the sun is rising, the light is diffused, the valley down below is enveloped in fog and the mountains in the distance are hardly visible…

The Young Shaman is splashing water all over his body and face with a brass bowl, and then rubbing himself vigorously with a cloth. Afterwards, he starts spreading on his naked body all kinds of oils, creams and herbs. "He is such a beautiful being, inside and outside," thinks the Monkey, "healthy, strong, young, but also wise…"

While still rubbing his body with great care, the Young Shaman starts softly chanting, raising his arms occasionally in prayer. "I will never forget this sacred moment," the Monkey whispers.

After sitting together silently for a while, the Young Shaman smiles at the Monkey and says: "Let's go down to the cave, it's time to work…" The Monkey is more than ready by now. He has rested enough, and his little belly is humming with contentment. He follows his new friend, now wearing his ritual robe, to a large niche carved in the rock walls. "It's a dry and cool storage for my treasure of herbs and potions," the Young Shaman tells him with a tone of reverence in his voice. "This collection of boxes and jars are stacked full with different herbs – some local, some foreign, some others very rare, and some officially extinct."

He starts opening jar after jar, first smelling its content, then dubbing his finger in it and licking it. Then he closes them, shaking each one to see if its content sticks to the glass. Finally, he picks a jar that seems to satisfy his requirements and silently looks at it.

The little Monkey understands that he is reading the content of this jar. There is no actual label on it, but it's as if he can read what ingredients it contains, and what healing properties it has.

"The properties of each jar are never fixed, my curious Monkey friend…" the Young Shaman adds in a whisper, "they alter according to the subtle balance of each patient. They tell me every time something different."

Just then, the jar that he chose starts to glow in his hands. It looks as if the glass is becoming softer, and whatever is inside sparkles like diamonds. Even the ordinary metal lid suddenly looks precious. A thin gold dust hangs in the air, spreading everywhere inside the cave.

As its contents settle, The Monkey can see the inside of the jar: a golden powder with some bigger shards, as large as pebbles, mixed in. The Young Shaman murmurs some invocation, and then reaches for a shelf. He draws out a suede pouch embroidered with red and gold geometrical shapes.

The Monkey cannot help commenting: "Your mother or sister must love you very much to give you such gifts…"

The Young Shaman replies laughing: "No, no, no, man! Embroidery of sacred pouches and costumes is one of the skills you have to develop as a Shaman: you have to become very good at it. You also need to become a skilled poetry reader, a storyteller, a cook, and a good lover. You need to be an expert in all the good things of life…"

Initially, the Monkey is not sure if he is joking, but then he realizes that the peaceful ease that emanates from this young man is probably coming from the combination of so many different qualities…

After pouring some of the contents of the jar in the pouch and making an artful knot around it, the Young Shaman offers it to the Monkey, and says: "Listen, little Monkey: this is a very powerful remedy for your most beloved friend the Little Buddha. But I have to warn you about its properties. You will have to watch out…".

The Monkey gets a bit spooked, and replies: "Well, if you feel it is too private, it is fine for me to carry the pouch without knowing."

"No, man", the Young Shaman says, "You have to know what you are taking to the Little Buddha. This powder is a very ancient kind of golden dust, much more condensed in its molecular structure, much more valuable and extremely heavy. It is given to people who have a lack of Golden Merging Essence in their system. The essential state of Golden Merging is something that you experience as a small baby with your mother when she takes you in her arms and gives you her breast, or when she sings songs to you or talks to you, or when she touches you and massages you… The Little Buddha's body-mind system has a great lack of this Essence…"

"No wonder, he came as a ready-made bigger child!" says the Monkey, his animal nature understanding perfectly the need for a certain amount of baby cuddles.

"Exactly. My vision last night revealed that in the case of the Little Buddha the amount of Etheric Gold is almost to zero. This can become very dangerous. Once a body has no more Gold, it starts moving towards death. Without Gold there is no warmth and no flow in a person's system, and the body cannot feel at ease and discharge – it remains in a stress."

The Monkey is impressed: it is the first time somebody gives a feedback on his friend's health that makes sense to him.

The Young Shaman continues: "But you need to remember that this is also simply gold. It has an incredible potential but also a very bad Karma. People have killed each other for it. The greed for gold has created much havoc and destruction. But in reality, human beings are unconsciously attracted to gold because it reminds them of how they felt when they were babies and their mommy loved them…"

Offering him the pouch, he concludes: "Bring this to the Little Buddha. Remember to start off with small doses, several times a day, and then slowly increase them. After one week, maximum ten days, you will see the difference".

Then, looking straight into the Monkey's eyes, as if to imprint on him the last information, he adds: "Given to a clean and pure being, this powder can do miracles. It can heal the wounds of separation and restore the Golden Merging Essence. It can bring people back from the edge of death. But at the same time – and listen well, little Monkey, because you are taking a lot of responsibility by carrying this with you

– It can be very dangerous if it's used without awareness. It is only meant for Buddhas...what can heal can also kill. If given to an unenlightened person, this powder will provoke all his greed to surface and possess him entirely..."

The Monkey shivers at his friend's last words. From his animal perspective, he cannot really conceive why on earth people can even kill each other out of greed.

"It will be of such monstrous proportions that the person will be consumed by it... like that King, Midas was his name, whose desire to turn everything he touched into gold was granted. He could no more eat or love, because everything he touched became solid gold. So, man, keep this remedy well away from unprepared people..."

The Monkey looks at him seriously and says: "I understand".

"And more news..." says the Young Shaman, reverting to his friendly funky self, "what I am giving you now is just a remedy to bridge the final healing, of which my part is only one fourth. There are four of us fellow travellers, colleagues and soul mates, that operate in different corners of the world,"

"The mysterious four? Facebook? Can you explain to me...?" the Monkey is trying to catch back the fragments of conversation upon his arrival in Khabarovsk Krai, before he went with the Storyteller.

The Young Shaman waves his hand for silence, and continues: "Chill out man, you will meet the remaining three in due time. We are all already working on the talisman that will cure the Little Buddha."

The Monkey is for a moment shocked. This means that his journey is far from over; what will happen to the Little Buddha meanwhile, and how long will it take to get back on the island...

The Young Shaman notices his turmoil and says: "You are supposed to meet your challenges, little Monkey. They are also ingredients of the potion that will restore the Little Buddha to life. Just trust. Now you need to go and to find the next one of our foursome. Just look at us as a puzzle: each piece is complete in itself, but you will only see how we four fit perfectly with each other once you have all four pieces."

"How many hours walk do I go from here?" the Monkey puts all his determination in his otherwise shaky voice.

"Cannot be done on foot, my friend," the Young Shaman pats the Monkey on the shoulder, "You will need to reach Peru, South America..."

This is really new territory for the Monkey. He doesn't know much about South America, "There are loads of monkeys in South America, but non enlightened ones like you..." smiles the Young Shaman, somehow encouragingly, "You will need to find a human, though, an ancient fellow traveler of mine. He and I share quite a few past lives in that area of the world. It was not called Latin America then: this name was given much later to it, by the white conquerors. Before that, it had many different names, some poetic and some sacred. My friend still works as a Magician with the local people, the ancient ones, and they call him like they call each other, "Older Brother". He is difficult to find because he keeps on moving. I can only give you a list of places where he might be. But you will need to follow your intuition to really find him, and it will work only if it's meant to. But I am allowed to give you one clue: Follow the music …"

The Monkey is quickly packed and ready, a bit sad to leave his friend, but happy to continue his quest. He is off guard when the Young Shaman gives him a last jolt:

"By the way, you are meant to leave behind your Watermelon Mobile where you left it yesterday, before you walked here. It will be safe. You need to do this stretch of the journey without directions and without vehicle. It's part of the test. You will get it back at the right moment in the right place…"

The Monkey is speechless, but does not want to argue: if there is anything that will help saving his friend, he is ready to do it.

"One last thing!" shouts the Young Shaman when the Monkey is halfway down the slope towards the lotus pond: we will let you carry your Ipad. We four understand that you need to keep connected with the Indigo Couple about the Little Buddha's health. In the journey ahead, you might find yourself in the wilderness, where no Internet connection reaches. But whenever there is one, you are allowed to exchange mails with them and be updated on how things are back home. But you can only ask questions or talk about the weather. You cannot divulge any detail about your journey. It would interfere with the healing process…."

The Monkey lets out a big sigh of relief: the idea of not being able to stay connected with the Indigo Couple would make him too anxious. He would waste all his creativity in imagining the worst scenarios.

He slowly walks away, retracing his steps to a bigger path that will eventually, somehow, take him closer to civilization.

Chapter Sixteen

THE PERUVIAN MUSICIAN

Full Moon in Capricorn- Karmic Connections

Walking on foot down the main road in his slightly weathered appearance and with his backpack trailing some brambles, the Monkey is on his own again. It took him some time to finally hear from very far away the sound of a lonely truck that guided him here, on the Ussuri Highway. At least this is the name of this place according to the map he quickly Googled before leaving the Young Shaman's den.

"I don't miss my Lotus Mobile," he thinks, "After all I chose to be reborn as a Monkey because I like organic, natural…"

He stops. After cleaning his backpack thoroughly and readjusting his gear, he sits on it and waits, hoping for a ride. As time passes, he muses about the lack of contact that he has been experiencing amongst ordinary humans. Many cars whizz by without one look at him. "They go too fast," he thinks, and then he realizes: "Humanity lacks Golden Merging…" The talk with the Young Shaman has really impressed him: he sees how much in his monkey nature he loves sharing and enjoying.

"I won't be of any use to restore the Little Buddha's Golden Merging Essence if I don't live it myself…" he realizes. He has to slow down; he must enjoy the journey and relax about the goal…

As he breathes out all his anxious hurry, all his useless worries, and scratches his belly, he starts whispering "Peru". He lets the word roll many times, and then tastes the word in his mouth. He likes the sound of it; it is sweet…

"But where is Peru?" the thought jolts him out of his golden state. He hasn't had time to search more than the directions to the port of Vladivostok, where then he has to…" he suddenly can't remember…

For a moment he can see himself, a tiny helpless dot in the middle of this vast landscape stretching through fields and fields of wheat, trying to go to Peru.

Suddenly, it all seems absolutely hilarious. His tired brain, foggy with impressions, cracks. The Monkey starts giggling. Soon he is lying on the side of the road holding his belly and roaring with laughter.

When the laughter subsides, he is spent, but happy.

Just then, a huge lorry thunders down the highway at full speed. Seeing the Monkey standing again, with his thumb neatly stretched out, the driver steps on the break. After a few sighs and hisses the truck stops.

Unexpectedly, the driver comes out. He is a big guy, with slightly slanted pale eyes and a frown above them. The monkey is a little scared. He would not know how to defend himself. But as the big driver approaches, his expression alters, and melts into a big childlike smile: "обезьяна!!!![1] Ebizyana!!!" he says, pointing at him and giggling…

"Vladivostok?" whispers the Monkey, just a tiny bit more at ease with the laughter…

"Da!!!" shouts the driver genially, and lifts the Monkey with unexpected gentleness on the passenger seat.

It's a long three-day drive. In and out of sleep, the Monkey remains in a dreamlike state, while his driver happily sings in between bouts of vodka, remarking on the Monkey's exotic bananas, and then falling silent for a while.

At some point of the third day, the monkey starts to realize that the truck is stopping and honking more frequently. Then he sniffs the air around him. It seems heavier with car fumes. He opens his eyes, feeling the buzz of a larger gathering of humans.

"Vladivostok!!!" the truck driver shouts loudly, stopping at the gates of the harbor. He winks at the Monkey, who is by then fully alert.

"Spasiba…"[2] he tells him, this being one of the few keywords he has learnt in Russian. He leaves amidst the roaring laughter of the driver and the ominous sound of his hissing engine. He is alone again.

The harbor of Vladivostok is a big place. There are millions of people milling around, and it has that multiethnic atmosphere that you only find in port cities: you can hear everywhere different languages being spoken, and see many different boats and ships: huge ocean liners, passenger ships, cruise ships, and small fishermen boats, even sailing boats, crowding its entrance and docks at any time of the day. It stinks, mulls our vegetarian Monkey, gagging at the mix of harbor waters, smoke, burned oil, petrol, fried fish and human waste.

But he soon forgets about it. As he moves through throngs of people, some of them beautiful, most of them ugly, some quiet, others loud, he actually starts feeling at ease. Nobody seems to mind that there is a monkey walking amongst them, some even smile at him.

Finally he stops in front of a sign where the word Internet stands out in the middle

---

1 Monkey in Russian

2 Thank you in Russian

of foreign looking letters with lots of exclamation marks. He looks through the shop window: it's dim inside, and it's crammed full of outdated computers, so square and big that they remind him of the old and rusty generator stored in a corner of the Indigo land. For a moment, his heart aches as he remembers the sweet mornings spent with his soul family in their luscious garden, but when one of the many bypassers bumps into him, he quickly realizes that this is not the time to get sentimental. He steps inside, and a nerdy and pimply Russian boy at the counter gives him a number, and without even looking at him resumes the viewing of his Playboy online.

All these casual exchanges relax the Monkey deeply; big city life is new for him, and he likes it.

When his turn comes, the Monkey sits on the furthest stool, away from prying eyes, slowly unwraps his sleek Ipad, types into its screen the password, and carefully moves it out of sight, on his lap, under the keyboard the prehistoric computer. Just to be safe, he tells himself. Monkeys have always thought that humans have a propensity for theft, he thinks, laughing at his own joke quietly. Then he sits straight up and checks his emails.

There is a short message from the Indigo Man: "Beloved, some hopeful news. The Little Buddha is stable, as if he has touched rock bottom and now is very slowly coming up again. We miss you and wish you the best wherever you are. Let us know how you are."

The Monkey types away happily: "Beloveds, I cannot reveal where I am, but I am good, and grateful for the amazing adventure..." he would like to say more, and then remembers: "the weather here is..." but he has not paid attention to the temperature outside, so he deletes and concludes: "I will be in touch when I can. It might take some days. The quest for healing continues...my love to you all". He presses, "send" and then kisses the screen, just for measure...

Then he sets off into a frantic intuitive tapping session on the screen until he finds the information that he was looking for: to get to Peru he has to first take a ship from here to Japan.

He gets quickly out of the rickety computer place and starts walking along the ships, studying the names on the crates and containers piled in front of each. He misses half of them because they are written in strange letters, but finally he sees a crate with the label: "Emergency Relief. Port of Tokyo, Japan". He checks around, sees no one, and quickly hides behind it. After a long outbreath, he looks all around the big box, finds a plank that is just a little loose and slowly bends it enough to create an opening for him to slide inside. In the semidarkness, he feels around with his hands: he is surrounded by soft and worn out second-hand clothes. This suits him very well: after so many days on the road he is exhausted, and happy to get a long undisturbed sleep. Carefully placing his satchel with nuts and fruits and his backpack with his Ipad amongst the clothes, he lets out a big sigh, closes the crate from the inside and waits...

Later that evening, he hears in his half sleep the sound of engines and chains. After an indefinite time, he wakes up to the sound of ocean waves against the flank of a ship. He has been carried on board! He is thrilled. Soon he is lulled by the sound of the sea, and enters again a pleasant trance-like state that will last the whole two days that the ship takes to reach the harbor of Tokyo…

When he is sure that the ship is moored, the Monkey repeats his Vladivostok stunt. He again quickly runs, from shadow to shadow, through the whole harbor, until he sees a crate with "Callao, Lima, Peru" written on it. He carefully opens the crate without breaking it, and climbs inside it. This time he finds himself sitting on a pile of old Japanese Tatami mats: they are very soft from wear and tear, and again very comfortable to rest on. He makes himself a cozy place, with his nuts and raisins at hand, and holds his breath until he hears the loud horn of the ship sailing out.

When all sounds, except the lull of the waves, cease, he decides to leave the crate and explore some of the ship. He gets out on deck, takes a deep breath, and looks into the starry night, so magnificent above the ocean.

He soon gets into a routine of hiding and coming out at night, taking care not to be discovered, to let the winds cleanse him from the odors of the storage below. During his nights on the ocean, he has time to contemplate many things. He remembers how in the rickety Internet café of Vladivostok he read that at the center of Peru there is the lush Amazon jungle, with its staggering diversity of flora and fauna. This once was the home of an extremely advanced Indian population, the noble Incas, who were said to have originated from the union of some inhabitants of the Pleiades with humans. They worshipped the Great Golden Merging with the Mother Goddess, and gathered gold nuggets and gold dust to offer them to Her.

"Until the Greedy White Man came…" thinks the Monkey with a shiver.

After two weeks, the mysterious land of Peru is etched at the horizon…

He wonders: by now he has a quite detailed idea of the country and its inhabitants, but he still cannot imagine how on earth he is going to find that one person, that nameless healer without a face who has the key to the next part of the journey, with just one clue: "Follow the music, follow the music", he hears the voice of the Young Shaman inside. After a while, he starts whispering, then singing softly: "Follow the music!" with a mixture of puzzlement and hope…

Once out of the crate onto the soil of Peru, the Monkey notices that he has never been aware of how many different types of music there are. One can listen to the sound of the cars and the boat engines in a rhythmic mix with the ancient singsong voices of the people just like one would listen to a symphony. "The Callao Rhapsody" he says, catching a distant bamboo flute in the mayhem. "This country is full of music…"

He absorbs the sights and sounds around the harbor for the whole day, and then decides to rest in an empty dockyard for the night.

On the second day, as evening descends, he decides to venture a bit further away into the town. A big full moon is shining over the alleys: everything is illuminated, thinks the Monkey, a good omen.

As he walks through the Zocalo[3], he sees a musician sitting on a small wooden bench, playing banjo and pan flutes. The Monkey instantly likes his strong music, so full of longing and sweetness, and sits somewhere behind him, in the shadow of a bush, to listen. After a while, the Musician shifts slightly, as if to acknowledge the Monkey's presence at the periphery of his view. Slowly, without interrupting the song he is playing, he turns his head and looks at him. The Monkey is completely absorbed, gently nodding with his little head in rhythm with the music and humming along with the song. The Musician looks surprised: he has obviously never met a monkey that could sing in tune. He smiles at him and resumes playing, while the Monkey edges a bit closer, more than happy to sing along.

A couple of hours are spent in this way. The Musician plays, and the Monkey joins in with his soft hum. No word is exchanged, while a musical trust grows between them.

When the bypassers become more rare and it's really dark, the Musician walks up to the little Monkey, and asks him in a deep and melodious voice: "Would you like to come for a meal with me?"

The Monkey accepts enthusiastically, bored as he is by his dried up raisins and hard nuts, and feeling good about having a good meal with a new friend. This Musician seems to be a good guy, an artist with a sincere heart. And who knows, maybe he can help in some way. He gets up and starts following him.

Together they go into a back street, to an old pub, and choose a corner table in the shadow, away from the street, where they can disappear.

The Musician asks him: "What would you like to eat or drink?"

"Fried Bananas..." are the first words that the Monkey utters. They exchange a smile.

The Musician orders for the Monkey a huge plate of fried bananas, and for himself some local food, with strange names like Papa a la Huancaina or Humitas ...

The Monkey is surprised at the ease that he feels around the Musician. It feels like catching up with an old friend. He starts eating his fried bananas with gusto, and meanwhile watches the Musician with the corner of an eye: he is not so young anymore; his hair is white, long and braided in the traditional native way. He has a quite pronounced profile, with a large aquiline nose. In many ways, he looks like the local Indians, but his face is a bit longer, and he is much taller than them. He has a more of a Caucasian body: lean and tall, with long limbs. Even at his age, he is youthful in the agile way he moves, lively, full of juice, full of melodies and songs.

"This is my life attitude, dear Monkey friend," says the Musician, gently leaning towards him as if revealing a very important secret, "whenever I have nowhere to

3   Main square

sleep or nothing to eat, I improvise a song about it and play it loudly. I forget myself in it, and people seem to like it. I almost always get enough coins to buy exactly what I need…"

"So you move without a plan?" asks the Monkey, happy to have found someone that shares his dislike for structures…

"Well, let's say that the plan unfolds as I move along. As a matter of fact, I start to feel that you, my new friend, are part of the plan…" he adds, smiling and raising an eyebrow enigmatically, "And what about you, are you on your way to somewhere specific?" he asks.

"Would you like to travel with me?" asks the Monkey, almost chocking on his last piece of banana out of sheer happiness

"It's Ok for me, as long as the music keeps us connected…"

The Musician produces out of his backpack a well-worn tourist map of Peru: "Take your pick, where would you like to go?" he asks

The Monkey, by now a veteran in intuitive tapping, places his finger on the map somewhere: he looks down and recognizes instantly the name of the place. It's the only name he remembers from the list of all possible locations of the Peruvian Magician.

For a moment, the Musician's expression becomes very intense and serious. But then, he smiles again, and turns his chair close to the Monkey's, pointing at the location he has chosen: "This place is far from the coastline. We'll have to cross the Andes and reach the edge of the big jungle. There are ancient ruins of cities and temples there, and some places are flooded with tourists. But this particular spot on the map is not famous. So far, it has been completely spared from tourism. It still contains the vibration of ancient rituals."

The word ritual sounds promising, thinks the Monkey. He hasn't yet told the Musician the whole story behind his journey, "But that's fine," he thinks, "one step at a time. He is anyway in tune, and he seems to know a lot about the territory…"

For the next few days they are on the road. Once outside the dusty city and through the endless string of vendors with improvised stalls selling all kinds of poor people's delicacies, they slowly hitchhike their way through the vast planes and across the Andes. They sing a lot, talk a little and eat wonderfully in the local villages, where they are always welcomed: everyone seems to know the Musician, and offers them shelter in a variety of adobe houses and huts.

But when the first sounds and scents of of the Amazon Jungle reach he Monkey, he really starts feeling at home. For the last stretch of the journey on foot, the Monkey jumps happily from tree to tree, letting out wild shrieks that provoke sudden flights of multicolored birds. The Musician laughs, and responds to the shrieks with loud cheers of his own.

Once they reach destination, they stop. The Musician looks interrogatively at the Monkey.

"I guess that now we should just sit around and wait," sighs the Monkey, "Truth is that I have no idea how to go on from here…" and tells him his whole story, from the Little Planet until the curse, omitting his visit to the Young Shaman. He wouldn't want to reveal any details that could interfere with the healing in progress…

The Musician nods many times during the Monkey's story, and when he hears about the Little Buddha's state his eyes are humid with compassion. Then he sits up, his aquiline profile regal and still, and almost sniffs the air, and says: "I have an idea. Not far from here there is an Indian Village. I have many friends there, musicians like me. Let's just set up camp here, and you can keep watch here while I go to my friends. I am sure that they will know something, and if I play a bit with them they will be happy to tell me anything they know about the Magician…"

He doesn't sound convincing, the Monkey thinks, feeling defeated for the first time in this journey. Maybe he has had enough, and just wants to meet his usual company and…but then, he sighs one of his big sighs and relaxes: "I will anyway have to wait, what else to do? I don't see any alternative…"

The Musician leaves saying "Hola…" in a very casual way, and the Monkey is on his own.

Later that night, after a few hours of waiting, the Monkey falls into a restless half sleep. He tosses and turns, feeling cheated and abandoned. When the first light filters through the foliage all around, he is inside one big knot of blankets. The Musician's face is smiling over him.

"Ahem… How was your jam session?" the Monkey asks him, feeling still a bit resentful.

"I had much fun, I hope next time you come along. It is really very beautiful to play with the locals!"

The Monkey, feeling included, instantly drops his grudge: "Did you find out anything of the whereabouts of the Magician?"

"I have. One of the locals told me that he has been seen recently close to the ruins of an ancient city in the jungle, not that far from here," he answers, and adds a bit apologetically, "To tell you the truth I am not even fully sure that the Magician he mentioned is the same as the one you are looking for, but it's worth a try…"

The Monkey looks a bit disappointed, but ready to give it a go.

"Anyway," concludes the Musician, "I am happy to continue the journey with you and help you to meet your destiny". In spite of all the insecurity, a warm feeling spreads in the Monkey's heart: for now, he is happy.

They don't lose any time. They first take a bus to the last post reclaimed from the jungle, a seedy village full of traders of all sorts of legal and illegal goods. From there, after bargaining with the driver for quite a while, they hire a battered old taxi, going deeper and deeper into the rainforest. At some point, the road is just a little more than a footpath. The taxi slowly drives them through many spots with ancient ruins: some are still standing, beautiful and impressive, while others are eroded by time and half hidden by the vines. The Monkey can see glimmering auras around all of them, as if they are still imbibed with divine energy.

Finally, at dusk, they arrive at the ruins of the old city that was mentioned by the locals the evening before. It is a deserted place, slowly being reclaimed by the jungle. They make their camp in a clearing under a large tree, and prepare a little fire to warm up the food they brought with them. At this precise point, the Monkey feels elated, at home in the jungle; he is happy about traveling with his new friend.

"I am grateful for what you have done so far for me," he says to the Musician, But then he adds with uncharacteristic seriousness in his voice: "But I am also glad to move on with my healing quest. The Little Buddha is waiting for me. I have two more unknown healers to meet after this one", and then stops on his tracks, unwilling to break his agreement of confidentiality with the Young Shaman.

The Musician notices his abrupt interruption, but doesn't pursue the subject. He tells the Monkey instead: "Don't worry, go to sleep. I will stay awake and keep watch. Tomorrow morning, by the time you wake up I will be gone to get us some breakfast. Meanwhile, you will simply have to follow the directions that I will give you now, and we'll see what happens".

This time, the Monkey doesn't want to forget any part of the directions. He quickly opens his Ipad ready to write them in, while the Musician smiles at the incongruous sight of a monkey typing away in the Jungle…

"Do you see that narrow path in between the dark green foliage at the edge of the clearing?" the Monkey nods a very attentive yes, "tomorrow morning follow it, until you reach the remains of a pyramid. Wait there."

The Monkey closes his Ipad and, after wondering for just a few seconds what this is all about, falls into a deep dreamless sleep.

Chapter Seventeen

THE PERUVIAN MAGICIAN
The Yellow Essence

When the first light filters through the thick foliage, the Monkey wakes up. He is alone. He rubs his eyes, eats the cold remains of yesterday's porridge, and sets off. He follows the narrow path over a mountain and through virgin rainforest. It's a magical surrounding, it reminds him of his fertile Little Planet: some plants have huge leaves, as large as average size human being. The jungle echoes with the songs and screeches of hundreds of colorful birds.

The Monkey, in contrast, becomes more and more silent, more and more peaceful as he continues. Shortly before reaching destination, he falls into a state of blissful contentment, just walking, swinging his arms, resting here and there… He would have loved to share this experience with his good friend the Musician, but he has the clear feeling that this last stretch of the journey is for him alone. He is anyway sure by now that they will meet again…

When the path ends into an inextricable tapestry of plants and vines, he immediately notices the still tall ruin of an ancient pyramid, just visible underneath the moss and bramble, casting a soft shadow all around.

Nobody is there. Not knowing what else to do, the little Monkey starts preparing for himself a little bed of leaves. "The sun is still high, but I could use a little siesta after the long walk," thinks the Monkey, "and then we'll see…"

A few hours later, just as the shadows of the tall trees start getting longer, he suddenly wakes up. He has picked up a sound from far into the jungle: as it gets closer, he can hear a chant, accompanied by an instrument that sounds like a pan flute…

The Monkey, still drowsy in his post-siesta state, has no time to decide whether to worry or not: the big leaves at the end of the clearing open up to let through the Musician. The Monkey is touched: his friend has caught up with him; he has come all this way, in order to support him to find this unpredictable stranger …

But the man standing in front of him is not the same as the one he left behind at the campfire. The Monkey rubs his eyes and looks in surprise. For a start, his usual outfit, suede jacket and jeans, is gone. Now he is donned into an incredible ceremonial outfit, decorated with embroidered beads and feathers, with many symbols painted on it in vivid colors. It looks so old and worn that it could disintegrate at any moment; the Monkey can sense around it the presence of the ancient world that produced it a long time ago.

He doesn't greet the Monkey with his usual "Hola". He lets out instead a sound that gives him goose bumps. It is definitely a sacred sound, the Monkey recognizes, it is as if the Musician is uttering an ancient magic spell. Even his voice is different, deep and booming, as if some higher source is speaking through him.

The Monkey is utterly overwhelmed: "Are you the person that I was looking for all this time? Why did you keep this secret from me?" he says, while his mistrust spreads through his system like a poison: he feels again cheated and wants to leave. But when he looks once more at the Musician, he meets his eyes. In spite of his otherworldly appearance, the Musician's eyes remain soft, friendly like always. This is enough for the Monkey to relax again. After all, he realizes, he has been guided right from the moment he set foot onto Peruvian ground. He finally bows down and says: "Thank you! Thank you!"

The Musician gently helps the Monkey up, and replies: "Dear little Monkey, from now on you will address me as the Magician. I am the one you were looking for. For now, forget about my other identity as the Musician. You can think of him as my twin brother, who is still on his way to join you… but let him be gone for a while. Tune into me as a new being,"

He beckons the Monkey to sit down, and continues: "The Young Shaman from the Siberian steppes is not so young as he looks, he is my most ancient brother. We have spent many lifetimes in each other's company, and we have gone through many adventures together.

Over the centuries, we have added to our duo two more healers, the ones you will later meet. We became what the older tribes call the Mysterious Four. It has not always been for us as easy as it is now, in this modern day and age, to stay tuned into each other, but we always kept on learning from each other through enormous distances and years of separation. Together, we have developed unique healing methods for people on the spiritual path…"

"I guess the secrecy is your way to keep low, and not to get in the way of pharmaceutical companies…" the Monkey adds, unable not to show off his own sources of information.

"Not only, dear friend Monkey," the Magician replies, his eyes getting a shade darker, "at this point I must warn you: even though I know the purity of your heart, it is important for you to remember what the Young Shaman already told you: what can be a great benefit for one person can be a curse to another. Be sure of your intention. If you are not, please leave. I don't even want to describe what could happen if magic rituals are misused".

The Monkey shifts in his seat, and looks serious: "I promise to be respectful."

The Magician continues: "In a few hours we will perform a ritual. I want you to pick a place somewhere here in the clearing where you can perform a ceremonial washing." Handing the Monkey a highly polished wooden bowl decorated with ochre designs, he continues, "Fill it up with water from the small source that runs just there, near the ruin. I will leave you some herbs and a sponge: scrub every part of your body and wash your clothes. It is still warm enough for them to dry; just remain naked for a while. When they are dry, put them on again, and wait for us to come. While waiting, simply meditate on what you want to ask on behalf of your friend".

"Us...???" the Monkey's question remains unanswered. The Magician has just disappeared into the foliage, and the sound of his Pan flute is already very far away.

After thoroughly washing, the Monkey sits and waits. Time seems still in the silence of the jungle. He has entered a kind of reverie about his tribal home and his parents when he hears the rustle of the leaves.

The Magician is back, beckoning him to follow. They take a small path, almost invisible through the thick jungle. Even for the Monkey, it is steep and treacherous. But the Magician hops ahead with ease; it's obvious that he knows his way around here. At some point, the Monkey, scared to continue going down what seems like an endless ravine, starts unceremoniously holding on to the Magician's robe. When the way gets even steeper, he finally climbs up on his shoulder, just like he often does with the Little Buddha. The Magician allows it, and in that way they reach another clearing, very shady and secluded.

It is completely empty. The Magician silently points at a smooth rock in the middle. The Monkey nods, sits there and closes his eyes. After a while, he hears the ring of cymbals. Almost as if in response, from all around comes a rustling of leaves mixed in with the sound of branches snapping. His skin prickles as he recognizes hushed human voices.

He opens his eyes: there are people, many people coming, maybe all together twenty. They are all clad in white or off white: most of them are women, clearly from all kinds of social backgrounds. Some look like Spanish educated ladies from the coast, immortalized by cosmetic surgery, and others are indigenous women from the rainforest, looking ancient in their hand woven natural colored robes. There are also a few men. Everyone present, the Monkey notices looking at their auras, emanates a beautiful peaceful yellow glow, and their eyes are smiling and joyful.

The Monkey is happy to meet them. Good people that will help him for sure. All the exuberance that he has had to contain so many times on his journey suddenly bubbles over, and before anybody reaches him, he stands up and enthusiastically shakes hands with each person.

"We, my friend and me," he says, indicating the Magician, "are happy that you could be here with us tonight. We hope that you will enjoy this evening, and that your spouses and your children at home are fine..."

After his impromptu speech, he walks among them, answering questions, and patting here and there on people's shoulders, looking like a campaigning politician.

The people, who have been obviously invited by the Magician, look at the Monkey with a mixture of incredulity and mirth. They look at the Magician, whose expression does not give away any personal opinion. But then, a tender smile appears on his face, and everyone relaxes…

When the Monkey returns to his seat, he looks satisfied. He feels proud to have honored the Little Buddha by welcoming everybody personally. He is ready to start.

The Magician opens the gathering by drawing everyone closer with a sweeping gesture of his arms.

"Let's make a circle", he says softly in a language that everyone, including the Monkey, seems to understand: "Come, everyone", and he sits on another rock at some distance from where the Monkey is again seated. Everyone makes a circle around the two of hem.

He starts: "Dear Monkey, I shall explain to you what we are going to do tonight. We are going to conduct a Spiritual Constellation Session for the the Little Buddha. With the help of all these friends gathered here, we are going to explore what has really happened to him.

Since the Little Buddha cannot be physically present, you, his dearest friend, will be his representative. By the power of this ritual, you will become his vehicle, and speak, think, feel as if you would be the Little Buddha. From now on, forget about your own identity, and trust that it will be returned to you at the end of the ceremony.

In the same way, the friends in this big circle have gathered here to represent the people that affected, either positively or negatively, the state that the Little Buddha is presently in. They will also forget their daily identities and become those people and speak for them.

The Constellation will reveal if the Little Buddha is meant to survive. We cannot perform miracles, but even if your dear friend were meant to die, this ritual would help him to leave his body in a peaceful way…"

The Monkey is impressed. His curious mind is instantly attracted to this method: he loves the idea of representing the Little Buddha. In all his own years of enlightenment, he has never done anything like this. He realizes that he is not very updated on spiritual techniques. In fact, the only method he remembers is Gibberish, he thinks with a private giggle. He takes a deep breath and replies solemnly: "Thank you!"

The Magician continues: "We are going to work with the constellation of energies that were active at the precise moment of the Little Buddha's collapse. This technique is ancient, and has only recently made its way to the larger public under the name of "Family Constellation". It is a very powerful and transformative tool when used with intuition and the right intent. We do not know what wants to be brought out into the open, so we will allow with open hearts whatever resolution wants to unfold…OK, little Monkey" he says, indicating the people in the circle: "Choose a person who can represent you".

The Monkey looks around, thrilled: who could be a monkey here? He scans the audience, and points at one man in the far end of the circle: he has bowlegs and a rather big head: "He looks like a monkey!" Everyone laughs. The Monkey is a bit embarrassed, because he does not understand the joke. But when the bow legged man also starts laughing, the Monkey finally joins in, and the collective giggles become an uproar of laughter.

"That was a great beginning", the Magician says. He invites the man to stand next to the Monkey. "So now we have the two of you, the Little Buddha and the Monkey".

"It's very strange to stand next to yourself," declares the Monkey, staring at the bowlegged man that strangely starts looking more and more like him…

The Magician continues assigning a role to each person in the circle. Everyone gets a part, even if only as the shoes that the Little Buddha wore on that day or as the food that he ate that morning… Everybody is either something or someone else. The Magician gives full attention to each representative whether he or she has the role of a person, an animal, or an object. They are all significant for the unfolding of the story.

Then he asks the Monkey to lead each one of the representatives to the place he feels was theirs in relation to the Little Buddha when he collapsed. This takes a while, because of the large number of people but also because in the beginning the Monkey is not confident with it. As time passes, though, he finds it easier and starts enjoying it. It's a bit like his intuitive tapping on the Ipad: he just needs to trust that things will happen by themselves.

When everybody is positioned, the Monkey stands back in the place of the Little Buddha. "How do you feel, Little Buddha?" the Magician asks him.

"I feel…I feel drained," the monkey whispers in the same flat voice of his sick friend, "I have much pain in my body, and no energy…it's devastating…" he answers, perfectly recognizing the Little Buddha's symptoms, this time from the inside. This tool, he realizes, works in very mysterious ways.

Then the Magician starts moving to different representatives and asks them what they are feeling. Everyone has something very precise to say. Even the Buddha's shoes talk at length about how that fateful morning was for them: how fast and light they had been walking before the curse, and how heavy they had felt in contrast afterwards. At some point, he has to stop "the shoes" from talking, because their representative doesn't seem to want to stop talking.

Then he moves around like a true Magician, creating new situations by placing the representatives in different positions, turning them to face others they couldn't see before, giving them sentences to say to each other.

For a while it looks as if it's going nowhere; it all seems a chaos with no apparent direction, people being moved here and there, and then moved back again. It all looks completely experimental. The Monkey, who does not mind chaos, is actually enjoying the mayhem. He giggles when an upper-class woman is chosen to represent the Buddha's shoes, while a very innocent looking Indian woman is given the role of one of the evildoers. It all looks a bit absurd, but by now the Monkey trusts the Magician unconditionally. Like many other times, he will make sense of it in the end…

At some point, a beautiful red haired woman that represents the Madame is placed right in front of the Monkey-Little Buddha.

The Monkey-Little Buddha is overwhelmed by emotions. In a rapid sequence, he first feels attraction and love towards her, then sadness, and then a strange kind of cold distance. It all culminates into a sharp pain in his heart.

"It feels like the story of a lifetime concentrated in few seconds," the Monkey-Little Buddha says with a broken voice. Then he starts feeling numb all over his body, and slowly falls into a heap on the ground.

The 'Madame' has been watching him all along. First she looks shocked, but then she takes a challenging stance and looks down at his inert body.

When the Magician asks her what is going on, she takes a deep breath, and straightens up. Still on the ground, the Monkey-Little Buddha feels her presence towering over him. He tries to get up but falls back, helpless.

The 'Madame' starts talking: "As the person I really am, I would almost want to apologize for what I am going to say, but as the Madame I am feeling very resentful and bitter. I look at the Little Buddha lying on the floor and I am shocked at the power of my spell. I did not mean to kill him, but I certainly wanted to give him a lesson in humility. I don't really know why, but I am sure that this goes back to a very long time ago…"

These words reach the Monkey-Little Buddha lying on the ground like an arrow. He doesn't know why, yet, but his numbness is washed away by regret and guilt.

She pauses for a long time. Her last words reflect her inner struggle: "But I did not want to kill him. I did not expect such a violent reaction from his side…"

The Magician intervenes, and says softly: "Even kitchen curses are too strong on the body-mind system of a Buddha…"

Suddenly her body starts shaking and she falls on the ground. All the women in the circle run to her, trying to help her… they all cry and hold each other for a long time.

The Monkey-Little Buddha is suddenly released. He stretches his aching limbs, and sits up. "I understand the confusion you must have felt when you saw me as the Little Buddha …" he hears himself saying to the 'Madame', and realizes that his voice is like the one of a big and powerful man. But this sensation is quickly gone as it came.

"I smell Karma,"[1] whispers the Magician.

---

1 Unfinished business in a past life

The Monkey-Little Buddha realizes at that moment what enormous distance he has created for lifetimes on end between him and women. He respects them, he even loves them like with the Indigo Woman, but he never comes too close to them: "I don't know, I don't know if it's me, the Monkey, or me the Little Buddha talking… but I just want to say I am sorry, I apologize, forgive me", he says, standing up and running towards the crying women.

They all look at him a bit dazed, and reply: "It is not your fault!"

"But you have to stop crying because of me! I don't want to hurt you anymore…" he continues, sobbing louder than them, his monkey nature taking over.

"Stop being sorry, Monkey-Little Buddha, you are disturbing us! We want to cry; crying while holding each other is the best way to let go for us women. That's how we can transform our pain into love…"

At this point the Monkey-Buddha has lost touch. He doesn't know who he is anymore, and to whom these women are speaking to. He runs to the Magician, jumps under his coat and crawls under his arm, he cries and shivers until he starts getting warm again.

Meanwhile, the Magician completes the Constellation: "The Law of Love is restored. What needed to be said has been said. The guilt and regret that petrified the Little Buddha have started moving again through his system. They will be dissolved in due time. More steps are be needed for the final healing, but what we could do here tonight is complete"

From under the Magician's coat, the Monkey sees how now suddenly everybody is hugging and connecting. In a soft wave, he feels the weight of the Little Buddha's burden lifting, and then he is again just the Monkey. The Magician takes him out of the folds of his coat and holds him gently, rocking him and whispering reassuring sounds. He falls asleep like he did when he was a baby-monkey in the safe arms of his father.

Next morning, the Monkey wakes up unusually late. He feels refreshed, much better than he has for a long time… His friend, now back in his Musician outfit, greets him with a cup of banana milkshake and says: "Hola! I am your friend the Musician…"

"Can I still call you Magician?" the Monkey sleepily says, "it makes me feel safer, and with him I have no secrets…"

"OK little Monkey, I am your friend the Magician, but, man, can I pick any tune…." They both laugh.

After a short pause, the Magician's expression changes: "You received from my friend, the Young Shaman, a powder in a little hand embroidered pouch. Do you still have it?"

The Monkey nods: "Yes".

"Do you remember the daily dosage for the Little Buddha?"

"Yes, I wrote it on the Ipad…"

The Magician cannot stop himself from smiling, and continues, "I have prepared another powder for you," he says, handing him a small bright yellow dropper bottle, "It is an extract of several Indigenous plants, harvested on special nights during certain moon phases. In a low dose, it is a mild stomach relaxant. With the addition of some secret ingredients, it is used to counteract shock and trauma. It acts on the solar plexus, and slowly relaxes the deep cramps of fear that are stored there. Once the belly starts functioning again, all the toxins are flushed out, and the body-mind system will flow again.

Have you ever seen a small child when it starts discovering and exploring life all around? Those delighted shrieks…ah, well, you do know, as a monkey…"

The Monkey happily nods, "I think I do, it's like flying around from tree to tree, playing with each other…"

"Exactly. This is the Essence of Joy, sunny and Yellow. When we lose touch with it, we become despondent, unmotivated and serious. This potion brings the Yellow Essence back into the system; it restores enthusiasm for life and ease in the body…" The Monkey remembers well those yellow moments with the Little Buddha before the curse, and also the deep gloom that has now replaced them.

"I will now call upon our Pleiadic ancestors for blessings," the Magician says, standing up to his full height and raising his arms:

"Dear older sisters and dear older brothers,

We are sorry for whatever wounds we have created without knowing.

Please support us in finding many ways to heal and transform our own wounds and those of others.

Thank you for being here in disguise last night…"

For a moment the Monkey perceives a subtle light moving all around them. He becomes very quiet, and hears a faint giggle. And another one. And many more. The spirit forms of what looks like a mixture of humans and monkeys with some other indefinable traits, are dancing all around them.

"Thank you, Pleiadic ancestors…" he giggles.

After a delicious breakfast with all kinds of tropical fruits and juices, the Magician tells the Monkey: "Soon it's time to continue your quest. So far, you have met two male healers. Now it's time for you to experience the female way. The third healer you will visit is the Lady, who lives in Istanbul, Turkey. This time we'll make it easier for you, you deserve it," he says, handing a note to the Monkey, "here is her address. The Lady is originally from Persia; she is a beautiful healer," and adds with a mischievous smile, "and woman…"

The Monkey feels very relieved. Truly, to again cross the whole planet in order to find an unknown Lady would be too much for him at this point. He carefully folds the note and puts it in the back pocket of his pants, where it's easy to keep track of.

"Would you play my favorite song for one last time?" the monkey is getting a bit sentimental, but this seems to suit the Magician. Soon the two of them are singing louder and louder, clapping their hands and dancing together.

After singing, the Magician relaxes completely; now it's just the two of them, the Musician and the Monkey, enjoying their last hours together.

"I have a little home at the feet of the pyramid. You haven't seen it yet, but it's there, behind that crumbling wall, hidden from view. I come here when I need to recharge. Only very few know about its existence." He gallantly bows and adds: "Before you leave, I would like you to be my guest here for a day".

The Monkey is so touched that he cannot reply in words. He just jumps up on the Magician's lap and gives him the greatest hug of all.

The Magician's home is small but very well equipped. Amongst his prize treasures, there is a chest full of fancy attires, from which he produces a very handsome black velvet suit, charmingly faded by time. Showing it to the Monkey, he announces: "I will wear this tonight. We are going to a very elegant restaurant in a nearby resort, and you will be my guest…"

The Monkey feels a bit embarrassed: there is no place in his backpack for something as fancy as a velvet suit. He is wearing rather boring cut-off jeans and an almost clean t-shirt.

The Musician notices it, and swiftly dives again into the chest.

He comes back and hands the Monkey a folded garment, "for you…"

It is the most stunning suit he has ever seen, made out of cream raw silk. It makes a great contrast to the black velvet of the Musician. It is vintage, with narrow sleeves and lapels, tight to the body.

The Monkey's eyes fill with tears, "It's a precious gift…"

Magically, of course, the suit fits him perfectly, "Flashy clothes…" he giggles.

"I was once a very famous pop star," the Magician replies, a never ending source of surprises, "World famous…One day I will publish my memoirs, and then, dear friend, you will get to know my whole story. For now please simply accept my gift".

And off they go, like two shining gentlemen in the late afternoon…

The Musician has reserved the two best seats of the restaurant, from which they can admire a magnificent view on the sunset. When they come in, all heads turn. The ladies are specially fascinated: many of the waiters earn good tips by constructing all kinds of intriguing answers to the much whispered question: "Who are the two gentlemen enjoying the sunset?"

Now that it's almost time to say goodbye, they both seem to cherish very much their time together. They laugh, remembering how on their first meeting the Monkey had found his singing voice, and the Magician confesses how many times he has been on the verge of revealing his identity to cheer him up. They also talk about the Little Buddha, both with tears in their eyes. In the end, over a glass of Pisco, they gossip in a friendly manner about some of the participants in the ritual of the night before. But what is really happening all along is that they are letting their hearts open up to each other, in mutual respect and trust.

They walk out of the restaurant a bit drunk. On their way home they sing, and stop and look at the waxing moon. Although the Monkey would like to experience more of the Magician's home, he is so tired that already twice on their way he collapses under a bush snoring, and his friend has to retrace his steps to help him up.

After a good night sleep, they both wake up excited, happy to know that they still have one whole day together.

After his first cup of Peruvian coffee, the Monkey is already speaking non-stop. Although by now he is familiar with his attitude, the Musician still marvels at the Monkey's mind: enlightenment or not, it has maintained all the inquisitiveness and talkativeness of his tribe.

"We need some peaceful time of integration after all the intensity," announces the Magician in a short gap between the Monkey's words, "Nature always helps. Come with me to the veggie garden."

But even there, in the stillness of the early afternoon, the Monkey can't stop being a monkey: he has gathered a bunch of carrots, put them in a row, and is now doing a constellation session with them…

The Magician gives up and laughs. "You certainly don't lack Yellow Essence!"

As the sun starts going down, it's time for the Monkey to leave.

He tells his friend: "I cannot express how grateful I am to you. I hope to see you again! You are in my heart forever, you are the most precious jewel of existence…" he would like to go on, but realizes that anyway no words can really convey what he feels now. He just looks at his friend.

They hold hands, and the Magician says: "I am going to stay here a bit longer to relax and meditate. One of the ladies from the coast will be shortly here with her limousine and driver to take you to the airport. Go to the check in counter with this paper, and you will be given a boarding pass to Istanbul. You have the Istanbul address in your back pocket." He puts an envelope in his hands and adds, "Here are enough Turkish Liras to pay the taxi fare to the Lady's home. Once you get there, she will take care".

At that point the Monkey, speechless with gratitude, falls on his knees and kisses the feet of the Magician. Knowing that this is his way to express the inexpressible, the Musician allows him to do it. Whether they will meet again or not, their friendship is forever.

Chapter Eighteen

SHADOWS OF THE PAST

It is early morning on the other side of the Earth. The Little Buddha is resting in the Zen Hut. The Indigo Man is just outside, lounging on an easy chair, looking at the squirrels playing through the branches.

The air is fragrant with herbs, and a distant birdcall echoes in the air.

When the Indigo Man starts nodding off and his breathing becomes even, the Little Buddha gets up. He moves a bit better, specially after he experienced a few days ago a mysterious golden glow around his body. But he still tires easily.

He sits back on his futon and listens: after what happened last night, he can hear the whisper of the beyond even now.

He looks at his new gift on the small cream-colored coffee table: an Ipad, a gift from the Indigo Couple. It is a shiny white twin model of the Monkey's black version. It's meant to entertain him, now that he is strong enough to stay up a few hours a day.

He takes it in his hands but doesn't open it. He just keeps on staring out of the open sliding doors for a long time. The Indigo Man hears him shifting uneasily and comes in quietly, sitting next to him on the futon.

After a while, the Little Buddha starts talking. In the beginning, his voice is like a faraway murmur, but then he slowly catches himself back, and begins in his usual soft voice: "Last evening in my contemplations before going to sleep, I realized that the curse is part of a longer story. I tried to remember, but the only thing that became clear was that it all happened long ago in a past life in Bhārata, now known as India.

I always get exhausted when I soul-search like this, so as the night came I decided to give up any effort and just trust that I cannot do more than what I am doing already. I went to sleep early.

Then, a dream came to me. Its images were crystal clear. It revealed that I am still carrying a great grief from a long time ago. I can still feel it all over this body now. But strangely enough, the dream was cathartic for me: I feel somehow lighter after it, and grateful for what it showed"

He slowly turns with some difficulty to the Indigo Man, and smiles: "Up to last night, I couldn't connect much with this Ipad. It just made me miss the Monkey even more. But last night, when I woke up from my dream, it was calling me. I opened it and started writing what I had seen.

Then, while typing with one finger, more memories started to come. I was so slow, that I had time to remember many details…"

Turning back towards the Ipad in his hands, he asks: "Dear Indigo Parent, could I read to you what I wrote? It would be very important for me."

The Indigo Man smiles, and answers: "You have my blessings, and my attention… Tell me, please". He reclines on the cushions, next to the Little Buddha, ready to listen.

The Little Buddha reads: "I find myself into what feels like a vivid dream, in a space on the border between matter and spirit … I am walking in a jungle amongst the ruins of ancient pyramids. Suddenly, out of the thick foliage appears an older gentleman with long braided gray hair. He smiles directly at me, as if we were old friends. Then suddenly the Monkey is there, staring at me with an expression of surprise while pointing at a group of women behind him.

One of them looks very bitter, and all the others seem to form a protective circle around her. They all start moving towards me. I suddenly feel very guilty. But I don't know why.

This "why" starts resonating inside me deeper and deeper. It becomes a vortex that pulls me through many layers of consciousness, until I am back in another life…

At first, I start recognizing only fragments, random sounds, flashes of colors, and whiffs of perfumes. Then I look at my feet: they are donned in the finest leather sandals, with golden clasps.

I hold my breath as I look at the garments that cover my legs: a long robe, bordered by threads of silver and gold, embedded with precious stones.

I know who I am: a King. I reign over a mighty kingdom. I can feel the burden of responsibility on my broad shoulders.

I look around me: I am sitting on a throne, surrounded by courtiers and what seem like foreign delegations. They all look at me with respect and a measure of awe. But I know very well that amongst those strangers are those who would happily plot my demise. Only my fame as a warrior keeps them out of the boundaries of my kingdom…

I notice on a tapestry hanging on the wall a large painting of myself, younger and fiercer, sitting bareback on my ink black Arabian stallion in my ink black battle clothes. My face, arms and legs are bare, painted with elegant miniatures of battle scenes. Either I must have been quite an arrogant and courageous young man to face the enemy without armor, or the artist must have wanted to flatter me…

"I am very much looking forward to being initiated into your famous Art of Battle, My Lord…" a young man, clearly from another country, bows down in front of me, surrounded by an escort of lesser nobles.

I smile back at him, and pat him on his shoulders. I have a good heart, I can feel that.

Then it comes to me. I have created an Enlightened Art Academy, where all the Arts known to men are taught to royalties from all over the continent by a hand-picked selection of teachers in…Asia, yes, Asia. I have glimpses of poetry and music classes, and flashes of swords hissing in simulated duels. I see students and teachers absorbed in debates in the middle of open rolls of parchment…

Someone hands me a tray laden with fruits. I pick a slice of perfectly ripe mango and savor it. I am a sensuous man, and I love beauty.

There is a quiet hush as a subtle perfume of jasmine mingled with some fresher spice announces the entrance of whom I immediately know to be my beloved. I lift my gaze to meet hers.

She is a young woman, half my age, with deep green eyes, blond locks falling to her waist. I remember: she comes from Mesopotamia.

She joins her hands in a graceful greeting and speaks to me with a foreign accent: "My father sends you greetings…"

I also remember her father: he is one of my greatest friends, and has personally overseen her education, something almost unheard of for a girl child, and something that has made her brother very jealous of her. When we agreed upon the marriage of his daughter to me, I promised I would keep her safe from her brother, who had meanwhile disappeared abroad to gather an army against his father.

She is so beautiful. Her bright eyes are full of intelligence and inquisitiveness, and she doesn't look down or through me like my other…yes, I realize I have many wives.

I can see them, each one in her special pavilion, commissioned by me according to the taste and dictates of the royal family that has sent her as a token of their alliance to me. They seem contented enough, living in luxury and having a safe future for their offspring. But there is no love spent between any of them and me, except for my occasional performance of marital duties, which keeps them pregnant.

I look at her again, and feel the intense love and dedication that streams though her green eyes. My heart responds with equal intensity, maybe just a bit tempered by age, which makes it more…spiritual. I am suddenly aware of an unknown door in my heart: it feels as if some force is elevating my soul. For the first time in this life, I sense what is beyond power and practical wisdom…"

The Little Buddha stops, taking a long breath and looking at the Indigo Man: "You know that feeling, don't you?"

The Indigo Man silently nods, and their eyes meet.

"I did not know it before that moment. She opened my heart for the first time. This is when my search started. I had forgotten…"

The Little Buddha turns again to his Ipad and continues: "Then I suddenly feel lifted upwards, and I am passing through another vortex, but this time it's a warm one. I feel gentle angelic hands carrying me to the next scene…

I am standing at the entrance of the main temple of the city. Colorful flags are waving in the warm breeze, flower garlands are decorating the tall gates, and incense fills the air. My robe is exquisitely simple, made out of the finest white cotton in the Kingdom.

"He should be arriving any moment…" a sober young man, a secretary, whispers to me.

I am looking with pride at the beautiful statues covered in gold that adorn the temple when the sound of bells brings me back to the present moment.

The crowd waiting outside the gate gracefully parts, and I catch my first glimpse of Him: a wise looking old hermit, dressed in a saffron robe, accompanied by a handful of disciples.

He approaches me slowly. He is so light that his feet barely touch the ground. I bow down to receive his blessings.

His trembling hands touch my head, and I experience a wave of compassion and peace streaming through my being. I lift my eyes and I see him smiling with a slight questioning nod.

My mind stops. This man sees my soul to its core. I feel very small, for the first time since I was a child. His eyes tell me that there is much more to my life than being a king. In that very moment, I surrender, and I become very quiet inside.

After a simple blessing of the crowd, the Holy Man leaves. A silence is left in his wake. And then, as life resumes in the main square, I rush to my beloved wife. She is nursing our baby boy.

"I can't really explain," I start telling her, but she interrupts: "I can see the yearning in your eyes. I knew that at some point you would have to retreat in contemplation…it's our age difference…"she sighs, "but it's fine, I have your child and your undying loyalty as a husband…I let you go; this is how deep is my love for you…"

The rest is again a blur. We find out where the Holy Man lives: outside our kingdom, in a hidden cave on a plateau surrounded by mountains…a whole night spent with my wife talking, making love, the candles flickering until dawn…

"We will keep it secret, "I tell her, "not to panic my subjects. In case of emergency, you know where to reach me. I will come back immediately. And here is a private message to the Head of the Council: I grant him full powers until my return". As I say these words, I can hear my voice faltering: I am taking a big risk. But I am also elated, excited, eager to go…

I am now at the foothills of the Plateau. My feet are chipped and my saffron robe is dusty and torn at the edges. And I feel tremendously alive. I am going to meet my Master…

Then a stream of golden pictures follow: the silence of the Plateau, the sound of the even breathing coming from my body sitting in a Lotus posture, the suave presence of my Master. Days are rolling by in an endless sequence of ordinary chores, chopping wood, making tea, and long times of meditation. The only discordant note in all this is an occasional high-pitched worry that creeps into me from time to time. I watch it, and every time decide that it must be my mind, trying to trick me back into action. My wife will certainly warn me if anything goes wrong..."

There is a long significant pause. The Indigo Man can almost hear the wheels of Karma turning…

"I never saw her again." The Little Buddha adds in a whisper. He turns to his Ipad and continues reading:

"I find myself much later in time, my long beard gracefully waving in the wind has some silver in it. My Master is leaving the body. He is telling me in a barely audible whisper: "Your have karmic responsibilities to attend. Keep on moving. Some layers of your heart have still remained untouched: they can't be reached by just sitting in meditation…"

His eyes sparkle for a last time with a compassionate grin, and he is gone.

I see myself burning his body in the ritual way, and building a shrine, a Samadhi for Him. And continuing my serene routine of daily chores and long sittings, just as if He would still be alive, there, with me. I am at peace and I have no feeling for moving. Whenever I catch a glimpse of the life I have left behind, I always picture my wife sitting in her Pavilion, enjoying life and faithfully waiting."

I am now on my deathbed, embraced by the windy silence of the Plateau. My disciples line up to be blessed by me for the last time. A young monk approaches, and murmurs a prayer while lowering his head. I recognize his accent: he comes from my kingdom; I might even have known him as a small child. For the first time, I ask what has become of my land.

He looks at me with deep sadness: "I have not set foot in my country for many years. I would be persecuted, if I tried. All spirituality is outlawed…"

I hang on with my last breaths to hear more. All my peace is gone. But it's all blurred…I hear him saying: "the former King's wife and her brother, and now her son in her footsteps, have created a very powerful military state, where no freedom of speech or worship is allowed…"

I feel a tremendous shock pulling me towards a dark and numb space. I want to forget, as I actually did when I died in that life…but this time around I am going to stay conscious.

I am standing in my spirit body, right after my death, at the edge of my kingdom. I don't recognize anything. Hostile looking guards stand at the new immense iron gates. I slide through the wall and catch the first glimpse of what had once been my city.

All art has gone: the golden statues have been removed from the temples; the fountains are stripped of their ornamental sculptures. No trace of the pavilions: in their place stand ugly square grey buildings that look like fortresses with narrow windows. The park looks neglected and bare. All the beautiful flowers and exotic plants have withered and died. The majestic building of the Academy of Enlightened Arts has become a ruin, with its entrance nailed shut.

What has happened to my kingdom? What has happened to my beloved wife?

The grief is so strong that everything blacks out for a moment.

When I come to, the city around me is exactly as it was on the day I left it. I hear people shouting. Breathless messengers are bringing to the royal palace news of the sudden death of the king of Mesopotamia, my wife's father. Her brother has been crowned. His army is already marching on my kingdom.

I am utterly helpless to what I already know must happen. I have left my wife in the hands of my sworn enemy.

I hear the first hooves of his gigantic army on horse. Soon they become a rumble that shakes the earth.

My wife is in her pavilion, hastily scribbling a note and giving it to a young boy that she hopes will pass unnoticed through the roadblocks. It's a message for me, with only two words: "COME BACK!"

The boy rushes out. Shortly after, I see him lying lifeless on the ground, having been run over by the stampede of horses and left to die on the battleground, like many others.

Again, I have to struggle with all my spirit to remain present, the shock is so great…I hang on to a last flicker of consciousness as best as I can.

I see my wife in her pavilion. Her brother, a stern and joyless man, is pleading with her to surrender.

"I have enough honor in me to let you live, and even rule at my side," he is saying, while she is turning her back to him. Behind him, at the entrance door, stands the Head of my Council. He is blubbering: "Your husband, with all his extravagant expenses on art…very unpractical…I dare say he had a selfish streak…"

I feel betrayed, and then I start wondering about my share. Selfishness: yes. This thought forces me to realize that all my other wives have gone, probably sent back with dishonor to their royal homes.

My beloved turns around, and quietly replies: "I will always love my husband and wait for him"

I feel humbled, and again bitterly impotent. I try to touch her but she gracefully chases away my invisible hand, mistaking it for an insect.

I realize that the room around me has subtly changed. The beautiful Persian vases full of fragrant flowers are gone. My wife is slightly older, her hair gathered in a sober bun: she is still very beautiful, but a stern expression has altered the lines of her face. She is looking at her hands, composed on her lap: "It would have been much simpler and fairer if Father would have just let me be a girl like every other. I became his only student and admirer, I can see that…"

"And then he married you away in an unknown land, to a much older man, his age…" her brother, now more plump and sure of himself, waits for a beat before going on. Her usual protests are no longer coming. He has convinced her.

"I will protect you now," he says, drawing with effort a smile from his tight lips. He has obviously spent quite some time and effort to gain her trust.

When she lifts her face towards him, there is a new look in her eyes: I recognize the loving expression of a much younger girl towards her big brother.

"I always regretted the way you were pushed and disciplined by Father. He was too strict with you…" she says, patting his hand.

"And remember how he discarded Mother for his latest young wife, and how he forced us to treat her with indifference, just like any other women of his Harem," he adds, and whispers:" it would have probably been your fate too, if I hadn't come."

It's finished. He has gained her to his side. And he had the right to do so. I was gone …"

The Little Buddha is silent for a long time. The Indigo Man takes his small trembling hand into his own, warm and large. It's the only reassurance he is capable of at the moment. "Stories like this one, my beloved Little Buddha, are universal. It seems that sorrow is sometimes the only way to really open our heart…"

The Little Buddha looks at his Soul Father and nods, "I can feel it. This sorrow is opening something inside me that has remained guarded for centuries…"

He looks down and resumes reading:

"I allow my spirit to leap forward, to the moment of her death. She is in her bed, surrounded by a very simple retinue of ladies and some dignitaries. Her brother must have already died. She calls a round old woman, whom I recognize as the servant that she brought along from Mesopotamia, a kind of mother figure for her, and takes her hand. She starts talking softly to the crying woman.

"The day that my imprisonment ended, my brother came to the pavilion with a gift for me: a beautiful robe, sober and with a simple design. He called one of my ladies in waiting and ordered her to dress me with it and tie my hair in a single braid. I could see how much authority he had gained by the way my servant blushed intensely and bowed very low.

My brother was dressed in simple black clothes. His only adornments were his weapons. After months of confinement, he invited me out. He wanted to show me the new country that was being built by him over the ruins of the old one.

It was the first time I left the pavilion. The world had changed completely.

It brought tears to my eyes to see the beauty of it all gone. But I could not cry in front of my brother, who was beaming with pride at the long straight roads he had built, with no shade and no decoration except for some enormous marble arches at regular intervals, to be engraved with the military feats and victories of his kingdom. That's when I thought of my husband for the last time. I remembered him at a street corner, where once stood a market, full of flowers, street food, colorful birds in cages, musicians of all sorts. One night we had escaped from the Palace in disguise, to just enjoy this feast for our senses and then make love through the night…"

One solitary tear descends from her hollow eyes, and she continues: "That's when my brother offered me to rule the country next to him and to sign all the kingdom's fortune to my name. He explained that for some ill fortune he could not father any children (he anyway favored men), and the succession line could be carried only through me and my son, whose education he would take into his hands."

At the mention of the Queen's son, the old servant's face clouds with pity and fear…

"I made a mistake in accepting this offer, maybe…" she continues. Then she suddenly sits up with an unexpected outburst of energy, everyone rushing to help her: "But where was my husband then!?!?" she starts screaming, "Men, always men, using you, leaving you, moving you around like a pawn!!!!"

Everyone in the room backs up: she suddenly looks crazed by rage, "My father who sold me, my jealous brother who used me, and my son, my disgraceful son who has become a depraved despot!!!! Where were they when I needed them!!! I will never, ever let this happen to me again!!!!"

And with that she dies. Her spirit seems in a hurry to leave behind this place and leaps into the night like a red flame. This is it."

The Little Buddha is sobbing quietly. It is the first time that the Indigo man sees him crying after the curse. He is so relieved about it. After such a long time of hardly eating and sleeping, of walking around lifeless, his Soul Child is feeling again. He gently takes him in his arms and holds him for a long time.

After a while, the Indigo Man goes to the main house to brew a soothing tea. The Little Buddha sits back in his bed, alone, and closes his eyes. He is aware of the images and feelings that linger around him, and he is in no way fighting them. They slowly dissolve by themselves, and his inner focus is back to the eternal, that which is never born and never dies.

When the Indigo Man comes back with a steaming pot of early evening tea, the sun is just setting on the sea. The Little Buddha is asleep, with a soft smile on his face. Not wanting to wake him up, the Indigo Man tiptoes out of the Zen Hut and finds a quiet place under the oak tree. Sitting silently, he sips his herbal tea, staring into the surrounding hills and wishing the Little Buddha all the best. Then he gets up and returns to the Hut.

A bit later, as evening descends, the Indigo Woman comes to the Hut and finds her husband deeply asleep, with the Little Buddha curled up in his arms. She finds a comfortable nook for her head on her husband's shoulder and silently lies close to them.

That next morning, a special feeling connects all three. They refrain from speaking until their morning tea break under the pergola, with a fresh fig pie and a spicy chai.

The Indigo Couple is deeply touched by the Little Buddha's story. Fear of betrayal and abandonment are something they know in their relationship: they are unavoidable side effects of opening up to intimacy. That's why it is so difficult to surrender…

After the refreshments, the Indigo Woman brings to their table a printed copy of the newly arrived email messages... All of them jump up when they see the Monkey's latest message. They know that he is not allowed to let them know what exactly he is doing, but they strongly feel that there is a connection between the Little Buddha's vision and the Monkey's experience: he was there at the beginning of the dream, after all...

"He is now in Peru, and has attended yesterday a very powerful healing ceremony", reads the Indigo Woman, "He wants you, the Little Buddha, to know that deep work is being done, and asks you to take special care to be kind to...the Indigo Woman...?" she smiles, a bit puzzled.

They all fall silent again. It is clear to them that the connection is there, waiting to unfold in its own time.

They decide to let the Monkey know what has been happening here meanwhile ...

By the time the next email comes from the Monkey, a few days later, his tone has changed...he is in some Lady's home in Istanbul, and he sounds head over heels in love with her...they chuckle...but he also confirms once more that there is a link between the Little Buddha's dream and the work that is being done on him. He cannot say more, he concludes, than sharing with the Little Buddha that the past is the past and that there are many beautiful women whose blessings could counteract the curse given to him...

Specially in Istanbul...

Chapter Nineteen

ISTANBUL: A TALE OF LOVE
The Pink Essence

After a very long airplane ride across half the globe, the same kind woman in uniform that has been offering the Monkey delicious drinks throughout the flight announces on the loudspeaker that they will soon be landing in Istanbul. Due to the eastward direction of the flight, the sun has been rising for the last two hours or so, overdoing itself in an endless pink dawn, and the Monkey is totally dazed.

When it's time to leave the airplane, he is so tired that he can hardly stand on his feet. His old monkey instinct, compelling him to go down on his fours in order to walk faster, almost gets him into trouble: people stare at him puzzled. He suddenly realizes that since he has left the Magician's lady friend at the airport in Lima, no one has ever questioned the fact that he is a monkey, traveling in perfect human style with human papers...probably some spell cast by the Magician has contributed to protect him, but now he is on his own: he needs to be very careful not to blow his cover...

He makes it through the enormous line for passport control, and even through customs. Just on his way out, he hears behind him a shrill child's voice, saying: "Who is that? Is it an animal? That's a mon...k...e...y..." but already by the "mon...", our friend has made one of those jumps that only monkeys can make, and is now running as fast as he can.

After speeding like a bullet through three or four long walkways, he catches his breath and looks behind: nobody is following, nobody is shouting after him. He fingers the piece of paper with the Istanbul address in his pocket, and knows perfectly well that it would be time to find a taxi and show that piece of paper to the driver. But he is simply too tired, exhausted by the excitement and the fear, sleepy and jet lagged. He looks around and likes what he sees: a large café with many plants that provide good secluded corners. None of the customers sitting around pays him any notice. He orders some börek (which he knows is sticky and sweet and very comforting), and dozes off for a while on the armchair.

When he wakes up, he feels refreshed and determined to go on. After typing a short email to the Indigo Couple confirming his safe arrival, he stands up, dusts the specks of börek from his coat, puts some Turkish Liras on the bill, and moves towards a sign saying: Çık, that somehow sounds similar enough to Exit.

Outside the terminal building, he finds himself in the middle of people coming and going. He once more choses to rely on his animal instinct rather than following the human plan: people are too speedy for him. On impulse, he hops on a bus with the sign: Taksim, finds a seat and leans back, looking from this safer perspective at the endless stream of traffic on both sides of the highway to town.

When he steps off, he is himself again, curious and ready for adventure. He begins to look at the city all around him. This is a big city, teeming with life, where - like in the jungle where he grew up - one has to learn to blend with the surrounding, and go about one's business as silently as possible.

As he walks through the many neighborhoods, he starts noticing with amazement that what is known as Istanbul is in fact a kaleidoscope of many different smaller cities. Some areas are super modern, with tall skyscrapers, shopping malls, and wide avenues full of traffic; others are more quiet and residential. In some other districts the houses are ancient, made out of wood in the original style. Then, suddenly, you find yourself in a 16th, 17th or 18th century copy of a Parisian arrondissement, with masterful brickwork and aristocratic facades…

Hours go by, and the sun is no longer high in the sky. Just as he is wondering what will be his next move, a taxi stops right by his side. Without hesitation, he silently opens the car door, slides into the back and hides underneath the back seat. The usual belly dance music is blaring in the background. The cab is full: a rakish looking man in front, obviously Turkish, is directing the taxi driver; behind sits a foreign couple: he is blond, and she is dark. They are laughing and telling stories to each other in a strangely accented English. At some point, the gentleman in the front points at the car radio asks something in Turkish. The taxi driver nods, and tunes the radio to another station. The Monkey recognizes the song played: it's Sufi Music, like he has sometimes heard in the Indigo Couple's home. It's so full of longing that it feels like a caress to his heart. For an eternal moment, cramped under the backseat of a small cab, he forgets his tiredness and feels elevated to another dimension. In the back, the two foreign friends have become very quiet. Even the taxi driver, a talkative guy, has stopped. All five of them disappear into the music, into the experience of the last glow on the evening horizon, the cool breeze, the traffic, all of it together. All is so perfect that tears start veiling the Monkey's eyes.

When the taxi stops in an ancient and beautiful district close to the waters, everything slides back into normal mode. As the three unknown friends disappear into the dark evening, the Monkey sneaks out unseen, and stands at a busy crossing. He takes the address once more out of his pocket and looks at it. He has memorized it long ago, but it's as if he believes somehow that by looking at it again he might find a clue...

In the end, the clue does come to him, from a public map hanging at a bus stand along the road. He squints at it, climbs all around it to follow the turns of the road, until he finally finds the Lady's street address. He traces his itinerary once more with his finger. He will have to cross just a few streets with complicated names. Less than a couple of miles, it seems. With a last big effort, he starts walking down the road, which is becoming steeper and narrower, towards his destiny.

The Lady's residence is an old building restructured into smaller units. From what he can see through the lit windows of different floors, some apartments are beautifully renovated in a rich bohemian kind of way, while others are still maintaining the old local style, with wooden shutters and clothes hanging in the alley. He enters through the heavy doors of the main entrance and starts climbing the stairs. She lives on top...he reaches the last floor with his heart in his throat.... The door is open. Inside it's dark.

He slips into the apartment and in the dim light of the hallway looks around for somewhere where he can hide. Standing in a corner at the entrance, there is a big vase full of multicolored umbrellas: the perfect place.

Just as he wiggles himself into the narrow space between the vase and the wall, he hears a sweet voice saying: "Mercury conjunct to Pluto...mmmh...Mercury in Scorpio".

At first, he doesn't understand from where the voice is coming, and whether it is talking to someone else: after the constant hum of the city, this soft sound confuses him. But he is too curious, and quickly sneaks a peak from behind the umbrellas.

On the wall right opposite him, he sees the dark silhouette of a woman, surrounded by the halo cast by the streetlights below. Her features are not visible, and she remains of undefined age.

"Mercury conjunct to Pluto", she repeats, walking on. She switches a standing light near a big library and browses through the shelves, taking out a book. With a satisfied sigh, she sits on a chair and starts to leaf through the pages. After a while, she stops at a passage, and starts reading it out loud: "Mercury conjunct to Pluto. Individuals born with this conjunction have the tendency to want to remain unseen upon first meetings. They favor hiding in corners at the entrance of homes, more specifically behind vases containing a lot of umbrellas. Even more specifically, they remain hidden but keep their ears very stretched, in order to hear everything that is happening outside".

Ashamed and angry at being caught, the Monkey speaks out from behind his vase: "This is too much!".

The Lady promptly answers: "Do you think so? I don't! It is quite normal for someone who has such a conjunction by birth to be a bit fearful!"

"I am not fearful!" he retorts. "I have been traveling all around this Planet, not only this lifetime, but for many more lifetimes before. I dare anyone call me fearful!"

The Lady starts laughing. It is as if a thousand little bells are ringing! So pleasant, so beautiful, so sweet!

She says: "Little Monkey… little Monkey! Come out from behind the vase!" But with those words she hits a stubborn streak in the Monkey. He won't show himself if he feels made fun of. He retreats even deeper in his hiding place.

"Come on, little Monkey!" the Lady continues, sounding even gentler, "Don't be so stubborn! I've got bananas here, and honey, all your favorite food! I just received a long email from your friend in Peru with an exact list of the delicacies you like, and today I went and purchased them in the best stores in town."

The Monkey's belly, faster than his pride, betrays him. It's grumbling and gurgling so loud that the Lady's laughter starts again, even louder…

A bit defeated and shy, the Monkey comes out from behind the vase and stands in the hall for all to see, tired and red eyed, dragging his backpack. The Lady is very young, more of a girl, really…she comes closer, her eyes misty with love, and whispers with arms open: "Little Monkey, come here!"

The Monkey, who usually does not like following instructions, this time surrenders: he would want to listen to her voice all the time, forever. Moved by something stronger than his will, he steps closer. He becomes aware of a delicious perfume around her; a bouquet of iris, chocolate, rosewood incense and many other mysterious ingredients… The Monkey remembers the Young Shaman and his many smells, some divine, some awful …

But to be seduced by a fragrance! The Monkey has never experienced this before. In his lives as a Lama he has never given much importance to beauty. But as an enlightened Monkey, things are different; he cannot shut off his senses. He realizes that his body has started to tremble, and it's spreading from his legs up to his knees and thighs. Soon his whole little body is trembling in a strange but not unpleasant way.

The Lady leans over and touches him. Her touch is making him swoon, and his whole body stretches out for more. He finds her hand, holds it, pulls himself closer and slips into her lap. He is drunk with her fragrance, with the tone of her voice, with the softness of her skin. Our little Monkey has completely fallen in love!

This is a first for the Monkey. In his previous lives he had partners and tried out all the tantric postures. He even remembers writing books about this… but he has never fallen in love in this way, completely, helplessly, like a baby!

When the first light comes in through the bay windows, he realizes that he must have fallen asleep in her arms, and that she must have gently slipped away, leaving her bundled fragrant shawl as a pillow for his head to rest on. He squints around the apartment. It is ancient, with large wooden floorboards and huge windows overlooking the Bosporus. The strait is so beautiful in the early morning light: it looks like a river, but it flows much more powerfully; it has strong presence, like a watercourse in the Bardo that divides lives, something that you cross never to turn back.

The apartment is full of pink and orange and red hues; the cushions, wall hangings and carpets, are all beautiful to look at and to touch. Many of the carpets are ancient Kilims[1] that are passed on for generations until they reach the exact degree of 'worn-out-ness' that makes them perfect. There are incense sticks everywhere, and oil lamps; beautiful books are piled high on every surface, none of them dusty, all obviously treated with respect. In a special corner he sees a computer, a printer and a scanner, the invaluable toys of modern life.

Holding his breath, he turns around very slowly to look at the Lady. She is sitting on an armchair near the window, bathed in the pale morning sun, sipping her tea and looking at the roofs of Istanbul. Last night he couldn't find out if she was pretty or common. Now that he sees her in daylight, he gasps at her beauty. She has a very refined face, with a long, narrow nose. Her mouth is like a rosebud. Her hair is wavy and curly, of many different colors: deep mahogany, red-brownish colors, some golden streaks and even some silvery hair. Her body is slim and round at the same time. She is very feminine, and her clothes emphasize her curves; she is wearing a long skirt with ethnic patterns, a blouse in hand-woven silk mixed with linen and a short brocade jacket on top.

She hasn't seen me yet, thinks the Monkey, relieved to have time to regroup. He notices next to him a freshly brewed bowl of tea that she must have brought while he was sleeping, and he suddenly starts feeling self-conscious about falling asleep in her lap. He tenses up. His involuntary shift of position attracts her attention, and she turns towards him.

For a moment, she looks as if she is still far away, in another world, staring unknowingly at him through a glass wall, but then recognition appears in her eyes, and the sweetest smile illuminates her face. It is the same smile that sometimes shines on the lovely features of the Indigo Woman back home: they could be sisters…

"Hello, little Monkey!" she says," Welcome to my humble apartment."

The Monkey feels awkward, something he has not felt for centuries; he grins back, looking quite a bit goofy. The Lady holds the laughter that is threatening to burst out again, and says: "Would you want to help me with breakfast?" The Monkey is relieved, and shouts overenthusiastically: "Yes! What shall I do? I can do anything, I am very handy, I am very good at making breakfast, I am the best at making breakfast, I have made breakfast everywhere, all over the world!" and then stops and thinks: "What am I doing again? I am blubbering at the top of my voice about being the best at breakfast when it is not even true!"

All he knows is that he wants to be loved and admired by her, and would do anything for her. "By all the Buddhas and sentient Beings!" he mumbles, "I am enlightened; I am not supposed to lose my head for a girl! I have transcended all this! Help! What is happening with me?"

---

1   Turkish carpets

The Lady notices his struggle and brushes over it with a smile: "Would you like to taste some of these delicious Turkish traditional dishes, with some additional bananas and coconut powder sprinkled on them to please your taste?"

The Monkey cannot stop eating, oohing and aahing at each different combination of spices and sweets. In the end, he has to unbutton his pants and vest, and feels again embarrassed: maybe she does not like fat bellied monkeys …

With such a big amount to digest, he falls asleep again like a child, on the couch. Hours later, when he wakes up, he is gently wrapped into a soft cotton blanket. With one eye, he sees on the screen of his Ipad close to him a blinking notification. Rubbing his eyes, he thrusts his finger on the screen, and a recorded video message of the Lady appears. She is saying: "Dear little Monkey, I have gone to work. I'll be giving some astrology sessions and an early evening group about the Enneagram[2]. I will be back at around nine in the evening. We can decide then if to eat at home or to go out to a local restaurant".

The Monkey has always been happy to be free and alone, but this day on his own feels like the longest of his life. He is constantly looking furtively out of the window and checking the wall clock. At some point he starts convincing himself that some disaster must have happened to the Lady; who knows, maybe an aggressive client, maybe an accident…and he doesn't even know where to look for her … By eight o'clock, when all kinds of shadows start moving around the old city under the eerie light of the neon signs, he is a wreck, half hanging out of the window, almost in tears.

Just then, the familiar comforting soft bleep of his Ipad brings him back: he has mail. A message from the Indigo Couple …

Eager for contact, he starts reading:

"Beloved Monkey, we hope you are in good health and in good hands…" The Monkey sighs," We know that you cannot tell us exactly what is going on. Still, we wanted to ask you if there is any connection between your trip to Peru and the vision that the Little Buddha had few nights ago.

He is still very feeble and needs to rest most of the time, but since he remembered some unfinished matters in another life, a smile has returned to his face …". What follows is a detailed account of the little Buddha's dream.

Distracted from his worries, the Monkey reads the full report. It's not so easy for him to imagine the Little Buddha as the King of that life… but there is something he can recognize in both: the same tendency to be very extreme in whatsoever they do, regardless of the consequences they have on others around them. He knows that kind of male independence in himself too. He just lost it to the Lady…

He would like to shake off that feeling of being in love, but after reading the Little Buddha's story he cannot take himself as seriously as before. On impulse, he starts jumping up and down, shouting: "I don't want to wait…I don't want to wait!!!!",

---

[2] A sufi method that divides personalities in nine different types

almost falling over mid sentence, until only " I don't" remains. He continues with abandon, breathless, until he feels again calmer, and whispers: "want to wait…want to wait…I want to wait"…

When his last whisper dies down, the Monkey is back to himself. He sits down on the couch and looks around for the first time today…the open kitchen counter is an assortment of ancient copper pots, beautiful porcelain plates and the latest appliances: in the middle of it all, there is a chrome and glass blender standing like a trophy. He gets an idea: he is going to prepare a smoothie, a delicious one, like the Indigo Woman prepares at home.

While making the drink, he relaxes into waiting. It's like kindling the flame until the guest comes, he thinks with a smile…

When the entrance door opens at nine in the evening, the Monkey is sitting in a clean and tidy flat, holding out a smoothie to the Lady and welcoming her with a sweet grin. She is surprised. He can see a moment of hesitation in her, as if it's not so easy for her to receive. But then it's gone, erased by her sweet smile.

"Venus in Libra…a sensitive heart that is opening up to women…" she murmurs under her breath, leaving the Monkey wondering if he actually heard it.

"Shall we eat here?" they both ask at the same time, and laugh.

They feast on a delicious Turkish meal, veggies mixed with dried fruit, rice and some curry, and top it off with a water pipe filled with apple tobacco. From his time with the Young Shaman, the Monkey has learnt never to refuse a smoke. They savor the water pipe together while nibbling on biscuits dipped in honey-flavored tea… and they start talking.

First she asks him questions about his tribe, the jungle on the Little Planet and how he met The Little Buddha there, and if the Indigo People are really as unique as she has been told. Then, she asks for some news about her fellow healers: "How was it in Siberia? How is the Young Shaman? As handsome as ever?"

The Monkey is no longer surprised when he hears himself saying: "No, he gained quite a few kilos, and doesn't smell so good. I don't think that any girl could come close to him!" He has to smile at his own words: he is learning to treat his temporary insanity with humor and compassion. The Lady registers all this with a little sigh, and moves on to the next question: "And how was it with the Peruvian Magician? I haven't seen him for such a long time, and I wonder what he looks like now. The three of us, the Musician, the Young Shaman and I, go back a long long time…"

The Monkey replies, confused: "But the Peruvian Magician is much older than the Young Shaman, and both are older than you!"

She looks at him with a quizzical smile, and replies: "No, we are all the same age. We simply don't get older: we found the elixir of youth, and our outer image shifts freely in accordance on how we feel for that period of time. Sometimes we appear older, sometimes younger. We just enjoy being whoever we feel like being."

The Monkey understands: age is a very relative phenomenon…

"It was fun traveling first with the Musician and then with the Magician," he tells her, "And the healing ritual was very powerful. I still feel confused about how it ended, though, with the women being so murderously angry with the Buddha because "he betrayed them like all male seekers", they said," the Lady sighs in recognition, and the Monkey continues, "Then, they started crying, but when I wanted to console them, they pushed me away!"

The Lady straightens up a bit, and asks him: "What do you mean by consoling'?"

"It was too much for me to see them cry…I felt bad about it for me and for the Little Buddha."

The Lady looks at him, and says: "We all need to cry, not only us women, but also men! If this planet wants to survive, we all have to grieve for what we have done to it … we need to cry because, if we don't, existence is going to give up on us!"

"Isn't it better to watch, or even do something about it, rather than indulging in emotions?" the Monkey argues, surprised by his own vehemence

She replies with equal intensity, staring straight at him: "But for sure you must understand that this is exactly what creates disasters in the world! If even enlightened males judge us women because our way goes through the heart, then there is no hope for humanity. We are half of it!"

The Monkey, touched, looks down. She takes his small hand in hers, and continues:

"My parents come from Persia, Iran as it is called now. My mother was a young rich girl when the Shah ordered that the women should drop the veil, the burqa, and adopt the Western style. That's how she grew up, relatively free.

When the Shah was deposed and the burqa returned, my mother's family escaped to Turkey, where my grandparents had established a silk business, taking my pregnant mother with them. My father stayed behind, never to be heard of again. Istanbul is where I was born, to a very sad and embittered young woman. She died when I was a teenager, and my grandparents took care of me…Apart from my unreachable grandfather, I grew up in a women's world. I know well the pain of women who don't feel respected …"

"But you are not one…" the Monkey smiles at her sheepishly, "you have your own self respect… But there is more I have to tell you about that night in Peru. While we were performing our ritual in the early evening, the Little Buddha was having a dream in Greece. Here, I have his full report," he says, reaching for the Ipad, and starts reading out loud …

"Wait a moment," the Lady interrupts him midway, "where did he say the queen came from?"

"Mepopotamia." the Monkey says, struggling a bit with the word, having no idea about where this country would be.

"MESOPOTAMIA!" she corrects, smiling at his obvious resistance to be corrected.

"Or maybe it is just misspelled" he quickly improvises, pointing at the screen, "maybe he meant Amsterdam!"

"Don't bullshit, little Monkey!" the lady laughs, "You said Mesopotamia!"

The Monkey, chastised, shrugs his shoulders: "What difference does it make anyway…"

"All the difference ", she says. The tone of her voice is now serious. The Monkey realizes that there is much more to it than he thought.

"Mesopotamia is the ancient name for the area in between two big rivers, the Tigris and Euphrates, which contained Syria, parts of Turkey, and parts of Persia, or Iran as it is called now.

"As far back as recorded, the women in my family have passed on from one generation to the next the story of one of our female ancestors from Mesopotamia.

"She was a princess, that was given away in matrimony by her father to a faraway king in a country called Bhārata, now known as India. This king was presenting himself as a wise spiritual leader, but he turned to be a coward in the end. One day he disappeared, leaving his wife unprotected and his kingdom at the mercy of the princess's evil brother, who invaded it and turned it into a military state. She had only one child, a boy, who was adopted by her brother. Her son became infamous in history as a hater of spirituality. He destroyed countless monasteries and had a strange peculiar taste for going to battle in woman's clothes. After waiting for several years in vain for her husband to return, our princess became an old resentful queen, trapped in her court and very unhappy.

This story has been deeply imprinted on our entire female lineage as a warning against trusting men blindly. It has never been mentioned to our husbands, fathers, or sons. It bonds us all women in a secret covenant to protect each other from such abuses. We have all been taught by our grandmothers to keep a distance from men and to cherish our independence above all. That's why most marriages in my family were unhappy, and many of us decided not to marry, like me.

"My mother's sister was also unmarried. She was a great role model for me, a real militant against the male race. As soon as she could, she left Turkey, and in the space of a few months set up a movement of solidarity and support for abused and abandoned women with headquarters in Paris. It was so successful that it expanded beyond belief, and became a world foundation. She called it as a pun the Belladonna Foundation: in Italian, this word means beautiful woman, but in Botany it's the name of a poisonous beautiful flower, a deadly nightshade.

For some reason my aunt, who became known herself as the Belladonna, had inside an unjustifiable rage against men: no man that I knew of had ever really mistreated her, although throughout the years of her militancy she did witness injustices and brutality towards many women…but she seemed to want revenge. Later, I also came to know from others that she could be really mean.

But I never met her mean side when I was little: she was the example for me. She was the only one who addressed me as a grown up, and would take me seriously. She was beautiful, tall and stately, with long blond hair and mysterious green eyes…wait a moment: what did you say the woman that cursed the Little Buddha look like?"

"She was a tall, stately woman, with long blond hair, and very deep evil green eyes… and wait…she had a strange accent, from faraway…"

The Lady jumps up: "Wait a moment. The last time I heard from my aunt, she told me that she was going on a Belladonna mission to Greece…I remember that distinctly, because I love the Greek islands…. oh my God…Do you remember what she exactly said to the Little Buddha?"

"Let me think…" for some reason, the Monkey does not like people to know that he has a razor sharp memory, because he likes keeping certain things to himself for the surprise effect. But in the end he answers: "Something like: 'Qued por Staz! Refus ad Morpad!' But I also remember very clearly that she was surprised at the devastation it created in the Little Buddha…kitchen curse, she called it…"

There is a long silence. The Lady is staring down at her feet. Then, she seems to come to a decision, looks at the Monkey straight in the eye, and declares: "It is a kitchen curse, true. Women in my family are taught to use it to put men into place when they are too arrogant. It has the same effect of a scorpion sting: it first leaves one numb, and then it aches a lot for a day or two at the most. But everyone in our field knows that it's impossible to predict the effects of a curse on the extremely sensitive body of an enlightened being… I guess my aunt did not believe that the Little Buddha was truly enlightened, and maybe she wanted to expose him as an imposter…

"But now I suspect that the story that was told in my family is only half of the truth: If you add the Little Buddha's other half, it all appears to be be a huge misunderstanding. The king never got the message of his wife…"

"No he did not!!!!" the Monkey shrieks, in shock and relief at the same time,

The Lady looks deeply into his eyes, and adds softly: "Of course, this doesn't excuse him for never returning, and he is paying for this, but…are we women cursing men too lightly, without hearing their side of the story?"

They look at each other stunned. Then again the Lady snaps out and shouts: "The antidote!"

The Monkey, unable to contain his agitation, is jumping up and down, saying: "What about it? Is there an antidote? Do you know which one?"

The Lady's voice comes in a broken whisper: "No. In these modern days, the curse has been almost forgotten. Only the Belladonna knows the counter curse."

"Can't you ask your aunt to give you the password…hem… the counter curse?" asks the Monkey

"It's not so simple. I would need to explain why, and from what I hear I do not think this would be successful. But do not fear, beloved Monkey: our ring of healers, which also includes men, will find a way to restore the Little Buddha's health. We are working hard on it, and it looks promising…"

The Monkey closes his eyes for a moment, sending out good wishes to his ailing friend, and then says: "Dear and most beautiful Lady, thank you for speaking out. The ritual performed by the Peruvian Magician was no doubt very powerful: it exposed how men can hurt women by being selfish, but it was incomplete. Now I am hearing the other side of the story. It makes my heart lighter to hear that also women have their dark sides…"

Chapter Twenty

A HEALING PRAYER

The following morning after breakfast, the Lady takes the Monkey's hand in hers and says: "I know a prayer, the 'Oponopono Prayer'. It comes from Hawaii. It has been recently rediscovered, dug up like an ancient treasure. Prayers like this are always in the human field. They become more and more powerful when we remember them.

The Monkey has not much experience with prayer. Only now he realizes that it must have something to do with the female approach to spirituality, and is for the first time curious: "Let me hear it".

The Lady chants the four verses of the Oponopono prayer on and on: "I am sorry – please forgive me – thank you – I love you… I am sorry – please forgive me – thank you – I love you…" After a while, the Monkey joins in with the chant.

A half hour passes by. The Monkey starts seeing the countless faces of people he has hurt in his many lives with his carelessness, with always being busy with the sky and hardly looking at the earth and its living beings. The prayer continues, going deeper and deeper on every utterance. Every once in a while, he looks at the Lady, who is completely absorbed in her own prayer: tears are running down her cheeks, and at the same time there is a blissful smile on her lips.

After a couple of hours of chanting, they look at each other, the beautiful Lady and the little Monkey, and speak out the prayer again: "I am sorry – please forgive me – thank you – I love you".

It is as if it's the male and female sides of existence speak to each other through the two of them, asking one another for forgiveness.

They cry and cry… It goes on for the best part of night. As dawn approaches, they are still crying, now just because they feel touched by existence, and it is anyway all out of their hands, and nobody really knows what is right… Finally, when the pink rays of the sunrise light up their faces, their tears become tears of gratitude and tenderness.

Blessed by the promise of a brand new day, they sit together to whisper the Oponopono prayer one last time: "I am sorry – please forgive me – thank you – I love you". They both know that the love that they are now experiencing will go on forever. Even if who they are, a woman and a monkey, keeps them apart, their hearts have become one.

The Monkey is amazed how clean and soft he feels. There is no hardness left in him: that's the female path, he realizes, the most tender and compassionate path he has ever travelled on.

With her sweet eyes still puffy from all the crying, the Lady goes to the kitchen counter and takes out a large wooden bowl and a jar of flour. With masterful gestures, she assembles and mixes cocoa powder from another jar, vanilla extract from a precious little vial, a cupful of rice and a dollop of butter. She takes some eggs and beats them with the butter and then pours the rest. The Monkey helps her. There is a new synchronicity in their movements. The Lady choses a baking tray with a heart shape and puts the mix in the oven. This cake is going to be for their goodbye celebration, and they both know it.

Together they take the heart-shaped tray from the hot oven, and pour cold milk over it. When it cools off, they pour a large jug of delicious dark chocolate pudding on it. She hands him a fistful of crushed pistachio and together they make drawings of each other on the pudding surface, and many hearts all around them.

"Now our Cukulatali Puding Kaplamali Kek is ready…" The Lady says, ceremonially placing their masterpiece in front of them on the table.

She closes her eyes and adds: "This is my contribution to the healing of the Little Buddha: I gave you my heart, now you take it to the Little Buddha. Let him drink this vial," she says, handing the Monkey a precious little bottle full of pink juice, "It activates the Pink Essence, which stands for unconditional love. Tell him that some day he will also have to follow his heart, wherever it leads him. Tell him that I deeply respect him for the courage he showed in leaving Shambala and coming back to the world: it is not an easy task, specially when coming as small and defenseless as he did. But please warn him that this is not the end of the journey: one day he will need to fall in love, and face women again. Share with him the love you and I have shared, open him up to feelings."

The Monkey knows that he will have to leave after eating the cake. He fantasizes doing it so slowly, crumb by crumb, so that this moment can last forever. But women are more practical: the Lady cuts it in four pieces and says: "We will eat one piece a day!"

On the first day and slice of cake, the little Monkey asks the Lady: "What is that strange symbol on your cup? It looks like a cross but also like a circle…"

She says: "It is the symbol of Venus, the feminine energy."

"Venus?" he says. "Aah… interesting! Is there also a symbol for masculine energy?"

"Yes," she says, handing him another cup with a different symbol, "it is Mars, you know, a circle with an arrow shooting upwards"

"Aah," says the Monkey. It's a stretch for his monkey synapses, but he manages to follow, "so energies can be indicated by symbols."

"Yes," she says, " this is exactly what I teach. Planets, Enneatypes, Chakra systems, are all magnificent tools to understand what moves us, from what inner space we relate, and what makes men and women complementary."

"Wow!" says the Monkey, "Don't you get confused with all these symbols?"

"It can become very confusing if you try to understand them with your head. But when you feel them through your heart, you simply see them as patterns of reality. The heart perceives existence through love. Love knows no judgment: it includes everything. Relationships teach you this, in joy and pain". Sadness veils her eyes for a moment. The Monkey sees it, but remains silent, in respect.

On the second day and second slice of cake, the Monkey arrives at breakfast a bit disheveled and distracted. He has been wondering during the night if there is someone special in the Lady's life. As they sip their Turkish coffee, he picks up the subject without preliminaries: "I thought you were against relationships!"

She replies with a hint of sadness: "It is not always easy"

The Monkey suddenly hesitates. He doesn't want to know.

She continues: "When love is your guiding light, you cannot use too much reason. There are never enough solid reasons for love, simply because if you analyze it, it disappears. Metaphors and symbols are more appropriate tools to convey love; they make you feel it, like when one says: 'Whenever I look at you, my heart flies like a bird rising up higher and higher'"

"That's exactly what I feel when I look at you!" the Monkey is in utter amazement, "How did you figure that out?"

The Lady laughs and says: "It is not so hard to figure out! When I see you tripping over everything and falling over your own feet."

He blushes and she smiles. They clear together the table and let go of the subject…

On the third day, at breakfast, the Monkey's Ipad sends out its soft beep: mail.

The Monkey taps the screen, and a short message in Brush Script appears. It is from the Siberian Shaman, of all people. It says:

"Dear friend, I hear from my beloved that you are doing great. You have opened your heart, which is the door to all healing. I will be shortly in Istanbul, to spend a few days with my Lady. I won't see you, but I wish you the best for this last…challenging stretch…" The Monkey is first pleased about his friend writing: he can almost hear his chuckle. But then he reads again: his beloved? His Istanbul Lady? He is suddenly intensely jealous, and feels betrayed on top of it. He is on fire, his little body tense beyond belief. The Lady looks up from her own breakfast: she sees him fuming and struggling…and she understands.

"Beloved little Monkey, love knows no boundaries, it can make a woman and a monkey feel like one. In the higher realms of Love, there are no differences. But in my body I remain a woman…and I share my life with a man. One day, it will happen to you too: you will find your partner, maybe even a few of them, to live all your dreams with. I am sure of that."

The Monkey gets shy, lowers his eyes, and fights back some tears. She does not console him; she just holds his hand in true empathy. In that silence and closeness, the Monkey lets go.

On the fourth day, the Monkey packs his backpack. Everything is washed, amongst the neatly folded clothes there is incense to keep them perfumed, and all his favorite snacks are beautifully wrapped in different cloth bags. He is ready to go now. Even though his own healing feels complete, he knows that there is still one more healer to visit, and wonders where this stretch of his quest will take place…

That evening, when they sit for their last evening meal together, he asks: "Who is the next healer? Is it also a woman? Do you know her?"

The Lady starts laughing. She says: "Do I know her? I certainly do, and I love her! She is beautiful in a different kind of way: she is a hundred percent unique."

The Monkey is trying to read through the Lady's words: "Are you telling me that she is very ugly?"

The Lady giggles, and says: "No, she is not, but she wouldn't go out of her way to please men's eyes. She is lesbian."

"A lesbian?" he says. "I don't know how to behave with lesbians…"

"She is cool. She is a Zen person: she does what she wants and shocks people into awareness. Zen people do not care at all about morals or traditions: for them, enlightenment has nothing to do with sexual preferences…Now you need to get out of my love field and wake up, little Monkey! Go to the Zen Master and get a big whack on your head, and take it back with you to the Little Buddha! So that you can both wake up!"

The Monkey is shocked by the change of her voice: from soft and sweet, it has become very strong and direct, although at the core it remains the same.

He surrenders: "I will go. Where does she live?"

"In New Zealand, a very magical place, recently discovered, vast and empty…you will learn to like it!"

When the following morning it's time for goodbyes, they both don't dare crying. Strength and focus are needed now, so they just briefly embrace and look into each other's eyes one last time. Then, she hands him an envelope, with boarding passes and documents: "Beloved friend of the heart, I will miss you. Be strong on your next adventure and let yourself be surprised. When you land in Auckland, look out for the Zen Woman. She should be there, although you cannot rely on her timing…just wait until she comes…"

And with that, she opens the door. Downstairs, the taxi is waiting: it's the same chatty guy of the Sufi radio station, this time welcoming him with a big grin…

Chapter Twentyone

ZEN: FROM NIGHTMARE TO NIRVANA

The White Essence
New Moon in Leo – Reason obscured

This time the journey feels different for the Monkey. Adventure doesn't pull him at all: he is too vulnerable, still digesting his last few days with the Lady. He realizes he has to watch out on the road.

Alone in the crowds of Istanbul airport, his usual cool is gone: he fears that all these emotions might make him too visible. But it's too late to turn back: something has woken inside him, a new passion that feels more true and important than any of his past spiritual achievements…

The flight to New Zealand is long, with a couple of dreary stopovers in airport halls that look all the same. His heart is not fully in it, he realizes, and he cringes at the idea of visiting a woman that doesn't care for men…

Nobody seems to notice him amongst the disembarking passengers: the guards don't seem to realize he is a monkey. After all, he sighs, being full of feelings does not necessarily give you away…

He gets out of the terminal a bit groggy, and is blinded by the intense morning light. A big black Porsche jeep, shining like a spaceship, is waiting for him. The driver gets out: it's the Zen Woman. He can see with his own eyes now that "unique" is the only possible way to describe her. She is at least two meters tall, muscular, and handsome in a kind of wild way. She has bleached dreadlocks and a strong boned face, sunglasses with broken frames glued together the wrong way around, and wears black pajamas with a loose cotton shirt that reveals and impressive bosom. She just stands there, her right hand dangling the car keys, looking at the Monkey with a disquieting stare…

"This can't be happening…it looks like I am not so welcome," he thinks, while fidgeting with the strap of his backpack and forcing himself to walk on.

When he reaches the jeep, he just mumbles something without looking up. Her reply doesn't do anything to improve the situation: she responds with a grunt.

"Where are we going?" he asks brusquely. She hisses something incomprehensible, opens the door and shoves him in. After a short drive through an endless stretch of scrub, she turns into the concrete car park of a huge supermarket, gets out slamming the door, and disappears without a word. The following two hours are a nightmare for the Monkey: the air is hot and sticky, he is hungry and itchy, and he is stuck in this car, without knowing how long it will take before she returns.

By the time she is back, he is simply exhausted, hardly able to sit up, his whole body in pain. She opens the door, barely looks at him and does not apologize; she just throws the shopping bags in the back seat. The car starts reeking of bruised fruits, and splattered chunks of bananas cover the floor. The Monkey is in shock: if this woman is meant to be the fourth healer, there must be something disastrously wrong with existence.

She hops with surprising agility on the driver seat, takes her sunglasses off and looks straight at him. Only now he notices the blinding blue of her eyes. Their expression is merciless: "I am not going to change the bed sheets for you," she says, "because you are a Monkey, and male monkeys are neither hygienic nor sensitive – just big showoffs."

The Monkey slumps back in the passenger seat, fuming.

Once they arrive, she shoves him out and slams the car door. He stands in front of a rickety adobe building, with a big sign on it: "Sappho's Inn". After screeching the car into the parking lot, the Zen Woman is again behind him. When they both reach the entrance door at the same time, she pushes him to the side to enter first: he doesn't give in, and they both get stuck in the opening. She curses at him in a strangely accented English, pushes him out of the way and disappears inside the building.

The Monkey stands alone and bewildered in the entrance hall, and seeing that no one is coming to either welcome or instruct him, he just sits down on one of the easy chairs scattered around until a bell rings repeatedly. "Smells like food…" he tells himself, in dire need of something warm to settle his stomach. Leaving the backpack under his chair, he gets up and roams around the building, a labyrinth of rooms and patios, until he finds the canteen, where several women are sitting around eating their evening meal.

They all lift up their gaze at the same time when he enters. He feels extremely small and uncomfortable, but won't back off from this challenge. He picks a free seat at a table with some quite pretty looking dark haired girls. As soon as he sits down, the conversation drops, and the Zen Woman appears at his side, dumping in front of him a plate of mean looking steak. "But I am a vegetarian, of course!" the Monkey shrieks his longest sentence since landing.

The Zen Woman hisses back at him: "What 'of course'? There is no 'of course' here and now! Why can't you eat meat like everybody else? Do you have to be special?"

The Monkey pushes away the plate and looks at her defiantly: "I will go without food…" cleverly thinking of the Turkish cloth bags full of delicacies in his backpack…

When everyone is gone, the Monkey, very hungry by now, reaches for his luggage under the easy chair in the hall. It's open. Nothing is missing except the food. He would like to scream. He cuddles into a little ball of despair, and falls asleep on the floor.

A couple of hours later, waking up all achy and cold, the Monkey is past any care. "Women bullshit you. Look at how it ended in Istanbul," he grunts to himself, "She was in love with the Young Shaman all along! How stupid of me to think that the Path of Love was my way! It was all a mistake…"

If it wouldn't be for his commitment towards the Little Buddha, he would leave immediately, he realizes. He is fed up with women and all their strange ways…

He climbs on one of the sofas in the reception area, and covers himself with a dusty carpet. It's pitch dark; there is no moon in the sky. The Monkey feels the darkness reaching deep into his mind, obscuring it. Halfway through the night, while tossing and turning and scratching himself angrily, he starts giving up. It's all too much: he is going to leave, first thing in the morning. Anyway, he argues, being here in this company cannot possibly be of any help to the Little Buddha. Aren't these damn women the reason for his sickness now? What with curses and fancy spells?

When the sun comes up and the hall becomes alive again, the Zen Woman comes back and offers him some grub for breakfast. He turns away, starved, refusing any contact with her. She does not even seem to notice or care. Never in his life has the Monkey experienced such anger, such disgust, and such hate towards another human being.

"She cannot be a healer!" he thinks "She is an insensitive bitch!" he mutters, with a vehemence that stuns him. "I am losing it…" he whispers. He is getting scared of his possible reactions. He has to go!

When she comes back for the plate, the Monkey tells her in a very official clipped tone: "I have decided that I am going back to the Little Buddha. I feel he really needs me. I need to go now".

"Do you expect me to take you?" she replies with another one of her incinerating gazes, "I don't have the time. If you cannot stick to the agreement, then you have to arrange your own way back. You can reserve a taxi; there is a list of telephone numbers there, on the wall. You will have to pay for your trip, I won't".

The Monkey, baring his teeth in an obviously fake smile, says: "That's fine. Thank you for whatever you have given to me already…" He dials the number for a taxi, books one, and walks out into the dusty road. He sits at the curve with his backpack, waiting. He regrets dropping out of his healing quest, but there is no way he can continue.

After some time, a taxi stops in front of him. The driver is a man, the first other male he sees after twenty-four hours of being mistreated by women. The Monkey is really relieved. The Taxi Driver smiles at him in a friendly way; there seems to be an instant rapport between them: while settling the Monkey's backpack in the trunk, he even whispers: "They should lock them all up!" The Monkey is surprised at how glad he is to hear it. He has always considered himself as a kind person, but now he is loudly laughing with the Taxi Driver…

Just as they are ready to go, there is a commotion at the entrance of the Inn. The Zen Woman walks out like a fury, stomps to the taxi, opens the trunk, takes out the Monkey's backpack and throws it into the bushes.

"The vile Monkey can walk!" she hisses to the Taxi Driver, who is now shivering under her intimidating stare, "You take my two friends now, they need to be at work this afternoon, and don't try to cheat me with your money! I know you fucking male taxi drivers…". She turns to the Monkey and without really looking at him she grunts from the side of her mouth: "Get out of my way and walk!"

The Monkey sees red. All his restraint and watching are gone…every fiber of his body is inflamed with pure rage. He jumps up, and with a piercing shriek runs and he grabs her throat in a flash, closing his strong hands around it. Suddenly, the large hand of the Zen Woman whacks him on the head with full might. As soon as the Monkey, stunned, lets go of her throat, the Zen Woman lets out a mind shattering sound that pierces through the air: "QWATZ!"

Absolute silence follows. It is like the eternal silence of the Himalayas. All emotions have evaporated, like clouds that cannot obscure the luminous peaks for long.

Nobody is moving; even the Taxi Driver has stopped. In that gap, something happens to the Monkey: he feels a brilliant, diamond-like awareness rising. It's pure and sharp, and pervades all and everything. It is the essence of Zen.

The Zen Woman is the first to move. She looks straight at the Monkey. As soon as their eyes meet, the Monkey experiences a new kind of love, a much cooler one… He has never felt anything like this, anywhere. It feels like falling with arms wide open, in trust, like a homecoming. When he finally turns away from her and looks at her friends, they all appear sweet and innocent, like freshly bathed babies.

Then daily life takes over again, but the feeling of peace remains in the background, less intense and more embedded in ordinariness. They all go for lunch together, the Monkey, the Zen Woman, the Taxi Driver (who is in fact a friend of hers), her two friends (in reality two seekers that are just about to start a Zen retreat under her guidance), and the Zen Woman.

The table is prepared with extreme care for details. There are small vases of wild flowers and colorful plates with native design, and the food is macrobiotic, purely made out of biological veggies and grains. There is much silence while they eat, just some minimal conversation and many smiles. The Monkey is seated on the right of the Zen Woman, who picks the most delicious bits of food for him, and puts them on his plate.

After lunch, he is shown to his room, a beautiful space with a view over the wide green hills of New Zealand, with that same quiet and collected atmosphere as around the table. Nothing can disturb him; everything is just perfect as it is.

He rests peacefully, and for the first time in ages he has a dreamless sleep until dusk. One of the women, a small and brisk lady, gently awakens him with a lovely twinkle in her eyes: "you are invited to our meditation practice before the evening meal", she says, pointing in the direction of a large open space in the backyard, surrounded by bamboos and covered by a strong canvas that elegantly stretches in the four directions.

He can feel its sacredness as soon as he enters the place. All the women are sitting in serene composure, their backs straight and the shadow of a smile on their lips. He takes the empty place near the Zen Woman, closes his eyes, and is instantly pervaded by a sweet feeling of lightness and surrender. The wind softly picks up, the leaves quietly whoosh on the roof, and a distant cuckoo calls. He is at home on the path of meditation. Now there is no longer a dilemma in him: he has experienced that love and meditation are not two separate paths; they are more like two streams leading to the same ocean…

The evening meal is full of laughter and jokes. The Monkey realizes that, even when the women tease him, he can take it good naturedly, and can also tease back. It all feels no more than pretty ripples in a quiet lake, because he is in the company of fellow seekers that he can trust.

When the meal is finished, in the satisfied afterglow, the Monkey clears his throat, and asks the Zen Master the question that has been buzzing on and off inside him since the morning: "Why "QWATZ!"?"

She answers: "There is no reason. "QWATZ!" is just a sound that works. It cuts through the split that we carry inside. In our minds, everything is divided into compartments by an inner invisible wall. Sometimes it feels like a glass wall, that keeps us separate from the world around us. Even if sometimes it is very dirty and foggy, we still can look through it, and this will affect how we see things on the other side. But we can't ever feel real behind this wall, and the world remains out of our reach. The truth is that we are not really separate: the glass wall is our mind that wants to protect itself from disappearing… "QWATZ!" shatters this glass wall and brings us into reality…suddenly, two opposite poles bang into one sound, a sound that bears no comparison to anything our mind knows already. Having no way to associate this experience with past experiences, the mind completely stops, and for that moment there is just emptiness, no content. We stop searching for a solution to our non-existent dilemma."

He is really impressed, and his overenthusiastic monkey nature wants to put this immediately to test: "QWATZ!" he says, "Thank you! Do you think that if I shouted it very loud it would work, even for me?"

The Zen Woman laughs, but she replies seriously: "Little Monkey, don't play around with these things! You saw what happened to you, when I brought your anger to a peak: it just was a matter of seconds before you would strangle me, and just then I shouted… this is the Zen way: it's not so easy to simply stop the mind, you need to bring it to its extreme before, and that is a risk not to be taken lightly, even for an enlightened Monkey like you. It's a question of timing: if you do it at the wrong moment, it can drive people crazy… These are sacred methods. Pass them on to those that deserve them, pass them on to the Little Buddha, and explain about all of us healers and about the different methods we use to reach to our innermost core. But don't entertain yourself or others with them. Please respect."

For a moment, the Monkey feels really embarrassed about being an enlightened soul with a monkey mind…Then he remembers: it was his choice for this life to leave the safe path of being a monk and embrace his "lower" animal nature. Now, true to that nature, his monkey mind will never give up jumping, like from tree to tree, from one truth to the next.

The following morning he wakes up to the soft peep of his Ipad: there is an email from the Indigo Couple: the Little Buddha, still weak, seems to have regained a spark of life. He has gotten out of his retreat in the Hut, and for the first time is asking to help in the house. The Monkey smiles at the simplicity of life, and how vitality often returns through ordinary chores, like carrying water and chopping wood…

Just then, the Zen Woman comes into his room and shows him a little cloth bag: "This is for the Little Buddha. What's inside is very precious. There are people who would do anything to steal it, but you must remember that it is specially made for him," she says, pausing to nail him with her penetrating blue gaze, "If someone tries to take it away, the thief will die instantly."

The Monkey takes the bag, and feels again the noble weight of his responsibility: it suits him. He asks: "Can I look at it?" She nods. After untying the multiple knots, he stares at the content resting in the palm of his hand: it is the purest white diamond he has ever seen, sharp and shining as the consciousness awakened in him by the "QWATZ!".

"Tell him to wear it on his forehead at night. It favors the expansion of the White Essence, which stands for presence and awareness."

The Monkey is flooded with gratefulness and falls on his knees in front of her. He whispers: "I am sorry for doubting you! I am sorry I was so righteous and inflexible…I was still busy with my unrequited love for the Istanbul Lady, I am still feeling hopeless and rejected, as if life had no mean…."

She cuts him in mid sentence, looks at him with a lovely smile and says: "This, too, will pass!", and then shouts again "QWATZ!". Everything stops. When after a few eternal seconds activity resumes, the Monkey, with his eyes still closed, thinks to himself: "It is as if she has found a way to switch the light on and off, there is no other way to describe it…"

When he opens his eyes, both the Zen Woman and the diamond have vanished. He is on his own when he literally hears the Zen Woman talking inside him: "The final remedy for the Little Buddha will emerge out of the combined magic of each one of the four healers. Just like in a diamond, there are many facets to the healing, all reflecting the same light…"

The Zen Woman is there again when he reaches the entrance door, his backpack on one shoulder, ready to leave with the Taxi Driver. She hands him the cloth bag, now again carefully and tightly knotted, and calls him aside: "I have a special personal message for your friend, the Little Buddha. But wait until the right moment to deliver it: you will know when."

Tell him: 'your son is doing well. After a lifetime of destroying the same Monasteries that you cherished so much, and going to battle dressed up as a woman, he moved on through many other lifetimes. One day, he found Zen as a way to stop his mind, and realized that he had come home. He has now reincarnated in the form that best suits him to transcend the duality of his mind: a Zen Woman'." Unperturbed by the Monkey's puzzlement, she continues: "You may not yet understand, but the Little Buddha will. Now I have reached where I wanted to be and I can feel grateful to him. Tell him that I bow down to him. He is not my father any longer, and I am no longer his son. We are simply emptiness."

The Monkey is for a moment confused. But then, he remembers. Could that be…

But when he looks up, the Zen Woman is just the Zen Woman, a rare and fierce beauty. He replies: "I will tell the Little Buddha, and I am sure he will be grateful. Maybe this will help to set him free."

He lets himself be enveloped by the embrace of the Zen Woman: it smells like earth, veggies, incense and air…he lingers for a moment, and then steps into the car.

Just as the door is closing behind him, he hears her giggling in an amused voice: "More surprises are on the way…"

They ride in silence for a while, the Monkey and the man, enjoying the vastness of the landscape and each other's company. The Monkey is just dozing off when his inner sense of timing jars him out of his reverie: they have driven past the airport, and are now heading towards a completely deserted stretch of fields. He wants to say something, but he is afraid of falling back into his old mistrust. The Taxi Driver reads his mind: "Do not worry, little friend, we are heading in the right direction. You will fly home sooner than you know…"

The stretch ahead seems endless and empty…except for a glimmering object in the far distance.

As they drive closer, the Monkey cannot believe his eyes: his Watermelon Mobile, polished and serviced, is waiting for him. He feels the call of home in his bones, in his heart, and his soul is dancing!!!

As they stop, he can barely contain himself. The Taxi Driver smiles appreciatively and compliments his vehicle. The little Monkey, free to give space to his male nature, nods proudly and answers a few technical questions.

After shaking hands and giving each other a bear hug, the Monkey is standing there alone, waving the car off, and breathing in the open space, infinite with possibilities.

He then examines his vehicle, sits inside the comfortable padded seat and notices a large envelope resting on the dashboard close to the touch screen. He opens it and starts reading:

"Beloved little Monkey, you have successfully finished your part of the quest, and the transmission we gave you is complete in itself. Now carry back our gifts and remedies to the Little Buddha.

Meanwhile, we will continue to communicate amongst us until we agree upon the complex nature of the final remedy which will be an amulet.

The amulet will be ready for you on the Full Moon in Pisces, a bit less than a month and a half away from now. It will be delivered at the home of the Indigo Couple. It will come in a little golden box with purple amethysts on top. You will need to open it exactly at the moment when the full moon starts rising above the mountains. At that auspicious time, our four essences will merge into the object that the box contains. You will need to place the amulet on the Little Buddha's neck, and healing will happen. Just remember that if anybody destroys or steals it there will be great disaster and great pain. But do not fear: we will protect you.

Be blessed

Your older brothers and sisters

PS For the next three days, we want you to take a good rest with your Monkey Tribe, and your monkey parents: you need to get nourished and recovered before the next stretch of journey…. Afterwards, go back to the Greek Island: after one more week of rest there, you and the Little Buddha will attend a meditative process in the center of the Controversial Master nearby: it is called the Mystic Rose, and it is a deeply cleansing and revitalizing process. It will create the right ground for the final healing."

The Monkey sheds a tear or two: he will miss all of them, with their colorful methods and above all with their wondrous souls…

He is also surprised how happy it makes him to have a holiday with his family, and how hungry his body is for some intense cuddling up monkey-style…

Chapter Twentytwo

LAUGHTER AND TEARS

Full Moon in Aquarius – Friends

Refreshed, and a few kilos rounder after his visit to the Monkey Tribe on the Little Planet, the Monkey is now ready to go home to the Indigo Land. Sitting into his sparkly Watermelon Mobile, which has been highly polished by his many cousins, he opens the envelope from the 4 Healers and reads it again. He wonders about the meditative process. He has been a few times with the Indigo Couple at the Center of the Controversial Master, and liked the people there. Let's see… he tells himself, happily tapping his touch screen for takeoff.

Leaning forward from his vehicle to take in the deep blue of the Aegean Sea, the Monkey is elated. It's sunrise, and the first seagulls are going fishing, letting out their screeches into the new day. He deeply inhales the iodine air, as refreshing as any shower, and gets ready for his descent.

He can catch whiffs of coffee and honey pastry from the sea village nearby, and the sounds of humanity waking up. He takes a sharp turn towards the golden hills, framed by the red mountains behind, and lets the Watermelon Mobile float downwards, until it lands gently in the open space near the orchard of the Indigo Couple. The inhabitants of the cottage are awake, and both the Indigo Man and the Indigo Woman run to greet the Monkey. After a short moment, the pale face of the Little Buddha peeps from the Zen Hut… he is smiling.

Many hugs and tears follow. The Indigo Woman silently takes indoors the monkey's dirty backpack and reemerges from the house with a tray of delicious smoothies. Everyone settles under the shady pergola overlooking the rose path.

The Monkey looks upon his friends with utter tenderness.

"Your eyes," notices the Indigo Man, "they seem wiser."

"I can feel around you the presence of the healers you met," adds the Indigo Woman, lowering her head in a bow.

The Monkey can clearly see that the Little Buddha is feeling better; still smiling, he asks him questions about his journey. As he starts answering, he can feel the change in the air: there is hope.

After a few anecdotes and descriptions of the different countries he has visited, the Monkey shows everyone the latest message of the Four: "In one month from now, at Full Moon, the final healing amulet will be presented to the Little Buddha in a golden box…."

The Indigo Woman smiles at the mention of the Mystic Rose: "We have done this process. It's wonderful, I love it. It is a deep cleaning: you will find yourself laughing and crying about your whole life and beyond it…"

The Indigo Man chuckles: "Sometimes it is hell…sitting there waiting for something to laugh and cry about, but then…what a joy when laughter or tears start coming down like waterfalls, leaving you afterwards clean and fresh…"

The Little Buddha softly speaks: "I remember when what seems like ages ago I received the CHARAVEDI note…I would have never imagined to learn so much about myself. Just before receiving it, I thought my journey was complete, and nothing would ever change any more…" His expression is older than his looks, when he says: "I am ready to open up to the new. I have come all this way to learn something…"

The Monkey, suddenly no longer tired from the journey, feels very happy and excited. He gives himself full freedom to jump up and down, animal style, causing general laughter.

The Indigo Woman adds: "The Mystic Rose will start in one week, and will end exactly the day before the next Full Moon…perfect…"

When the first nightingales start their melodious calls and a majestic Full Moon rises from the hills, the Little Buddha and the Monkey are alone in the Zen Hut. The Indigo Couple has prepared a comfortable bed with soft blankets for the Monkey next to the Little Buddha's. A beautiful wooden vase full of fruits and nuts is displayed on the coffee table. The air is pregnant with the night scents, and it's as if a golden glow surrounds them.

In the intimacy of that moment, the Monkey starts sharing with his friend about the Lady in Istanbul. He tells him about the rivers of tears they shed, sometimes alone and sometimes together, holding each other: "Our bodies were releasing layer after layer of forgotten pains, and meanwhile our souls were grieving for the for the whole of humanity. I slowly disappeared: the toughness that kept me aloof from all that is tender in life went away. I felt completely defenseless…" After a long sigh, he adds: "And that was just the honeymoon: when I came to realize that she was in love with someone else I even had to let go of my possessiveness, and that hurt…"

The Little Buddha is listening very keenly: it is different to hear about love from his enlightened friend. Seeing so many people suffering for love, he has always assumed that love causes suffering. But now the Monkey is talking about a higher love, which causes bliss: embracing the pain into one's heart and letting it stay there until it transforms itself into compassion …

"I can see the transformation in your eyes," he says, "When I look into them I remember something that has to do with mother and woman, a soft and warm area that I have not touched for a very long time…" for a moment, the Little Buddha remembers again his past life and sighs, "Something is incomplete, still… but also something new is happening…"

The Monkey can see a new longing in his friend's eyes and chortles: "You are starting to miss women…"

The next morning, the Little Buddha feels as if he is waking up to a whole new world. Everything inside him feels fresh and cleansed like after a big storm.

The Monkey is already up. He has taken one of the easy chairs and is reclining in the early morning sun. His slightly perked ears indicate that he is not sleeping, but guarding. From time to time, he opens one eye and looks left and right. When he sees his friend coming towards him, he opens his eyes and smiles at him with some concern.

"Don't worry, my friend, it's looking up, I am getting better..." the Little Buddha tells him. Let's share some breakfast and then it's my turn to talk…"

"I want to tell you how it was for me to receive the curse," the Little Buddha says a bit later, putting down his empty bowl.

"When it fell on me, I disintegrated. Suddenly, everything went blank and I lost consciousness. When I came back, I felt as if my will to live had been robbed from me."

The Monkey is devastated. Guilt and shame are written all over his face: for not being quick enough to protect him, for naively thinking that he could…

"But this is the way, my friend," the Little Buddha tells him, "most of the times what seems like a misfortune is leading us instead exactly where we have to go. Without the curse, you would not have accomplished your magical quest, and I would not have stopped long enough to feel that my heart needs healing…"

Healing…the word brings the Monkey instantly out of his collapse: he remembers the very important news…

"Now I have to tell you something", he says, "which I didn't feel safe to write about. My beloved Lady of Istanbul is not Turkish: her family is from Persia. She has an aunt…" and tells whole story of the curse, and how the Belladonna herself is the only one that knows how remove it. "But this is going to be difficult," he concludes, "because we strongly suspect she might be the queen of your past life…"

A long silence follows: "Yes, she might well be…" the little Buddha answers. No further explanations are needed.

In the days that follow, the two friends slowly resume their philosophical walks around the orchard in between long rests. The Indigo Couple watches over them from the cottage, meeting them only occasionally, when she brings them food, or when he goes to sit with them for a little while, mainly in silence. The peacefulness of everyday life on the island gently hums around them, and everyone rejoices in it.

The day before the beginning of the Mystic Rose, while they are sitting in the shade of the oak tree, the Monkey whispers in a conspiratorial tone to the Little Buddha: "I think I had enough of crying for a while. I wish I could skip the first two stages of the process and go straight to the last stage, one week of just peacefully watching…I like that! I could just sit here under the pergola and look into the valley. But then, knowing myself, in the end I would get bored…"

"Charavedi…" giggles the Little Buddha, and adds, "You can't skip them! I read the description: first you laugh for a week: that frees up all the rigidity in your system, then you cry for another week, and let's see if there is nothing more for you to cry about…"

The Monkey sighs. The Little Buddha is obviously getting stronger: he has not been teasing him like this since very long, "I know, I know, there is still much to cry about…" he replies, lowering his eyes…

"It's because of these two parts that the silent sitting in the third stage goes so deep. It's unencumbered…"

"Seriously?" the Monkey asks with a glimmer in his eyes. Unexpectedly, he jumps up and starts tickling the Little Buddha, who tries to stop him at first, and then lets go into a whoop of giggles. Then he starts making all sorts of funny and distorted faces that make the Little Buddha roll on the floor with laughter. In the end, he jumps over him, and they both lie in a heap, spent. Their bodies are tingling, and their silence feels alive, fresh, clean. When they help each other up after a while, they are convinced: this Controversial Master must be a genius.

A day later, at the gate of the Meditation Center, they are welcomed by an alive buzz: people are meeting and hugging everywhere. In this colorful crowd of seekers, the two friends do not particularly stick out. Everyone knows them anyway from the Evening Meditation…Soon it's time: they all gather in a tower like round room with a circular view on the fields and the distant sea. The meditation leaders, a young and tall couple whose smell the Monkey finds delicious like fresh fruits and nuts, make a brief introduction, after which everyone launches themselves into laughter. "Just like this…" says the Monkey to the Little Buddha, and it's the beginning of endless series of giggles for the rest of the first session.

On the second day, sitting in his corner of the room and doing his best not to feel the ache in his jaws, the Little Buddha starts realizing how serious his past life as a king has made him: since then, he has been subtly punishing himself and retreating from life, without even knowing why…

But there is no way for him to keep suffering in an overheated roomful of colorful people, all crazed by laughter. How to remain unaffected by the fat laughter of a voluptuous Greek woman, or by the melancholic giggle of a sunburnt Northerner? Slowly slowly, he opens up. He finds himself laughing about his own saintliness, and about his tendency to anticipate disaster…

Meanwhile, the Monkey is having a ball, jumping from one person to another, clinging, scratching, pinching. Everyone laughs with him, and together they laugh about the meditation leaders, who in their turn fall over on the floor with laughter just by looking at the Monkey, who has meanwhile started swinging over the beams. He is finally free to be a monkey! For him this is a miracle, since he has never felt free to fully behave like one because of being already enlightened at birth. Now for the first time he is just like all the other monkeys: shrieking, running around, laughing hysterically, teasing those who try to hard and get red in their faces, repeating "ha, ha, ha" methodically, who then can't help really laughing. Initially, he remains a bit careful with the Little Buddha, but when he notices him laughing and playing with others, he feels the beginning of a deeper friendship between them, a more intimate connection than the loyalty he always felt towards him. It's physical, warm, like two male friends relaxing with each other.

On the third day, the Little Buddha has to laugh about how scared of women he has always felt. The women here are not scary at all: they are shrieking in bliss with laughter…he goes to each one of them and laughs with all of them. But when the session is over, he has a big setback: he feels deeply ashamed of having been such a coward. For the rest of the day, he takes distance from everyone at home, including the Monkey. He needs time to experience the shame to be able to let it go.

But it doesn't last long. The following day, enjoyment replaces shame. He really likes these women, all of them…An elfin blond girl looks at him and bursts into peals of laughter, and he starts laughing back, just happy to experience that there is no longer a wall of separation between him and her or any of these women…

For a moment, he starts thinking of what he knows about the Mystic Union, the meeting of male and female…and then realizes that these holy thoughts are again creating a wall between himself and the warm funny people around him. A deeper laughter, a compassionate one, springs from his heart: he smiles for all the past seekers like himself, too busy with the Absolute to notice that human beings are its most precious manifestation.

New Moon in Virgo – Turning Inwards

On the seventh day of laughter, the Little Buddha regrets that this is the last day. He feels full of life. But then, when that night he retreats in the Zen Hut, a shift seems to happen by itself. In the stillness of the invisible New Moon, he feels that his energy is changing direction: it's moving inwards.

When the crying starts the next day, weeping comes as a relief to everyone in the room.

Again just a brief introduction by the meditation leaders, and tears start rolling. Everyone lies or sits on soft mattresses. There is not much relating: all are searching for their forgotten tears.

The Little Buddha is ready to cry. Gently loosened by the laughter, his soft belly and heart have many tears to release.

He cries for the pain he caused to his Queen, for the loneliness of his path, for all the times he silenced his heart, for all the teachings he missed, for all the times he hurt and got hurt, for the hate he saw in the eyes of the woman who cursed him… He tries also to cry for the Monkey, but he ends up instead smiling at him, on the other side of the room, just to be reminded by the meditation leaders that the focus is on crying.

Meanwhile, on the third day, the Monkey is hitting upon some deep resistance. He compares this experience with his time in Istanbul: suddenly, everyone here looks fake. Nobody, he is sure, would resist one of his pranks… The other participants start looking disturbed about his smile and jokes. The Little Buddha, a bit embarrassed, finally signals him to stop. The Monkey retreats in a sulk.

After the session is finished, the Little Buddha sits next to the Monkey and puts his arm around him.

The Monkey lets out a deep sigh.

"It's not that I cannot cry," he says, "I have cried plenty, recently…" and hiding his head in the nook of the Little Buddha's shoulder, he deeply sobs for one last time about his Lady.

The next day, the meditation leaders invite everyone to sit around them. The man starts talking: "We would like to share with you how acceptance is the key to this process. There is no guideline to how tears come and how many there should be…"

The woman continues: "I sometimes get caught up in wanting things to run the way I think they should. It's a great pain", she adds, tears welling her eyes.

Everyone is so touched by their sincerity that people are crying even before the bells ring.

This time the crying seems to go deeper for everyone.

The Little Buddha cries because he misses Shambala, and weeps for the strange destiny of the Twelve, whose task seems to keep everyone moving, except themselves. He cries for his and everyone's loss of trust in enlightenment, for the dark night of the soul…

Suddenly, he stops at the realization that his chronic boredom in Shambala has been covering the pain of leaving his beloved behind. He needs intimacy.

He doesn't want to become a recluse.

When he starts weeping again, his warm tears touch and melt a cold and dark place in his heart. He feels the warmth spreading through his body, and it's pleasurable.

After four days, the collective quality of the crying goes through a quantum leap.

The Little Buddha is no longer crying for himself. He feels part of a universal heart together with everyone present. Everyone is crying out the pain of the whole planet.

As the sobs become progressively softer, the atmosphere in the room becomes sacred. The pain has turned into a sweet sensation, almost like a blessing.

The Monkey stays close to the Little Buddha; they often weep together without having to share why. It's not needed: they know each other so well by now that they have become like one soul.

At the end of the crying, the Little Buddha feels more relaxed than he ever felt in his entire life, as if the big burden he has grown used to carry has been removed from him. He has released many impressions and old feelings, none of which are worth remembering any longer: they are all gone with the tears.

The Monkey's last tears are spent in gratefulness for the Raidas family, which has created his Little Planet, and for being allowed this life as an animal…"

In the silence that follows, he hears a message, spoken out with authority by a sweetly American accented female voice: "One day, beloved Monkey, you will meet again many of your kind, with your same courage and curiosity. You will see with your own eyes that enlightenment is not just a human privilege, but that it is everywhere. Every living being has the potential to become enlightened…"

Just then, the bells ring to end the crying stage. A shy smile appears on his face, and when nobody stops him, it becomes a huge beaming grin. He feels it from the inside, like sunshine rising through the thick foliage of the Jungle.

For the Monkey and the Little Buddha both, the third week of sitting silently and watching feels like a homecoming. In the peaceful silence of the countryside, highlighted by the occasional tingling of sheep bells and shrieking of seagulls, they gracefully ease themselves into the sitting. It's a peaceful time. By just sitting together for many hours, a special sense of intimacy grows between all the participants.

"I told you he is a genius," the Monkey whispers to the Little Buddha on the last day.

"I agree. There is too much mental activity in the modern world to be able to just sit down and watch. The Controversial Master knows this humanity well," the Little Buddha says, "and he realizes that it needs to de-stress and understand how its mind functions before it's too late…"

At the end of the group, there is a big celebration in the open-air bar of the Center. Light music is played, and people linger on just to catch the afterglow of their experience together. Before going home, everyone receives an invitation, handed by the Monkey, for a Full Moon party at the Indigo Land in two days. "Many of the local friends are also invited. It is going to be a special healing event..." he says, without giving away any details, "You will be surprised..."

It's already dark when the Little Buddha and the Monkey come home. The Indigo Couple has already gone to bed. Thousands of frogs are singing full heartedly their symphonies. The moon is rising, almost full. "Forty eight hours to go..." whispers the Little Buddha.

The Monkey, trying to hide his worry and excitement, answers coolly: "Oh, really?"

Chapter Twentythree

THE FINAL HEALING

Full Moon in Pisces – Healing into Oneness

"Being stuck in the early morning traffic jam on the ring road around Paris under a violent rain does not exactly feel very promising as a start" the Istanbul Lady thinks, while sitting in a cab from Charles De Gaulle Airport towards Montmartre. She is in a hurry: only twelve hours to go before Full Moon…

For the whole month, the four healers have been pooling all their resources to create the healing amulet for the Little Buddha.

In the beginning, the Young Shaman got everyone's attention by posting on his Facebook page a cryptic statement: "More light is required to heal light…" It didn't take long before the other three understood: their usual methods would not be enough for someone so spiritually advanced as the Little Buddha.

"Call upon your spiritual resources, brothers…" the Zen Woman had replied, while the Peruvian Shaman had posted a video clip of a Tibetan chant, commenting: "May all our spiritual guides stand by us and create a vast field of healing…" The Istanbul Lady had added a short: "Inch' Allah" to the post. With that, all four had launched themselves in their favorite spiritual practices, which were many and from all over the world.

The Lady from Istanbul, in spite of being a Sufi at heart, had made a special place in her room for a very simple Buddha statue, and sat silently in front of it every morning, letting all the noise of the city recede. Every single time she looked at the way the Buddha sat gracefully in meditation, she felt a great tenderness in her heart.

Through prayer and practice, the field of light around each one of the four healers has been growing like a golden halo. And the amulet is now almost ready…

"Almost…" the Istanbul Lady sighs, still sitting in her taxi, surrounded by a cross fire of horns and pelting hail…

The amulet is now with the Young Shaman, waiting to be shipped from Siberia to Greece. It looks really precious and powerful. But it doesn't work.

An almost invisible circle of yellowish vapor creates a field of pollution around it. They have tried everything: the cloud almost evaporates, but always returns full force.

"It's because of the curse…" the Istanbul Lady has told them in a hasty videoconference last night, "That yellow ring is poison!" It's the first time she actually sees the Zen Woman crying.

"I am going to Paris," she concluded, already typing in a search for an early flight to France, "I am going to confront my aunt…"

The traffic is easing as they enter a large boulevard, lined with majestic trees. It's still early, and the Cafés are just opening, while a constant trickle of people surfaces from the elegant looking Metro Station exits, with their rounded cast iron and glass. As they drive on, the streets become narrower, paved in cobblestones. Left and right, high steps lead up to even smaller streets, like in a maze. Looking at the lines of stalls on the ancient pavements, selling sheets and linen, or prints and old books, the Lady is reminded of her own area of Istanbul, where ancient whispers hide in every corner…

Finally, the taxi stops off a small square with paved floor. Some artists are setting up their canvases and easels for painting and exhibiting their ware to the tourists that will show up in a little while. But at this time of the morning it's still quiet: there are only a few locals up and about, whistling their way across the square and carrying fresh baguettes under their armpits.

The driver tilts his head in the direction of a small alley closed to the traffic and mumbles something about "la rue"…

It's a relief to be standing outside the cab, breathing in the fresh morning air, after such a rush…the Lady takes a moment to relax in the pale sun, and then moves towards the alley.

Her aunt's home is on the third floor of an old building, perched on a slope. Once through the main entrance, she is surrounded by the plush comfort of artful renovation. Everything is elegant, classy in an understated way. The Lady is at home here: since teenage, this has been her refuge countless times. It was to her aunt that she would go when things were getting difficult for her as a woman in Turkey. Her aunt has been her door into the wider world…

The Belladonna, still in her silk dressing gown, is surprised to find her niece at the door of her apartment, standing there, looking a bit frazzled.

But as customs amongst educated Eastern women commands, no mention is made of this. They first embrace, and then go through the welcoming ritual of tea and biscuits. Talking will come when everyone feels at home.

Throughout all of it, our Lady keeps on reminding herself to breathe. She relaxes a bit with the familiar smell of jasmine tea and the cinnamon taste of the biscuits, but another part of her remains in high alarm. She knows that time is running out, and all depends on what will happen in the next few minutes.

She manages to appear interested when the Belladonna shows her on a huge home cinema screen a beautiful clip of her work with women in a remote region of Africa. She even manages to ask a few questions here and there…

After all pleasantries are completed, the deep green eyes of the Belladonna suddenly turn towards her in her typical fierce way, which reassures whomever she protects and terrifies her enemies… "Why are you here, my dear?" she asks, with a loving smile on her lips…

The Lady hesitates for a moment: she wonders if she has been fabricating this whole story and nothing of it is real. Maybe her aunt is just the courageous and outspoken woman that she has always known…

But then, she replies: "Do you know anything about a childlike being that goes by the name of Little Buddha?"

"Childlike! Playing little boys is one of the worst forms of manipulation that men inflict on women. It's a scam to seduce them into slaving for them!"

The Lady is shocked back into awareness: the charge in her Aunt's voice is proof enough of her involvement…

"Do I take this as a yes?" the Lady keeps going, a bit scared of her aunt's volatile moods.

"Yes, he was one of the worst examples of this, but I think I set him right…"

"You? Did you curse him?"

"My child, it's not the first time and it won't be the last that these ancient methods are used to put a stop to male arrogance… It was time to expose his pretenses, and I did…but don't worry, it's after all just like a scorpion's sting…"

Suddenly, the Lady feels nauseous. She can almost taste her aunt's sourness in her own mouth: "Scorpion sting? He is dying! You cannot curse an enlightened being!!!!"

"He is not enlightened, he just pretends!" the Belladonna hisses back, her face distorted and her eyes glazed. She is clearly out of reach.

The Lady steps back, and takes a long, deep breath and looks lovingly at her: "Aunt of mine, I need to tell you that you are and have always been my favorite Aunt. You protected me, you were my ideal: I wanted to become like you. I am afraid that what I am going to say now will alter our connection, but I have to take this risk… I am doing it out of love."

The Belladonna finally looks at her and nods. Taking a step forward, the Lady starts: "In all respect, I give you back the burden of revenge. From this moment, I take the risk to step out of the circle of women that are known as the Belladonna. I open myself up to a new system, where men are accepted as friends and fellow travelers on the path…"

It all comes in one wave. As she symbolically puts at the feet of her Aunt the burden of revenge, the Lady hears a very loud static crackle. She looks up, and sees in front of her an explosion of yellow particles, flying around like volcanic ashes: they hang in the air and then gather, forming a sentence which the Lady has barely the time to read before it dissolves: "Qued por Staz! Refus ad Morpad!"

When the sparks cool off, a silvery dust lingers on and dances itself for a brief moment into the word: "Love", vanishing after one heartbeat. Then, the air becomes transparent again, leaving the room fresh and light.

The Lady understands: the ring of the curse has been broken. By stepping out of the circle of the Belladonna, she has altered the system, and created an opening for love to enter. Now healing is possible. She can only do one thing now: run back to Istanbul, as fast as she can, to the safety of her home.

She is already sitting in a cab towards the airport when she texts the other three healers, and receives confirmation of the final disappearance of the yellow ring of vapor around the amulet.

Meanwhile, the Belladonna has remained standing in the middle of her apartment, completely dazed. The rage has left her, vanished in thin air, and in that disappearance her whole world has burst like a bubble. It is as if now she sees herself from above as a dance of light particles creating patterns…She feels weightless, and disorientated… and strangely free…

Everything she has gathered around her all these years seems meaningless: the beautiful antiques, the trophies, the photos of smiling women and babies…She has only one thing in mind: "I must see him. I must go there".

The sense of disassociation doesn't leave her even when she boards her plane to Athens. People notice her because she is very pale and a bit absent, but then decide that she must simply be another one of those eccentric ladies living in Paris…

That same morning, back at the Indigo Land, the lifting of the spell is unconsciously felt by all: it is as if a new wave of fresh energy fills up the place. Preparations for the final healing ceremony for the Little Buddha have started the day before already, but until this morning, everyone was stressed and distracted. The soup got spilled, a few cups got broken, and not much was accomplished. By the end of the day, they all had gone to bed feeling exhausted.

Today everyone moves around smiling. "Some major shift must have occurred somewhere," the Indigo Man says, polishing his collection of crystals for the ceremony.

"It must have. I haven't felt this happy for a long long time…" says the Indigo Woman, rearranging the flower pots in the courtyard.

"I am glad that we decided to have this party. Remember how in the beginning we were worried, and the Indigo Woman had to convince us to do it?" the Little Buddha tells the Monkey, while they move around little tables and easy chairs in the shady corners of the property, "Having many friends is new to me, but I don't need to worry. I have cried and laughed already with most of them…"

"And they come from all over the world…which means that they are going to bring all kind of exotic plates for the buffet!" The happiness has made the Monkey hungry, not only for food but also for life, "and so many exotic beauties, and so many live performances…"

The morning unfolds in an easy flow. From the open windows of the cottage, sweet music accompanies all four friends while they go about their chores. The Indigo Woman is inside, preparing a light snack; the Monkey and the Indigo Man are carrying rattles and crystals to the Zen Hut for the Full Moon ritual. But as noon approaches, everyone becomes increasingly busy with the amulet: how, and when, will it come? By now no one doubts that it will, but waiting is not easy…

The Little Buddha is watering the orchard. While regulating the watering drips at the roots of the small sturdy fruit trees, he has time to review his last two months after the curse. It has been a deep process. Whatever coldness or aloofness was left in him has been erased forever. He experiences in his body and soul a warmth that wasn't there before. Thanks to the healing powders of the Shamans, the cleansing effect of the Mystic Rose, and the unconditional love of the Monkey and the Indigo Couple, he can already deal much better with the devastation that the curse has provoked in his body and mind. Now the amulet will eradicate it completely from his system.

Just then, the Indigo Woman emerges from the house, calling and smiling and waving her Ipad for everyone to see…the three interrupt their activities and gather around her to listen: "The healing amulet has been successfully completed. It will be delivered to you today, late afternoon. Prepare yourselves as best as your hearts tell you to. With all our love and power, the Four Healers. PS The method of delivery will be unusual."

From this moment onwards, a feeling of sacredness descends on the land: every movement, every breath of our four friends becomes full of focus and intention: everyone wants to stay as present as possible.

As the heat of the day wears off into a golden afternoon, the distant splutter of some local mopeds announces the arrival of the Mystic Rose friends. A colorful group of all ages and nationalities, they dismount their vehicles and immediately start helping. Trees are decorated with festoons and colorful sarongs that flap in the soft breeze, and a big table for food and drinks is placed under one of the almond trees in a corner of the courtyard. In no time, a unique cocktail of scents and fragrances fills the air: the comforting smell of German potato salad, mixed with Greek fried pastry and honey, embracing the sweet and sour smell of a Chinese dish. The banquet table is a feast for the eyes: fresh salad bowls, full of green herbs and red tomatoes and vases of bright violet and pink zinnias glow in the late afternoon sun.

The rest of the courtyard is left empty for dancing, and a special stage on an upper terrace is created for the musicians that will play live.

All is in place before sunset. As the mountains in the background start turning pink, everyone gathers in the empty courtyard, sitting in a circle.

The Indigo Couple greets everyone: "Beloved friends and neighbors, tonight is a very special night. You are invited to be part of a great healing event. If you contribute to it with your meditation and your joy, you will be blessed a thousand times … thank you!", and with that, they turn towards the circle, signaling to a Greek woman with the bearing of a priestess to start. She speaks out in her turn: "Now we will hum all together. Our souls are like instruments; they need tuning, and humming does just that…" she says with a smile. She starts humming and everyone joins in, with eyes closed. It's as if all the mental dust raised by the anticipation and excitement for this moment finally settles, and everything becomes very quiet.

After a while, the Indigo Man stands up silently, followed by the Little Buddha, donning a new raw silk saffron robe, and the Monkey, wearing his cream satin suit. On cue, the Indigo Woman steps back from the circle, and gestures to a red haired wild-looking woman, a Local Shaman, and her partner, a Snake Charmer, to join them. The six of them quietly move away, towards the Zen Hut, while the others continue humming, sending them peaceful vibrations.

They come to a halt just outside the Zen Hut. The Local Shaman draws symbols in the air to shield the exterior of the building, while the Snake Charmer stands protectively by her side. Then, they all go inside. "It's like stepping through an invisible threshold into another world," is the Little Buddha's last thought before entering the ritualized space.

The Monkey draws out of his backpack a magnificent ceremonial costume - a gift from the Peruvian witch that brought him to the airport -, decorated with tropical bird feathers, shells and beads. While he puts it on with extreme care, he deeply inhales the jungle smell that lingers around it. From the large display of percussions on the tatami floor, he picks up a rattle adorned with strings of colorful wooden beads and starts to vigorously shake it, "It's to chase away negative energy…" he whispers with a wink to the Little Buddha, who has jumped up at the sudden sound. When the last echo of the rattle is lost in the shadows, the Monkey plays a soft tune on a flute, to bring back a more peaceful feeling. When the melody fades, the Indigo Man stands up and starts placing crystals, Tibetan bowls and other magical objects in each corner of the room. Then he bows down to all four directions, while the Indigo Woman starts chanting Mantras.

In the end, they all start humming again, joining the steady hum of the friends in the courtyard.

Without even exchanging a sign, the six in the Zen Hut stop simultaneously. The Local Shaman and the Snake Charmer leave the Zen Hut and signal to the larger circle in the courtyard to stop humming too. When the sun starts its descents into the sea, the little Soul Family takes back their seats in the larger circle. Everyone is perfectly silent as evening descends.

The bells ring. The Indigo Woman closes the ceremony with a sweet and deep chant that awakens in everyone's heart a longing for goodness, beauty, and truth.

But, human as everyone there is, once the ceremony is over the bubbly chatter and the sensuous hugging are quickly restored. There is a buzz of happiness amongst the friends, and a sense trepidation for the four who are waiting for the delivery of the amulet…

The Indigo Man, well known for his keen sense of hearing, is the first to pick up the distant rumble of a motorbike with an intermittent honk. Everyone is looking in the same direction: in a cloud of dust, they see one of the Sappho priestesses from the sea village below, dressed in black leather, driving up the dirt road and honking at the same time. A small hairy white dog is sitting on her lap. She parks at the gate and dismounts with a nimble gesture. The dog follows her close. The whole company present knows her: her incredibly deep blue eyes seem to have captured a summer sky.

She takes with uncharacteristic care a parcel tied to her back seat, and starts walking up the slope in the direction of the Local Shaman, handing it to her with a bow and a twinkle in her eyes. The Local Shaman reads out loud for everyone to hear: "It's addressed to the Monkey, care of the Indigo Couple". Before anyone can stop her and ask her anything more, the Sappho priestess jumps back on her motorbike. At the very last moment, she turns around and whispers, loud enough to be heard by everyone: "We have our ways…" and she is gone with a loud bang of her exhaust pipe.

The ensuing silence doesn't last long…there is relief in the air, and the last nervousness trickles away while everyone hugs and smiles. The Indigo Couple and the Little Buddha escort the Monkey with the parcel in his hands to the house, closing the door behind them, and keeping a respectful distance from him. He reads out loud the note taped on the outside of the package: "The box contained in this parcel has to be placed at the center of the ritual space that you have prepared, and must be opened only when the first rays of moonlight touch it"

When the Monkey opens the cardboard box, a powerful fragrance is released. He recognizes the musky smell of the Young Shaman, and a variety of healing herbs and pungent roots laced with flower essences… for a moment the Monkey is back in Siberia, being initiated into the magical world of plants and powders. Then, he detects another familiar smell, sweet and enveloping, the Tea Rose Essence that the Istanbul Lady wears, and smiles. He lifts out of the box a bundle, wrapped in a large leaf from the Amazon. He gently unknots the strong grass blades that keep it tied and lifts up for everyone to see a small hand crafted round golden box, studded with diamonds and amethysts.

Everyone comments in a hushed voice about the beauty of the box,

"I can feel that its content is powerful," says the Indigo Man,

"Look…" the Little Buddha whispers touching his heart, "even closed, this little box emanates a stream of healing qualities and blessings, I can feel them…"

It's getting darker, but there is still one hour to go before moonrise. The Monkey, holding on to the box like to dear life, and his three friends go out to join the party outside. New guests are arriving in a steady flow: the lower field of the property is full of vehicles. The guests, holding their drinks or paper plates, are mingling. Although everyone is aware to different degrees that it's a very special evening, this doesn't seem to be reason enough for anyone present to hold back on enjoying. A constant sing song of greetings and laughter mix with the soft live music played on the upper terrace.

In a quiet corner of the property, away from direct gazes, sits a beautiful, seemingly very fragile woman, with deep green eyes. She is absentmindedly caressing a big tom-cat that seems to have taken a special liking to her. No one present could associate the Madame of the curse with this pale woman: her charismatic aura has vanished, she is a bit unkempt and the long skirt and Indian blouse that she picked up sometime earlier in the local sea village are faded and a bit frazzled at the edges. More than anything, she looks like an ageing hippie. People pass her by without a second look. A few stop by for a moment, and seeing her so unresponsive, decide that most probably she is just resurfacing from a long silent meditation retreat.

But in truth the Belladonna is not interested in meeting anyone else than the Little Buddha. While she scans the crowd from her quiet corner, she is surprised when her attention is drawn to the Monkey. In her present state of confusion, she doesn't really remember who he is. She just likes him: he looks warm, full of enthusiasm, like someone that can devour life with a gulp. She can literally see the stream of warm red and orange energy spreading from him. Every shocked bone and organ of her body feels drawn to that warmth. Just then, she catches a glimpse of saffron silk, and spots the Little Buddha. He is standing a bit aside from everyone. He looks fragile, as if he has been through a very deep cleansing: the light around him flickers a bit, but it's pure gold. It reminds her of something…something royal, something noble…a saffron robed majestic presence, monks, a visit to a temple…. the effort to remember causes her an instant headache…She closes her eyes, and lets all these impressions settle inside. Two guests pass by, looking at her and whispering to each other about the hazards of excessive Vipassana…

As the clock ticks on, one of the Mystic Rose friends, an ageless man with big gray mustaches and the soul of a child, starts chanting Sufi zikhrs…the musicians instantly adjust, playing the drums to the rhythm of the heartbeat, while everyone chants and sways. The Little Buddha, remembering the Dervish in Shambala, joins in, grateful to be able to experience bliss again.

Twenty minutes before moonrise, everyone sits down on chairs, cushions and benches, and listens to an audio talk of the Controversial Master. His words resonate high and clear all around: "You have to keep moving. Slowly slowly, you will understand that there is no home, that movement itself is the home; that there is no end to the pilgrimage but the pilgrimage itself is the end".

The little Buddha whispers, "Charavedi…"

As silence follows, the Monkey grips the box closer to his heart and signals his three friends. It is time to move…

Enveloped in the darkness of the still moonless evening, the four friends silently climb to the upper part of the property. It's wild up here, uncultivated, left for nature to compose it as it pleases. Crossing bushes and scrub, they reach an octagonal platform under an ancient olive tree. From there, the view spreads around for 360 degrees, and the sky feels closer, almost in reach. The Indigo Woman is the first to look up at the vivid twinkle of millions of stars. She points at the golden Jupiter, and then at the glowing red Mars: "Let's lie all together and look at stars and planets," she says, "if you really watch, you will see how each one of them has a different color, from pink to yellow to green…like us, each one a colorful light onto ourselves…"

As they lie down, the Monkey places the golden box at the center of the platform, and the Indigo Man whispers: "Look at the constellations…so many patterns, symbols, figures. They all reflect the same source of light in their own way…just like us…"

The Little Buddha remains silent. He just enjoys the sweet sound of their voices, the intimate gesture of lying together under the sky. It is a moment he will never forget.

Meanwhile, the celebration on the lower level has picked up again. The sweet voice of a Bard is singing songs in praise of divine love, while his band rocks on…

Five minutes before moonrise all the lights are switched off. The entire property is bathed in absolute darkness and silence. Standing up on the platform, surrounded by his three friends now sitting with their eyes closed, the Monkey looks taller than his usual self. He raises his arms, and starts chanting an invocation. It is spoken in a guttural, primeval language. The Little Buddha picks up a few times the word "Shaman". When the Monkey stops, even the frogs in the nearby pond have ceased their racket.

When the others open their eyes again, they are in for a surprise: the Monkey is no more himself. He looks transfigured. He looks like a young man, his pantomime indicating that he is mixing herbs and doing incantations at the same time. Everyone smiles with recognition: it's the Young Shaman! Then suddenly he turns into an older man, playing a string instrument and singing in a voice full of joy, while everyone claps to the rhythm. But when he turns around again, he has become a beautiful and sensuous young lady, who suddenly metamorphoses into a female fury shouting: "QWATZ!".

In deep synchronicity, the four healers, spread through four continents, hear the monkey's shout, and join hands in their spirit bodies.

Then everyone on the Indigo Land sees a silver lining over the mountains. Everyone joins their hands in a salute. The Moon is about to rise.

When its first diaphanous ray touches the little golden box at the center of the platform, the box starts shimmering, as if brought to life, and then opens with a click…

Inside, lying on the deep blue velvet lining, the Monkey sees something sparkling. With the slightest nod, he invites the Little Buddha to take the content of the box in his hand. It is a golden chain with a golden heart pendant studded with a diamond. Everyone is dazzled by its beauty. There is a note that comes with it. The Little Buddha opens it, and reads it with a clear voice:

"To the Little Buddha:

This is the outcome of our combined effort. This amulet has challenged all of us to go beyond what we already knew. We are eternally thankful for the great transformation that working with you has provoked in us.

Young Shaman – alchemical gold

Peruvian Magician - the chain that connects us all forever

Istanbul Lady –the way of the heart.
Zen Woman – diamond awareness."

While everyone holds his or her breath, the Little Buddha lifts the chain into the moonlight, and then places it around his neck.

He does it very slowly, taking time to let go of the last residues of the curse that almost killed him. He looks around with tender gratitude at his three most beloved companions, thanking them silently for their immense loyalty. Without them, he would have certainly been annihilated.

As the golden heart pendant touches his heart, he feels an incredible sweetness entering him layer by layer, through muscular tissues, blood, nerves and molecules, until it reaches the core of his life energy, his Hara. The Little Buddha feels gently nudged back into himself. All is well again.

He turns to his friends, and whispers with a smile:

"Remember that you are all Buddhas. Walk like a Buddha, talk like a Buddha, sit like a Buddha… and dance like a Buddha!"

With these last words, he feels an explosion of joy, like an inner sunshine rising, and starts dancing. First, he dances with arms up towards the stars in the sky, and then he reaches out in his dance to the universe beyond. Then he dances for his first friend the Cosmic Creator and the whole Raidas Family, and, one by one, for all the marvelous beings he has met on this journey. He goes to the Indigo Couple, takes them by the hand and dances with them, letting go into delighted shrieks. He finally turns towards the Monkey, who is loudly sobbing of joy, and draws him into a frenzied jig. He has never looked so free and light…

In perfect cue, the lights go on, and the music picks up from the lower level. This time everyone is singing, men and women seem to be involved in a musical dialogue; it sounds very alive. It is the Little Buddha who leads back the friends to the lower courtyard. Everyone, led by a Mediterranean woman who seems to know her way into their childlikeness, is dancing and singing funny songs.

As soon as the Little Buddha, now glowing with good health and smiling, returns, everyone moves away to the side, leaving an open space for him at the center. The music picks up again, and the Monkey draws the Little Buddha with him in the middle.

Out of nowhere a violin starts, drawing the passionate chords of a Gypsy tune, and the two dance in full abandon. The Monkey can almost hear the Little Buddha's heartbeat growing stronger and steadier as he whirls blissfully. Everyone joins in again, dancing to the music, reaching peak after peak of wildness. When the tune finally fades, everyone feels recharged and alive: the healing energy has been shared by all.

It's getting cooler. Some clouds of humidity are hanging low in the September sky, and there is a luminescent halo around the moon…Some people start going back to the warmth of their homes, others linger enjoying the comfort of chit chatting or just sitting quietly for a while.

From her safe corner somewhere amongst the rose bushes with her tomcat, the Belladonna has watched it all. She has not joined the dance: it was too much for her, just thinking about it made her dizzy...she still needs time to get a grasp on herself and understand what is her purpose here. She is struggling, trying to reassemble all the different pieces of herself...one part of her wants to let go, while another is absolutely stressed about accomplishing a mission that she doesn't even remember, one part of her longs for love and another is addicted to hate. For a while, though, the celebration, has tipped the balance towards love: her heart remains touched even now, but she is not very comfortable with it. As more and more people leave, she recedes further back into the bushes: "the rose thorns don't hurt me," she tells herself rubbing the bloody scratches of the plants, "they just help me to stay awake..." When the last guest has left, she has made herself completely invisible.

When everyone is gone, The Indigo Couple joins the Little Buddha and the Monkey outside, under the stars. They have brought a tray of aromatic tea and a plate of chocolates, biscuits and walnuts.

For this moment, it's back to them four. But they all feel that sooner or later this perfect moment will come to an end, and their ways, as hosts and guests, will part. On the other hand, it is obvious to everyone that wherever the Little Buddha will go, the Monkey will follow...

They sit in silence for a while, sipping their teas and nibbling on the snacks, until the Monkey stands up. For the second time this evening, he seems to grow in height. With arms raised and a deep voice that seems to contain the voices of all four healers, he declares: "To all the sentient beings, visible and invisible...Hereby I declare this ritual complete, and with gratefulness I release back into existence all the forces that helped us accomplishing it"

When the Indigo Couple retires, the Monkey whispers to the Little Buddha: "All four healers said that you will be extremely open and sensitive after the big healing. Now you need to return to the Zen Hut, have a good sleep, and let the amulet do its work. Meanwhile, I'll check the property and make sure no one is still around..."

"I cannot think of a better suggestion," says the Little Buddha, "I am looking forward to my first healthy rest..."

"I'll be watching over you," the Monkey tells him, "I will make myself a comfortable seat outside the Hut, my friend", and hugs him, before disappearing into the darkness...For a while, he moves around and checks all corners. He dismisses the tall rosebushes as a very unlikely hiding place, too thorny, only a crazy person... The Belladonna draws a sigh of relief...

Then all is silent, back into the womb of existence. When the Monkey comes back, the Little Buddha's breathing is regular. The necklace is lying on a cushion next to him. The Monkey settles on a comfortable easy chair, and the big day seems to be over...

Chapter Twentyfour

ALL IS WELL

It's getting darker. The full moon is not far from setting: it's the silent hour where the doors into other dimensions open up. The Belladonna, who has not budged from her rosebush hideaway, is frozen and aching: "If I don't move for just a little longer", she has been thinking, "I will remember why I came here...", but the only things that keep coming to her mind are that cute Monkey and her short glimpse of the Little Buddha. Her whole body is in a tremor: her muscles and nerves, so finely trained for lifetimes for vengeance, are now at a loss. That feeling has almost disappeared, and different cellular memories, older ones, are surfacing to her dazed consciousness. She feels on the brink of a very big ancient pain: her whole system goes on alarm trying to push it back into her unconscious. She tries to hold on to her hate, but cannot find it anymore. With a last monumental effort, she tries to recreate it: she tenses up her whole body and tightens her jaw. It works to a certain degree: at last, she has the impulse to come out from the bushes and walk. Before she knows it, she is standing just a few steps away from the Zen Hut.

Then it dawns on her: she is here to steal the Little Buddha's amulet and make justice. She doesn't remember the details, but the feeling of having a task ahead makes her feel better.

As she approaches the Zen Hut, she can hear the Little Buddha's regular breathing. "He is sleeping, " she tells herself, "Like an angel...easy for him, healing has been brought to him on a silver plate, no risk at all...he has never had to suffer and survive on his own...." As her litany continues, she almost falls back into her lifelong steel determination, but something prevents her. She wants to understand: "But why such malevolence from my side? He doesn't seem to deserve it..." Her head spins, but this time she wants to get to the bottom of it.

Without one sound, she reaches the sliding doors. She is so silent that not even the animal instinct of the Monkey detects her: he continues to peacefully snore on his easy chair.

Slowly, she lets herself in. In the darkness, the diamond on the heart pendant is sparkling with a life of its own. Just by looking at it, an impulse takes hold of her: she is infuriated by the perfection of the amulet and she wants do destroy it. Without one more look at the Little Buddha, she slides under his bed, reaches for the amulet, and grabs it.

Just at that moment, the Monkey stirs in his sleep. The Belladonna stops on her tracks and quickly hides under the bed. Her heart is thumping. Suddenly, it occurs to her: "Somebody or something is knocking at my heart". In a fast sequence, she is flooded by intense sensations of pain and love. It's all too strong for her system. Barely able to stand up, she comes out from underneath the bed, puts the amulet back on the cushion and sneaks into the oak grove facing the Hut. The coolness of the night steadies her. She feels again empty of revenge, but in a different way: there is a warm beating heart inside her.

Just then, she becomes aware of the Monkey on the deck above her, tossing a bit on his easy chair. He looks exhausted, but contented. He has a loyal and devoted heart, she can feel it now; he would never abandon his beloved…Tears stream along her face, and honey-like tenderness floods her heart. "I could never hurt you, little Monkey," she whispers.

She turns in the direction of the Hut, where the Little Buddha still lies unmoving in his sleep, and notices how her feelings get instantly complicated. The energy is too dense for her around him at this moment. She needs more space for herself.

She stretches out, and feels her body for the first time since her niece's visit yesterday. It's the same body as before, but it's more vibrant, less tense, and quite a bit more fragile. She suddenly feels like dancing, and forgets her caution by tip tapping over the fallen leaves. Their crackling wakes up the Monkey, who sits up looking straight down in her direction. She freezes. He climbs out of his easy chair and steps off the deck, towards her. She is surprised: there is no sign of recognition in his eyes. She can remember how on the fateful day of the curse she dismissed him as a dirty animal after just one look. Now she is flooded by guilt: she would like to throw herself at him and say sorry. But he sees her just as another stray guest; like someone that maybe fell asleep in a corner during the party…

He comes closer, slightly hunched from tiredness, but she no longer sees in him only the innocent and warm small creature that he looked like when asleep. It's a male standing in front of her, a warm hearted and sexy male. Attractive. She is aware of an unusual sensation: her belly is getting incredibly warm, and it feels alive.

As their eyes lock, the current between them gets stronger. She can sense that this is unknown territory for her. Then, with an unexpected leap, she crosses an invisible barrier between them and surrenders to him.

He suddenly starts to whistle a vaguely familiar tune. Then he takes a dance step, and she recognizes it: Sirtaki! She reaches out to his outstretched hand, and joins him. Even though he is less than half her size, it doesn't matter. She can feel the magic of the Greek music, going faster and faster, all those notes going into rivulets of sound, and lets go into the dance. They whistle and giggle together, and sometimes slow down just to enjoy each other's company. Finally, they stop at the same time, and fall into each other's arms. She inhales his warm scent, fragrant of nuts and fruits, and she likes it. Then she hears a soft sound.

To her shock and surprise, the screen door is open, and the Little Buddha is sitting up on his bed, wearing the amulet. He is looking at them. Sensing that this is something important, the Monkey steps aside.

The Belladonna, frozen in her steps, holds on tight to his hand, but he lets go of her. The Little Buddha's expression is difficult for her to read. His eyes twinkle, but the rest of him doesn't move. A horrible guilt seizes her: he is certainly going to curse her back to death. She is terrified, and tries to shut down her feelings like she always did. But his smile prevents her: he stands up and invites her in. It doesn't look like he has been sleeping, she is sure of that. "He knows who I am, and has known it all along…" it is her first clear thought after the shock. In a flash, she realizes that he simply chose to do nothing when she stole the necklace earlier.

She moves slowly forward, taking each step with solemnity. Her head is no longer bowed in fear. She is standing straight and looks at him. She trusts what she sees.

The Little Buddha sits back on the bed, making space for her next to him: "I know you are the woman who cursed me, I recognized you earlier this evening. But I would have let you steal the amulet if you would have wanted to. It was your right to do that, and whatever else your heart needs to do to balance the wrong I did to you when I left. I am ready to pay for it with my life, if necessary."

As he talks, she pays no longer attention to his outer childlike appearance. He sounds like a mature and noble soul, tempered by failures and successes.

The Little Buddha continues: "I have to tell you a story that happened a long time ago. Thousands of years back, in Mesopotamia, lived a young and beautiful maiden. She had green eyes and a wisdom far superior to her age and gender…"

But the Belladonna stops him. Putting her index finger to her lips, she whispers: "Sssshh, let's wake up, Little Buddha…" She takes his hand with extreme gentleness and continues: "My ancient beloved one, I remember the last morning we made love. Afterwards, you went away, leaving our baby son and me behind. You followed your heart, and did something that I respected then and still respect now as impossibly courageous. You surrendered to your Master and followed him on the path of meditation, which knows no time limits. I completely supported you in your choice. I knew that you would return immediately if I called you. There was no reason for me to worry."

Her eyes veil with tears and the Little Buddha's hand tightens around hers.

"When my brother invaded the country I sent you a message to come back. You didn't, and he destroyed all the beauty that we had created."

"I never received that message," the little Buddha whispers.

"I felt it." She says, and sighs: "But what could I do? I was imprisoned in my pavilion, and my brother was my only visitor. He soon started talking to me about his childhood. I came to know another side of him, the one that had suffered under our father's rejection. I felt touched by it, and slowly gained respect for the way he had grown out of it into a powerful man.

He treated me with respect, like an equal. This was new to me: you had been much older than me, I had always felt cherished and worshipped by you, but never truly treated like an equal. I had never objected to that, and surely it would have happily continued, had you not gone. It was my brother that made me aware of the disbalance between us"

The Little Buddha listens carefully. "I am sorry if I used you…"

"You didn't. You just saw me as your favorite child bride, which was true from your perspective. My brother was different: he preferred men, both as lovers and as enemies. He was not afraid of my feminine power, in fact I represented for him the perfect solution: a Queen who could rule at his side without the complications of marriage and sex."

"And you came to love him…" says the Little Buddha.

"For a while, in a sisterly protective way…but that stopped when he estranged my son from me. He didn't do it all at once, but slowly, with flattery and bribes. Against my wishes, my brother took my son, still far too young, to ride to war with him. I suspect that he also took him to his bed. My boy changed. I still remember the day that he started wearing women's clothes. There was no way to talk him out of that. Later on, his female attires became as famous as his cruelty on the battlefield.

I could not accept what had become of my boy. Secretly, for years, I had kept finding reasons why you couldn't come back. I excused you in all sorts of ways, but it was enough now. I suddenly saw you as selfish and exclusive: there was no place for your son and me in your spiritual world.

That's when my rage blossomed. And I cursed you then just as I cursed you here a month and a half ago…"

The Little Buddha doesn't move an inch, "Whatever you need to do, do it now…" he says. But she interrupts him: "I am sorry, please forgive me. Up to now, I could not see my part in the whole story. Truth is that when I married you, I took with you the same role of spoiled daughter as I had with my father. I liked it and it was convenient.

In a subtle way I abandoned you too. I sometimes desired younger men, more my brother's age. After I was freed, I deceived you once in a while with one of them, taking our son along with me as a cover. I did not want to expose my need for you and feel how much I missed you..."

There is a long silence.

"I knew all this," the Little Buddha says, "That is why I left."

The Belladonna looks straight at him. Time stands still.

Then they lean forward simultaneously, and fall into each other's arms.

In that embrace, they can both feel a burden lifting. "We don't have to be anything special for each other anymore…" whispers the Little Buddha, giggling: "I am not a sugar daddy any longer, I am not even this child. I am just your fellow traveler, equal to you."

They sit silently for a moment. Now that the full story has been told, and both have owned their share of responsibility, there is nothing left unfinished: only love remains.

Just at that moment, the Monkey jumps up on the platform, agitated: "Wait a moment" he shouts, "Hold on to the Happy End!"

They both turn around startled.

"I have a message for you both: it's from your son, the one that liked to dress up as a woman," he says with a big grin on his face, "he, she, he...wants you to know that after experimenting for lifetimes with all the different gender possibilities, he has found the one that suits him. He is now a very happy lesbian Zen Woman, and one the Mysterious Four Healers."

The Belladonna lets out a happy shriek of surprise, but the little Buddha looks troubled.

"Do you think this is okay?" he asks, "Or would he need to search for professional help?"

The Monkey and the Belladonna exchange a quick glance and a smile, and the Monkey speaks:

"It's a new world " he says, "Better remain deep frozen in Shambala if you want to keep everything under control, beloved..."

The Little Buddha gets the joke. He laughs, and in that laughter also that story dissolves.

Then the Belladonna surprises the Monkey with the same prayer that her niece has taught him. She looks at the Little Buddha and tells him: "Forgive me. I am sorry. Thank you. I love you."

While she says the prayer once more, the Little Buddha starts repeating it with her. As they continue, a last wave of emotions cascades over them. Tears of sorrow, gratefulness, blissfulness, stream down their faces. The pain, the anger and the fear that have accompanied them for so long have just become a shadow, a necessary contrast for unconditional love to shine even more.

When the tears subside, even the surrounding trees seem to have been washed clean; the air seems more transparent, the glow of the approaching dawn looks psychedelic. The Little Buddha and the Belladonna are empty, looking at each other with deep compassion and friendliness.

He bows down to her, and she returns his bow. It is still odd for the Belladonna to see her once big king in the form of a childlike Buddha, but she understands his choice. With it, he has obviously decided to move on. It is courageous to become a child again and see the world with whole new eyes. A good counterbalance to many lives filled with spiritual ambition.

Only now it dawns on her that their story must have happened thousands of years ago.

"How long can a karma last," she says in awe, "How many lives did I carry this feeling of incompletion, how many of my love stories ended tragically..."

"As many as the lives I spent alone, protecting my heart..." replies the Little Buddha, "Now it's all eradicated, like a poisonous weed pulled by his roots."

"I am free now". The Belladonna says, stepping outside. It's getting light, and the sun is about to rise. For a moment, she feels concerned about her new friends, but she knows perfectly well that it's time to leave them and be alone for a while.

As she walks on into the field, everything is full of light. The rainbow auras of the trees dance in front of her vision. One young plum tree dancing in the morning breeze seems to call her. She dances with it for a moment, and in that gesture her sense of separation disappears. She has become one with existence.

From inside the Hut, the Little Buddha and the Monkey witness it all. They know what is happening to her, and they don't interfere. It's the Divine at work.

When the sun is higher in the sky, mellow and ripe as it befits a perfect September day, the Belladonna returns to the Zen Hut.

Her transformation is obvious to the two friends waiting for her. She looks as radiant and golden as this late summer light, full of true feminine warmth.

The Belladonna looks back at them: they seem two life size crystals. The Little Buddha is like pure clear quartz, reflecting white light through all its tiny prisms; the Monkey is more like a smoky crystal with a peaceful and darker shine.

She feels that she is also becoming like a crystal, absorbing more and more light by the second. The light is entering her heart, which gently reflects a pink glow, like a rose quartz, very soft and feminine. She sits next to them and closes her eyes.

When she opens them again, she joins her hands in a Namaste. It's time to go her own way, she says without speaking. "Remember now that you are a Buddha…." the Little Buddha whispers to her, while the Monkey simply takes her hand.

She comes close to the Little Buddha, gently lifts the amulet from his chest and holds it in her free hand, uttering a blessing: "May this amulet give you the health and strength that you need…there is a new stretch of life ahead of you. One that will open you to another great love. We will meet again, but this time only as dear friends and fellow travelers." Then, with the palm of her hand she places the amulet back on his heart center: "It's absolutely yours, made for you. It has the perfect combination of frequencies for restoring balance in your body…"

"And for you, little Monkey…great adventures are ahead…", she says, squeezing his hand, "I will be forever grateful for your warmth: it brought me back to life…"

Finally, she looks at both: "It will take me some time now to learn how to live in this new state of consciousness, but trust is the force that truly brought me here, and I will let it carry me to my next stopover…"

"Your way is the way of the Heart, beloved friend," The Little Buddha says, and the Monkey adds: "You are a Sufi, beloved soul sister…"

And with that, they part. Silently, unseen by the Indigo couple, the Belladonna leaves. From the Hut, the Little Buddha and the Monkey see her briefly stop in front of the rosebushes, thanking them for having given her shelter. Then with a twirl of her faded Indian long skirt, she is gone.

That day, everyone in the Indigo Land seems to want to take it easy. It's only late morning when the Indigo Couple, hand in hand and looking refreshed from their quick dip at the sea, joins the Little Buddha and the Monkey on the deck outside the Zen Hut. The two friends update them with the happenings of the night, having the grace to anticipate the happy end of the story first and then go into details, to be sure to diffuse any possible worry.

"It was not by accident that we weren't there with you, Little Buddha: it had to be between you and the Belladonna, and the Monkey on the deck asleep was enough of a protection." The Indigo Man turns towards the Monkey and continues, giggling: "It must have been something for your exuberant nature to be restrained for hours, watching out for the Belladonna!"

Without words the Monkey stands up, and clicking his fingers in an utterly male way, starts to dance the Sirtaki, showing how the Belladonna could not resist his charm and danced with him, causing general laughter.

"She is fortunate," continues the Indigo Woman, "She had the trust to let go and move on," she inwardly sends a blessing to the Belladonna, "She feels more like a sister to me now than like a threat" she adds, smiling.

Later on around the dinner table, the Indigo Man asks the Little Buddha: "I meant to ask you this for a while: how is it going in Shambala? Do you have any news? What has become of the Operation Charavedi?"

"I received some news from my former neighbor, the Samba Lady," the Little Buddha says. He speaks loud, life seems to overflow from his each and every pore," She is very satisfied with her stay in Brazil. She is amazed about the interest for meditation that is flowering all over the country. Now she is offering meditation in a Samba school for children, and people are crazy about this unexpected combination. She also writes that many of the Shambala Buddhas have found ways to prolong their stay on Earth. A group of them, spread around the globe, joined in with a new movement, MedMob, that promotes spontaneous meditation events: they gather in beautiful locations around the Earth and sit in public places, silently sending out an invitation to whoever passes by. It's surprising how many respond and stop to sit for a while with them."

"It's a bit like becoming prayer flags flapping in the wind, sending positive vibrations to the world!" exclaims the Monkey, somehow surprised by being so pleased with this analogy. Tibet is forever etched in his heart, but he also feels excited about all these new rituals open to everyone...

"She also writes" the Little Buddha continues, "that even those who have returned to Shambala look very different than when they left. They don't wear the same robes anymore; each one of them has adopted a unique way of dressing, and very different hairstyles. They make quite an impression, I hear. A colorful, funky bunch, very alive and quick in learning the ways of technology and communication. They chat through Skype, send each other messages through Facebook, and just generally enjoy using these toys to spread more consciousness in new ways."

Chapter Twentyfive

JOURNEY TO THE MANSAROVARA AND BEYOND

"I am glad our trek is almost over," sighs the Monkey, hanging his soaking wet clothes in front of the fireplace, "I am a tropical animal, cold is not for me…"

"Yes, but it's your Tibetan Lama memories that saved us from the worst cold," answers the Little Buddha, "thanks for teaching me the "Tummo", the Tibetan breathing technique that kept us warm through the worst snowstorms…"

The Monkey has to smile. He also had a great time walking through the mountains, mostly in silence and sometimes philosophizing for a while.

Relaxing in the warmth, he starts looking around. The glowing gold of the oil lamp and the incandescent red of the fire logs piled high in the chimney give their little cabin an ultimately cozy atmosphere. Outside it's the permanent twilight of the Himalayan peaks at the beginning of the winter season, small snowflakes persistently making their way on the already frozen ground…

They are the only ones up here: the passes are closed, and no one ventures further up this time of the year. For the last stretch uphill, their Sherpas have turned around and left them to their own resources.

For the Little Buddha, this is home territory; he knows perfectly well all the secret passageways from here to Shambala.

Three weeks or so ago, shortly after the final healing ceremony, our two friends' lives have taken a turn.

One day, while he was lounging after a long swim with a group of his Mystic Rose friends under a makeshift shed, the Little Buddha heard the Monkey screeching at the top of his lungs from behind the dunes. When he finally appeared, he was waving frantically and jumping up and down at the peak of excitement.

"Little Buddha, my friend!" he said out of breath when he got close enough. Everyone was staring at him and all conversation had dropped: "Surprise! We are leaving the day after tomorrow!"

Without a shadow of hesitation, the Little Buddha got up, wrapped his orange sarong around his small body, and asked: "When? Where to?"

"Have you noticed the Yacht with the Turkish flag moored in the harbor?"

The friends all nod, and small conversation breaks out about who the owners are, "some of them were with us in the Mystic Rose…they all are friends of the Controversial Master…Lots of pretty girls…"

"Wait," the Monkey signals everyone, "I was just enjoying my favorite banana and chocolate crêpe at the Zorba the Buddha Restaurant nearby, when I saw a very pretty Turkish girl dressed in colorful silks, with a beautiful round belly and tingling bells all over…"

The Little Buddha smiled. He knew already where this was possibly leading.

"Don't anticipate me!" the Monkey told him, blushing, "well, she came to the restaurant and I asked her to belly dance for me. She did it! But that's not all: afterwards, she handed me a written invitation for both of us to join her and her friends on a long cruise…in two days from now! All the way to India!"

"Existence has its timing…I have to leave, beloved friends," the Little Buddha told everyone, "together with the Monkey. I hear the call from the Himalayas…"

That evening, the sudden goodbye to the Indigo Couple was touching.

"On a cruise? Tomorrow? And then back to Shambala through India…on a motorbike?" the Indigo Man exclaimed when they announced their departure, "this is real life, my dear friends!"

But the Little Buddha could detect in his eyes the same sadness that he also felt, and added, with a little tinge of apology in his voice, "I need to experience fun: it's my dedication to this second life that was granted to me through the healing…"

The Indigo Man observed him while he was talking. Although it was not technically possible in such a short time, the Little Buddha has grown a lot. He almost looked like a young man, and behaved like one. He decided to ask the questions that he had been holding back already for a day or two. They all erupted in a fast sequence:

"Do you know more about holographic reincarnation, Little Buddha? Do you know what will happen to you when the summer season ends? Did you notice how much you have started growing after your last meeting with the Belladonna? You look and talk almost like a young man! Isn't it a bit too fast?"

The Little Buddha looks down at his hands, and shrugs: "No, I do not know more, but I trust. I feel stronger than I ever felt…"

"Wait a moment," the Indigo Woman said, looking in the direction of the Monkey, "Look at the Monkey, he looks bigger too…"

"As a matter of fact, I was seeing him shrinking," replied the Indigo Man

"No, I feel bigger than you!" retorted the Monkey.

At that point everyone had to stop trying to make sense, and laughed. Nobody knew the answer anyway. The best approach by far remained the Little Buddha's: continue moving and trust the process.

They spent the rest of the evening reminding each other of the happy and funny moments in their lives together.

At the end, just before going to sleep, the Indigo Woman handed the two friends a few jars of her homemade fig jam, saying: "Enjoy it during the cruise, and explore the world before you go back to Shambala…"

A few hours later, in the solitude of the night, the Monkey had woken up thinking anxiously about the sea voyage. He didn't like water at all and could not really swim. The fig jam provided instant comfort, and before he knew it he had eaten half of his share for the whole trip. The rest of his night was spent in fast excursions to the toilet and belly cramps. When the time to sail had come the following day, he looked washed out and gaunt. He was barely able to stand on the peer for the last goodbyes.

"Did we hurt you in any way?" the Indigo Woman asked him before hugging him for the last time.

"I just ate too much jam, I should have saved it for the journey, "but it was so good," he told her, rubbing his aching belly, "it almost tasted like fresh …enlightenment!"

The Indigo Man replied, "Don't be sorry, you lucky Monkey, who knows the taste of the beyond!!!"

"The house will feel empty without you…" the Indigo Woman told the Little Buddha while holding on to her man and crying softly, and added, "Beloved Little Buddha, beloved Monkey, you are forever part of our human hearts"

Just as another river of tears was beginning to rush down their faces, the voluptuous Turkish belly dancer came down, announcing with a giggle that the captain was ready to sail.

"We will meet again", were the last words that the Monkey heard from the Indigo Couple, disappearing in the distance.

"I was sad to let go of my Watermelon Mobile, I had just found it back!" The Monkey constantly repeated on his first days on the Yacht, fighting against seasickness. The Little Buddha, more at ease with the lulling of the water, calmed him down by reminding him often of the wondrous dematerialization ritual performed by the Indigo Couple, and how both their vehicles had become again just beautiful drawings.

Once his stomach settled, the Monkey could satisfy all his desire for food, except figs, and for dancing, while the Little Buddha started making friends, specially girls. They disembarked a few times to visit ancient places like Alexandria of Egypt, which both the Monkey and the Little Buddha remembered from former lives, and also strange futuristic cities on the edge of the desert, like Fujairah....

Here, surrounded as they are by the eternal show of the Himalayas, all these memories warm them up from the inside.

"Do you remember our arrival in Mumbai?" asks the Little Buddha, while stirring a pot of steaming porridge on the fire.

"How can I forget? The smells, the perfumes, the stench, the colors, the sounds... in that heat, every cell of my body relaxed instantly ..."

The Monkey shivers, more than anything from the memory of the unforgiving ice on the last stretch of journey. Then he sighs, recalling the day following their arrival one week ago in India. They spent most of it in the Juhu Beach district of town, haggling to purchase an old Enfield motorbike.

"I loved Juhu Beach," the Little Buddha says, "full of life, elephants, children, oxen, women in colorful saris, snake charmers with turbans, vendors everywhere, I loved even the young teenagers speaking loudly into their cellphones"

"And the fluorescent sunsets, and the delicious Masala Dosas[1]..." the Monkey almost swoons at the memory of so many spices in the food, and concludes: "As polluted as it may be, I smell Nirvana in the air even in Mumbai ..."

Both friends can merge with India like nowhere else in the world.

The purchase of their motorbike was easy. The Monkey made friends with a local, who then introduced him to his cousin brother, who had a friend whose Auntie's husband owned an old Enfield motorbike, which was brought to them almost immediately. It was a rusty but sturdy old model, which could carry both of them and their backpacks. Under the hundred staring eyes of curious bystanders, they took off on it with loud spluttering noises, leaving a big trail of smoke behind them.

The Little Buddha was driving. In the beginning, the bike felt obsolete to him, like an old coughing ox chart compared to his Lotus Mobile. But then he started enjoying the zigzagging through crowds and stalls, the sudden open stretches, and the closer contact with the surrounding. He was quickly becoming more male and rough in a cowboy kind of way.

For the first three days, they leisurely moved northwards, alternating the crossing of spectacular landscapes, waterfalls, rivers and jungles, with the more dangerous crossing of cities, avoiding the stunts of crazy rickshaw drivers and observing the passive resistance of cows and oxen blocking the way.

Almora, perched high on the slopes of the lower Himalayas and surrounded by tall maritime pine forests, was the last big town they reached before the higher mountains. They arrived there from Nainital, welcomed by the rare sight of the three peaks of the Mount Trisul looming immaculate in the distance.

---

1   South Indian dish

Since leaving the planes behind, the Little Buddha's whole composure had grown more confident by the minute. He was closer to his home, and it was visible. Moving with ease through the crowded marketplace, he sold in no time their motorbike to a couple of ageing hippies, and found fair priced porters that could lead them up to the feet of Mount Kailash.

"We have a problem, Little Buddha: the season," the Monkey complained to him, "no one in their right mind would cross the high passes beyond Mount Kailash at the beginning of winter!" But the Little Buddha just smiled in reply.

They joined a larger caravan of trekkers and porters up to the shores of the Mansarovara Lake, where the dark sky at the horizon indicated that the first heavy snowstorms where already falling on the Mount Kailash ...The white swans flying south and the clouds overhead were a dazzling sight, enough to distract them from noticing that everyone else, including their porters, had meanwhile turned around and disappeared. They were left alone, standing there, 4550 meters high, two small dots in the eternal snows.

The Little Buddha, unruffled, had just joined his hands in a Namaste and had stared at the vast steel blue expanse of sweet water, the biggest in the world, against the mist that was hiding Mount Kailash. He bent low enough to take a cupful of water from the Lake with the brass bowl purchased in Almora, and drunk it slowly. He filled it up again and offered it to the Monkey: "Drink this water, it is energized by the prayers of thousands of pilgrims who visited this Lake. It purifies your mind and prepares you for the ultimate journey…"

"Ultimate?" the Monkey exclaimed, worried that their present situation meant sure death… "I don't know if I want that!"

"Shhhh, trust me, my friend," the Little Buddha said, "There are specific guidelines about entering Shambala. For its portal to open, you need to empty your mind and open your heart. This water helps you to do just that."

While instructing him, he looked at the Monkey: his resistance to rules was plainly visible on his tight lips and slightly clenched fists. But the Little Buddha knew that the rebellious Monkey would ultimately bend to these guidelines to make him happy: after some dignified silence, he started slowly drinking.

Wiping his mouth at the end, the Monkey sat on the shore, musing: "This is exactly the reason why in my so many lives as enlightened I never made it to Shambala. I had to become a monkey instead, and follow my own way. I just do not like rules. When I hear 'You have to drink this water to purify your mind and open your heart in order to enter Shambala' I have an allergic reaction…"

"But," the Little Buddha was about to patiently explain his point once more,

"I know it's true, but it feel…it feels too holy…" the Monkey interrupted

They smiled at each other in deep recognition. The Little Buddha himself could see how his own sense of religiousness had been forever altered by his last visit on this Planet. Things could be said in a friendlier way, now…

"But also your Tummo technique," he added in a provocative tone, "sounds so absolute, but who knows, maybe it's just self deceit…"

The Monkey jumped up, balancing himself on a high rock, and did a perfect representation of what could have been himself many lifetimes ago:

"Dear ignorant seekers, I will teach you the Tibetan Tummo technique", and continued in an increasingly hypnotic voice, "Close your eyes, and just recognize that the outer phenomena are the mirror of your mind. That is enough. Now your body heat will increase to a very comfortable degree even in freezing conditions," and suddenly he reverted to his usual voice, adding with a smile: "it also might make you feel blissful, as a side effect, although that could be also a sign of approaching death by freezing…"

When they stopped laughing, the whole lake seemed aglow with colors. "Did you see that?" the Monkey asked astonished, "Do you think that we are experiencing side effects from our Tummo meditation?"

The Little Buddha had replied seriously: "It is a common phenomenon on this Lake. It is said that the water functions like a prism, capturing and reflecting colored lights at certain moments of the day…"

"Oh….." the Monkey replied, deep down preferring his own hypothesis to the more scientific one that the Little Buddha was offering, "you are so serious! You know the explanation for everything! I am an animal, I don't understand science…"

"But my dear friend," the Little Buddha answered, "you know better than me that your true strength lies in the heart. Your monkey mind is your challenge: even in front of the ultimate truth, it just can go on arguing forever, just for the sake of it…. you know it!"

The Monkey felt exposed, and started sulking. After a while, the Little Buddha broke the silence with a laugh, telling him: "Now, who is serious here?"

A moment later, being so occupied as they were with each other, neither of them noticed that, as they stood up and turned away from the Lake towards the Mount Kailash that they still had to cross, a small boat appeared from the mists. All the colored lights that had been shimmering in the water gathered around it, and disappeared with it back into the fog.

"I must say …I admire your knowledge of snow and mountains…." says the Monkey in the warmth of their cabin, already half asleep, "how do you know where exactly to put your foot in the high snow….and… not to fall down…".

The Little Buddha smiles silently, seeing how his friend has already fallen asleep sitting, leaning to his backpack with an untouched cup of tea next to him.

He is a bit concerned: how will it be for the Monkey in Shambala? Will he be able to adjust? He is such a free spirit. Then, he suddenly understands: he is not only talking about the Monkey, but also about himself. He hasn't given much space to his hesitations during the whole journey, and now, on the eve of the crossing, he has to face the fact that he is not sure if he wants to live in Shambala again.

Something still feels unfinished for him on Earth; he is not yet sure what it is. This summer has been such a celebration of life for him, no matter where he was or how he was feeling. He remembers even the darkest moments as suffused by love and care and friendship. He thinks with affection of his first friend, whom he still secretly calls the Trash Giant, and the whole Soul Family of Raidas. They must live nearby, on the Lake that they just left behind, fulfilling their destiny of creators. Will he be able to see them again? And above all, the burning question: will he be able to continue being so alive also in Shambala?

He goes to sleep with all these question marks; he is anyway sure that he wants to visit his cottage, the Council of Twelve, the Dervish, and all the Buddhas who have returned after Operation Charavedi.

Dawn is spectacular. The clouds have dispersed, and the sky is turning a pale shade of pink. The embers of the fire are still glowing when our two friends leave the cabin and set off for the final stretch.

They walk through high snow for a few hours, while the wind picks up and grazes their faces. They finally reach an area that is blindingly white: sky and earth are of the same hue: just by an inner sense of gravity they can tell that they are standing on the earth. The Monkey visibly tenses up: for the first time he really doubts his friend's capacity to lead them to safety…

"Don't worry, little Monkey," the Little Buddha says," we are very close now…"

"I only see a never-ending wall of snow and ice ahead!" replies the Monkey.

Just then, he notices from far what looks like twin boulders, parallel to each other and standing out at an odd angle, casting a silvery shadow on the snow.

After another hour of walking, the Little Buddha stops in front of them, waiting for the Monkey to catch up.

"The first time I came to the land now known as Shambala, it was just a trek away from what is known now as Katmandu by open road. Now it's a different story, it's hard to enter. The portal to Shambala shifts all the time: now it is right here, between these two boulders. There is no use in trying to remember what the portal looks like or where it is, because it takes a different shape every time you want to enter. Its location has more than anything else to do with where you happen to be when you are truly ready to enter. It's enough for us to know that this time it looks like twin boulders, and it has materialized this way just because it's our time …"

"So, what's the password?" asks the Monkey, fascinated

"Shambala. But it's not saying the word itself, it is experiencing its meaning: Shambala indicates a state of consciousness: Sham means tranquility, Bala means virgin -- virgin tranquility. That is the inner space, which always remains virgin. There is no way to corrupt it. In your honor, my friend, let's do some minutes of Gibberish, and then sit and close our eyes: this will be enough to bring us home.…"

Chapter Twentysix

VISIT TO SHAMBALA

The sound of meditation bells and a soft humming coming right from the earth tell the Little Buddha and the Monkey that the crossing has been successful.

They open their eyes to a green and sunny landscape. The snowy mountains are still there, proud and high in the background, but the soil is covered with tall grass and thousands of flowers: delicate Lilies with purple borders, explosions of yellow marigolds, intense blue poppies, elegant bushes of deep red rhododendrons… after all that stark white of the snow, they are dazzled.

As they start walking through the meadow, the Little Buddha looks at the Monkey: "We must really look wild. At least that's what I see when I look at you: ruddy, healthy, and unkempt…"

The Monkey is about to reply that the Little Buddha looks also uncharacteristically tanned and bleached, when they are alerted by the sound of voices.

The German accent is unmistakable. The Little Buddha speeds up towards the two figures that are now visible in the open field ahead. He recognizes the other one as the Buddha of Technical Support and Maintenance, with his typical stoop and distracted attitude. They are busy measuring and fencing with ropes a large perimeter on the ground; they haven't noticed the arrival of the two friends.

Finally, the Monkey catches their attention with his peculiar way of hopping and zigzagging ahead, something unseen in Shambala. An Enlightened Animal is a first, even in the Land of the Buddhas. They stop talking and stare. Behind this strange creature they see the Little Buddha, waving at them.

By the time they have carefully placed on the ground their tools, the two friends are standing in front of them. The Little Buddha runs into the open arms of the German Buddha, and after a warm embrace he introduces the Monkey to his Shambala friends.

"There is obviously much for you to tell us, dear Little Buddha" the German Buddha, unable to hide his curiosity, is still peeping at the Monkey while talking, " and much for us to tell you, but first let us go back to town, settle you and your friend into your cottage…"

The Buddha of Technical Support and Maintenance is already calling the Cleaning Department of Shambala instructing them to prepare the Little Buddha's home, with all the necessary adjustments to his present size. "And fresh linen and a second…bed?" He looks questioningly at the Monkey, who nods, "for his honored guest the Monkey!"

The Monkey has never seen such a beautiful town. From above, it looks like a luminous pearl diadem.

As they descend, he notices the people in the streets: they all walk calmly, with a soft smile on their faces. Everything is absolutely clean, no traces of garbage anywhere. "Everything is so…. perfect!" he exclaims, and the two hosts smile, taking his comment as a statement of appreciation.

Knowing the Monkey, though, the Little Buddha knows that this it is not a good sign: perfection is not his cup of tea: when everything is too organized, he gets unhappy. His brain is more at ease when the surrounding is, well, organic, with smells and tastes.

The Little Buddha looks around: Shambala looks as beautiful as ever. Everything glows with that pearly shine, and the buildings are all in immaculate order. But he sees fewer Buddhas around.

"Gone on Charavedi Missions…" the German Buddha answers to his thought, "there will be time to hear about it all later. For now know that everyone is doing good." The Little Buddha smiles, remembering how hard it had been for him as the Buddha of Long History to keep his thoughts of boredom away from his twelve mind reading friends.

As they walk on their way to the Little Buddha's cottage, many Buddhas stop by to greet him, hug him, and ask questions about his journey. To each one of them, he introduces the Monkey, who is gaining by the second quite a reputation as a formerly illustrious Lama and a presently enlightened Monkey.

"There is a lot of smiling here, it's nice," says the Monkey, "But not so much loud laughter, if I observe rightly. People keep a little distance from each other. Nobody walks hand in hand. Not much gold essence…" he adds, showing off his recently acquired shamanic insights…

"True," whispers the Little Buddha to him, "but give it a chance before judging…" the Monkey nods, looking a bit chastised.

The Little Buddha's cottage, perched on one of the highest locations of town, is ready to welcome them. The temperature inside is pleasant but not too high, in order to avoid getting lethargic; the furniture is simple but tasteful. The Monkey sighs and gladly sinks into the comfortable bed made for him, while the Little Buddha takes in the familiar view from the large window next to his bed. Sprawling below him, interspersed with smaller personal dwellings, are the many religious buildings: Stupas, Gurudwharas, Churches, Temples of all sorts: here in Shambala, he thinks while looking at the Buddhas coming in and out of them, the essence of every path is represented not only by these buildings, but also by the living mystics that visit them all the time.

After a three day long and satisfying rest, interrupted only by light delicious meals, our two friends decide to have a stroll to the Meditation Hall on the outskirts of town.

"Here there is a constant flow of Buddhas, day and night. Everyone is free to come and go according to his or her own inner rhythm", the Little Buddha tells the Monkey when they arrive in front of the elegantly built large hall.

As they enter, the Monkey is deeply touched: there is none of the atmosphere of austerity that he knows so well from his former lives as a High Lama. The Buddhas look light; after their personal Charavedi mission, many of them have adopted colorful modern clothes and hairstyles. They all sit with closed eyes wherever they feel on the marble floor, while the wind in the pines around the building creates a constant sweet background melody. He whispers: "I can feel it in my body: this is a consciousness power plant!".

The Little Buddha is relieved to hear it: the love of meditation is something he always shared with the Monkey; at least here in the Hall his little friend feels at home.

They go on in this way for a few more days, alternating rest to good food and meditations, until the Little Buddha notices that the Monkey is starting to get restless: "My friend," he asks, "what is going on? You are not sleeping for such long hours any more, and when you do sleep, you often whimper. What is it?"

"My dear, beloved Little Buddha...I must confess that I am getting a bit bored here," the Monkey is just starting the long answer that he has been rehearsing for quite a while, when a loud gong coming from the center of town reverberates through the valley of Shambala.

"This sound usually announces an important meeting of the Council", the Little Buddha explains.

Before he can say more, there is a knock at the door. He rushes to open. The whole Council of Twelve, dressed like a rainbow in colorful satin and silk ceremonial robes, is standing at the entrance.

"Greetings to you both," commences the German Buddha, "Are you now ready to come to the Council Hall and tell us about your journey? It seems that the appropriate lapse of time has passed, and we would be very glad to hear your stories..."

The Little Buddha replies for both: "We would be honored". Meanwhile, he is surprised to detect a resistance inside him about readjusting to Shambala. He takes mental note of it, and turns to the Monkey, who is instead visibly excited about having an audience to tell his adventures to.

After a few hours of breakfasting and talking around the Council table, there is a long gap. The Monkey is spent after all his mimics and acrobatics, while the Little Buddha cannot help longing back for the freedom he experienced on his journey; he misses the Indigo Couple.

At the end of the Little Buddha's tale, the Twelve, usually quite composed in their attitude, are flushed and wide eyed. "Let's take a little break and close our eyes," suggests the Waif Buddha, trembling with overexcitement. As everyone settles back inside himself or herself, the atmosphere instantly cools off. The Monkey takes a long overdue outbreath.

After a while, the notorious German voice brings them all back to the moment: "Dear beloved Little Buddha, we are impressed by your stories and by the wisdom you gained through your experiences. It is clear to us that something new needs to happen to us too, because without adventure we are slowly becoming predictable. We love our life in Shambala immensely, but it became clear through your stories that we members of the Council of Twelve also need to follow Charavedi and move on. This is why we would like you both to become our advisors. We would meet with you once a week, to deepen with you, Little Buddha, our understanding of the New World,"

"And to discuss the effects that the Charavedi Operation has had on you," intercepts the Buddha of Technical Support and Maintenance, eagerly.

The German Buddha resumes talking, "We would also like to hear more from the Monkey about his visits to the four Shamans, and talk about the connection between Healing and Meditation. We would be very happy if you would accept our invitation. It would be starting tomorrow."

The Little Buddha and the Monkey look at each other, and reply in one voice: "Yes, we would be honored to accept…"

But their smile has something forced: they both don't look so happy.

That same day at sunset, two beautiful brocade sky-blue robes are delivered to the cottage. The two of them try them on: they both look stunning in them. The last rays of the sun and the silvery shine of the rising moon bring the cloth to life. It looks like a flowing river; it glitters like the sun on sea waves. It's new for the Little Buddha to don a different color than orange, but then the Monkey reassures him by saying that this new color sets off his blue eyes…

As the night falls, they talk. "I cannot stay here," says the Monkey, looking with his liquid dark eyes at the Little Buddha, "it's not my climate, and my appetite for life is too big, after so many centuries in Monasteries."

"I understand, little friend," replies the Little Buddha, "It's hard for me to say this, but I feel the same…"

The following morning, after the ritual greetings and another good breakfast at the Town Hall, the Little Buddha and the Monkey, dressed in their blue robes, announce their decision to the Twelve: "Beloved Council," starts the Little Buddha, "Honored Gathering of Enlightened Beings. As a sign of respect for your invitation we are wearing our ceremonial robes. But the Monkey and I cannot stay here. It is a perfect place for you, as it was once for me. But now I need to move on. I will always long back for this emptiness, for this virgin tranquility, but I need to go back to the world. I have already learnt a big lesson this time on Earth, but I feel I have been granted a second chance. I have to get back to fulfill a longing inside me that I do not completely understand yet."

The Twelve nod, respectfully. He continues: "I want to let go of my childlike form and become a man. I long to walk on Earth as a fully-grown male human, and meet the challenges and gifts that this will bring. I ask for your blessings to follow this path."

In the silence that follows, the Monkey speaks out: "Dear Enlightened Ones, this lifetime as a monkey has been so far a really beautiful gift. I would have never thought that to be an animal and enlightened at the same time could be so precious. In this monkey body, I feel a freedom that was previously unknown to me: my animal nature is blessed with the golden dust of enlightenment, and there is nothing more that I want than continuing my adventures in this form."

The Twelve look at each other. By the way some are smiling and some are shedding a few tears, it is clear that everyone understands and accepts.

This time, a dark skinned woman Buddha, known for her relentless pursuit of Truth, says with an American accent: "Do not waste this precious life, dear friends. We give you our unconditional blessing to follow your path, and thank you for the inspiration that you gave us by doing it..."

Everyone stands up, and the German Buddha declares with an amused spark in his eyes, "Don't worry, we will meet again when the time is right..."

Later in the afternoon at home, the two friends take some time to rest and prepare for the journey ahead. But the Little Buddha is too excited to sleep: while the Monkey is gently snoring on his bed, he keeps on tossing and turning. Finally, he gives up trying, and decides to go to the Library to pay a visit to his old friend the Dervish and deliver him personally an invitation for their evening farewell party.

As soon as he reaches the entrance, he knows that something is different. The Library is usually the most silent place in Shambala, normally emanating a dense field of contemplation and focus.

But this time it's the sound of loud Middle Eastern Music, belly dance type, that wafts through the open doors. Intrigued, the Little Buddha looks inside: whole bookshelves have been pushed aside, pages are flapping around, and the Dervish is in the middle of all the chaos, dancing. He is not whirling, though, he is freely moving, like a happy madman. He is not alone: he is dancing with a woman. The Little Buddha cannot see her face because she is turned away; but going by the exalted expression of the Dervish, she must be very beautiful and somehow special. Then something in her movements stirs his memories: he knows her, but can't really place from where. When she finally twirls around and her face comes into the light he recognizes her: it's the Belladonna. She has made it to Shambala!

The Little Buddha regrets that the Monkey is not with him: he would have loved to see this. The Belladonna looks more beautiful than ever: she is a bit rounder and moves in a more sensuous way than before, her thick long hair is full of luster and her wild green eyes are focused on the Dervish.

It doesn't take much for the Little Buddha to figure out that this is not a good time to interrupt them. "This must be what the Sufis call Ishq', Ecstatic Passionate Love …" he tells himself, puzzled and also strangely stirred, "Is this what is waiting for me when I become a grown man?"

Making sure not to be heard, although chances are slim that they would notice anything else than each other, he tiptoes out of the Library.

As he walks out, he bumps into the German Buddha, who is standing at the Library entrance with an impish smile on his face: "Hello dear friend," he says, "We think that the Dervish has fallen in love. But we can't ask him; he doesn't want to talk to anyone, and doesn't read books anymore: he is only interested in her. We do not know who the beautiful woman is; she arrived here more or less one month ago. It was during a very quiet period, many Buddhas were gone, and there was plenty of space. She was obviously in a deep process of awakening. We showed her around, assigned her one of the empty homes and invited her for a communal dinner that same evening. She said yes to the invitation but never came. Later we came to know that she had met the Dervish. From that moment on, they haven't been seen apart even for one second. They are in rapture. We all love the energy that they spread around, it's great!" He pauses for a moment. Is he blushing? The Little Buddha wonders, as the German Buddha lowers his face and continues: "We are just not used to this anymore"

Then he reverts to his usual no-nonsense tone and continues: "I was anyway just looking for you, dear friend", he says, leading the Little Buddha towards the outskirts of town, "I want to show you our new project. Do you recall that upon your arrival you met me and the Buddha of Technical Support and Maintenance taking measurements and fencing off a construction site? We are building something new there, more in style with the Charavedi principle than the old Council building, so full of massive furniture and mementoes from the past."

The Little Buddha is surprised to find himself in the open field where they met upon his arrival. He can see that the works have been progressing a lot in just one week. There are stainless steel poles bent at angles waiting to be assembled, and a very big striped canvas, still folded: presumably a roof.

The German Buddha continues: "This will be a temporary structure of exquisite beauty, made of strong ropes, steel, canvas, and all the latest amenities. We are not yet sure whether we Twelve will live in it, or if it will be used for other purposes that are not yet revealed to us. But we are not lacking in vision: each one of us has beautiful ideas of how to decorate it and make it more functional…"

The Little Buddha is impressed: he can see that something of the New World has entered Shambala.

"It's thanks to pioneers like you that this is happening," the German Buddha replies, reading his mind once more.

The evening party is a feast of surprises for the Little Buddha and the Monkey: each one of the Twelve improvises a small performance in honor of the two. The dark skinned American Buddha gets a big applause by singing a song full of rhythm and juice, and the Buddha of Technical Support and Maintenance impresses everyone with his magic tricks. When asked to also contribute, the Monkey is more than willing to take center stage and present a funny pantomime of his journeys. The Little Buddha, on the contrary, remains shy, and hides behind his Ipad while mixing a great variety of tunes from all over the world for everyone to dance to.

When the evening is finished and it is time for the final goodbyes, the Little Buddha tells the Twelve: "I wish you much success and pleasure with your plans this winter here…" He is again not fully sure, but he might have caught a glimpse of a mischievous smile on the face of the Waif Buddha. But all is soon forgotten into the river of good wishes and blessings that are showered upon the two friends.

As soon as the two friends reach home, they both fall into a deep dreamless sleep.

Chapter Twentyseven

REBIRTH

Full Moon in Aries – A New Beginning

The day after, with their backpacks full of biological snacks from the Enlightenment Store and still clad in their blue robes, the Little Buddha and the Monkey cross the portal back into the world.

Once on the other side, they open their eyes on an icy but gloriously sunny panorama. Down below, the Mansarovara Lake is shimmering like an enormous mirror.

"Queen Maya conceived Gautama the Buddha on these shores," says the Little Buddha while admiring the view, "This Lake is like a womb that can give life to the spirit"

"Look!" shouts the Monkey, "It's happening again! The prisms of light!"

They speed up their pace, wanting to get to the Lake before the phenomenon ends. As they approach, the display of colors becomes increasingly intense: they become twirling flashes of rainbow lights that constantly create new shapes.

"The Lake looks alive..." the Little Buddha exclaims.

By the time they have run all the way down to the water, the Lake has become again the still mirror that it always is. But the colors and shapes remain floating in the water, like reflections on glass...

"Aren't these...our Indigo friends?" the Monkey points out at a particularly deep blue shape, close to the shore.

"You are quick, my beloved Monkey...yes, now I see them too: look, they are painting themselves while relaxing in the Zen Hut. And look there! That man with intense eyes and unkempt hair...and those flowers that he is painting, the way they catch the light!"

"It's Van Gogh," declares the Monkey, very proud of his expanding worldly knowledge...

They just sit on the shore for a while, completely absorbed into the play of lights that keeps on creating images on the water to dissolve them again into new ones: a Japanese woman painting cherry blossoms turns into a poet who makes lovers embrace in the sky, who then changes into a computer graphic releasing algorithms from his screen into the world...

"It's like a slideshow," murmurs the Monkey, who loves watching such things on his Ipad.

The two friends are so taken by the endless sequence of images that at first they do not notice the boat gently moving towards the shore. It's the Monkey's keen sense of hearing that alerts him. He looks up and sees it: it's a small one, with one person aboard.

"Is this a real person?" The Monkey says, pointing towards the boat, "Is he pouring colors into the water? Wait...look at the way he moves.... It seems like a very large monkey to me!!!"

The Little Buddha smiles. There is only one person that he knows who might look and move like a big monkey.

"No, my dear friend, I understand your first impression, but already from this distance I can see a human body. I have a real good friend who moves exactly this way" the Little Buddha is almost stuttering with excitement, "he has reddish blond hair just like this man..."

Now the boat is close enough for them to also see his outfit: he is wearing several layers of colorful second hand bath coats, mostly faded.... and yes, he is pouring colors into the Lake.

"Just like when I first met him," says the Little Buddha, laughing at the memory, "when he was moving mountains of Trash and sculpting them..."

"Whatever you see in the water is a reflection of your soul..." shouts at them a booming voice from afar, followed by a hearty laughter...

"Your voice is as booming as ever, my friend!" the sweet voice of the Little Buddha cuts in, "Hello, Trash Giant!!!"

While his old friend wades his way from the boat to the shore, the Little Buddha notices the change in his appearance: he looks even larger now, bigger then a normal human being, radiant like the Sun on its zenith, like a Michelangelo masterpiece.

"Now called the Cosmic Creator, at your service..." shouts the burly man, towering over him, "And is this not my best friend the Little Buddha?"

The Little Buddha is beaming while the Cosmic Creator continues, "and this must be the illustrious hero, the Monkey: I have heard a lot about you!"

To the Little Buddha's surprise, the Monkey lowers his eyes and looks suddenly shy.

"So what's up?" the Cosmic Creator asks casually, as if they had meetings like this every morning.

He is really cool, the Monkey thinks, still keeping his eyes downcast. For the first time ever, he is wondering how it would be to be so big and so funny. Then he looks sideways at the Little Buddha, and notices the change in his attitude. He knows him well, and it's only with the Indigo Couple of with himself that the Little Buddha allows such display of emotions. They must be really close friends, he thinks. Before he knows it, he finds himself he is in the relentless grip of his monkey mind: first jealousy erupts, and then the deep despair of abandonment explodes, causing big tears to stream down his cheeks. He does his best to hide them with his downcast eyes.

The Cosmic Creator notices the Monkey's tears immediately.

"Little Monkey," he says, "I look big, but thanks to our friend here the Little Buddha I found back the child inside me: it's very colorful and creative, but also easily wounded and possessive, like yours…"

The Little Buddha stands back immediately, trying to tone down his enthusiasm for this long awaited for reunion, not to hurt his friend.

The Cosmic Creator, taking in the whole situation and not knowing what else to do, puts his large protective arms around both of them and gently changes the subject: "How do you guys make breakfast here? Little Buddha," he says, giving him a conspiratorial wink, "I bet you both love pancakes …come to my humble boat and I'll prepare you some"

It's the right approach: soon tears and embarrassment are forgotten and everyone is busy on the boat, preparing the mix and adding different sauces from a variety of jars that seem to materialize out of little twirls of color.

"I want…. blackcurrant jam!" the Monkey screams at the top of his lungs, and there it is, dark and inviting. "Ginger Candies!" giggles the Little Buddha, causing a waterfall of golden sweetened morsels.

At the end of their meal, the Cosmic Creator clears the table with one splash of black paint, and all is clean and empty.

"The sun is getting high in the sky. Help me set up this awning for some shade over the boat…" he says.

Being busy together in the middle of nature and with a happy belly brings the three of them very close in a simple way. Lounging afterwards under the outstretched canvas, the two friends relax while the Cosmic Creator launches in one of his favorite activities: telling stories.

"Did you know that one of the shifting portals of Shambala is always somewhere close to this Lake? Sometimes it is even inside it. This is why there are so many folk stories about innocent peasants disappearing into the waters and returning after a while with unbelievable stories. The religious types would talk about paradise, celestial music, and angelic touch, while the ones that were known for their greed would tell about golden temples and naked women…"

The Little Buddha giggles: "I don't think I ever saw any naked women in Shambala, except at the hot springs…"

"The local Shamans" continues the Cosmic Creator, "had to hypnotize them to erase from their memory the location of the portal and the whole experience of Shambala to protect its secret…."

After a few more fascinating anecdotes, the Little Buddha sits up, rocking the boat a bit, and asks:

"Something has changed in you since we last met. You were always beautiful to me," he says to the Cosmic Creator, who shrugs with modesty, "but now you are radiant, like a god. You are as fully human as always, but also more than that. What happened to you?"

"The path of Buddhahood was never for me. Even in my childhood visits to Shambala I always felt different than the locals: I perceived myself more as an artist, a dreamer, a visionary. I did not feel any attraction to waking up, which seems the main teaching of you Buddhas. Maybe this is the difference between a mystic and an artist."

The Monkey sits up. He can relate: each one is free to choose their way, just like he did.

"People like me are not Buddhas. For thousands and thousands of years, we were called Gods: we always remained earthbound, involved in life. We lived intensely and created passionately, and embodied the essence of humanity's dreams.

Buddhas don't believe in dreams, they have gone beyond them into the ultimate reality…"

"Wait a moment," says the Monkey," I did follow my dream to become an animal! What does this make me, then?" he says with a little challenging grin.

"Maybe a new type of Buddha," answers the Cosmic Creator, grinning back,

"One that can indulge and watch at the same time. But," he stops and looks at his tiny friends, "there is a difference between us and you: you are small and we are big. We live on a constant high level of intensity; our senses and our nerves live permanently at the peak of experience. We have to be so large and strong for our bodies to cope with this, and even then sometimes this intensity drives us crazy for periods. You two, on the other hand, can be any size you like, because you move with a different grace: the one that comes from knowing your limitations and embracing them in your heart. For example, take our beloved Buddha brother here…" he says, suddenly snapping his fingers. A holographic life size image of the Buddha of Technical Support and Maintenance appears right in front of the two stunned friends and bows down to the Cosmic Creator, who continues: "He used science to produce your holographic image as the Little Buddha. But he cannot alter the laws of nature and go beyond the limits of duration of such a complex hologram. He doesn't mind that," he says, while the image complies and nods in assent, "because he knows that life is impermanent, and sooner or later all forms will anyway dissolve", he adds, while the image vanishes into thin air.

"I am no longer afraid to tell you, dear Cosmic Creator," the Little Buddha replies in a firm voice, "that being a Buddha has its setbacks too. Boredom is the one word that sums them all up. Not so long ago I was still ashamed of feeling it. Now it's become my friend. It's there to tell me that I have slipped into complacency and I need to move…"

The Cosmic Creator smiles at the Little Buddha: "It's a whole new world that we are living in!" and takes his tiny hand in his, frowns, and continues in a more serious tone: " I have heard all about the curse that fell on you. As Maya hinted in your astral meeting with all of us, we saw it coming. It's a simple law of universal balance: when light intensifies, like it did when you started using your healing capacities, darkness also intensifies. That cannot be prevented. But we did not expect that the darkness would have such a devastating effect on you...."

The Monkey comes closer to the Little Buddha, and puts his arm around him protectively. "We could not prevent it either, neither me nor the Indigo Couple..."

"But you held the space for the healing to happen, and this wasn't easy." the Cosmic Creator tells him, "When someone touches the Dark Night Of The Soul," and he stops there, with a long unexpected sigh. The Little Buddha can see that he is remembering his own journey through darkness and loss, "nothing can help, because it is meant to happen as a purification..." but then the frown on his forehead disappears, and his face lights up in a smile: "I was lucky to meet the Garbage Collector in my own dark times. I don't know if I would have managed to get through without him. Just like the Monkey has been for you: an unwavering support in your moments of hopelessness and despair. A monkey is full of joy..."

The Monkey cannot hold back any longer. He starts pulling the Little Buddha by his robe, and then giggles, hiding his face into the folds of the cloth.

"Just like a small child..." the Cosmic Creator concludes, and asks, "Tea everyone?"

While they sip their warm herbal brew, they chat about the Belladonna and the Dervish.

"It's good that she found such an intense fellow traveler. He will help her to stay present and learn to measure her powers. That same energy that almost killed you, Little Buddha, can be also used for healing," says the Cosmic Creator.

"Is she a Buddha or a Goddess?" the Monkey asks, increasingly confused.

They all laugh.

In the easy silence that follows the laughter, the Cosmic Creator announces: "And now, my friends, would you like to meet the Raidas Soul Family?"

"Yes!" the Monkey is thrilled, and eager to see them all in person.

The Cosmic Creator jumps out of the boat and pulls it to the shore, inviting the two friends to step out. They all sit on a formation of flat rocks enjoying the afternoon sun.

For a moment there is great stillness in the air, then starts a gentle humming that seems to come from everywhere. Far away on the horizon a small group of what looks like specks of gold is moving in their direction.

"There they are..." the Cosmic Creator says happily.

"Look" the Little Buddha says to the Monkey as they approach, "they all walk in one rhythm, even the children..."

"They look graceful and also powerful. I get it; these are Gods" the Monkey states, while the Cosmic Creator nods.

Now he can see them better: in the middle of the group, there is an older man who exudes authority and wisdom. He is dressed in black, with long white hair and beard, and deep shimmering turquoise eyes. Next to him walks his spouse, a tall proud woman with noble bearing, soft eyes and long dark braided hair. She holds a young boy by the hand. He looks like both his parents, and has a Tibetan puppy with silver fur in his other arm.

Protectively close to them follows a young couple dressed in emerald green, looking healthy and natural and very much in love with each other. Around this group, the whole tribe follows a bit back, at a customary distance.

The Little Buddha waves in recognition, and joins his hands in a salute, "See the man in the center?" he tells the Monkey, "It is Raidas, my old friend from Shambala…he looks so different…"

"They all move with animal grace…" the Monkey whispers, recognizing their sensuous movements without any trace of stress. They are….making love with life!" he adds, blushing.

"Like a herd of lions…" say the Cosmic Creator with unmistakable pride, and giggles, "look at my grandfather, as strong and rooted as the Alps that we come from… little did I know that this was the essence of Tirol, when I was a child…"

"You really found your home…" the Little Buddha tells him.

When the group is within hearing distance, the booming voice of the Cosmic Creator welcomes them: "Welcome to all of you. Little Buddha, dear Monkey, I am honored to introduce to you my Soul Family, my dearest friends, teachers and fellow Gods."

With a bow, he steps back, letting Raidas, who stands now in front of the Little Buddha, continue: "My dear ancient friend, things have taken a turn for me. I have become a God, and I like it this way. These days my family's creative endeavor is to grant wishes and respond to prayers, although often people don't really know what they ask for…" he lets out a bellow of laughter that shakes the ground. "But here in your case, dear old friend, we are simply more than honored to fulfill your wish. It is in the service of love and light."

The Little Buddha's heart beats faster. He knows: the time has come.

"We offer you two possibilities: you can revert to your former shape as the Buddha of Long History. You would find yourself back as you were but richer in wisdom from your experiences on this Earth. The other option is for you to become human, truly human, and continue your life here in the world as the man you can be. Your body will grow up all at once, and you will have to completely let go of being a child. It might be quite confusing at first. It's your choice. Take some time to decide."

The Little Buddha looks up at him, and answers without hesitation: "I want to become fully human!"

Raidas nods, and the Cosmic Creator steps up again, saying in a voice slightly broken by emotion, "It is my honor to be the one who is assigned to the fulfillment of your wish to become a man…"

The Little Buddha marvels at the perfection of existence: to be transformed by someone who has gone himself through such depth of transformation! He goes to hug his friend.

The Monkey stays a bit back. He silently wonders what it is that he would truly wish for himself.

"The Little Planet where I found you, dear Monkey," the Little Buddha interrupts his thoughts and takes his hand, "was the outcome of the Cosmic Creator's transformation. It's thanks to him and his Soul Family that you found the right place to be reborn free…"

The huge Cosmic Creator looks fondly at the little Monkey, who affectionately grabs him by one leg.

"Ehm, OK, let's keep the focus," announces the Cosmic Creator, "it's time. Only you, little Monkey and I, will go by boat with the Little Buddha to the center of the Lake. The others will remain on the shore, praying for us. You, little Monkey, are going to protect the space around the Little Buddha while I work at the metamorphosis. The transition we are about to perform will leave him for a moment very exposed, in between worlds. Practice your Tummo and create a warm field of serenity around him…"

The Monkey, happy to be part of the experiment, nods. He immediately jumps aboard and starts breathing evenly with eyes wide open, taking in the vast lake and the shore beyond it.

Maya and the Cosmic Alchemist step forward, and hug the Cosmic Creator. They all look young and beautiful. It's strangely stirring for the Little Buddha to notice the strong current between the three of them as they embrace.

"Is this kind of thing going to happen to me?" is his last thought before climbing on the boat.

After giving a few instructions to the couple, the Cosmic Creator turns around and also climbs on the boat, causing the waters to splash at being displaced with such weight.

Out on the Lake, the three become very quiet. The silence is deepened by the gentle swooshing sounds of the Cosmic Creator at work in the Lake, which is once more aglow with colors around his boat.

"It's time to open your eyes, Little Buddha", he whispers," "Look for the last time at your childlike self," and invites him to the side of the boat.

The Little Buddha sees the reflection of himself as a child, bursting with health and liveliness, and bows down in thankfulness for the experience that he is about to complete.

"And now for the first time look at your new self…"

He notices another larger reflection: a man, a fully-grown male with blond curls and slightly slanted blue eyes. He emanates strength and gentleness.

He is exactly what he was wishing for.

"Dive into the water towards the reflection, Little Buddha," he hears the somehow distant voice of the Cosmic Creator beckoning him, ". When you are there, dip with your whole body under water. I will be there to hold you: you will reemerge transmuted."

The ceremony that follows is basic and ancient, no high tech, just a simple human affair: the Little Buddha jumps into the water, the hem of his robe floating on the surface. When he reaches the larger reflection, the Cosmic Creator is there, waiting for him. Held by him, the Little Buddha dips completely into the Lake.

For a moment, all is quiet. The Monkey holds his breath.

Then, a strong wind starts blowing, creating ripples on the Lake and shivers down his spine…

The body that emerges with a large gulp from the water is much bigger, taller and stronger.

"Welcome to the world, Big Buddha," the Cosmic Creator says, helping him up and gesturing to the Monkey to row back towards the shore.

Once out of the boat, surrounded by the silent tribe, the three of them stand half in the water, sharing a deep sense of wonder. The Big Buddha is touching his body, testing the strength of his arms, looking confused at the Monkey, so small in comparison to him. The Monkey's first response is just pride. He loves his friend's new appearance, and is happy about his new size: it makes him feel protected; he can take the passenger seat now…

Their Divine friends slowly come closer. One by one, they congratulate the Big Buddha with a few words and hug him.

When all of them have gone, the Cosmic Creator takes his leave with a promise: "We will always be connected…" and disappears into the night.

The golden full moon seems to smile at the Lake, amplifying its glow.

Chapter Twentyeight

ALL ROADS LEAD TO GOA

New Moon in Scorpio- A True Meeting of the Heart

The district of Goa in India is pretty. It has it all: beaches, lovely Portuguese bungalows, tall coconut forests, and a multicolored community of backpackers, traditional tourists, Japanese tour groups, hippies and seekers of all kinds mixed in with the local dark Catholic Indians.

Every Wednesday all of them with no exception go on a pilgrimage to the local Flee Market, using whatever means of transportation they can find: some come by foot through a rocky cliff over the ocean, others by squeezing four on one motorbike, the richer ones by taxis driven by overfriendly drivers or even by boat, crossing the sometimes capricious waters to the next bay.

The Anjuna Flee Market sprawls over a long stretch of inland under palm trees and close enough to the beach for a dip in the Indian Ocean. It's teeming with humanity. The bright Indian colors of the cloths waving in the breeze on so many stalls create a festive atmosphere, and the perfect background for the variety of people's skin colors, from bright pink to leathery brown. Vendors and hustlers of all types push their goods on the by passers who slalom across them. The smells of food, spices, and incense blend with smoke and dung. The Tibetan bells mix in with shrill voices of Indian female pop stars, while loud vintage rock music alternates to booming techno beats. This is the heart of Goa.

A tall handsome blond man is walking around with a small monkey in tow. He stops at a stall to look at white embroidered cotton shirts while drinking a hot chai from a paper cup. Although his bleached hair is just as long as many other men's here, and he wears faded Indian clothes like everyone else around, he somehow stands out. To begin with, he talks all the time to the monkey, and the animal seems to talk back to him just like any human friend would.

"This place is timeless", the Big Buddha tells the Monkey, "OK, now there are cellphones and gadgets everywhere. But it's just remarkable how India manages to maintain its essence…"

The Monkey replies: "I simply love it…Does my new brocade vest with glitters suit me?" He asks, puffing his chest proudly and showing off for the hundredth time his fancy new purchase, bargained down to nothing, from a street-clever young Indian girl that has caught his attention by calling him: "Hey you, sexy monkey!"

The Big Buddha kindly nods, offering no further comment on the flashy taste of the Monkey. He definitely prefers a more understated style for himself.

The two have been on the road for a couple of weeks, just wandering through India, the safest place for the Big Buddha to get accustomed to his size and appearance: there is more tolerance for extravagance and oddities here than anywhere else in the world…

They left the North as soon as they could, looking for warmer weathers to ease the Monkey's dark moods. They alternated walking to hitchhiking. The Big Buddha felt that this was the best way for him to exercise and get grounded. The Monkey didn't mind the constant moving: monkeys are anyway always on the go, and always enthusiastic about change.

"Hey little Monkey!" a familiar, melodious female voice reaches them from the dense crowd of the Flee Market. It takes a moment for them to locate it, until the Big Buddha catches a glimpse of an upraised hand and a flash of color from a scarf waving.

The Monkey is beside himself: "It's the Istanbul Lady!" he screams and starts running, bumping the crowd, stumbling over himself to reach her. But as soon as he comes close to what seems to be her market stall, he stops short. The Young Shaman is also there.

Luckily, the Big Buddha comes right behind him. Guessing the situation, he jumps to the front to divert the Young Shaman's attention from the Monkey's expression of dismay. The stall is glittering with crystals and precious stone pendants. There is also a round coffee table in a corner, covered with an indigo blue velvet cloth. Several books, decks of cards and an Ipad are neatly displayed on it.

"It's my working corner," says the Istanbul Lady to the Big Buddha, who is more than happy to cover for his little sensitive friend.

"Hello," the young man greets the Big Buddha. He has a broad smile, and the air of a friendly rascal. The Big Buddha likes him instantly.

"Do you also work here?" he asks, not knowing what else to say

"I sell my potions, you know, for bad bellies and hangovers, which is what people suffer from the most here, and my magic pendants…" He then looks lovingly at the still brooding Monkey, and tells him: "Little Monkey, I am so glad to see you, no harm done, are we cool, hey, friend?"

The little Monkey is in a reaction: he likes the Young Shaman, but there is no way he is going to accept his condescending remarks …

The Istanbul Lady comes to his rescue: "My dear beloved Monkey, come and sit with us. And...is this man whom I think it is...?"

The Big Buddha is overwhelmed by emotions: "I am so grateful to you...." His voice is only a whisper, but the intense feeling in it seems to silence the market's noise for a moment.

"We are also grateful to you, man, we learnt so much in our journey to create...", says the Young Shaman with a broad smile.

"Let's not talk about it in public," interrupts the Istanbul Lady, "for now, let's just celebrate our reunion. I am so happy to see you again dear Monkey!"

The Monkey's resistance completely evaporates. The people he loves most are here, together, and it's not the time for grudges.

"It's closing time," she adds after checking her IPhone, "Wait for us at the cappuccino stall over there, we'll join you as soon as we have packed up."

A few hours later, the four of them are sitting under a velvety moonless sky at a gourmet Vegetarian Restaurant inland. They are chatting and enjoying the soft breeze after a delicious meal. The Big Buddha, still puzzled by the size of his appetite in this new body, is trying to digest his three courses while the Monkey leans between his two old friends and tells them about their trip through India.

"And what is your plan now, friends?" asks the Young Shaman.

"We don't have any, our savings are dwindling, and we are waiting for guidance. We trust it will come at the right time..." replies the Big Buddha.

"We might just be its instruments, with the blessing of Allah," the Istanbul Lady answers with a chuckle...

And so it happens that the Big Buddha and the Monkey settle in the small but comfortable hut adjoined to the young couple's cottage on a nearby stretch of empty white beach.

One evening, after a whole week of leisure, good dinners and interesting discussions on the subject of healing and meditation, the Istanbul Lady produces for everyone to look her Ipad, open on a page full of colorful lines crisscrossing a world map. She is definitely in a working mood, the Monkey thinks, noticing her serious expression.

"I have made some calculations," she says, pointing at a particular spot on the map where a blue and a green curve meet, "According to your rebirth horoscope, Big Buddha, Istanbul is a very good place for you. It is the crossing point between the Mars and Jupiter lines. It will strengthen you as a man, and make you adventurous, full of energy and enthusiasm. It's a perfect place for a new start..."

"I love Istanbul!" butts in the Monkey, unable to contain his excitement.

"And so Istanbul it will be..." joins in the Big Buddha, with a happy trusting smile that echoes the child, still alive inside him.

"Would you like to be my guests?" asks the Lady, casting a glance of complicity towards the Young Shaman, who chuckles and replies: "I will go back to my cave in Siberia, but mark my word, my Monkey friend, I'll be watching you…"

"Istanbul is so different now in November from last time I was here… I am freezing…" the Monkey is shivering non-stop. The big city seems to be sulking since a couple of days: it's gray, rainy and it feels miserable. Down below, the Bosporus has turned into a dark angry cataract of water.

Inside the Lady's flat, though, there are roaring flames in the fireplace and comfortable couches and cushions to lounge on.

The Monkey wonders: the place is exactly as he remembers it, even the infamous vase with umbrellas at the entrance, but it all feels different. He cannot shake off the itch to move on: his life has just started, he feels, and there is much more for him to experience out there.

One week has already passed since they left Goa. After a touching goodbye at the Mumbai airport with the Young Shaman, looking so different in his Siberian attire, the remaining three of them took their flight to Istanbul. The Big Buddha utterly enjoyed his first experience on an airplane: it made him feel again closer to the cosmos.

After a couple of days, the Lady resumed going out for sessions while the two friends remained in her home, eating and resting.

The Big Buddha was totally absorbed for some time into browsing through the vast assortment of esoteric books piled up here and there in the apartment, while the Monkey seemed to never get tired of sleeping.

For their whole time in Istanbul, their evening dinners with the Lady were the highlight of the day. While eating the delicious food that they prepared together, the three of them discussed all sorts of topics. There was a particularly hilarious moment around the table when the Big Buddha, looking sincerely puzzled, declared: "If the Belladonna was my wife in a past life, does that make you, Lady, my past life niece?" Everyone, a bit tipsy from the bubbly French Champagne opened in honor of the Lady's Aunt transformation, roared with laughter.

But this afternoon, maybe because of the persistent rain or just because their traveling spirit is waking up again, the Monkey and the Big Buddha are both fidgety. "I am tired of reading," says the Big Buddha, walking up and down the apartment. "And I am tired of…sleeping…" the Monkey giggles at his own absurdity, "but it's true, it feels like that…"

"You two," says the Lady on her way out, "go for a walk, you need it. I have an inkling that this coming Taurus Full Moon night will shed a new light on your path ahead…"

And with the flash of a smile and a swoosh of her long satin skirt, she is out of the door.

"Let's go to the old part of town!!!" the Monkey says with the tone of an expert, "I know my way around here…"

The Big Buddha, happy, throws on the overcoat given to him as a gift by the Young Shaman, and is ready to go.

As they walk up the steep cobblestoned slopes crammed with small apartments they look carefree, like two friends on an adventure. The late afternoon sun is breaking through the clouds, creating a kaleidoscope of colors in the sky.

"Look here! Such a pretty layout!" the Big Buddha has stopped in front of an ancient brick wall plastered with flyers and posters advertising all sorts of services, from Yoga classes to pet care, from night parties to morning concertos. He is pointing at an orange poster with a beautiful headline embossed in gold: "Dwija Circus on the Road again".

The Monkey looks at it casually, and then stops, stares, and starts pointing and laughing hysterically at the same time.

The Big Buddha is nonplussed, waiting for his friend to recover:

"Look carefully at the people in the poster," the Monkey finally gasps, "Do you recognize them?"

Smiling at them from the paper is the German Buddha, wearing a fancy leopard print long coat. Next to him on both sides, is the whole Council of Twelve, dressed in colorful Circus attires. Behind them, there is a large Circus tent with a striped canvas roof.

"Dwija…I remember…" the Big Buddha whispers in amazement, "Dwija means Twice Born in Sanskrit. It is a term used for those who have attained a second birth in their lives. Parents give you the first birth, but only you can give birth to your real self and become a Dwija, a Twice Born."

He turns to the Monkey with a big smile full of wonder: "I should have known, when I saw that temporary structure in Shambala…"

"Of course, it was a Circus Tent!!!" the Monkey, forgetting completely his Turkish manners, is almost screaming.

"Shall we go tonight, little Monkey?"

The Monkey nods his head fiercely in assent…

They jump, skip and hop on one leg, laughing like kids, for the rest of their way home.

That evening before dinner they dress up really fancy; the Monkey dusts out of his pile of clothes his elegant cream silk suit, and the Big Buddha wears a hand embroidered saffron kaftan bought for him by the Lady in the Gran Bazaar.

"You two look really elegant, tonight! What is the occasion?" asks the Istanbul Lady coming home from work, "any special blessing from the coming Full Moon?" They tell her the surprising news and invite her to come with them. "No, thanks, beloved friends, this is part of your story, not mine…" she replies, and, turning to the Monkey, she changes the subject: "Your dress code has evolved since we last met, little Monkey!"

"You have been the inspiration for it all: you were the one who bought for me new unusual clothes…remember the red shirt? And the tights?" he stutters, looking away towards the mirror to adjust his lapel, "Little did I know when I was a Lama about showing off!" he says, surprising everyone. For a split second, they all can see through his animal appearance the highly evolved being that is having so much fun watching his monkey self…

Soon, it's time to go. After dabbing the nape of their necks with some fragrant sandalwood oil, the Lady sends the two friends off into the city that never sleeps with some directions.

Just as they close the door, they hear her sweet voice whispering: "Happy "rebirth day", Big Buddha…"

Chapter Twentynine

THE DWIJA CIRCUS

Full Moon in Taurus- Mystery unveiled

The Circus Tent stands in a wide-open stretch of green along the Bosporus. The people waiting outside don't seem to mind the cold wind; the steam of their breaths creates around them a warm cozy cloud of protection. The area is fully illuminated with festive lights, and invisible loudspeakers diffuse an artfully modernized version of an ancient Sufi tune. During his last visit to Shambala, the Big Buddha has grown to admire the many talents of the Buddha of Technical Support and Maintenance; now he can recognize his hand at work in the perfection of sound and lighting.

The first surprise waits for our two friends at the box office. Sitting behind it is the enigmatic longhaired Waif Buddha. She is known more for her strong presence than for talking. When she greets him with a conspiratorial smile, the Big Buddha suddenly remembers how much he likes her: "We were hoping you would come soon! We'll talk later. Meanwhile, enjoy the show!" she says, winking at the Monkey and handing him the tickets for the best front row seats: "These have been waiting for you two since quite a while…"

Once through the heavy velvet drapes into the Circus Hall, it is like stepping into a Fairy Tale. The ground is covered with gold dust, the seats are plush and comfortable, and the dome of the tent is alive with large holograms that keep on shifting shape.

From their front row seats, the Big Buddha and the Monkey can see the audience of all ages coming in. Once inside, everyone becomes silent. There is an unusual hushed quality in the air. Even small children stare silently at all the glitter. Without really knowing why, some even close their eyes as soon as they are seated.

When the Hall is full, the lights are dimmed to almost dark. A lonely violin starts playing. The man playing it slowly emerges from the shadows and walks to the center of the ring. Suddenly, a bright spotlight illuminates his features.

The Monkey gently taps the Big Buddha's elbow: "the German Buddha!"

They both stare open mouthed: he is wearing a long Leopard print coat, and is playing with abandon. As his music picks up, all the lights go on, and the other eleven

Buddhas appear in the ring, taking turns to introduce their act. The Waif Buddha, in a light baby blue tutu riveting with clouds of gauze, is standing on her pointed toes over a holographic unicorn, while behind them the Buddha of Technical Support and Maintenance is materializing countless musical lotuses floating in the air…When the music reaches its final peak, the Twelve, including the German Buddha whose violin is now playing by itself while floating in the air, start whirling in unison, creating around themselves tornados of color and light.

Then, everyone stops, the audience draws a long held breath, and from the loudspeakers a voice announces:

"Let the Show begin!!"

The acts that follow are all a genial mix of entertainment and meditation. Like in most Circuses, people become children again and have fun, but here, in addition, each performance ends with a meditation technique, to which both actors and audience participate.

"And now allow yourself to feel that there is no separation between us… feel a honeylike substance penetrating your heart and expanding all the way to your armpits…" the Eternal Child Buddha, a girl with the sweetest nature, guides everyone into a deep relaxation after her dolphin performance.

"She is evoking the Golden Essence of Merging!" the Monkey exclaims, noticing how slowly everyone relaxes into his or her seat with a contented smile.

When after her dance show with tigers the Dark Skinned Buddha leads the audience into Baby Gibberish our two friends are deeply touched. They are stunned about the leading male tiger, which becomes like a sweet cub and goes around licking people's face while they blabber like babies and pet him.

The performances continue, each one surpassing the previous one.

The Monkey is deeply impressed by all the animals on stage: "They have a human quality in their eyes. They are not obeying to commands, they are also performing! I bet that with the right training they could start talking very soon…."

"Who knows? Maybe some of them have chosen like you to be reborn as animals…." The Big Buddha replies, with one of his grown-up-man chuckles.

In the next act, six Buddhas, standing on a tightrope close to the roof, form a human pyramid, while the other six freely float around them. The loudspeaker is broadcasting a reading of the Lotus Sutra about timelessness. For a moment, the audience is entranced, transported mid air with the performers, free from gravity and structure.

"Never in my life…" the Big Buddha is just saying when the final act is announced.

The final act of the evening is a collective underwater dance performance. A very large transparent tub starts rising from the glittery floor: it fills itself as it comes up with rainbow colored water and colorful tropical fish. When the tub has reached its full ten-meter height, the Twelve, all dressed in gauzy robes, dive into the water. After a few minutes, it is clear to all that the performers have the capacity to stay underwater much longer than normal.

"Training, lifetimes of training, this is what this is," the Big Buddha whispers into the Monkey's ears, "And it really brings you in touch with your life source…"

The Monkey, reminded of his Tummo, winks at him and sits back to enjoy the last show. First the Twelve freely dance on high energy Disco Music, creating whirlpools around each other, and then, as the music turns into a soft Indian tune, they let themselves drift around peacefully in the water.

The final applause seems to last forever. It becomes a standing ovation, and the Twelve keep on bowing, sending kisses in the air and joining their hands in a Namaste.

When the clapping dies down, the Eternal Child Buddha steps forward. She sings with her angelic voice the closing song, a blessing for the Earth, inviting the audience to join in.

Outside along the Bosporus, late hour bypassers hear the faint echo of the people singing, and see the Circus Tent glowing with a pink pearly light as bright as the full moon in the sky. Few of them realize how surprisingly good they are feeling, for no reason at all.

Inside the Circus Tent, while everyone stands up to leave, the Big Buddha and the Monkey remain seated. They both have teary eyes, and are still holding hands, speechless.

"You look fantastic in your new appearance, Big Buddha…We expected you two sooner," the unmistakable German voice from the back catches them by surprise; "You look like you have had a great time this last month…"

The two friends stand up and turn around to find the whole Council, with their stage makeup in all sorts of sorry states, smiling at them.

"It was quite something to step out in the world…we did not realize how much it would leave us exposed. It was a bit like stepping off a pedestal," tells them the Dark Skinned Buddha.

"I never ever dreamt in my whole time in Shambala that one day I would lead a full human audience into a song of blessing," the Eternal Child Buddha remarks.

"Let's give them a moment," steps in the practical Buddha of Technical Support and Maintenance.

"Let's just sit for a moment all in a circle and close our eyes," whispers the Waif Buddha, anyway more at ease with silence.

The Big Buddha, still holding the Monkey's hand, looks at the circle surrounding him. While he opens up to the warm wave of love coming from all sides, the last debris of concern still clouding his soul vanish. He feels at home with his fellow Buddhas, but no longer in an ivory tower…

Later that night, they all move to the comfortable trailer of the Empress of Poetry Buddha, well known for her taste for design and luxury.

"Sorry, Big Buddha, sorry, little Monkey," the rather large Empress of Poetry Buddha talks for all of them with her kind, deep voice, "We could not tell you that we were preparing to leave Shambala when you were there with us. We would have told you in due time, because we needed your advice on how to make it in this New World…but you both told us that you wanted to go, and we did not want to burden you…" She waves her bejeweled hands as if to sweep the past clean, and continues: "But now we can see that it was meant to be this way, in perfect synchronicity as usual. This last month we had to face arrest on our way down in Almora. We hadn't thought about bringing any ID, and the police stopped us. Luckily the German Buddha speaks a few words in Hindi, and this charmed the local police. We had to anyway spend the night in a common cell with people who were there for all sorts of different reasons, but they let us go in the morning." She looks at the others, and adds with a perfect smile: "After our release, we had to find ways to leave India, which included making contact with many surprisingly beautiful people and receiving from them invaluable information about the ways of the New World. Some of them in fact knew you -from the Center of the Controversial Master in Greece- as the Little Buddha and the Monkey. They were on their way back to Greece from the big Resort dedicated to their Master in Maharashtra…"

"They have a festival in summer in Greece, you could come…" the Monkey chips in enthusiastically. The Big Buddha gently nudges him with his elbow, and whispers: "later…"

"We also met some very interesting professors from a recently established University of Mystery and Science in the Valley of Manali, that seems to offer a fantastic winter program," says the Buddha of Technical Support an Maintenance, "They showed us slides of the place: a combination of enchanting Tudor architecture and tall tainted glass pyramids. It all runs on solar power and wind."

"We all liked them very much," adds the German Buddha, dressed again in his usual plain robe. Suddenly, he laughs out loudly, something unheard of: "and we did something really new: we told them that we were from Shambala, and we invited them there next summer for a Cosmic Festival…You can imagine their response: honorable teachers crying and laughing like babies…"

"It was touching. We opened up Shambala for Buddhas-to-be…" adds the Waif Buddha.

This last remark wins the Big Buddha's heart once and for all. He is about to speak when the German Buddha jumps back in, clearing his throat and saying: "Returning to the here and now, with all due love and respect for you Big Buddha and you, Monkey, we ask: would you two like to join our traveling Circus?"

Our two friends look at each other: there is no trace of doubt in the Big Buddha's eyes, but the Monkey, normally so overenthusiastic and dramatic, looks down at the ground, silent. When he finally lifts his eyes, he looks flushed: "Dear Council, dear Buddhas, even in my wildest dreams as a Lama I could have never imagined that something like this would be possible…thank you. And I am so happy for the Big Buddha that he found you all again. There is something I would like to say before responding to your invitation…"

The Big Buddha interrupts him: "And I am delighted and honored to participate to this experiment."

Everyone smiles at his words, and the Empress of Poetry Buddha responds: "We too feel honored, dear Big Buddha, to have you again amongst us. You have been the great inspiration that made this jump possible."

Everyone gets up, and surrounds the Big Buddha with a collective hug. He is overwhelmed, amused, and curious about all the new sensations that this warm body contact provoke in him.

But the Monkey is not in the embrace. Emerging from it, the Big Buddha's eyes immediately start looking for him. He is sitting in a corner, looking sad. "My sweetest friend," he says, leaning towards him," Did I interrupt you before? What did you want to say?"

The Monkey can feel the Big Buddha's loving concern, and how his previous enthusiasm is a bit dampened by it. He does not want this to happen: he gives the Big Buddha a lopsided smile and says, sounding exactly like the Young Shaman: "No harm done, hey friend " They both laugh, remembering him with great affection.

"We will have to take our bags and say goodbye to our hostess," the Big Buddha tells the German Buddha, "and...where will be heading next?" he asks, barely able to contain his excitement.

"We usually set up the Circus Tent wherever we feel a good potential. So we'll move and we'll see..." the German Buddha explains to the Big Buddha, who nods understandingly.

"And this time we'll announce a brand new act: the Big Buddha and the Monkey!" exclaims the Eternal Child Buddha clapping her hands.

"Me? And the Monkey?"

"Well," comments the Waif Buddha, in a never-heard-before long string of words, "sooner or later you will have to get used to your new looks...you are now a handsome guy. With a bit of glitter and makeup, you will look like a rock star and dazzle the audiences! Then you can do anything and it will look good..." The Big Buddha, a bit uneasy about the compliment, blushes and looks away; but when he looks again, he sees only kindness in her deep blue eyes. Everyone, including him, softly giggles. The Monkey relaxes into a smile.

The following morning, after a long goodbye breakfast, the Istanbul Lady tells the two friends on their way out of the flat: "We will all anyway meet soon again in surprising circumstances, Allah bless you..." and gently closes the door behind them.

They are welcomed at the Circus site by the loud clanging of metal tubes assembling themselves, and the "swoosh" of the big circus tent deflating and folding itself. The Twelve, in simple and graceful traveling clothes, are standing on the side in admiration while the Buddha of Technical Support and Maintenance directs the whole operation from his laptop. Everything else is already neatly packed in the trolleys attached to the colorfully decorated caravans.

The Buddha and the Monkey are shown to their own separate caravans. "It's the Shambala way," the Big Buddha tells the Monkey, who in his animal nature would be much happier to sleep nice and warm in one space with him.

"Today you look like a ripe peach…or maybe like a juicy mango…or…" the Monkey has gotten into the habit of teasing the Big Buddha about his blooming appearance. He sighs in response. It's the end of their first month with the Circus, and the combination of physical exercise and life outdoors has created a vibrant sheen of good health on both their faces. The Big Buddha looks like a healthy man, although he remains boyish and virginal in the way he keeps to himself and shuns intimacy. While on stage, he is a natural, and he looks flamboyant and charming in his performances with the Monkey, but with women he remains shy, reserved.

It's nighttime: the air is quite cool, but with a good coat on it's still pleasant. They are sitting outside their caravans under the stars. The others, tired after the long road trip from Brindisi and one night on the ferry before that, have gone to sleep. Stretching in front of the two friends, hill after hill, is the city of Rome, dotted with cupolas, lined at the edges with the dark silhouettes of tall stone pines.

It's the Monkey's turn to sigh: sometimes he longs back for his adventures on his own, for that sense of total freedom that comes when one travels alone. It's like an inner itch for going his own way that he doesn't want to confront just yet. He loves his friend, and appreciates the glamour of Circus performances combined with meditation. The Big Buddha and him have had fun creating their act together, a mixture of his own shamanic rituals and subtle body healing events by the Big Buddha, all of it spiced up with slapstick and clownery provided by the Monkey. They recently added also some occasional outbursts of rock music alternated with ethnic tunes from all over the planet, which gained the Big Buddha the extra function of Circus DJ. Children are always mesmerized by their act, and adults become like children again watching it. But somehow the Monkey cannot completely find himself in this new life.

"I wonder how my parents on the Little Planet are doing," he says, looking with dreamy eyes at the panorama.

The Big Buddha can feel that this communal lifestyle that he is so at ease with doesn't suit the Monkey's rebellious nature, "Too bad that most of the intelligent animals in the Circus turned out to be just holograms…I am sorry about that," There is a little strain in his voice. He has tried just about everything to cheer the Monkey up. But the Monkey just lifts his head and sighs again.

A few days later while rehearsing, the Big Buddha tries another approach. He asks straight out to the Monkey: "My dear little best friend, what is happening? I can hardly reach you. We don't talk and we don't laugh anymore. We have become just working partners. Does this have something to do with the fact that I have grown in size and that you look so small in comparison?"

The Monkey does not immediately respond or deny. He is weighing friendship against freedom: "Ehmmm," he finally says, deciding for friendship, "I do feel that we are out of balance in our Circus act. You are so large and I am so small that it might not be easy for the audience to see us both at the same time. I don't know if there is anything we can do about this…"

The Big Buddha secretly smiles. He has an inspiration. Early this morning, he went for a hot chocolate in a nearby typically Roman Bar. While paying, he noticed a new poster on the wall behind the cashier that read: "This Sunday special offer at the Porta Portese Market. Birds, cats, dogs and monkeys almost for free, available for adoption by loving and caring humans that can respect their background and private history, and want to foster their unique talents". Some deep understanding for our animal friends, he thought, on his way out. Now he is happy that he saw it.

There was no specific number or directions on the poster. Porta Portese is big, the Big Buddha thinks, but it's worth a try…

"Maybe it's not something, but somebody that can help us…" he says, jumping up, "what day of the week are we?"

"Sunday…" shouts the Eternal child Buddha, skipping by.

Chapter Thirty

SOULMATES

Full Moon In Gemini – Twin Souls

"Everything looked so simple when I first thought of it…", the Big Buddha thinks, as he makes his way jostling through the crowd of Porta Portese, the huge Flea Market of Rome. Families on their Sunday outing mingle with young people dressed in all sorts of fashions, while petty thieves and shady dealers loiter in the corners. He is on his own. He wants to find good company for his friend the Monkey and surprise him.

He likes the market instantly. He prefers the human contact and exchange happening here to the new over-lighted and impersonal shopping centers.

There must be some logic in the division of the stalls, he is sure of it, but he has no patience to figure it out. Relying on his intuition, he starts wandering around, browsing through colorful clothes, stainless steel pots and Chinese gadgets with no apparent aim, until he hears the sound of an accordeon played with virtuosity.

Almost hidden in this very alive and noisy corner of the market is a gypsy, sitting on a stool and playing his instrument. It is as if his music is born by itself, effortlessly rising above all noises. The man looks absorbed in it, with a faraway look in his eyes. The Big Buddha realizes that the gypsy is sitting right in the middle of the area where the animals are sold. He is surrounded by stalls loaded with cages of all sizes. Multicolored birds respond with their chirping to his music, while dangerous snakes and reptiles slither lazily in their glass boxes, and puppies and kittens piled up together in large cartons seem to relax on top of each other with his tune.

This man looks different, thinks the Big Buddha. He is not from here. He is taller than him, and wears his long white hair in a braid. He has a sharp profile, like an eagle…the Big Buddha jolts in recognition.

"Are you really the Peruvian Magician?" he asks, coming closer and talking loudly over the music, unable to contain his surprise.

The 'Gypsy' nods ever so slightly. That's enough of an answer for the Big Buddha's heart to start beating faster.

The Peruvian Magician stops playing and carefully places his accordion in its case.

"My work here is done," he says with a singsong accent. He picks up a cloth sack nearby and slowly opens it, revealing its content. It's a monkey.

He is smaller than the Monkey. Its fur is of a glossy silver grey, and it has pale blue eyes.

It looks around, stares silently at the Big Buddha, and then turns away.

The Peruvian Magician pats it on the tiny head, and turns to look at the Big Buddha, "Although I never saw you before, I have met you intimately," he says, "each time our friend the Enlightened Monkey spoke about you, I could see you through his heart."

"But how did you…" the Big Buddha asks, trying to tie loose ends together.

"After the Monkey left for Istanbul to my coven-sister, I remained a little longer in my house close to the pyramids taking care of my vegetable patch and enjoying my aloneness. One of the women of the Constellation Ritual, the wife of a local zoo owner, came to see me there for advice about a silver grey monkey, who had been brought to the zoo by the police almost dead. She had brought it slowly back to life with good food and care, but it was not healing on a deeper level. Nobody could touch it, and it could only move sideways to protect itself from a possible beating. Recently, it had even started to refuse food again."

The Big Buddha can see the fear of violence in its constant subtle trembling. The blaring sounds that have taken over the Market since the Peruvian Magician stopped playing are obviously too much for the grey monkey.

"I told her to bring the monkey with her, and she came the day after with a large bamboo cage. When I looked inside, I couldn't even see it at first. It was lying in a little heap in corner, shivering. I started to call him "Grey", and took him to live with me. It took lots of care and patience from my side before he let me touch him, but it never went beyond a certain point. He remains scared and isolated."

"It does remind me of myself in my dark period…" the Big Buddha smiles with gratefulness, remembering his own healing.

"But in this case we Mysterious Four did not seem to be enough…" the Peruvian Magician continues, "I asked everyone of them to help, but none of us really knew what to do. That's how I heard that, after becoming big, you met the Istanbul Lady and the Young Shaman in Goa, and how initially the Monkey got upset about seeing them together…"

"He has very strong reactions," the Big Buddha says with a sigh about his friend, "and he doesn't seem happy at the moment either…"

"This is where I am getting at…" smiles the Peruvian Magician, "Last time I was on Skype with the Istanbul Lady, about a week ago, she told me how happy she felt about you joining the Dwija Circus, but added that she had some doubts about the Monkey. He seemed unusually quiet…"

A big cloud of guilt crosses the Big Buddha face.

The Peruvian Magician waves it away with a gesture of his hand and a smile: "Never feel guilty about your happiness!" and continues, "Anyway, the night after our conversation, I felt troubled about our friend the Monkey. I tried to think about what could make him happy and boisterous again, but I could only see in front of my inner eye two sad and lonely monkeys, lost in this large human world.... Until suddenly the solution came to me like lightning bolt. I could only wonder why I had not thought of it earlier. I asked one of my lady friends to book for me a ticket to Rome, the city of romance and love.... I was going to visit my friend, the Enlightened Monkey, and take the little grey monkey with me!"

One of his lady friends, he says…the Big Buddha is looking at the Peruvian Magician from a new angle, considering what he could learn from him…

"I also sent an email to a former lady student of mine in Rome," he continues, "asking if I could stay with her for a few days," and adds with a rakish smile, "and she said yes!"

"For the travel I chose a long winter coat, which allowed me to hide the little grey monkey in its folds. It was definitely a good idea…the cold north wind in this city can really drive you insane!" the Big Buddha nods, rubbing his freezing arms. "After leaving my luggage in the lady student's home, I kept warm by filling all the bars around the Circus neighborhood with my poster. I knew from the Istanbul Lady how fond of Italian hot chocolate you are. I was sure you would find my message…"

The little grey monkey has meanwhile again retreated in his cloth bag. Not a movement could be detected in the small bundle. The Big Buddha approaches the bag, and opening a tiny sliver on top, he gently lifts it in his arms. The little grey monkey just looks up at him from the opening. He seems to have a well of sorrow in its beautiful pale blue eyes. The Big Buddha opens the sack a bit more to reveal its whole face. It's thin, emaciated, but the silver grey of its hair shines like the moon.

The Peruvian Magician sighs with relief, and hugs the Big Buddha: "It's all yours now, I'll be in touch…" he says, stepping back.

For a short moment, the two humans and the monkey, still half in the sack, fall completely silent. The Peruvian Magician joins his hands in a Namaste and the Big Buddha responds with the same gesture. From the half open sack in his arms, the tiny hands of the grey monkey respond with the same salute.

As he starts walking away from the stalls with the grey money, the Big Buddha hears a commotion behind him. He turns around, and sees the Peruvian Magician handing a wad of notes to the owner of the bird stall.

"What? Do you want me to free them all?" he hears the surprised shout of the vendor. Suddenly, the sky is filled with multicolored flapping wings and a symphony of birdcalls. In the middle of it all, the Peruvian Magician is waving him goodbye with a big grin, shouting on top of his lungs: "Please don't tell my friend the Enlightened Monkey that I was here, I will connect with him at some other point!" Only now the Big Buddha notices that all the reptiles are free too, slithering all over the Peruvian Magician while he is busy buying freedom for all the puppies and kittens. He doesn't seem to mind: it must be a Shaman thing, the Big Buddha tells himself, happily on his way back to the Circus Tent.

The expression on the Monkey's face is one of shock and delight when he peeps into the sack that the Big Buddha is holding in his arms. The silver monkey's eyes shine like two feeble lanterns in the darkness.

"I thought that this little monkey, I call him Grey, could create a new balance in our act. It would take some training, of course…" says the Big Buddha with a questioning smile. Looking at the fragile bundle in his arms, he adds: "It will take some care and love to bring him out of its shock, but I trust we can do it…"

The Monkey reaches out and touches the silver fur gently: "We will call him Grey, and he will be our friend". He is deeply touched, and also excited by the challenge of teaching him something. The Big Buddha smiles: he has managed to make his friend happy again…. with some secret help, of course.

Everyone in the Circus celebrates the arrival of Grey. They all try their best to make contact with the sad and beautiful little creature. Finally, the German Buddha fishes out of his vast knowledge the memory that he somewhere read that some musicians are said to have monkey blood in them. Laughing, he grabs his violin and sets off into an irresistible Gypsy tune. Everyone around is up on his or her feet, keeping rhythm with the music.

Feeling unwatched, Grey starts also moving: first carefully, then slowly letting go and joining the dance. But as soon as one of the dancers tries to make contact with him, he shrinks away in some safe corner of himself: he still dances, but his steps are mechanical and his pale eyes void.

The Waif Buddha, who has suffered lifetimes of food disorders before her enlightenment, goes out of her way to try and find out what are Grey's favorite morsels, but he won't eat anything.

The last one to fail is the Dark Skinned Buddha: when her tiger tries its sweet little cub number on him, Grey retreats terrified into his sack for a whole day.

But our Monkey is not going to give up on his new friend. Since Grey is there, a new energy has entered him. He wants to take care.

A couple of days after his arrival, the Monkey softly knocks at the door of Grey's new little caravan. Hearing no answer, he gently opens, and looks inside. Grey is sitting in a corner, staring at the wall, a big platter of bananas and coconut slices lying untouched in front of him.

The Monkey tiptoes closer until he can hold his hand.

For the first time there is a tiny reaction. Grey is whispering in a strangely accented monkey language: "I don't want to see you"

"Come outside in the sunshine, everybody is friendly here, this is not a cage!" says the Monkey, scratching his back gently.

"No, I cannot, I am locked up in here!" comes another barely audible whisper.

"No, you are not! I have just opened the door!"

"No, there is no way to open that door! The door is inside me, I am locked up in this cage inside of me!"

Grey looks so scared. The Monkey experiences a big pang in his heart: "What happened to you?"

"I don't want to talk about it," there is such weariness in his soft voice, "I don't want to tell anybody, but, let me tell you, I have reasons enough not to want to feel anymore."

With a little intake of breath, Grey lifts his gaze to meet the Monkey's eyes. In contrast with his liquid brown eyes, Grey's eyes are very pale. At that moment, a warm current that connects them beyond words passes through them. The Monkey is amazed at how attracted he is to Grey's beauty.

"What is your name?" the Monkey asks after a long spell of silence: "What is the name your parents gave you?"

Grey hesitates, almost retreating, but then speaks: "My name is Samantha."

"Samantha? Is this a boy's name?" the Monkey asks.

"Come on, silly!" Grey replies with a lovely giggle: "I am not a boy, I am a girl! Can't you see?"

The whole world around the Monkey seems to crumble. A girl monkey? What is he supposed to do now? He has an impulse to run to the Big Buddha, but he suddenly fears that he might want to send her away, and he wants her to stay at all costs.

One step at a time, he thinks, although this is the most difficult thing for him to master in a monkey body. He takes a deep breath and replies sweetly: "Samantha! What a beautiful name! Come, let's go for a walk together."

"I don't want my old name anymore, call me Grey, it's like being reborn..." she tells the Monkey with a shy smile.

It is amazing how she changes when she is a girl, the Monkey thinks, while he reaches out for her hand. When he touches it, he feels a high voltage running through both of them.

"This place is so beautiful..." she says, enthralled, "everyone is so free here, even the animals..."

"Sorry to disappoint you, my darling", the Monkey replies, surprising himself with the "darling", "but most animals here, except myself, the good old male tiger and a couple of horses, are holographic..." he jumps on the opportunity to show off his knowledge, and launches into an approximate explanation of holograms...

They continue walking around the Circus compund, looking here and there, while everyone including the Big Buddha tries not to stare too obviously. They do not talk, they just walk hand in hand until they stop at a corner, piled up with puppets and dolls that the Buddha of Technical Support and Maintenance likes to operate from time to time on stage. One of the dolls is wearing a very pretty little pink brocade dress.

The Monkey touches the material with appreciation, and turns to her: "Grey, let's get you that dress! I am sure it fits perfectly!"

She gasps: "No, I don't want!"

"Come on! You will look so pretty! You will look like a girl!"

Her beautiful eyes are brimming with tears when she weakly nods. He gently takes off the dress from the doll and hands it to her.

It does fit perfectly: her thinness is suddenly elegant, and her reserve becomes charming. There is no way back: the Monkey falls in love with her.

This time he recognizes the feeling: it's like in Istanbul but stronger, and less scary at the same time. This girl is not towering over him: she is like him. All the molecules in his body are rushing towards her: he wants to kiss her and hug her, and tell her that everything is going to be all right. But her eyes are still full of fear and pain. He realizes how fragile their connection still is, full of untold stories that maybe only time can heal. So he just takes her by the hand and walks on.

They find the Big Buddha all sweaty and dusty in the back of the Circus tent, happily preparing for the evening performance. He lifts his blond head from the stage prop he is creating and squints against the light. At first, he only sees the Monkey: "Hey dude, hello beloved friend!" he says with a newly acquired funky twist to his speech. Then he notices that his friend is holding hands with someone else smaller than him, who is wearing a lovely pink brocade dress.

"Who is that girl?" He whispers

Grey retreats in the shadow, but the Monkey holds on to her hand.

"This is the monkey you brought home, Grey!"

"But... he was not wearing a dress when he came! Why would you want him to look like a girl?"

"Big Buddha..." says the Monkey with a chuckle, "it's not a 'him'! Have you been in celibacy for so many lifetimes that you can't remember what girls look like anymore?"

The Big Buddha has to admit: he has completely forgotten how to connect with women: he fully honors their Buddhahood, but he is aware of still treating everyone, man or woman, with the same neutrality: "Is this true? Is she a girl?"

"She's a girl and her name used to be Samantha!"

"Samantha!" The Big Buddha echoes with genuine surprise. There is not a hint of criticism or accusation in his voice, notices the Monkey, relieved.

Instead, he kneels down and tries to make contact with Grey. She initially looks away, scared. But then she grips the Monkey's hand firmly and bravely looks up towards the big man. Used as she obviously is to be badly treated by most humans, she is thrown off guard by his eyes, so gentle and compassionate. She relaxes a fraction, but never lets go of the Monkey's hand.

In the language that animals and Buddhas equally understand, she speaks out in a tiny brave voice: "Yes, Big Buddha. I am Grey. I am a small silver-grey female. If you don't want me, you can set me free."

"No, no..." the Monkey starts, but she stops him and continues: "I lost my whole family. I cannot really remember them. I just remember escaping from the evil smugglers, and walking endlessly -without water or food- through many dangers from the jungle to the coast of Peru. When I was brought by the police to the zoo, I was full of fleas and crusts, on the verge of death…"

The Big Buddha looks angry, raging inside at the futile cruelty of humans towards animals. Grey misreads his expression and shouts in pure panic: "Please, don't bring me to another zoo or an animal shop! I am just a girl, but I will not disappoint you. You won't regret keeping me!" she forces herself to smile and adds, "I may look weak now, but I promise, I will start eating again! I will be the Monkey's partner in whatever you want us to perform in the Circus!!!"

The Monkey feels dizzy. Did she really say…US!?!? He hears loud trumpets from the sky, and then horns, violins and flutes. He is on a stairway to heaven, with golden balustrades and diamond chandeliers, dancing with his beloved on the beat of happy soul songs…

The Big Buddha's voice brings him back to reality: "Beloved Grey, you are welcome to stay! You are already part of my heart, and I respect your suffering and your innocence. The way you spoke for yourself shows how brave you are." Turning to the dreamy Monkey, he adds with a smile, "and I give my unconditional support to you, beloved Monkey: it is time you make new friends of your own kind. You have challenged the laws of your spiritual tradition to fulfill your longing. I guess Grey is very much part of it…"

He smiles at both, satisfied with himself. Maybe too satisfied, the Monkey suddenly thinks, irritated. He looks too big, like a benign patriarch looking down on his favorite children. He is just about to start brooding again on the size issue when he remembers Grey. He doesn't care anymore: he just wants to be alone with her. He closes his eyes and resumes for a moment his happy daydream until it climaxes in a long romantic kiss…

The Big Buddha just stares at him, while Grey softly giggles. He clearly wants to go back to his practice, but patiently waits for the Monkey to open his eyes again.

The Monkey finally comes back with a long sigh, and looks at his big friend. He is loyal and considerate. "Thanks for arranging this meeting…" he tells him, realizing for the first time that they both have their different paths to follow.

While the Big Buddha returns to his people, the Monkey sits in a corner with Grey in his arms. "Enlightenment has infinite expressions," he sweetly whispers to her.

Chapter Thirtyone

MARRIAGE

Full Moon in Libra – Balance Restored

For the next four months, the Dwija Circus continues traveling in what looks from the outside like random circles. In fact, the Twelve have started following an astrological chart, recently drawn by the German Buddha, that indicates at any given time which place is most receptive to what they want to transmit through their Circus acts. They first travel to Copenhagen, then to Vilnius, then they suddenly plunge to Spain, and then they go north again through Paris and Prague and south again to Athens. It works: everywhere they go, they are welcomed and praised.

As the days pass by, the Monkey and Grey develop their gig. They use their monkey skills at swinging, jumping, and doing summersaults. They love what they are creating, and they are good at it. Both are also excellent dancers and comedians with an occasional melodramatic touch.

But above all they are in love. It is visible in their every gesture; in the way their eyes lock, in the sparks that set off when they touch each other, accidentally or not.

Only the Big Buddha remains blissfully ignorant of their love affair. Even though the air around them is thick with sensuous love, he continues seeing the Monkey as his best friend, and Grey as a kind of buddy. The three of them work well together: the Big Buddha appears in their show and they appear in his. The Big Buddha looks happier when he performs with his friend rather than alone, and Grey is always glad to include him.

Meanwhile, Grey herself has brought a new element of grace into their joint performance: she is very flexible, and with her acrobatics she can keep the audience breathless for quite some time. Next to her, the Monkey looks a bit clumsy, but that also is good: it cheers up the public. The Big Buddha is not totally at ease with people laughing at his friend, but the Monkey is in the seventh heaven. He spends all his free time with Grey, smiles a lot, teases her and hugs her while she giggles with her tinker bell giggle.

Everyone else in the Circus knows that they are in love, but nobody mentions anything, giving them the privacy they need to get to know each other.

One early spring evening in Athens, under a beautiful golden Full Moon, the Big Buddha goes to visit the Monkey for some advice about the new act that he is putting together. On his way, he realizes how long it has been since he last visited the Monkey off duty. Nothing to worry about, he tells himself reaching The Monkey's caravan, our connection is as strong as ever...

It's drizzling outside, and the door is closed against the rain. The Big Buddha gently knocks on the window. No response. He rubs off the sheen of condensed vapor on the glass and looks inside. The Monkey is sitting in front of his Ipad, and Grey is leaning against him with a steaming cup of tea in her hands. A tray with an empty cup rests on a small table covered with lace under the window. The two are as physically close as they can get, all cuddled up in a heap of arms, legs, bums, backs, faces. Even the virginal Big Buddha can finally see that they have become lovers. He pulls back his hand from the window and turns around very silently.

Once back in his own caravan, a big wave of sadness crashes over him. He doesn't know what to make of it: it's an unknown kind of sadness for him. Like a big sense of loss but also a deep longing, right in the middle of his chest.

He needs help. He goes online and tries messaging the Young Shaman. No reply. The same happens with the Istanbul Lady and with the Peruvian Magician.

That night, the Big Buddha stays up until late, meditating on his new feelings. He cannot deny them any longer: it's as if he has just woken up from a deep trance. He sits and watches, riding waves of emotions, staying with contradictory thoughts until they disappear, and breathing in his belly not to get hooked back into them. It's a bit like sorting rice, he thinks at some point of the night with a smile. He suddenly remembers that any outer or inner event is part of a larger evolution, and finally relaxes. Charavedi, Charavedi...keep on moving, he whispers.

Happy to have found himself again, he falls asleep just as the sun rises above the white Athenian skyline.

When he wakes up a few hours later, his whole body seems to be singing a happy melody. He takes time to bathe and cream himself, consciously touching and exploring each part of his body. Feeling sensuous, he decides to dress up for the day. He throws on his best Afghani caftan and casts an appreciative look at himself in the mirror. Then he automatically runs to his door to go and tell the Monkey what happened. He stops before opening it: "Wow," he says, stunned by the realization, "The Monkey and I have almost been a perfect couple...just the sex was missing..." he laughs out loud at the silly idea, and opens the door to a new world.

The Waif Buddha is outside, waiting for him. He blushes, and lowers his eyes, afraid that she could read him. Truth is that she is so focused on herself that she doesn't notice anything. Thank god for narcissism! He giggles.

"Is it your birthday, Big Buddha?" she asks, looking through him with her otherworldly expression.

"Not that I know of...why?" the Big Buddha answers, a bit thrown off balance. "Four different people have called this morning for you. They all want to meet you urgently..."

"Did they say who they were?"

"Let me think..." she suddenly laughs, looking straight at him, "yes, a Peruvian witchdoctor, a Siberian healer, the Lady from Istanbul, and a Lesbian Zen Woman..." and adds hugging him, "your friends are always such interesting people!"

All pink and warm after the sensuous hug, the Big Buddha runs back to his Ipad to check his messages: none. He wonders what this is all about.

He feels suddenly stressed at the idea of meeting the four, especially his past-life-son-now-Zen-Woman, whom he hasn't yet seen in person. The mellowness that he just experienced before all over his body is gone. "What would the Monkey do in such a situation?" he wonders. For a few seconds, he goes blank, and then bursts out in a hearty laughter: "I have to find the Monkey inside me!" he shouts, to no one in particular, while he walks out again. It's time for him to create his own adventures and have some fun.

"This could be fun..." he says, and right in the middle of the Circus morning activities, he starts jumping up and down like a huge gorilla, baring his chest, growling and shouting. An instant response comes from the other side of the compound: two shrill monkey voices call back in unison. Soon everyone around catches up, and starts acting like an ape. The German Buddha, looking like a big baboon, hops to his violin and starts playing a dizzying tune.

Suddenly, from a distance, an accordion joins the violin, the two instruments creating together a wild and romantic melody. The Four must be here, the Big Buddha realizes.

The Zen Woman is the first to enter through the gates. In front of everyone's gaping eyes, she turns into a big black panther. She looks ferocious. Everyone freezes. The Monkey breaks the spell by running towards her and growling a panther-like greeting to her, remaining unafraid while she playfully bares her teeth in response.

The Istanbul Lady and the Young Shaman enter next. They slowly metamorphose into two enormous lions, pounding together on the Monkey, who lets out an ear-shattering shriek that stops them on their tracks. Grey joins in, bringing the screaming to an unbearable pitch until the two "lions" beg them to stop.

At last, the Peruvian Magician walks in. He wears a huge winter coat, open to reveal inside it what seems the body of a Tiger. The Monkey runs in his arms.

The Big Buddha, unable to utter a word, is feeling happy, realizing that his new world is full of surprises.

Later on, in front of a steaming cup of coffee, the Peruvian Magician tells the Big Buddha: "The meeting between sentient beings and animistic forces is the SALT of this Earth..."

Since they met on the market in Rome, the two feel like friends. When earlier on the Monkey introduced them proudly to each other, they just smiled, glad to share their little secret. There had been also another moment of confusion when Grey was introduced to the Four. The Peruvian Magician had to look sideways and quickly whisper to her: "Shhh…" But the Monkey, happy as he was, didn't notice anything.

"Good that we could keep up the pretense," the Peruvian Magician whispers now to the Big Buddha, "Especially the two ladies amongst us Four thought it would be extremely unromantic to reveal how Grey got here. Maybe in future, when the right moment comes, you and her can tell him the truth, but not now…"

The Big Buddha nods, and comes back to the fascinating subject that they were discussing: "Tell me more about shamanism…." he asks his new friend.

"Once we were all animals." he replies, "When mankind came on the scene, the other animals did not expect these young and inexperienced siblings to become so powerful so fast. Men started claiming that having a soul was a privilege bestowed only upon them by their god. Animals, plants, nature, were just tools for their ambition. We Shamans want to heal this big wound of disrespect that is killing this Planet. We care for nature, and for the soul of every living thing. Without it, there would be no home for anyone, including mankind…."

He looks at Grey, who has quietly snuggled in his familiar coat: "I am sorry for all the mistreatment and abuse inflicted to animals by humans. For their indifference and the denial. For all of us forgetting that we are one soul…"

"But how did you manage to literally appear like a tiger?" the Big Buddha is fascinated, "this is a new area for me…"

"It's not as new as you believe…" the Peruvian Magician replies, "It's in the human DNA, in its memories. You have an animal inside yourself too…"

"We Four, dude," butts in the Young Shaman, holding a large glass of very dark beer, " originate way back from the same feline tribe. It was eons ago; at that time, nobody cared for color or size: lions, panthers and tigers and many more felines peacefully coexisted and hunted together in the same pride.

"Since then, we saw many new worlds being born and many old worlds dying, but we never lost touch with our feline nature: we can still shape shift back to it, even now that we are human," says the Zen Woman, relieved that the Big Buddha has dropped staring at her, and happy to contribute to the conversation. "Humanity, though, has less and less tolerance for what is natural. To shape shift like we do has become dangerous. There is hardly any wilderness left, and many species of animals are disappearing…."

"If you don't count the brainwashed ones that vegetate in the zoos…" whispers Grey from inside the Peruvian Shaman's coat. The Monkey, for a change, is not jealous: he just enjoys what he thinks is an instant friendship between two of his most beloveds, while sitting on the lap of the Istanbul Lady.

"I heard the Circus was in Rome some time ago…" the Peruvian Magician stands up, suddenly changing the subject, "I also visited Rome recently. You might know the symbol of this city: two twin baby boys, Romulus and Remus, at the breast of a she wolf. She saved their life. Now, I would like to introduce to you all the one you who saved MY life in Rome...my hostess..."

He lets out a piercing howl, and moves towards the gates to open them: a she wolf with unsettling slanted eyes comes in softly growling, and starts walking towards the rest of the company. Under their gaping mouths, she slowly turns into a pretty girl.

"This ancient wolf soul in a pretty girl body," he says, looking at her with obvious desire in his eyes, "has moved with me to Peru. We are working together now."

The Wolf Girl smiles at everyone, hooks her arm to the Peruvian Magician's, and looks straight into the Big Buddha's eyes, who blushes intensely but stands his ground and says, "Thank you all, beloved friends, for coming and teaching me so much...and thank you for what you did for the Monkey too..." He winks at them and continues, "and...I pray to the Wolf Goddess, so beautifully embodied by this lovely girl...that what happened between her and the Peruvian Magician will one day happen to me too."

The Waif Buddha, who has not moved one inch since the arrival of the Four, lets out a sigh and announces them: "Please enjoy the Circus tonight. We have reserved for the five of you the 'Royal' seats!"

That night their performance is the best ever.

The five guests are seated in their 'Royal' places wearing clothes that hint at their animal selves, from the fancy designer shirt with tiger prints of the Peruvian Magician to a lion cub print all over the gown of the Istanbul Lady that matches the long shirt of the Young Shaman. The most stunning is the Zen Woman, with a black satin mini dress that reveals her curves.

The German Buddha, all dressed in emerald green, opens the show with a sweet lullaby on his violin. There is a lonely spotlight illuminating him. Suddenly, two fluorescent emerald wings open on his back, and he sets off fluttering like a butterfly across the ring. On cue, from the orchestra box below starts the deep and peaceful sound of Tibetan bowls. A loudspeaker broadcasts the Child Buddha's voice humming, and slowly the audience joins in, while the sound of the instruments fades and disappears. When the humming subsides, only an expectant silence remains.

Then the violin starts again, slowly. As it winds its way into a crescendo, the German Buddha whoops a yell of jubilation and all the lights go on over a masterpiece of holographic design: a full, thick jungle, occupying the whole Circus ring.

The five guests are in awe. It's the first time that they see what human Buddhas can create. "Truly, guys," the Young Shaman whispers to them all, "being human can be an equal gift as being an animal!"

"It all depends in whose hands it is," the Zen Woman reminds him.

"I love a bit of glamour..."the Istanbul Lady says, "especially if there is meditation at the end...The glamour of the performances combined to the silence that ends each meditation! This is a multimedia Satsang[1]!!!"

1 Spiritual Communion

The five are in utter admiration when, after a repeated standing ovation, they see the Greek crowd walking out with a new softness in their eyes.

The Monkey takes Grey to say goodnight to the Istanbul Lady and the Young Shaman. There is a lot that remains unsaid between them, but they all feel it's better to keep it at that. The Istanbul Lady looks at Grey, takes her tiny hand in hers and asks her: "Are you planning to marry him and have children?"

When she sees Grey's eyes filling with tears, she realizes that she has touched a sensitive point. "I would love to, but I don't know if I still can, after what happened to my body…" Grey finally replies, looking down.

Overhearing their exchange, the Young Shaman turns to the Monkey and whispers: "Hey dude, if their is anything wrong that prevents you from having a family, come to my place again, and we can explore together different treatments… Also, man, I need a good buddy there, a man to hang out with!" The Monkey remembers the soothing effect of his smelly herbs and answers with a big grin: "Thanks, man!"

After endless goodbyes, the five leave with a final promise to stay in touch.

Having given the best of themselves in the show, all the performers are spent. Everyone needs a break from the high energy and a good long sleep.

The next morning, the Big Buddha goes for a visit to his monkey friends. He finds them under the awning in front of their pretty caravan with flowers at the windows. They are slowly sipping their morning hot chocolate. As they greet him with a big smile that includes him in their pink cloud, the Big Buddha notices how through some mysterious alchemy they have become one. Grey is whispering something in the ear of the Monkey, whose eyes become rounder and bigger as he starts chuckling, soon joined by her in an escalation of giggles that culminates into hysterical laughter, that ebbs again into more whispering.

Just as Big Buddha is about to turn around and look for some more mature source of conversation elsewhere, the Monkey looks up, his face all red and sweaty and his hair sticking out to all sides.

"Big Buddha", he says, while suddenly tears start running down his cheeks, "I love Grey so much that I can not imagine a life without her! Grey feels the same. We are happy! That's why we are laughing so much." He turns to her with big dreamy eyes and continues, "She was just telling me that she will follow me wherever I go…." He stops, takes a big breath, and looks up at his best friend asking: "Beloved Big Buddha, do you think I am ready to marry? Because…" he suddenly looks insecure, and a bit guilty, "because if you feel I am not ready and you sincerely think that it is better to wait…I wouldn't know what to do…I don't want to hurt her in any way, so maybe if you see that I could harm her by marrying her…I honestly don't know if I could live without her but…"

The Monkey is building up to a big drama, the Big Buddha thinks, worried. He looks tearful and disheveled, as if something terrible is about to happen.

"My dear Monkey," he replies in his calmest tone, "There are times in our lives when we go through big changes… Marriage is one of those times. It requires from each one of the two partners a full 'yes' for the adventure they set off on together. For marriage to work, this 'yes' must be equally strong for both, unconditional. It doesn't mean that you will be forever bound to each other when you don't love each other anymore. It doesn't need to be a contract: it can just be a celebration of your adventure together…"

The Monkey is nodding his head vigorously. He hasn't followed the Big Buddha's words, but likes his friendly tone. He basically takes it as a yes. In his monkey nature, he cannot think of anything else than always taking care of her, buying her every possible present, kissing her, hugging her…

He looks at his beloved, takes her small elegant hand firmly in his big monkey hand and declares in the middle of sobs and giggles: "Yes, I want to be your divine husband. We will take care of each other through good and through bad!". He then sweeps her up in his arms and disappears with her back in their caravan for the rest of the morning.

Later at lunch, the Big Buddha stands up in front of everyone gathered around the big table and bangs a spoon against a glass to get everyone's attention: "I would like to announce the beautiful wedding ceremony of my friend here the Monkey and his beloved Grey…"

Everyone is enthusiastic, and a date is set with the astrological help of the German Buddha: "Tomorrow!" he gasps, causing an outburst of laughter and a flurry of sudden activity and conversation…

"Hereby I declare today and tomorrow official holidays for the Circus!" adds the Empress of Poetry Buddha, "let the preparations begin!"

The following morning at the auspicious hour of Midday, all is ready. The Circus tent is all festooned, and the Twelve are standing facing the stage curtains in a wide semicircle around the Big Buddha, dressed in a smart orange satin jacket and trousers, his long hair in a topknot. The loudspeakers play the Monkey's favorite music: Peruvian country and western.

When the curtains part, the Monkey and Grey appear in the middle of the Circus ring. There is a murmur of appreciation. She is wearing a lovely taffeta white dress, and he a fancy little suit with purple and yellow pin stripes. Their faces are black, pitch black, glinting in the spotlights. "It's custom amongst Monkeys to smear black ashes on their faces as a sign of beauty" the Buddha of Technical Support and Maintenance is close enough to whisper to the Big Buddha, who chuckles. "Why not," he replies, "they need to honor who they are…I just start to wonder when and with whom my turn will come…"

The celebration goes on and on for the whole day with performances, gifts and a never ending banquet. In the evening, the newly wed retreat in the privacy of their caravan, and everyone else sits around an open fire to talk and sing until late.

The Big Buddha is the last one to leave. He sits close to the embers, happy and light, blessing existence for yet another precious gift.

Chapter Thirtytwo

THE MYSTERIOUS ADVENTURES OF MISS SWUPI

In the days following the wedding celebration, a general mood of restlessness has set into the crew. The performances continue, but the real animals seem to need more space, while the holographic ones are starting to split from time to time into hundreds of smaller images of themselves. Also the Buddhas don't look so good anymore: they are a bit pale and haggard from all the traveling and lack of sleep.

"It's clearly time to move on", announces the German Buddha to the Circus crew on a bright spring afternoon, "The Circus experiment has been so far a real blessing. We have been welcomed everywhere by warm hearts and innocent souls, and we have shared what we could. I personally long to stretch my bones for a while back in Shambala, but of course everyone is free to do what he or she wants. We are going to dismantle the Circus in three days, and whoever wants can fly with me to New Delhi".

Although a few of them are crying, the other eleven Buddhas all nod.

"But let it not be the end of our adventures!" says the Dark Skinned Buddha with a surprising sweetness

"Once Charavedi, Charavedi forever…" adds the Eternal Child Buddha

"As for the holographic animals," adds the German Buddha, "we all knew that they wouldn't last forever, but…"

"There is good news for them from the Little Planet," adds the Buddha of Technical Support and Maintenance, grinning, "it is still all in an experimental phase, but everything seems to be in an accelerated growth and constant transformation. The Monkey tribe is even starting to develop humanoid features…"

"Where are we going with this?" jumps in the Monkey, not wanting at all to lose his animal soul…

"Don't worry, dear Monkey, it is not your destiny…" The Empress of Poetry Buddha tells him, looking through him into his future.

"And it seems that the basic Elixir that permeates the Little Planet can be also used to transform holograms into living things!!!!!" concludes the Buddha of Technical Support and Maintenance.

All the holographic animals respond with a loud "Hurrah!" and hug each other Even the Unicorn and the dolphin try to embrace, slipping and sliding on each other's glimmering surface and causing general hilarity.

The Big Buddha just stands there in the middle of everything, not knowing what to do.

"I will have to wait for some guidance," he tells the Twelve later, around the dinner table. "I don't really mind letting you go. My soul is forever connected with each one of you. But I have no clue about what is next…" For the first time in his new life, he feels alone, but in a good way.

On the final evening of the Circus, as the audience vigorously applauds and the crew bows down to the audience for the last time, the Big Buddha catches a glimpse of Indigo light in the middle of the public. The Monkey, who has noticed it too, is quicker than him: he grabs Grey's hand and runs to the benches, jumps in the middle of the surprised audience and lands in the arms of a couple.

"The Indigo Couple!" the Big Buddha shouts to everyone and no one, running towards them.

When he arrives, the Monkey, pulling his beloved with him, has already wiggled between them. He is pulling the hem of the Indigo Woman, telling her: "Look Nonna[1]," using the sweet word for grandma that he learnt in Rome, "this is Grey, my wife. And look Nonno[2]," he says, patting the leg of the Indigo Man, "isn't my beloved beautiful?"

"Yes, she is!" they both say with true appreciation. Grey relaxes in between them.

Then the couple turns towards the Big Buddha, who doesn't move, just stands there to give them a chance to recognize him and take in the big change. They stare at him for a while and then slowly bow to him. When they finally hug, everyone cries. "These are my first tears in a grownup body…" the Big Buddha whispers to his Soul Mother.

Later, after all the introductions are completed, the Indigo Couple sits under the sky with the Big Buddha and the Monkey Couple.

"I thought you never left the island," the Big Buddha, a trace of the child in his voice, says to his Soul Parents.

"We took time for you, beloved, that's why we didn't leave the island when you lived with us." the Indigo Man tells him.

"We normally travel quite a bit," adds the Indigo Woman, looking somehow differ-

---

1 Grandma in italian

2 Grandpa in italian

ent, maybe younger, or maybe professional? The Big Buddha wonders, "and work in many different places around the world, just like the Dwija Circus"

The Indigo Man continues: "We came to Athens because we saw on Facebook that the Dwija Circus was here. We liked the spiritual name, and we got curious. As we browsed through their masterfully done website, we saw photos of the Monkey and you…"

"Me?" asks the Big Buddha surprised.

"You do not look as different as you think, at least in my eyes," says the Indigo Woman, squeezing his hands.

"We came immediately", the Indigo Man says, and adds looking at his Soul Child, "I miss you these days. I loved so much the summer we spent together… After you left, we both wondered what would happen. We knew that your holographic form could not last much longer"

The Big Buddha feels touched, "We are connected beyond form, dear Soul Parents. I am the same as I was before, and love you as much…"

The Indigo Man tells him: "I already could see your potential as a man when you were still a child. I am so glad you found a way to grow into this man!"

"And I always could see the child in you, Soul Parents, you kept it always alive inside…that's why I love you so tremendously…"

Just as he is slipping back into the magical and tender space he used to share with the Indigo Couple, the Big Buddha stops. The Indigo Couple understands, and takes a step back. The path must go forward: Charavedi…

For a moment the Big Buddha feels very sad, as if he has to once more give up his childhood, but their little gesture is enough to remind him not get sentimental. "Keep on moving," the Indigo Man whispers to him, "this time you can be anybody and anything. Don't choose. Live it all with awareness!"

The Big Buddha smiles at his remark. He remembers a discourse of the Controversial Master: "There is no sin," he repeats, "The only real sin is unawareness."

The Indigo Couple smiles back, slightly bowing, happy to hear the words of their Master spoken out by another Buddha…

"Ehmmm…" the Indigo Woman says, suddenly reverting to the safe ground of practicality, "We also have a letter for you, Big Buddha. It came a day ago, here it is." She hands him a big sandalwood scented envelope.

"I will open it later," the Big Buddha answers, wanting to spend as much time as possible with his Soul Parents.

After a pleasant evening, the Indigo Couple leaves to grab some sleep at some friends' home before their boat trip back to the island. When their taxi arrives, everything suddenly goes very fast: they are gone in what seems to the Big Buddha the blink of an eye.

Alone and still awake in his caravan, the Bug Buddha finally opens the sandalwood envelope.

"To the Little Buddha", he reads, "from the Board of Directors of the University of Mystery and Science, Kulu, Valley of the Gods, India."

It's an official invitation to give a talk about his own process of incarnation. Their University, they write, is teaching both Science and Spirituality. Quantum Physics and Meditation, the ultramodern and the eternal. The Big Buddha has to laugh when he thinks of their faces once they see him in the body of a grown man telling also this recent part of his transformation. Then he remembers the Buddha of Technical Support and Maintenance mentioning this place, and how much the German Buddha liked them…"

He puts the letter down, closes his eyes, and knows instantly: this is it. It's the best start for his new life: large groups of people have never intimidated him, and by now he is well acquainted with big audiences. From there, something else will happen, he decides, and goes for a nap at last.

After a few hours, he is woken up by a knock at his door. He opens his puffy eyes to the sight of the Monkey Couple, as he calls them affectionately, hand in hand, unkempt and shiny eyed after a night of intimacy, For a moment, their warm and soft atmosphere envelops him, and his big male body loves it.

His two tiny friends straighten up to their full dignified height, and the Monkey speaks for both: "Big Buddha, we have a request for you."

Shaking off his tiredness, the Big Buddha nods attentively: "We are experiencing something similar to what you felt few months ago: we also have enough of being small and fragile. We want to explore something else. Please help us to become big. We would like to be the same size as you, but we want to be able to alternate between being big monkeys and average size human beings, according to where we are and what is needed. Could you ask your friend the Cosmic Creator to do this for us?"

He is speaking with such unusual certainty and focus for his otherwise besotted self that the Big Buddha is speechless: his little friend, who has been on his shoulders through so many adventures is asking him now to become a man like him. Then he suddenly remembers his own devotion for the Monkey when he was a wise Lama, and chuckles. Life is full of surprises…

His amused "Yes!" lights the sunshine in Grey's eyes: It's good that both become big, he thinks.

That's how the next stretch of the Big Buddha's itinerary gets finalized. He will join the Twelve on the flight back to India together with Grey and the Monkey, then trek with the two of them to the Mansarovara to pay a visit to the Cosmic Creator, and then…He will bless them for whatever lies ahead and be on his way, alone, to the University of Mystery and Science in the Valley of the Gods.

The travel to India all together is so much fun that everyone is disappointed when it's time to disembark. For most of the Twelve it is the first time on an airplane, and in between their giggles, their mantras and their deep breathing they attract the attention of quite a few passengers going to India to meditate.

It's a couple of days since the Twelve parted with our three friends at the Red Fort in Delhi and set off with elephants and porters towards the higher Himalayas. After waving them goodbye, they decided to take the most luxurious means of transportation and get themselves to the Himalayas as comfortably as possible.

It is almost a déjà vu for the Monkey and the Big Buddha when they reach Almora, but Grey makes all the difference. She has to stop at each market stall to browse through all the glitter and bracelets displayed, and there is no way to hurry her…

The two monkeys travel the final stretch towards the Mansarovara Lake on the Big Buddha's shoulders. "You walk so much faster now as a grown man!!!" giggles the Monkey, full of anticipation, holding his beloved's hand across his friend's neck.

When they reach the shore, the weather is fair and the sky is deep blue. They sit silently looking at the waters, until they are startled by a flock of swans flying overhead.

In the deeper silence that follows, they see the Lake changing color, and the familiar silhouette of the Cosmic Creator rowing his boat towards them.

"Hello my friends," he shouts from still afar, "This time I would like to experiment with a simple and elegant ritual which seems to me just right for these two beloveds… we don't want to spoil their animal soul with complicated human ceremonies…"

Grey nods vigorously…she is a bit afraid of water…

"Don't worry, sweet one, it's worth it," says the Cosmic Creator, now close, beckoning her and the Monkey to jump on the boat, "come…"

Once they are aboard, he draws in a circular movement one single golden line towards the horizon, where lake and sky merge. Quickly, before the line fades, he grabs both monkeys in his huge hands and dips them under water. First there is some spluttering and shrieking, and then just quiet bubbles.

A gorgeous Grey, as tall as an average sized human female, with a stunning mane of silver grey hair and human features, emerges from the Lake. Spitting a big jet of water, the Monkey comes out after her: He is very handsome, a few inches taller then her, with the lithe body of a dancer and slightly aboriginal features, looking like a man.

The Big Buddha on the shore is stunned.

The Cosmic Creator admires them for a moment, helps them up, and rows them to the shore while talking to them. After the couple disembarks, he winks at the Big Buddha and silently turns the boat around, waiting. The three friends know: it's done, it's time to say goodbye, at least for now.

The Monkey whispers something to Grey and moves towards the Big Buddha. She follows him right behind. Together, the three of them stand at the shore of Lake Mansarovara in a silent embrace that seems to last for eternity.

"We have decided that we will spend our Honeymoon on the Little Planet: the Cosmic Creator will take us there" the Monkey says, "I want to introduce Grey to my Tribe. And to tell you the truth," he adds with a grin, "I am myself very curious about the new developments there. It will be for sure a good way to practice a bit with our new bodies…remember our month in India, when you became the Big Buddha?"

"I will never forget" the Big Buddha replies

With these last words, they part opposite ways. When the Big Buddha looks back, the boat has become a tiny dot in the sky.

He starts walking on the shore towards the hut of Raidas, happy to have a stopover at the settlement of Raidas's Soul Family before continuing his journey to the Valley of the Gods. There are many stories he would like to tell them and many he would like to hear from them.

Full Moon in Scorpio-Whirling in Love and Gratitude

A week or so later, the Big Buddha is sitting on a train bound to the Valley of the Gods, surrounded by people who constantly offer him morsels of their meals. He feels excited, happy and in his heart. He looks at the large Indian families and feels their warmth: they share everything they have. He looks around at the girls, the young mothers, the daughters and sisters, and really likes them all: they look pretty to him, full of laughter and sensuousness. Their dark features are very soothing: he can imagine disappearing in their arms. Inside, he is starting to get used to his new longing to meet the girl of his life and to be in love, make love, kiss her, admire her, protect her, and start a journey together. As he sits there surrounded by life, noise, people and smells, he suddenly feels a warm current from his genitals all the way to his heart. It's a new sensation that unlocks something in him that has so far been inaccessible.

A couple of stops before the Big Buddha's final destination, the train gets emptier. All families have gone, leaving behind them a trail of peanut shells, rose oil fragrance, a whiff of beedies, and some local newspapers. On the seat next to him, there is a crumpled "Manali Gazette" with a large photo portrait on the front page. He absent-mindedly takes it in his hands, and a big rush of energy hits him when he looks at the photo: it's a dark young woman. She looks a bit defiant and very sweet. She has sparkles in her eyes, and a noble bearing.

"The Mysterious Adventures of Little Miss Swupi" reads the title. It's an interview with her and a presentation of her autobiography.

An invisible arrow strikes him straight to the core.

The Big Buddha is so shaken that he cannot really read the article in a coherent way. She is some kind of Princess, has had many adventures, and was raised by… Intelligent Animals?

"I know her, although I do not know her…" he whispers

She is a postgraduate student at the University of Mystery and Science. He is on the right train, he tells himself, still short of breath.

"Wait a moment! I had a dream last night right here on this train", he suddenly remembers, talking out loud in the empty compartment, "I was waltzing in front of an open window, the perfume of jasmines and queen of the night was almost intoxicating, and she was in my arms…the night sky outside was alive with whirling milky ways and comets, and inside, on the dance floor, our hearts were whirling in utmost love and gratitude.

THE END

ISBN 978-09928533-1-0
Copyright Premartha De Koning and Svarup Disegni 2014

www.primaltantra.com

The right of Premartha and Svarup to be identified as the authors of this work has been asserted by them in accordance with national and international copyright laws.
All rights reserved. No part of this publication may be reproduced, stored in a retrieval system, or transmitted in any form or by any means, electronic, mechanical, photocopying, recording or otherwise, without the prior permission of the copyright owners.

www.ingramcontent.com/pod-product-compliance
Lightning Source LLC
Chambersburg PA
CBHW080728300426
44114CB00019B/2519